Power and Resistance in Prison

Palgrave Studies in Prisons and Penology

Edited by: **Ben Crewe**, University of Cambridge; **Yvonne Jewkes**, University of Leicester; and **Thomas Ugelvik**, University of Oslo

This is a unique and innovative series, the first of its kind dedicated entirely to prison scholarship. At a historical point in which the prison population has reached an all-time high, the series seeks to analyse the form, nature and consequences of incarceration and related forms of punishment. *Palgrave Studies in Prisons and Penology* provides an important forum for burgeoning prison research across the world.

Series editors:
BEN CREWE is Deputy Director of the Prisons Research Centre at the Institute of Criminology, University of Cambridge, UK, and co-author of *The Prisoner*.

YVONNE JEWKES is Professor of Criminology, Leicester University, UK. She has authored numerous books and articles on the subject and is editor of the *Handbook on Prisons*.

THOMAS UGELVIK is Senior Research Fellow in the Department of Criminology at the University of Oslo, Norway, and editor of *Penal Exceptionalism? Nordic Prison Policy and Practise*.

Advisory Board:
Anna Eriksson, Monash University, Australia
Andrew M. Jefferson, Rehabilitation and Research Centre for Torture Victims, Denmark
Shadd Maruna, Queen's University Belfast, Northern Ireland
Jonathon Simon, UC Berkeley, California, US
Michael Welch, Rutgers University, New Jersey, US

Titles include:

Vincenzo Ruggiero and Mick Ryan
PUNISHMENT IN EUROPE
A Critical Anatomy of Penal Systems

Peter Scharff Smith
WHEN THE INNOCENT ARE PUNISHED
The Children of Imprisoned Parents

Phil Scraton and Linda Moore
THE INCARCERATION OF WOMEN
Punishing Bodies, Breaking Spirits

Thomas Ugelvik
POWER AND RESISTANCE IN PRISON
Doing Time, Doing Freedom

Palgrave Studies in Prisons and Penology
Series Standing Order ISBN 978–1–13727090–0 (hardback)
(*outside North America only*)

You can receive future titles in this series as they are published by placing a standing order. Please contact your bookseller or, in case of difficulty, write to us at the address below with your name and address, the title of the series and the ISBNs quoted above.

Customer Services Department, Macmillan Distribution Ltd, Houndmills, Basingstoke, Hampshire RG21 6XS, England

Power and Resistance in Prison

Doing Time, Doing Freedom

Thomas Ugelvik
University of Oslo, Norway

Translated by

Stephen G. Evans

First published 2014 by
PALGRAVE MACMILLAN

Palgrave Macmillan in the UK is an imprint of Macmillan Publishers Limited, registered in England, company number 785998, of Houndmills, Basingstoke, Hampshire RG21 6XS.

Palgrave Macmillan in the US is a division of St Martin's Press LLC, 175 Fifth Avenue, New York, NY 10010.

Palgrave Macmillan is the global academic imprint of the above companies and has companies and representatives throughout the world.

Palgrave® and Macmillan® are registered trademarks in the United States, the United Kingdom, Europe and other countries.

ISBN 978–1–137–30785–9

This book is printed on paper suitable for recycling and made from fully managed and sustained forest sources. Logging, pulping and manufacturing processes are expected to conform to the environmental regulations of the country of origin.

A catalogue record for this book is available from the British Library.

Library of Congress Cataloging-in-Publication Data
Ugelvik, Thomas.
  Power and resistance in prison : doing time, doing freedom /
  by Thomas Ugelvik.
     pages   cm. — (Palgrave studies in prisons and penology)
  Includes bibliographical references.
  ISBN 978–1–137–30785–9 (hbk)
  1. Prisoners—Norway—Case studies.   2. Corrections—Norway—
  Case studies.   3. Prison administration—Norway—Case studies.
  4. Authority.   I. Title.
  HV9732.U44 2014
  365'.609481—dc23   2014018855

For Synnøve

Contents

Acknowledgements

This book reports the results of a research project that started in 2006. First, sincere thanks are due to my translator Stephen G. Evans. Thanks to your work, the book is finally available to an international readership. I have not envied you the job, but I'm very glad that you did it. Thanks also to the Norwegian Research Council for generously funding Stephen's work.

Many people have offered comments on various versions of texts that ended up as parts of this book. I would like to thank Ben Crewe, Rod Earle, Sverre Flaatten, Yngve Hammerlin, Andrew Jefferson, Sune Qvotrup Jensen, Yvonne Jewkes, Nina Jon, Berit Johnsen, Gustav Erik Gullikstad Karlsaune, Stein Ole Ugelvik Larsen, Kjersti Lohne, Charlotte Mathiassen, Jim Messerschmidt, Dominique Moran, Cecilie E. Basberg Neumann, Iver B. Neumann, Marie Nordberg, Gerhard Ploeg, Torbjørn Skarðhamar, Øystein Skjælaaen, Sharon Shalev, Peter Scharff Smith and Torill E. Wistner for their important contributions. I would also like to thank Odd Lindberg, Annick Prieur and Tian Sørhaug for their thorough and challenging examination of my ideas. The list of colleagues and peers who have kindly given of their time is long. Any errors and deficiencies in this book remain mine.

I would like to express my gratitude to my colleagues in the Department of Criminology and Sociology of Law at the University of Oslo, who at various times have made life both pleasant and academically rewarding. I would in particular like to thank our head of administration, Turid Eikvam and librarian, Vibeke Lagem.

I was fortunate enough to be accepted as a visiting scholar in the Prisons Research Centre at the Institute of Criminology at the University of Cambridge for six months in 2012. I am grateful to Alison Liebling and all her accomplices at the PRC, especially Ben Crewe and Deborah Kant, for making my stay the most interesting and pleasurable kind of learning experience possible.

Many thanks also go to good colleagues at my former place of work, the Correctional Service of Norway Staff Academy, who taught me that prison was a subject worth being interested in.

I would like to express my gratitude to the Norwegian Correctional Services Central Administration, the Eastern Regional Office and the then governor of Oslo Prison, Are Høidal, for allowing me to visit.

I owe a special debt of gratitude to all the prisoners, officers and other staff who lived and worked in the two units in which I conducted my fieldwork. Without their goodwill, openness and curiosity, the result would, to put it mildly, have been very different.

Finally, I would like to thank my dear wife, Synnøve Ugelvik. Not everyone is lucky enough to be married to a good colleague. You have always read what I have written, and you have always critiqued, argued, praised, supported and laughed with, and at, me. You have kept my spirits both up and down, as the circumstances warranted. As my muse, coach and all-round life guide you have quite simply been invaluable.

Oslo, March 2014

Introduction: Power, Resistance and Freedom in Prison

It's a Monday morning in May 2007. I'm on my way to Oslo Prison for the first time. Not completely true of course; I have already been to three meetings there to discuss my research project. I also went on two tours of the prison when I worked for the Correctional Service of Norway Staff Academy. But today is not one of those days; today feels like the first time. Today is the day it begins.

The slightly queasy feeling in my stomach and my clammy hands testify to my nerves. How will I be received? What will be the result of all this? It feels like a lot is riding on today.

I cross the Sculpture Park and walk round the corner of the prison. The weather is fine and mild. But what do I care, I think, after all, I'll spend my day indoors? I walk along the high concrete wall down towards the main gate. I notice that wall is cracked in some places; you can glimpse a world on the other side. A message has been hastily scribbled on the outside of the prison facing the city: "Cops suck!" I arrive at the gate as a van is being admitted. Faced with this open gate, I am mildly bewildered. What should I do? I can't really just wander into Norway's largest prison, can I? What would happen if I just walked straight in?

I decide not to provoke anyone if I can avoid it on my first day. I wait. The gate slowly slides shut behind the van while the guard inside is busy talking to the driver. I wait a bit and then ring the bell. "Yes, hi, it is Thomas Ugelvik from the university, I have an appointment." The metal door next to the gate buzzes. Everyone who has ever visited a prison has had that feeling that they might never be let back out. That's what I'm thinking as I open the door and approach the prison officer behind the safety glass. The officer calls the wing and tells them I have arrived.

After a while one of the officers from wing four arrives to escort me up. It's one of the officers I met at an earlier meeting, a familiar face. She is nice, but our conversation feels a bit awkward. I'm definitely tense and nervous; she's probably wondering about me and what my arrival means.

1

We walk up the stairs and through the entrance to "Plata", the main communications and guard hub in Oslo Prison's B wing. The whole way there the officer has to unlock one heavy metal door after another; each time, I cross the threshold and then wait while she locks it again behind me. Attaching the black, oblong assault alarm to my belt feels strange. She looks at my green striped, civilian cloth belt and concludes: "Well, you can't wear that." I'm quickly fitted out with a new black leather belt with a sturdy buckle, prison style. We exit Plata, go through the corridor, up the little stairs, through another metal door and arrive on wing two. I'm here now. Inside the prison.

We take the lift up. It's the calm before the storm here; all the prisoners are locked in their cells and the officers are on a break. The elongated room is two stories high and has rows of white cell doors on both sides. Unit four is down here on the fourth floor and unit five is on the landing above us. The smell of the prison is unfamiliar: institutional, sweaty, soapy, enclosed and sweet. It's a totally unique smell, but not really bad. The wing looks recently renovated, although the building is showing its age in places.

I follow my escort, past weight-lifting equipment (worn and well used), a table tennis table, a so-called "foosball" table – best known in Norway from the TV show Friends *– and a pool table, into the officers' room. Here they are, the unit four and five officers who are on duty today. One is sitting at a PC; the rest are sitting around a table in the inner "break area". They are all nice and seem interested, but no one has heard I'm coming. "Who are you, are you going to starting working here or what?" So much for the circular I sent to the prison in advance that was supposed to be handed out and posted on the notice boards. I explain and explain and explain.*

Lock-up is over and the officers let eight or ten prisoners out for the afternoon social. A "social" is what they call it when every other day, on a rotating basis, prisoners are allowed access to the common area down in unit four for an hour. From visiting other prisons I know that Norwegian prisons usually let prisoners out of their cells for much longer. But four and five are remand wings, and, even though at any one time some of the prisoners are serving their sentence, the entire wing is oriented towards remand prisoners. And although, to some extent, things are better than they once were, remand prisoners spend a lot of time alone locked in their cells. Socials are welcome breaks.

I peek through the door. Five of the prisoners have started working out with weights. There are the familiar clanging noises of weights striking each other and heavy breathing from straining bodies. Suddenly the officers are not there and I'm alone. I take another stroll around the safe officers' room and glance distractedly at a newspaper. But, come on! I didn't come here to study the inside of this room. From experience I know that in such situations I will definitely have to take the first step and that it might be awkward. But, again, come on! Who am I? The reluctant ethnographer? Really, I should be rushing out enthusiastically to meet and speak with these people. So I pluck up a bit of courage and leave the room, walking as calmly and as relaxed as I can over to the weights at the other end. I try to make eye contact with some of those waiting their turn for the weights, but it's hard. I choose one and try to introduce myself, stretching out a hand. He looks at it. Then he looks up at me and stares, glassy eyed. "Do you speak English?" A poor first attempt, but okay, I can cope with that. I try again. I introduce myself and can see out of the corner of my eye that the other four are listening intently. He makes no attempt to answer. Instead, an angry shout comes from my right:

> Prisoner 1: *What the fuck? Are you saying you're police?*
> TU: *What, no? No, no! I'm not police!*

My mind is racing. I didn't say I was police, did I? That's not what I said, was it? Why did I say, I was police?

> Prisoner 1: *You are! You're saying you're police! I'm going to fucking tell everyone not to talk to you.*

The prisoner, who after all has started to talk to me, stares squarely at me, leaning forward, fired up. I have a vision of a research project in ruins. He turns on his heels, shows me his back and walks to the sofa group at the other end of the room and sits down. I follow and sit down opposite him. After all, at least he said something. Behind me I hear people resume their workouts.

So my first meeting with the prisoners in Oslo Prison is spent trying to convince someone that I'm not an undercover police officer. The more I protest, the surer he is that I'm lying. The man opposite me is skin and bones. He is in his forties, has a crew cut, is in a tracksuit, and has sunken cheeks and protruding eyes. He leans back in the green sofa and is totally serious when he asks me to stop lying:

> Prisoner 1: *You know what, I'm absolutely sure you're police so it doesn't matter what you say. You're here to gather information.*
> TU: *Well, yes, that's true in a sense, but not for the police or for their use, I'm a researcher, I work at the university, I'm going to write about what it's like here.*
> Prisoner 1: *So, you're going to write a book, are you? What are you going to use this book for then? Who is going to read it? The police will, won't they? That doesn't help, does it?*

> TU: *You're wrong, I . . .*
> Prisoner 1: *No, no, you can't fool me [shakes his head grinning].*

The conversation moves on to a series of tests. He says things to see how I react. But after a while I notice that he's easing up a bit. The questions are a bit more flippant, the mood relaxes. He grills me about my experience of crime and drugs. I answer honestly. We chat for an hour. I also get some assistance: another prisoner wanders past, nods towards my partner and looks at me with a grin:

> Prisoner 2: *Don't listen to him; he's full of shit, heh heh.*

Other prisoners come and go, participating in the conversation (or, rather, the examination). After a while my examiner admits that he might not really believe I'm police. Another prisoner interferes and tries to make him see the gravity of the situation:

> Prisoner 1: *I'm only saying you're police to see what happens, how you react. To see how tough you are.*
> Prisoner 3: *But you shouldn't, he could get a kicking in here.*
> Prisoner 1: *I know, that's why I'm doing it, heh heh. To see how tough he is.*
> TU: *Well, I'm not really that tough.*
> Prisoner 1: *Well, we'll see about that. We'll see. Heh heh.*

The project

This is a book about the interconnected and mutually dependent relationship between power and freedom. It is an analysis of how people actually behave, think, feel and react when they encounter power, and the consequences this has for them. The specific arenas that are the subject of the study are two remand units in Norway's largest prison, Oslo Prison. I will show how the prisoners, within the constraints of a prison wing, take liberties, construct free areas, find and explore secret means of escape, and creatively and productively put up resistance to, through and against the everyday routine forms of power in the prison.

What is power, and, more specifically, what is state power? Proudhon lists in the following quote all the means of exerting power that the state of his day had at its disposal in relation to its subjects; from observation, enrolment and counting, through taxation and (other forms of) extortion, to imprisonment, deportation and execution:

To be GOVERNED is to be kept in sight, inspected, spied upon, directed, law-driven, numbered, enrolled, indoctrinated, preached at, controlled, estimated, valued, censured, commanded, [. . .]. To be GOVERNED is to be at every operation, at every transaction, noted, registered, enrolled, taxed, stamped, measured, numbered, assessed, licensed, authorized, admonished, forbidden, reformed, corrected, punished. It is, under pretext of public utility, and in the name of the general interest to be placed under contribution, trained, ransomed, exploited, monopolized, extorted, squeezed, mystified, robbed; that at the slightest resistance, the first word of complaint, to be repressed, fined, despised, harassed, tracked, abused, clubbed, disarmed, choked, imprisoned, judged, condemned, shot, deported, sacrificed, sold, betrayed; and to crown it all, mocked, ridiculed, outraged, dishonoured.

(1989 [1851]: 294)

Proudhon's catalogue of forms of power is based on a traditional understanding of power and liberty as antonyms, of freedom as the absence of power. Taken together, his list reads like an almost total system for the control and suppression of a population; a system that leaves very little space for freedom.

Thus, it may seem paradoxical for a book about everyday life in prison to be based on the theme of liberty and freedom, but it is not. In contrast to the logic behind Proudhon's catalogue, Foucault shifts the focus to the productive aspects of power, to all the opportunities that must necessarily open up because the techniques of power are being put to work:

[T]he most intense point of a life, the point where its energy is concentrated, is where it comes up against power, struggles with it, attempts to use its forces and to avoid its traps.

(2000a: 162)

From a perspective inspired by Foucault's concept of power, there is no contradiction between power and freedom; instead, the two are interwoven and mutually constituted. Furthermore, there is no original unfree position that is then subdued and oppressed by power; on the contrary, power is an element that forms part of any social relationship, any meeting between people. Power is everywhere and is, therefore, something that it is not possible (or desirable) to avoid completely.

People who are put in prison are placed within a network of specific forms of power. Prison is a social space in which an attempt is made to create and maintain more comprehensive and rigid control over people than is normal in most other places, and where the dividing lines between groups are very clear. The prisoners are administered in more detail, and the various technologies of power they encounter in prison will affect them more directly and straightforwardly, than the more indirect forms of control one often encounters on the outside (even if the forms of control have, as I will show, become more indirect inside the walls of the prison as well). In prison, the line has to some extent already been drawn, the positions are clear and the game is basically relatively easy to understand. This makes prison a suitable arena for the study of power in practice, in its specificity and as it plays out in daily social interactions (Sykes, 1958; Sparks, Bottoms and Hay, 1996).

The point of departure here is that power and liberty are understood in their practical aspects. From such a perspective, both exist only as practice, as power and liberty *exercised*. Being subject to several layers of different forms of power could, thus, be a particularly favourable starting point for *doing* freedom when this is understood as *a practical and performative issue*. It is practical because it is only by performing an action that crosses some boundary or other that one can, in practice, show that one is free to cross boundaries. If power and freedom are inherent variables, it is precisely by confronting various forms of power that people can "do" freedom in practice. In these circumstances, the authorities' boundary that is crossed represents an absolutely necessary part of the free action. It is performative because boundary-crossing actions affect the actor. The prisoners *take* liberties, *do* resistance and *become* free. If freedom can, thus, be understood as a performative variable, the person taking liberties becomes free. And a person who is free is, in some sense, not really a prisoner at all. Understood like this, freedom is the practical outcome of successful forms of resistance. I will show how one of the goals of prisoners is to turn themselves into something other, or more, than prisoners; to challenge, alter or modify their prisoner status. This book is about the ways various acts of everyday resistance can be used to enact this form of practical and performative freedom.

In this perspective, which one could just as easily call Nietzschean,[1] there is no freedom without power or power without freedom. In other words, this study does not examine freedom in an absolute or metaphysical sense, understood as the totality of the forms of power listed by Proudhon. However, in a practical and performative concept of freedom, all of the authorities' techniques and mechanisms present opportunities for *doing freedom* and *being free* by evading or adapting to control. This book is about how prisoners, positioned as prisoners in prison, *do* freedom, and the consequences of this. It focuses on that aspect of power relationships that Foucault refers to in the second epigraph: freedom understood as what happens when life encounters power.

What sort of day-to-day acts of freedom, forms of resistance and means of escape are possible in a prison? Cohen and Taylor look back at their study of the high-security wing in Durham Prison:

> To accept the prison timetables or work schedules or systems of rewards uncritically, threatened the possible development of identity; they [the prisoners] could not readily show their uniqueness by accommodating to the "reality" which the regime presented. Once, however, they had constructed some type of alternative reality – cleared some small subjective spaces which were relatively uncontaminated by the institutional reality –

they then had sites upon which identity work might be mounted. They could display their specialness within the very style of dissociation from the regime.

(Cohen and Taylor, 1976: 20)

How do prisoners create free spaces and how do they maintain them? And how do they create their own space within the institution's walls (Duguid, 2000), an arena for individuality in a system that in some sense is based on the idea that all prisoners are the same? The prisoners' liberty projects can involve creating alternative realities that can be substituted for the old, with the added opportunities for turning yourself into something other, or more, than just "a prisoner". I will describe in more detail the various symbolic and material resources available to the prisoners in their work on transforming themselves, and I will show how various forms of resistance, in a broad sense, are effective tools in this work.

The question is what concrete actions can be seen as examples of freedom producing resistance in a prison context. In other words, this is not a study of general counter-power strategies in prison. One example of what I would call an act of resistance involves a remand prisoner called Ilir. He refused, for religious reasons, to give a urine sample after some cannabis had been found in the prison. As a Muslim, he said, he did not want to undress in front of the officers. The prison responded in line with its procedures by acting as if he had given a positive urine sample. Ilir received a reprimand and his confirmed used of drugs was recorded in his file. This made him angry and frustrated, and he chose to fight what he perceived as unnecessary harassment on the part of the institution. Since the urine test was a spot check that was not based on specific suspicion, he believed that he could not be forced to undress. He wrote a long letter of complaint and was willing to take matters "all the way":

I did not want to degrade myself because they wanted to check me, I haven't done anything wrong. They didn't really suspect me of anything. So I refused. It's undressing and pissing in front of an officer. I'm a Muslim, I don't do that sort of thing, you know? But then that one officer says, that bastard, he's at work today, he says that "Okay, then we'll just count it as a positive test and report you." That's not right! I haven't done anything wrong. And I'm not stupid, you know? I have checked the law and the Prisoner's Handbook.[2] It says in black and white that they have to prove that I have done something wrong. It's not me who has to prove that I'm innocent. There's no reverse burden of proof here! I will not degrade myself. The problem is that the prison has a file on m~ ~ it'll follow me, it'll have consequences for me, I might I might not get into an open prison. After all, my record s drugs, but it isn't true. I haven't done anything wrong! [.. six page letter of complaint to the prison. But I bet nothi

The school [Education department] helped me find the complaint form for the [European] Court of Human Rights online. It's not that hard, you know? The only thing is that I have to have tried all the national courts first. So I guess I'll have to go to court as soon as possible. [...] But it'll get sorted out; it has to get sorted out. I'll take it all the way. I ended the letter of complaint with that, I wrote that this is my first complaint, but it won't be my last.

Sometimes there is a lot of anger and frustration in Oslo Prison. But, in the midst of the frustration, a difficult situation also presents an opportunity to get even, to have an opinion, to stand for something. The most basic expression of resistance is to say *no*, to refuse, to turn your back or to sit down (Foucault, 1997). To refuse to fill the sample jar. Ilir said no, he stood his ground, and thus reopened a space filled with autonomy and self-determination, even in a prison context characterised by the fact that most of the decisions are already taken for you. The fact that there was a price to be paid merely increased the value of what he did.

But resistance can be more than just refusing. Thompson is onto something important in his description of the relationship between acts of resistance and autonomy: "To live autonomously is just to refuse the given, to uncover what is possible, and to have the courage to master one's life" (Thompson, 2003: 133). Everyday resistance is largely about refusing and looking past the given, finding and exploring opportunities, and mastering a situation. Analytically speaking, such a concept of resistance can be employed to hone in on precisely those expressive and performative aspects of resistance I am interested in, as well as the more traditional instrumental ones. Given this, when someone resists in situations such as in prison, they are always also doing something else at the same time. If you resist, you may turn yourself into someone who resisted. Erol puts it like this:

The day I submit is the day my heart stops beating. I'll be dead. Otherwise I'll always stand my ground until the final second, wherever I am, that's just the way I am.

Ilir's letter of complaint was explicit, open and written in the System's[3] own language. But if you stop there, you miss most of the resistance that occurs on a prison wing. In Scott's words: "[There is an] immense political terrain that lies between quiescence and revolt" (1990: 199). There are many ways of resisting, some more indirect and informal than others, as in this anecdote related by Nadir:

I just love coke in a glass bottle so much, right. I called my detective and said I couldn't hack it any more, prison was making me tired and depressed and I was ready to spill everything. He got really excited, heh 'eh. There was one condition, I said, come to the prison with coke in a glass bottle and a hamburger and then I'll tell you everything. It didn't take him more than 20 minutes. I got a message to go down because the police wanted to talk to me. I went down and all of sudden I had two glass bottles of coke and a full hamburger meal, proper McDonald's food. I ate up and had a lovely time. He was getting more and more excited; he was so ready to hear everything I had to tell him. I leaned backwards and said "...No...I don't think there'll be any interview today after all..." He went nuts, went crazy, you should have seen him, heh heh heh. A few weeks later I called him again and said that "Now, now I'm really ready to confess, I can't take it anymore and I want to get out. I don't want a coke or a hamburger, just come, I will tell you everything. Just bring waffles!" He turned up with waffles and jam, the lot. I ate up. Afterwards I just started to grin. He asked "I don't suppose there'll be any interview today either?" "I don't think so man." Heh heh heh. But that was that. The next time they wanted to talk to me it was down at the station. Heh heh, you have to mess with them a bit, you know? They get so excited that you are going to talk that it's so easy.

Resistance can be limiting and even destructive, but it can also be constructive, creative, inventive and playful when viewed in relation to authorities that want to restrict and control. Achieving something, despite restrictions, mastering a difficult context, turning your surroundings to your advantage: this can all work as resistance in relation to different, specific forms of power. Even saying *yes* can be part of a resistance strategy, as in, for example, go-slow actions. If the context is restrictive enough, it might be enough to open up space for action, to put your stamp on a situation, to create a feeling of autonomy and authority.

If there is overt and covert resistance, formal and informal, destructive and productive, a number of very different practices in prison can be understood as resistance (Hollander and Einwohner, 2004). At the overt end of the spectrum we find Ilir's letter of complaint. Other prisoners write letters to politicians or document and collect written evidence of the System's faults and deficiencies. More informally, and (at least so far) without the knowledge of the institution, Youssuf was writing a diary that he hoped to turn into a book about his time in Norway, and especially about what he called his fight with the Norwegian police and judicial system. The goal was for his story to be heard, and he also hoped that Norway would learn from what had happened to him:

One thing I've learnt here in Norway is that papers are never thrown away. That's also why, I don't care if anyone reads it, the most important thing is that it is there, that it exists and that it is archived. Perhaps it can change something, together with what you are writing, change small things. Such changes take a long time, slowly but surely, small drips the whole time. It is important to fight, it is very important not to give up.

This is a form of resistance that, at least there and then, was not made explicit and known to the officers. Many forms of resistance do not register on the officers' radar. At any given time there are a number of outlandish and semi-serious escape plans, fantasies about blowing up the prison or a police station, lonely outbreaks of rage or fits of laughter about all the stupid and irrational things the prison gets up to. These are expressions of resistance that never become publicly known on the prison wing. The reality is often like that described by Scott (1990): a prison can foster the impression of total and perfect order and agreement on the surface, while various actions of dissent lie beneath the surface.

What does it mean to become a prisoner? Being assigned the position of prisoner is to be assigned the position of someone whom society perceives as having been put in prison for understandable reasons; who is morally inferior, deprived of freedom and authority; who cannot decide for themselves; who has committed bad or incomprehensible acts; who has all sorts of problems and therefore needs help and to learn to take responsibility for their own life; who is, in the Norwegian context at least, one of the welfare state's most serious problems. Nietzsche describes the offender's perception of society's gaze as follows:

> If we generalize from the case of the criminal: we can imagine beings who, for some reason, lack public approval, who knows that they are not seen as beneficial or useful – that Chandala[4] feeling that you are not seen as equal but as excluded, unworthy, polluted. All creatures like this have a subterranean hue to their thoughts and actions; everything in them is paler than in people whose beings are touched by daylight.
>
> (Nietzsche, 2005: 219)

The status of prisoner carries with it a feeling of being placed on the margins, of feeling inferior, of being an object of society's disapproving glare. Being a prisoner is, in Nietzsche's words, to lack public approval. Being understood as one of the prisoners is to be ascribed a number of negative attributes – it is a *stigma* in the sense described by Goffman (1963). Such an ascribed position can be painful and can be understood as a being a fundamental part of what Sykes (1958) called *the pains of imprisonment*.

By objectifying prisoners and subjecting them to power and control techniques, the prison produces, as a more or less unforeseen consequence, a prisoner subject. A person put in prison becomes a prisoner. Conversely, the prisoner subject is a correlative of prison as a power technology, and its many techniques as they are adopted and put to work in daily life. The crucial thing in the following is how acts of resistance can be used to reposition

the prisoners as resistance subjects, something which is completely independent of any other results of the acts of resistance. Thus, planning an
escape attempt can be regarded as successful resistance, even if the plan is
never actually intended to be executed in actual practice. In other words, the
point is not necessarily to be someone who manages to escape prison, but
to make yourself into someone who *could have done so*. So, while it is right
to say that the prisoners' forms of resistance in prison are ways of escaping the monotony, boredom and impassivity of everyday prison life, one
can also say, and this is the particular focus of this book, that they are *an
escape from being a prisoner*, a form of resistance against the objectification
and "othering" that the status of prisoner entails. Everyday modifications,
translations and attempts to counter-attack, big and small, help the prisoners
create new symbolic and discursive contexts with the associated new positions for themselves. These are the sort of subject- or identity-oriented forms
of resistance I have studied: escape attempts understood not as attempts to
escape the prison's confines, but as the prisoners' attempts to escape from
their status as a prisoner.

Resistance also involves showing that you are a person who can resist,
someone who has not been deprived of all their autonomy and authority,
even if you have been put in prison. Modifying the situation, participating in the power relationship in a way that transforms it, at least to some
extent, and making yourself into an active subject who resisted, can be goals
in themselves. This desire to appear as an active and vigorous agent can
be found in much of what prisoners are interested in and say about the
prison and their situation. Understood like this, everyday forms of resistance become something far more than relatively harmless boundary testing.
They are actions that have fundamental effects on the level of the ongoing work on renegotiating and reconstructing your own identity within the
framework of the institution (Goffman, 1961).

Above, Ilir, the prisoner who refused to give a urine sample, staged the little man's righteous fight against the mighty, unfair System. He strongly committed himself to reconstructing himself as the freedom-fighting, oppressed
religious minority, someone who is not afraid of the superior power and
who would not allow himself to be picked on by the ignorant prison that
did not understand his spiritual needs. He had done nothing wrong and
would, therefore, not undress in front of the officers. Refusing to provide a
urine sample became part of a legitimate fight for justice and what is right,
a fight against oppression and persecution.

Youssuf's diary writing had the same effect for him. This can partly be
understood as resistance to the legal texts that affected his life as a remand
prisoner, an attempt to rewrite life using a non-legal and non-clinical
vocabulary. At the same time, he created a broader negation or counter-
ideology that resulted in all of his small examples of resistance becoming
part of an epic struggle against the unfair System and all this meant to

him as a subject who dared and managed to take on and continue the struggle. Prisoners are generally made passive and dependent on others. Youssuf did not allow himself to become a passive object: he took matters into his own hands and made himself, at least in part, the master of his own fate.

Nadir's anecdote about his cat-and-mouse game with the police detective was perhaps the most extreme example of this. His rendition may not be a perfect description of the meeting between him and the detective, but that is beside the point here (Sandberg, 2010). In Nadir's anecdote the power relationship between the hunter and the hunted has been reversed, at least temporarily. The anecdote tells the story of how he leaned arrogantly back in his chair, good and full, and watched, grinning, as his adversary absorbed the fact that he had been tricked, not just once, but twice. Instead of an anecdote about Nadir as the victim of a powerful System, the parties are relatively equal, although, of course, with Nadir slightly ahead. He didn't let himself be broken; instead, he masterfully took advantage of the opportunities he had, despite everything, and transformed himself into the master of a tricky situation – as well as a cheeky bastard making life difficult for the police, for added effect.

The fact that doing freedom in order to be free is a main project for prisoners, is perhaps, upon reflection, not particularly surprising. This book is about how this project is expressed in practice: about the prisoners' everyday forms of resistance (Scott, 1990), acts of freedom (Foucault, 1988) and escape attempts (Cohen and Taylor, 1976) in a Norwegian prison. And, yes, notice it says escape *in*, not *from*. This is not a book about prisoners tying sheets together, sawing through bars or scaling walls. The examples of the concrete forms of resistance I will present are (on the whole) not spectacular events that would fill the front pages of newspapers. Without denying that prison strikes, riots, escapes and violence against staff occur from time to time, also in Norwegian prisons, and without taking any of the dramatic power away from such events, it is important to say that these are very rare events in Norway (Hammerlin and Kristoffersen, 2001; Hammerlin and Strand [Ugelvik], 2005, 2006; Hammerlin and Rokkan, 2007). Even though such dramatic acts also can be understood as resistance, in the following the concept will mainly refer to practices that are far more common. Although a prison escape in its more traditional sense does actually appear later on in the book, I am, in this case, more interested in how the other prisoners discussed what had happened than describing who escaped and why. The focus is on what happens when individuals encounter power in their day-to-day lives, how these encounters play out in specific situations, why they play out in these particular ways, and their consequences.

Following this introduction, Chapter I describes the research methods and design. It gives an introduction to the particular field site that is Oslo prison and provides the general information about the institution and its people readers will need to make sense of the sections that follow. My position as an ethnographer in the specific field site is also explained. I describe how I was met by both prisoners and prison officers and how I (after a few initial problems) slowly managed to create the separate, distinctive position of "trustworthy visiting researcher" that I needed to complete the project. Chapter 1 ends with a discussion of the inevitable research ethics dilemmas all prison researchers have to face as part of doing research in such institutions.

Chapter 2 describes the forms and techniques of power in a prison and discusses their results. Foucault's thoughts about power, resistance and subjectivity are introduced in more detail and adapted to fit life on a Norwegian prison wing. The prison as a social technology is briefly introduced, with emphasis on the specific techniques and preferred outcomes. The focus is then shifted to life on the wings and to how the techniques of prison power play themselves out in practice. Following Foucault, I introduce the term "untrustworthy bodies" to describe the way the everyday re-creation of order and control seeps into the prisoners through the limits set on their bodies. The most basic of all the informal messages the institution conveys to the prisoners through the administration of everyday life on the wings is this: You are not to be trusted. This message is then connected to the Foucauldian framework introduced earlier and discussed as a subjectivity challenge.

In Chapter 3 I show all the different responses the prisoners have to being positioned as untrustworthy bodies by the institution. The prison turns people into prisoners. Prisoners try to change into something else. More specifically, I describe five different common resistance strategies:

First, prisoners reposition themselves through the use of so-called "constitutive others". These processes are not prison-specific; they can be found wherever people interact. I show how othering processes work in practice within the specific context of the prison. Common constitutive others employed for this purpose are agents of The System (most of the time, a term prisoners use to refer to the various agencies working to keep the prisoners incarcerated), the officers on the wing (after all, prisoners and prison officers are each other's most common topic of conversation) and Norwegians in and outside the prison (around 60 per cent of the prisoners in Oslo prison were foreign nationals at the time of fieldwork).

Second, prisoners re-create themselves through the physical and symbolic transformation of the space of the wing and its cells. A cell represents the institution as a power technology and, as such, the prison as a whole. But a cell is seldom just a cell; the empty space of an uninhibited cell is soon changed into something like a home when someone moves in. I show how prisoners transform the bare cell into a home surrogate.

Third, prisoners make themselves into free men through the various covert practices of illegal or semi-legal alternative food making that goes on behind closed cell doors. I show how prisoners experience the official prison food as a continuation of the more general attacks on their identity that imprisonment entails, denying them status as a person with competence and agency, forcefully removing them from family and friends, and positioning them on the margins of the larger community outside. The daily meals thus serve as painful bodily manifestations of the power the institution holds over the individual. As Foucault reminds us, however, power may be conceptualised as a fluctuating relationship of forces, not a property of powerful groups or individuals. From such a perspective, the prison food also works as an arena for prisoner identity work through practices of hidden resistance.

Fourth, prisoners react to being positioned as untrustworthy bodies made passive. The prison experience is one replete with restrictions. Prisoners try to negotiate and find ways around the limits to their freedom of movement through activities like weight-lifting and pool playing. The symbolic importance of scars is also discussed.

Finally, a prison understood as a moral space positions its prisoners as "immoral others" who should confess and repent. This ascription of low morality may, in fact, be seen as an important pain of imprisonment. I describe how prisoners reconstruct themselves as men of high moral fibre through their relationship with their children and through the exclusion of what they, in contrast to themselves, regard as the *real* "immoral others", like grasses and sex offenders.

Why write a book like this?

What is the point of this book? Why have I spent time writing it and why should anyone take the time to read it? The book can be read in many ways and may be useful to readers in a number of ways. Therefore, there are many possible answers to the question why. I will provide brief accounts of some partial answers that have been important to me during the work, although I would not wish to prevent the reader from finding other forms of meaning and use in the text.

One way of reading the book is to view it as a study of the state's most severe system of sanction and control, as it is working in practice. The prison is a means of, or a technology for, exercising the state's power over its subjects. Power must, writes Foucault, be caught off guard where it is exercised; it must be studied in its specificity in order to see its effects:

> [I]n thinking of the mechanisms of power, I am thinking rather of its capillary form of existence, the point where power reaches into the very grain of individuals, touches their bodies and inserts itself into their actions and attitudes, their discourses, learning processes and everyday lives.
>
> (Foucault, 1980: 39)

The prison is part – one could say an absolutely central and distinctive part – of the state's formal apparatus for managing its citizens. It pushes the issue of the state's power over its subjects to the extreme. How can ethnographers best approach a large-scale phenomenon such as the state? The answer is that the state can be described and studied using the practical level as a point of departure. Sim (2003) points at the obvious: it is never the state with a capital "S" that acts; it is always specific politicians, bureaucrats or other civil servants who are placed in specific situations at various levels of the apparatus of the state. The focus is thus displaced from the state's overall functions to its day-to-day operations. As an extension of such a perspective, this can be understood as a micro-study of state power.

Furthermore, the use of prisons is increasing in most countries with which it would be natural to compare Norway, and in most others as well (Christie, 2000; Cavadino and Dignan, 2006; Lacey, 2008; Nelken, 2010). At the same time as its use is increasing, the invisibility Foucault describes (Foucault, 1977a; cf. Wacquant, 2002) has increased: prisons are no longer built in city centres as a clear, tangible sign of the power of the state, as a warning to actual and potential offenders. Instead, they are hidden off the beaten track. From this perspective, I regard simply enabling people to learn more about the inside and day-to-day life of the institution as valuable.

The book can also be read as a form of translation, as set out by Cohen and Taylor (1976, 1981). The prisoners' thoughts, words and deeds are expressions of a particular context – with a concept that is thus taken out of its theoretical context, a specific "lifeworld". The goal is to make the prisoners understandable also outside the specific context of the prison. From an external vantage point, the local meanings and purposes ascribed to acts may be difficult to spot. Acts can, quite simply, look meaningless divorced from their original contexts. According to Geertz (1973b), one of the fundamental purposes of any ethnographic study is to facilitate understanding. Researchers need to understand the relevant culture so that they can communicate their findings in a manner that enables others without first-hand knowledge to understand it as well. As an extension of this, ethnography can demystify and humanise, and, in a certain sense of the word, normalise:

> The claim to attention of an ethnographic account does not rest on its author's ability to capture primitive facts in faraway places and carry them home like a mask or a carving, but on the degree to which he is able to clarify what goes on in such places, to reduce the puzzlement – what manner of men are these?
>
> (Geertz, 1973b: 16)

In prison, cognitive thinking errors, psychopathy and Attention Deficit Hyperactivity Disorder (ADHD) are terms currently in vogue (Duguid, 2000; Garland, 2001; Andersson, 2011). Given this background, the book provides an alternative way of understanding the prisoners and their actions. On the one hand, it is, of course, important that those who live and work in the arena I describe, both prisoners and officers, can recognise themselves. On the other hand, I hope they do not recognise themselves *too well*. The whole point is that it is I, an outsider with a totally different background and a completely different project from theirs, who has written the book. Even if prisoners and officers are around each other every day, there are many situations in which their different perspectives mean that they are living in different worlds. An alternative perspective from the sidelines may help both parties understand each other and themselves in new ways.

A secondary goal has been to help the "gendering" of prisons research. While gender is probably the single variable that best categorises the population by likelihood to commit crime, criminology has, like many other disciplines, been surprisingly gender-blind (Messerschmidt, 1993; Newton, 1994). Over time, criminology has, as part of a broader focus on developing women's and gender research, opened its gender-sensitive eyes. However, for a long time it was primarily women who had a gender. Men and men's actions are gradually starting to be analysed from a gender perspective (*inter alia* Newburn and Stanko, 1994; Sim, 1994; Daly, 1997; Carrabine and Longhurst, 1998; Cowburn, 1998; Messerschmidt, 2000; Hood-Williams, 2001; Hayslett-McCall and Bernard, 2002; Jewkes, 2002; Miller, 2002; Jewkes, 2005; Kupers, 2005; Bandyopadhyay, 2006; Klein and Chancer, 2006). I hope to continue this trend with this book.

Finally, the book can be read as an attempt to develop theory. It has been said that Foucauldian perspectives are unsuitable for empirical social research (*inter alia* Fox, 1998). Foucault himself was no social scientist; this is a form of study he never conducted. Nonetheless, he gave explicit encouragement that his concepts and perspectives should be tailored and put to work in new fields. Therefore, the book can be read as an attempt to "put Foucault in prison". I will try to explore opportunities for using his ideas and concepts, in particular the relationship between subjectification, freedom, power and resistance, as a source of inspiration and an analytical system in empirical social research, especially those concepts he developed towards the end of his life. The result is a sort of Foucault-informed – theoretically, empirically and analytically informed – analysis of a specific empirical field.[5]

Having said that, a small but important shift in analytical focus has occurred in comparison with classic studies of prison life (e.g. Clemmer, 1940; Sykes, 1958; Galtung, 1959; Klare, 1960; Wheeler, 1961; Mathiesen, 1965). The fundamental analytical level is, as an extension of Foucault, the continuous game of forms of power and resistance. I describe the social field constituted by a concrete prison wing, with the rules, norms and positions that the players of the game can utilise with varying effects vis-à-vis their subjectivity. As a social arena for this game I view the prison wing as consisting of many "things" on various levels, including relationships (of power, mutuality, equality and difference), objects and materials (to which the players, in turn, may have different relationships: of ownership, rights, affinity, identification), one's own body, opinions and perceptions and so on.

As a last point, I have tried to develop a theoretical and analytical basis that is not prison-specific. This is the result of a view that is both research-based and, in some sense, political; prisoners are not people who are totally out of the ordinary, nor are prison wings unique as arenas for social interaction. Therefore, I wanted to employ an analytical framework that might also function in other places and potentially tell us something interesting and useful about people who are not in prison. I will analyse empirical data, which I am keen to describe in all its prison-specific depth, but with the aid of general social analytical tools that allow both prison-specific and more general conclusions.

1
Implementation

I am hanging out with Brede. An officer discreetly knocks on the half-open cell door and tells us that we have to end our conversation because it is about to begin. We eagerly get up and start getting ready. First out are all the prisoners. They leave unit four and go through the metal detector gate and down the stairs as if they were just going out into the prison yard as normal; although they are perhaps more pleased and excited. The weather is good, luckily. Perfect for a barbecue. After the officers have made a quick inspection and checked that all the cells are empty, it's our turn. In the corridors we meet prisoners from other wings on their way out. Quick, expectant steps.

Just before the exit we are naturally and smoothly divided into different groups – prisoners to the right, officers (and me) to the left. For a split second I can see in his eyes that the officer who is posted to ensure that everyone chooses the right lane is about to ask me to move to the right. Then he sees the ID cards and the alarm and says "Move to the ... no, not you", and smiles at me. We all leave our keys down in wing one. The officers there can watch them. Keys are not allowed out in the prison yard with the prisoners. We move out into the sun, through the wire mesh enclosed passage that leads from the building to the prison yard.

Out in the yard the party has already begun. Long tables have been laid and, in a marquee at one end, red-clothed Red Cross workers are hard at work serving a long queue of prisoners plates laden with barbecued food, hot dogs and hamburgers. Two large barrel barbecues made in the prisoners' metal workshop are working away. Several prisoners ask what the burgers and hot dogs are made of and the cooks reassure them that they are only beef or chicken, not pork. Everyone is satisfied.

All the prisoners coming from the main building join the food queue straight away. All the officers move to the right, basically putting themselves on the sidelines, as outsiders. A small group wearing blue shirts are standing together, out of place and a bit tense, next to a hundred men in civilian clothes on the grass, benches, stools, and in the food queue, all with summer hamburger and hot dog grins.

What should I do? Stick with the officers? No, that does not seem like the thing to do. But whom should I approach? I look around and see a few familiar groups of prisoners sitting together. At the same time I see a number of hearty reunions between people who know each other. A number of wings are gathered here, people who are not used to sharing the prison yard. I feel I have to do something. But is there an empty stool next to anyone I know?

I pick out a stool, join the queue, get some food and a mineral water, and sit down. Fortunately, the stool is still empty. Several people around the table eye me suspiciously, but those who know me help break the ice. They tell them that I work at the university; that I'm writing about the prison. And apparently that's just great; people smile and give me the thumbs up. There is a great atmosphere around the tables; the band has started playing some classic tunes. "No Woman, No Cry" is played to great approval. "We Don't Need No Education" is also popular.

The officers are still standing on their own, still without any food. They are reduced to awkward visitors now; it's quite clear that the prison yard is not their territory. Red Cross girls, cute and highly visible in their red T-shirts, walk around handing out coffee and ice creams. The prisoners are lying around on the lawn chatting, relaxed. They are flirting with the ice cream girls. Small groups of prisoners glance up and whisper to each other, before they break out in loud laughter. The band has become background music. The girls smile and appear to be enjoying the attention. Doling out ice cream is not a job for those who do not enjoy being looked at.

I move over to Arfan. He is chatting with an older prisoner on crutches. He has broken two bones in his foot. It fucking hurts, he says, grimacing for emphasis. He has taken six strong paracetamol, but they aren't helping. But he is still going to party. The foot is not in plaster, it's just bandaged. Dark blue toes protrude from the peach-coloured bandage. In broken Norwegian he tells me that they have to wait for the swelling to go down before they can break the bones again and put a cast on. It had taken too long to get to accident and emergency. The prison's fault, he says, shaking his head.

The clouds suddenly empty. Warm summer rain pours down. Laughing, we seek shelter in the two, much too small, marquees – the one where the food was made and the other one used by the band. The mood is still light and pleasant among the random collection of prisoners standing under the drumming rain. Arfan thinks the rain proves that everyone who is outside right now is innocent. After all, the other block will take over the summer party soon, while we will have to go back in. They'll only get the rain and are therefore guilty. God is for us, not them. God loves us innocents, he says, laughing.

We return to the wing along the same two routes we took on our way down. The mood is still good; everyone is wet, stuffed and happy. But now lock-up awaits. A trustee asks if there will be dinner later, but no – this was dinner. A Spanish-speaking prisoner's eyes widen when he finally understands the message: the normal association time and all normal activities are cancelled for the rest of the evening. The reason is that the officers have to be on standby for as long as the barbecue continues for the other half of the prisoners outside (luckily the weather cleared up again). Therefore, it will be an afternoon in the cells for those for whom the party is over. The prison gives with one hand and takes with the other, says Arfan. That way everything evens out.

* * *

A book like this one must meet some formal requirements. One is that it must explain the study's methodology and the circumstances surrounding its implementation. In the ethnographic tradition it is normal in such cases to present the researcher's position in the field in some detail in order to provide the reader with some keys to understanding and drawing conclusions about the data material upon which the study is based. For many people, the methodology section is one of the most enjoyable sections – it can, in its own way, provide a lot of information about the field and the researcher, which is often somewhat tangential to the overall argument. For others, such sections often represent a diversion on the way to the real substance. For those who wish to go directly to jail, I have tried to frame the discussions of methodology in the context of Oslo Prison as much as I can.

The practical stuff

Oslo Prison is Norway's largest. With a capacity of 392 male prisoners in single cells, it houses over one-tenth of Norway's total prison population. When it opened, the prison stood on a hillside on the outskirts of the city. Today, Oslo has expanded well beyond its walls, placing the prison in a multi-ethnic residential area in the eastern part of the city centre. The prison has two wings. Wing A occupies the oldest part, the brick building that opened as one of six planned penitentiaries ("botsfengsel") built in 1851.[1] Unit A is, therefore, also called "Botsen" when there is a need to differentiate. It houses prisoners with sentences of up to two years. Unit B occupies the newer buildings in Åkebergveien on the way up to Galgeberg. These buildings were originally home to the Oslo Aktiebryggeri brewery and gradually became part of the prison through a renovation process in the 1930s. For this reason, wing B is often referred to by its nickname "Bayern"; the *bayer* is a type of dark beer inspired by Bavarian beer-making traditions. Bayern mainly houses remand prisoners. It was here, in units four and five located on the fourth and fifth floor of the yellow prison building closest to Galgeberg, that I spent a year.

So, who are the prisoners here? They are men. Oslo Prison is an all-male prison. It is also important to point out that remand prisoners represent a special section of the Norwegian prison population. The average time spent in prison by prisoners convicted in Norway is about 110 days, and most of them spend no time on remand at all. When remand prisoners arrive at Oslo Prison they are first sent to a special reception wing. It is only after they have been here for some time that they, if they are remanded for long enough, may be moved to the two wings where I conducted my fieldwork. The group of prisoners who appear in this book are, thus, not just remand prisoners; unlike "most prisoners", they are those remand prisoners who have been on remand longer than most. They are generally suspected of committing serious offences involving violence, murder, rape or importing or dealing relatively large amounts of illegal drugs. In such cases prisoners can spend a long time on remand, sometimes years, before their case comes to court. If they have been imprisoned on remand for some time, they will, as a rule, be convicted. And if they are convicted, they will, as a rule, be given sentences that far exceed the average.

Remand prisoners also represent a mixed group. At the time of writing, around 60 per cent of remand prisoners in Norway are foreign nationals. That figure is probably even higher in Oslo Prison. In addition to this, a large but unknown proportion of those counted as Norwegian belong to an ethnic minority. Looking at the overview whiteboard hanging in the officers' room, you will see that some of the names belong to Norwegian-Pakistanis with Norwegian citizenship who have been in the country since the 1970s, or who were born here, and whose entire network is in Norway. Some prisoners arrived in the country later, as refugees from the former Yugoslavia, and have also been in Norway for years; most of these also have Norwegian passports. Others, for example prisoners from North Africa, have often lived in Norway for some time and speak broken, but understandable, Norwegian. Some, from Romania or Africa south of the Sahara, rarely speak Norwegian, but can make themselves understood in English. Another group, often from the Baltic States, speak neither Norwegian nor English. This is the diversity represented by the remand prisoners in Oslo Prison.

The introductory description of my first day in the prison does not tell the whole story of how the project started. I had, by this time, been working on the project for a full year. There was a lot that needed to be done. Prison researchers often face big problems just getting as far as gaining access to a prison. Waldram (2009), who has carried out research inside a number of prisons, describes major difficulties in gaining access to some institutions. Even though he had the approval of the central prison authorities, at one place he had to wait at least an hour every day before he was allowed into the prison because his application for more permanent access rights was always still sitting on the prison governor's desk. It is impossible to conduct research in a prison without a certain degree of goodwill on the part of those who work there. The prison service, the prison's management and the officers on the particular wing all have to accept the researcher's presence, at least before and during the entire fieldwork phase. Thankfully, unlike Waldram, I experienced no sabotage. On the contrary, the regional level of the Norwegian Correctional Services approved the project without delay, and the management of Oslo Prison received me with interest and goodwill. I also quickly became part of daily life in the two specific wings where I spent most of my time, despite some initial challenges. I could come and go as I wanted and I could speak with whomever I wanted without clearing it in advance. Within the framework of the two units, I only experienced the restrictions I imposed upon myself.

I visited the prison three or four days a week for one year, usually for five–six hours at a time. I did not make observation notes while I was at the prison. In other fieldwork contexts a notepad can signify that what is being said is being taken seriously, that the researcher regards it as important. But when you have a notepad in your hand it is easy to be assigned the role of social worker, journalist, or, worst of all, police detective, and then the pad just becomes a distraction. This, of course, does not mean that I believe that a researcher without a notepad can assume some sort of neutral position – I will return to this later. The desire to avoid this sort of distraction resulted in my nonetheless, after weighing all the pros and cons, choosing not to use a notepad.

As the fieldwork moved forward I noted a series of events I wanted to know more about, and questions I really wanted to discuss. After I had been visiting the prison for about six months I asked some of the prisoners if they might be willing to participate in more formal interviews, which would be recorded. With one exception, everyone I asked was willing to do so. These interviews represent just a small part of the total data material, but they did afford me an opportunity to return to specific episodes and ask those involved what they thought about what had happened. They also gave me an opportunity to ask questions and open up areas for discussion in a different way than one usually would as part of the day-to-day interaction in the units. I conducted eight such interviews, each of which lasted between one and two and a half hours. All of the interviews were conducted alone with the prisoner in his cell. They were thematic and driven by specific events I had observed or conversations I wanted further comments on. At the same time, they were open and relatively unstructured: I had noted a handful of questions, but the interviews were just as much steered by the prisoners' interest.

The prisoners I interviewed were, without exception, among those I had known quite well for some time. Nonetheless, the interview situation felt tense and a bit formal. The prisoners underscored this new solemnity by taking their role of host extra seriously: they served mineral water, instant cappuccino, crisps or toast with fresh cheese and honey. The small audio recorder I used added to the formality. It sat there seemingly staring at us and emphasising that the situation was new and different, even though in most cases we had previously spent hours together in the same cell. With the audio recorder there, we were suddenly not alone; we had listeners. Some interviewees reacted by being more expansive when relating anecdotes. At the same time, conversations that normally would have been more fluid took on a more strategic character. I noted that the prisoners became more interested in the details being correct; who had done what suddenly meant more. And I noted that several of the prisoners I interviewed suddenly wanted to take about "their criminality", even when I tried to steer the conversation in other directions. This was probably an expression of what they thought I "really" wanted. All in all, the interviews were useful as an opportunity to discuss and correct my preliminary interpretations, and, therefore, they often stimulated reflection and helped with the formulation of new questions. Nonetheless, an interview situation presents clear limitations, which resulted in my choosing to focus on the observation data.

The indented quotes are either excerpts from my fieldwork diaries or transcripts of interviews. I noted my impressions from the day's visit to the prison on the same evening or the morning after, not just focusing on the meaning of what was said, but also expressing the tone and style of speech, as well as the relevant conversation situation. I have chosen not to use quotation marks around fieldwork diary excerpts (meaning they stand out from interview excerpts in the text) in order to show that the words cannot be read as a verbatim reproduction of what I observed. Quotation marks in the fieldwork diary excerpts are used to show direct speech and do not signify a verbatim quote either.

My position as researcher

I experienced my first day in the prison as an extremely chaotic jumble of loud noises and strange people, alleviated by (I must admit) a welcome silence when the prisoners were locked in their cells. Nonetheless, at the end of the day I was, despite my slightly unclear undercover status, a restrained optimist, given that things had gone better as the day went on. In the weeks that followed I gradually became part of a world that I grew to understand better and better, a world in which I had created a space for myself and which I could relate to and which related to me. This position, partly on the

inside and partly on the outside of the rest of life on the wing, was the result of a process of negotiation that continued throughout the fieldwork. Who and what I was in relation to daily life in the prison was important in how I perceived the institution, for what I could, as a result, see and not see, and, as an extension of this, the entire result of the research project. It was in their meeting with me, in the position I developed in relation to the specific context the two units constitute, that the prisoners thought as they thought and did as they did. Naturally, the presence of a researcher changed the field in various ways. However, such "control effects" are not sources of errors; they are key methodological tools.

Prison researchers have often been able to carry out their research via holding an official position in the relevant prison. Clemmer (1940) continuously interviewed prisoners in his role as a resident sociologist as part of the institution's knowledge production and other decision-making processes (his job title was "sociologist-actuary"). He also carried out his prison sociology surveys in this position. Coggeshall (2004) conducted his studies while teaching anthropology in the prison's school. Mathiassen (2004) returned as a researcher to a prison where she had previously been employed as a clinical psychologist. Former prisoners have also written about their experiences. The most common genre is the prison biography, although some prisoners also write research papers and monographs (Galtung, 1959; Lauesen, 1998; Ross and Richards, 2003; Bosworth et al., 2005).

I experienced Oslo Prison as a politicised field in the sense meant by Becker (1967), with a clear dividing line between prisoners and officers. The "perpetual conflict" that some (*inter alia* Sparks, Bottoms and Hay, 1996; Lindberg, 2005) have seen as characteristic of a prison per definition could not be misunderstood, although in Oslo Prison the conflict was far more moderate in daily life than, for example, the one experienced by Jacobs (1977) when he arrived at Stateville Penitentiary. He describes how he was thrown into an unstable social situation with rumours, factions, suspicion and more or less open conflict, all of which were like landmines he could step on at any time. But, even though it was somewhat more moderate, conflict was also the permanent basis for all interaction in Oslo Prison. Given such a situation, I made a point of trying to approach the field without "choosing sides" in advance.

I held no clear position when I arrived at Oslo Prison as a university employee. My behaviour and presence basically had no clear meaning for either prisoners or officers. I observed, but I was also observed. I had to sort out and negotiate a meaningful role. I had previously worked as a researcher for the Norwegian Correctional Services, which I was, of course, completely open about. At the same time, I represented a criminological academic community that for many people – officers as well as prisoners – is synonymous with prisons critique and even prison abolitionism. Given my background in the Norwegian Correctional Services, I risked the prisoners viewing me as an agent of the System who was working for the Ministry of Justice, while the officers might view me as a management man, since my previous job in the Norwegian Correctional Services involved doing evaluations. On the other hand, my university affiliation could result in the officers associating me with someone who speaks from his ivory tower about punishment being the intentional infliction of pain. Both the prisoners and the officers were initially sceptical about me in different ways. The prisoners viewed me either as a representative of the authorities or as their useful idiot, while the officers wanted to know more about the project, the criminological academic community in general, and *whether that weirdo Christie is still going on about that pain business?*[2] For me, therefore, much of my initial effort to adapt consisted of trying to disprove and refine both of these forms of preconceived affiliation.

The dividing line between prisoners and officers structures everything that happens in a prison. The actors are deeply committed to this difference and, to a very large extent, define themselves and others on this basis (Goffman, 1961). For example, as a general rule, providing some types of information across this boundary is strictly taboo. Both prisoners and officers have clear rules about what can be told and how it can be told to members of the opposing group. This taboo forms such an integral part of everyday life in the prison that it is joked about (which, of course, does not mean it is not real): like the time some prisoners put the clock back in the common area to trick the officers into extending a social. When the officer on duty – resignedly, but smiling – realised he had been tricked and asked a prisoner if he had had anything to do with it, the prisoner grinned slyly and repeated the well-known refrain: *I didn't see anything, officer. I know nothing.* Prisoners become snitches if they give the wrong piece of information to the wrong person. For their part, officers risk causing a political criminal justice scandal and the need for a public inquest should the wrong practice be described in the wrong way. Both sides in the game risk something by talking to a researcher. And there I was, somehow in the middle of everything, without a clear role, but pursuing this precise sort of information.

Neutrality as a research strategy is not without problems when it comes to its actual practice. You can easily be drawn into the day-to-day categorisations, whether you want to be or not. And, as an ethnographer, you really do want to be drawn in. Simply put, the problem is that being drawn in will challenge the desire for neutrality. The already politicised field requires a choice, and anyone who simply tries to walk the thin line down the middle requires good balance. I deliberately placed myself on a tightrope from which both the prisoners and officers invited me to fall down on one side or the other. Sometimes it felt as if I – rather than being a talented tightrope walker – was standing with one foot on the pier and one in a boat that was beginning to drift away. I experienced officers trying to use me as a mediator or "lightning rod" when they were in conflict with prisoners I knew.

One officer said to me that *it's unbelievable how much more cooperative he was because you were there as well*, after calling me into a meeting he had with a prisoner to clear the air. At the same time, prisoners deliberately used me to influence the officers. As the fieldwork was drawing to an end, one of them told me that he had made a point of ringing for the officers from his cell while I was visiting. He thought that the officers were far better at remembering that he wanted a shower when I was a "witness" to the request.

It was also interesting to observe how both prisoners and officers tried to make me an associate member of their respective groups. When there were too few people at work, the officers joked that I would have to go and find a uniform. If there was too much to do in the office, they sighed resignedly that it was too bad that I was so lazy that I could not be bothered to even answer the phone or unlock a door. Nonetheless, these were probably more attempts at inclusion than actual challenges. I was never seriously asked to perform prison officer tasks, apart from remembering to lock the doors that did not lock automatically.[3] For their part, the prisoners talked behind the officers' backs and laughed at them in my presence. They shook hands with me in the way prisoners do and stated that *You are one of us now Thomas.* And, when they talked about who had been on the wing the longest, they also asked me: *Nine months? Hell, you've been here just as long as me, Thomas. Remind me again, when is your release date?*[4]

Even though both prisoners and officers tried to include me in various ways, I could, of course, never fit in properly anywhere. Whether it was officers commenting on what they perceived as typical "academic" cloth- ing (*Really? Woolly socks and red shoes!*) or the prisoners who were envious because I could leave at the end of the day, I was regularly reminded that, as an ethnographer, I was a member of a group of one (Jacobs, 1977). More than genuine invitations, I guess I understand these examples of inclusion as confirmation that I was welcome; that it was nice that I was there.

From the first day I was a natural part of the officers' "back stage", with access to all the conversations to which the prisoners definitely should not be privy. Sometimes the officers experienced that I remained out of such conversations around the lunch table, especially when they discussed things that would have required me to break a confidence with respect to individual prisoners if I had participated. Even though they joked about it (*Oh, he's gone quiet again, eh? This will definitely be in the book!*), the officers probably reminded themselves and each other that the walls, even more than usual in a prison, had ears.

Sometimes the officers also wanted to bring me in as an expert. For example, I was asked for my criminological opinion on how the prison should organise a recently started initiative aimed at young offenders. Being asked for "diagnostic" opinions about prisoners I knew did not feel quite right. Given my attempt to be neutral, I was deliberately vague and therefore probably fairly useless. Many an officer who has sought academic advice from me has probably had all of their prejudices about academics confirmed.[5]

For a profession that attaches importance to control and knowing what is happening at all times, the prison researcher is a chaotic element, especially if he wants to talk to the prisoners undisturbed. The fact that prisoners have secrets is, of course, nothing new, but the secrecy is in a way legitimised as soon as a researcher wants to go in and talk to the prisoners, which means, of course, to some extent, talking about the officers "behind their backs". The fact that I was met with a certain amount of scepticism is, therefore, not strange.

On the other hand, I experienced a great deal of trust on the part of the institution. Every day I brought my backpack containing my gym kit and lunch box onto the wing. It was never checked. I therefore enjoyed the same level of trust as any member of the prison's staff, a fact that could possibly be linked to my former status as an employee of the correctional services. As a researcher working for the correctional services I had previously experienced being thrown prison keys before I had even managed to sign in. The staff of Oslo Prison (thankfully) did not view me as a problem. The title of "criminologist" appears to be invaluable for those who want to maintain a certain minimum distance from prison officers. All in all, I was again *in the middle*; not a real colleague on the inside, but not a strange, external critic who has misunderstood everything, either. In my opinion it was the perfect position, an appropriate mix of proximity and distance.

Trust must be earned and merited. A number of prisoners tested me to see whether or not I could be trusted. Some showed me a gradually larger number of kitchen utensils that breached prison rules to see whether or not I went to the officers with the information. Another prisoner asked me whether I knew an associate professor at the Department of Criminology and Sociology of Law, giving me a made-up name. I replied that that person did not work in the department. He smiled and was satisfied.

After I had spent some time in the prison I was included in both the prisoners' and the officers' respective informal joking and banter communities, as when the same prisoner who had thought I was really a police officer on the first day greeted me as follows:

Prisoner: Look, here comes our bookworm. Are the police going to be here today as well?

TU: You really should make your mind up; the police don't read books do they? Either I'm a bookworm or police. What is it to be?

Prisoner: Ha ha ha!

Such quick, witty ripostes between prisoners, between officers and between members of both groups are highly valued in the day-to-day interaction in the prison (Mathiesen, 1965; Nielsen, 2011). The officers had a lot of fun teasing the criminologist, who, they assumed, was critical about everything he saw. An officer who was letting prisoners in from the prison yard on a warm summer day said to me:

Officer: This really is the best part of the whole day. It's this and body searches.

TU: Yeah? Why?

Officer: It's when we take stuff from them [prisoners]. That's the best thing I know!

The officer smiled teasingly. It's fun to play up to prejudices he thinks that I might have, being a criminologist.

Officer: You know that I'm kidding right [smiling]?

TU: I didn't really hear what you said just now. I was far too busy remembering what you said about taking stuff from them. After all, that'll be a whole chapter right there [smiling].

Being teased and teasing back a bit means you have been accepted (Geertz, 1973a). Therefore, when I discovered that a photo of me that I had posted on the noticeboard had had devil's horns and a goatee added as soon as I had replaced an old one with a new, I took it as a good sign.

I wore, as the prisoners did, my own civilian clothes. An Oslo Prison ID card hung around my neck, the same card every employee in the prison carries. I also carried a university ID card. Attached to my belt was a black, oblong assault alarm, with a red alarm button, and a single prison key fastened to a long chain. In earlier meetings with the prison's various representatives I had said that I would rather not have this key, but the issue was never properly clarified. When I first arrived I encountered the prison as a practical world where officers had better things to do than open doors for a researcher. Would I have to be fetched from the gate every day? And what if I wanted to go to the toilet? I allowed myself to be convinced to carry a key, although I did not really have a choice. I was worried about the symbolism inherent in having the key in my possession, worried that I, as Waldram (2009) describes, would be dependent on the prisoners' trust while at the same time carrying visible symbols of mistrust on my belt. Control of the keys is important in prison. I shoved mine, with all the accessories, in my trouser pocket, mostly so I did not have to walk around jangling all the time. I soon understood that the prisoners associated this jangling sound with officers, a discovery that, of course, made it no less important to put the key in my pocket.

On the first day I wore a brown and beige checked shirt and a pair of jeans. I do not really know why I chose the shirt. I soon realised that it was probably a bit formal. I was not dressed up; the shirt was open at the neck and, anyway, it was not the formal sort. The problem is that there are only three good reasons for wearing a shirt in Oslo Prison: you are on your way to court, you are going to a funeral, or you are an officer. A shirt says that you are at work and therefore creates distance between you and the prisoners; it is a symbol of the difference between prisoners and officers. I therefore switched to something more like the informal style of most of the prisoners; I wore a t-shirt and a hoodie. All in all, the goal again was to come across as someone in between the established positions in the prison. The alarm on my belt marked me as a non-prisoner, the informal clothes as a non-employee.

For the officers I was a safety risk, first and foremost for myself. Sometimes the officers who were responsible for me said that I should not do something because it could be dangerous for me, or, they hurriedly added, not *really* dangerous, but, after all, they were responsible for me. When I visited a prisoner in his cell, the officers popped in occasionally to make sure everything was alright. Sometimes the cell door was locked by mistake while I was visiting a prisoner. Once we did not say anything right away. The officer who found me locked in a cell half an hour later was obviously both embarrassed and a bit flustered, while my host had a good laugh at the officer's mistake. As far as the prisoners were concerned, it was just fine that the officers were meant to look after me. My status as a non-officer could not be more clearly communicated: when young, female extra officers who weighed half my weight had to look after me, it was obvious that I was neither an officer nor an undercover cop. The officers' responsibility for my safety marked me as an unmistakable member of that helpless, unworldly class of "academics".

So what did I do for a whole year in Oslo Prison? Since I had no official duties in the prison, and since the one key I carried only allowed me to walk from the main gate up to the wing (I could not open or lock cell doors), I spent most of the time hanging around the wing. I drank coffee, played pool, and chatted about the weather, football, cars, and anything else that anyone wanted to talk to me about either in the small common area or in one of the cells. As a research strategy it is very close to what has been called "deep hanging out" (Geertz, 2000). This worked well as an ethnographic strategy in a remand prison where there is an abundance of time and not a lot to do with it, even though the strategy regularly provoked teasing questions about when my break was over and whether I did not have to do some work soon.

Choosing this strategy meant choosing not to take advantage of other opportunities. There were a number of arenas linked to "my" wings that could have formed part of this study. The adjoining prison school is the most obvious. Many of the prisoners in wings four and five were at school during the day. I had originally planned to make this part of the project, but after a while, as I developed more and better relationships with the prisoners, the school idea faded away. On the other hand, I would have liked to include the prison yard in the study. Yard time was the only part of the day when all the prisoners were locked out of their cells at the same time. For my own safety (or, more precisely, because of the prison's responsibility for my safety), I was not allowed to join the prisoners in the prison yard. I accompanied officers out to the yard watch tower a few times, but primarily to talk to them. Watching the prisoners as a researcher from a concealed position inside a watch tower would, to put it mildly, have been problematic. However, the two or three hours I spent in the yard tower gave me some insight into how officers view boring, daily, routine duties.

I do not know much about the structure of how decisions are made in the prison either. By hanging out in wings four and five I had chosen not to view decision-making processes at a level above the wings. I have only studied decisions as they have played out in the two wings. I participated in a few meetings at the explicit invitation of the officers, but, again, it felt strange to be part of the institution's official conversation about the prisoners and to be asked for my "professional" opinion. The regular meetings where the officers discuss the prisoners tell you a lot about the officers' viewpoints and their rationality and methods, and could, therefore, have been interesting. From a Foucauldian point of view, it would also have been interesting to study the institutional knowledge production about the prisoners, to look at archives and systems for collecting information and knowledge. This will have to be for another time. Even though I could probably have gained access to this type of information, it would, in practice, have placed me in a very difficult position in relation to the prisoners. The transferred symbolism of such access could have been the same as walking around in a uniform with a full key chain – which could, of course, have provided the basis for a research project, but which would have undoubtedly affected the results. The neutral researcher position I was striving for required me not to wear one.

For research ethics reasons, it was important that everyone in wings four and five during my time there knew who I was and why I was there. From the day I arrived and discovered that the information poster I had sent to the prison had not been posted, to when I greeted newly arrived prisoners on the very last day of the fieldwork, I constantly strove to tell and retell the story about who I was and what I was doing in the prison. This was not always easy, given that there was no forum where the prisoners were all together. There was no morning meeting at which I could present myself. The prisoners did not have a representative who could help me disseminate information either. Therefore, my most important tool was probably the prison grapevine. I realised that a good way of presenting myself to as many prisoners as possible was to be present during the daily letting out and in of prisoners for yard time. This was the only opportunity when all the prisoners were released from their cells at the same time (all except for those who were on report, and for that reason were not allowed out for yard time, and those few prisoners who, for some reason or other, wanted to stay in their cells). On the way between the wing and the stairwell you have to pass through a metal detector gate. Queues often form here. By positioning myself here, I had a good opportunity to shake hands with prisoners I knew and have a quick chat. Prisoners I did not know soon had their questions answered about who this bloke was. The prison grapevine was a particularly important tool, given that there were always prisoners on the wing who spoke neither Norwegian nor English. Getting help with interpretation via the prison grapevine was, therefore, invaluable.

Next, as I have described, I made sure I hung up posters on the wings' two cork noticeboards with brief information about the project in Norwegian and English, and a photo of myself. The poster was hung up in the middle of the respective wings, but I occasionally met prisoners who had not seen the information. Finally, the fact that I wore two ID cards around my neck helped. It made me unique, and the difference was so obvious that many people wondered what wearing two cards meant, which gave me an opportunity to tell them about my university affiliation. I just had to live with the fact that some people thought it looked a bit strange: *Two cards, eh? Was there a sale on?*

Meanwhile, I was mistaken for a lot of things during my year in the prison. Despite all the energy I expended on disseminating information, I was mistaken for a trainee prison officer, summer temp, new employee, teacher in the school department, recreation department worker, and social worker. This is, of course, only a partial list of the instances of wrong information I actually discovered and corrected. There is a practical aspect to questions concerning the quality of the information about the research project, but there is also a research ethics dimension. Prisoners are incarcerated against their will and placed together with a researcher whom it is difficult to avoid. Given this, I made a great effort not to force my company on people whom I did not know. With the exception of the slightly difficult first day, I did not take the initiative with respect to getting to know new prisoners; they had to come to me. If prisoners did not want to talk to me, they would not have to. For the same reason, I did not note down observations about prisoners who looked like they wanted to be left in peace. In some cases the officers tried to get me to contact prisoners who were having a hard time and had isolated themselves in their cells, because a chat would be good for the person concerned. I had to say no in such cases. It may well have been the case that the prisoner concerned would have liked me to visit him. But, out of respect for the idea that prisoners should be able to avoid me, as well as to avoid ending up in some sort of pseudo-therapist role whereby the research visit would be used to help someone who was having a hard time, I had to decline. The potential confusion about my role could have landed me with an impossible responsibility. This, of course, had an impact on the "sample" of prisoners I ended up talking with. The prisoners who were coping with remand the worst, who isolated themselves, who did not go out into the prison yard, who did not talk to anyone, and who were heavily medicated, are largely invisible in my data. This was not, however, a problem in my interaction with the large majority of the prisoners. The prison grapevine worked and the prisoners got in touch with me out of curiosity or because they wanted an easy win at pool.

Why were the vast majority of prisoners actually interested in talking to me? In an article she co-authored with four prisoners who had been her informants in a previous study, Bosworth (2005) describes how many different motives can lie behind a wish to talk to a researcher. Prisoners may want to help the researcher, to make the effort and be nice. They may hope to blow off some steam by talking about a difficult situation. As I mentioned, because of this, talking to a researcher can easily take on a therapeutic bent. There may be a political goal behind it; the prisoners may want to change the prison and society as a whole. They may want to get their story and perspective out and show people what the prison is *really* like. They may want to alleviate the boredom of remand, with the result that the researcher becomes a means of passing the time. Finally, they may want to live out a side of themselves other than the one that is relevant in the everyday life of the prison; talking to the researcher provides a break from the status of prisoner. What did those who chose to talk to me and share their thoughts feel they got out of it? What were their goals?

First of all, it was clear that many prisoners wanted to talk to me to help pass the time. Remand prisoners are locked in their cells on their own for large parts of the day. The hours pass slowly for many of them, with only the TV for company. I gave my time, and therefore ensured that for them the time passed faster. When I visited them the cell door also had to be open, or at least ajar. Many prisoners found the unlocked door that my presence entailed a relief. Some grasped this quickly and actively used me to avoid or delay being locked in. In some cases this was okay; in other cases I found it problematic, when prisoners who saw me arrive were disappointed to find that my dance card for the day was already full. As time passed I had to deal with a certain level of vying for my time. I had to try to spread myself in order to avoid conflicts and hurt feelings. Nonetheless, by the end of the fieldwork a day did not pass when I did not have to disappoint someone who wanted me to visit their cell because I already had an appointment. The fact that I understood how much it meant to the prisoners often made it difficult to end conversations with prisoners who, I saw, really wanted me to stay. It was not unusual for me to spend a couple of hours longer than planned in the prison. The giving of gifts to gain entry is a well-known ethnographic strategy. The opportunities for this are limited in the context of a prison. If any type of transaction did take place between me and the prisoners, it was primarily that we gave each other time. We both got something out of the conversation – I got data, they passed an hour or an afternoon.

Another reason many of the prisoners wanted to talk to me was that, since I was an outsider and independent of the System, it was easier to talk to me; I functioned as a break from the prison situation. Mark put it this way:

> One of the hardest things in prison for me is not being able to have a decent conversation or to communicate with people I understand and they understand me. You know, and with a conversation like this, with talking to you, expanding on certain issues, can sometimes give me a better insight into my situation, into myself, and somehow I might come to a new conclusion. And that's, in prison, that's very hard to find, people you can actually connect with and talk with. Because everybody deals with their own problems already. They also, the average prisoner is not exactly the most evolved human being neither. Which is for me very frustrating, to try to find a good friend in here that I can talk to, can share things with.

As well as having a chance to position himself as not an average prisoner, Mark got a visit from a polite and understanding listener. I was deliberately non-judgemental, but at the same time I had an opinion if I was asked. I assumed, both consciously and unconsciously, the role of the slightly naive researcher; I was the novice who needed instruction, whether it was at the pool table or about the ins and outs of the day-to-day running of a strip club. Høigård and Finstad (1992) describe how this role as a "novice from the straight side" legitimises ignorance and the asking of stupid questions. I found "making a fool of myself" when we were talking in their cells to be relatively unproblematic for both me and the prisoners. As an academic, I was often positioned as the person in front of whom you did not need to maintain a façade. I had not invested in the same things as they had, which made our respective investments less important in our interaction. At the same time, I wanted the relationship to be professional; I handed out business cards and encouraged everyone to contact me and discuss the project later as well. I wanted to tone down the role of "temporary friend" who could help the time pass so as not to make promises I could not or did not wish to keep.

The project benefited from my being rendered a harmless academic due to the officers having to watch out for me and be responsible for me. On the other hand, it was hardly a clear advantage for my position as a man. It soon became clear that many of the prisoners regarded me as something less than half a man, and wanted to do something about it. Being one of the boys can have its price, and it is a fact that fieldwork always also has a physical dimension (Coffey, 1999). Tom quickly initiated a regime of training and testing in order to toughen me up. This consisted of, for example, attempts to surprise or frighten me; either verbally or by sneaking up behind me and kicking the back of my knees or sticking fingers into my side. Such surprise attacks are common among prisoners, and to an extent it was a sign of inclusion. A pair of arms would suddenly grab you from behind and lift you up such that the air disappears both from beneath your feet and from your lungs at the same time. When this happens, it is important to react in the right way. At first I was told with a shake of the head that I seemed anxious and uncertain. As time passed and I learned that you must not look away, I was praised for doing better. In the end I could demonstrate that such attempts at frightening me did not bother me. I stared dumbly back and received recognition. At home I was told that my stance had perhaps become a little too macho. However, I was never subjected to the harder end of the play-fighting continuum. For example, no one hit me as hard as they could on my shoulder, which is not an unusual sign of friendship and superiority. I was in the middle again; I was included in ways the officers were not, but not as a *real* prisoner.

The functionality of my body was also tested. For example, Tom called me over to the weights to see what I was good for:

Tom: Come on then, let's see. You're a strong lad.
I try to get out of it, I'm not warmed up, I just arrived, I say, but I have to do it. The others working out watch curiously. I stand in front of the worn white equipment, grip the short bar and lift. The weights won't go past my waist. It's too heavy.
TU: No, I guess that's not for me [smiling].
Tom stares at me seriously, slowly shaking his head. He grips my arms and squeezes them through my jumper.
Tom: Oh no, that's not good. That's just soft.
The three others look sympathetically and uncomfortably away.
Tom: But there was something there. That's a bit better [he squeezes my triceps]. Look, try this instead.
The triceps curls go a little better. But I have to stop after five–six repetitions with the weights Tom works out with. The atmosphere eases a bit. Tom takes the weights from me, does a lot of repetitions after each other. But he also pulls a lot with his shoulders. "Your workout is wrong", says one of the other prisoners and smiles at me. A friendly gesture.
Tom: You weigh what, 92 kg perhaps? You should be stronger. It's not good.
TU: [I'm clutching at straws now:] No, you're probably right that I've neglected my upper body. I mainly exercise my legs, I cycle a lot.
Tom checks my legs and thighs, he squeezes and feels thoroughly.
Tom: That's not bad. It's much better. But, you have to exercise your upper body as well. That's not good, that isn't. You spend way too much time in your office. What condition will your body be in when you're 40?

As a young man I was expected to be able to stand my ground, at least a bit. Tom felt my body was making promises it could not keep. The situation can partly be understood as the physical subordination of a poor researcher. A more positive interpretation could be that he was giving me an opportunity to show that I, too, was a man. Given that a female researcher would probably not have been subjected to similar tests in the same way, the whole situation is, of course, predicated on my being viewed as a man. And I was taken seriously as a man; that, too, is at least something. A man, but not a *real* man, an academic man who needed help. On one occasion my body was also tested by a male officer to whom I had the pleasure of losing in arm wrestling. As a rule, the officers' relationship with the academic man was usually characterised by friendly ridicule rather than physical subordination.

Skrinjar (2003) has described how an attempt was made to assign her the role of love interest, in and after interviews with a male informant, which in various ways required the simultaneous neutralisation of the role of researcher. In my case, however, the position of researcher was fully compatible with the alternative positioning. For Skrinjar it was researcher *or* babe; for me it was researcher *and precisely therefore* a puny half-man. The ascribed lightweight position could, of course, be uncomfortable. On the other hand, it worked well in the work on clarifying perceptions and therefore producing knowledge about manliness and the male body's potential and limitations. Meetings between researcher and informant are an arena for staged masculinity: this is also true when everyone involved is male, but, of course, on other terms than when the researcher and/or informant are women (Schwalbe and Wolkomir, 2001). No attempt was ever (as far as I could tell) made to position me as a love interest, but I was obviously challenged and tested in ways that made the key to manliness and (not least) the peripheral areas of unmanliness visible. Masculinity's terms, as they apply in interactions in the prison, were made observable and analysable for a researcher who could therefore live with being called a lightweight.

Research ethics

I have already described how the field was basically a minefield. The attempt to appear neutral probably meant that some perceived me as vague and slippery. I was to some extent the "political eunuch" described by Vidich:

> He [the participant-observer] is socially marginal to the extent that he measures his society as a non-involved outsider and avoids committing his loyalties and allegiances to segments of it. This is not hypocrisy, but rather, as Howe has noted of Stendahl, "it is living a ruse". Being both a participant and an observer is "the strategy of deceiving the society to study it and wooing the society to live in it".
>
> (quoted in Jacobs, 1977: 270n)

There is also a research ethics dimension to choosing neutrality as a method-ological strategy. As a prison researcher, one, by necessity, steps into conflicts at various levels. As well as the perpetual conflict between prisoners and staff in the prison, you may be expected to take a position in relation to more local conflicts between individuals in different positions in the prison. You may also have to relate to conflicts between different criminal justice policy points of view in society as a whole, and you may even be drawn into con-flicts between different prison research approaches and traditions. Conflicts at different levels will often be intertwined.

One question that can be asked about a neutral vantage point like mine from a perspective that is more critical of prison is whether or not it is eth-ically defensible to take anything other than a thoroughly critical position when you encounter an institution that causes as much suffering as prison. Would not any focus that does not prioritise documenting the suffering be in danger of participating in the broader cover-up of criticisable practices behind the prison walls? Conversely, one could, from a perspective more in line with the correctional services' own, claim that any research effort that does not actively help the work of combating and preventing future crimes contributes to the suffering of future victims.

Becker (1967) examined these issues in a well-known essay. He describes how, by necessity, sociologists doing work on crime and deviance are gen-erally caught in the crossfire. Some would argue that in the interests of accountability you should not take sides, but instead produce correct and value-neutral research that others can use. Others would argue that research is shallow and useless without being based on an explicit value position. This is a false dilemma, writes Becker, because one of the bull's two horns is imaginary. It is impossible to produce research without its being "con-taminated" by personal and political sympathies, and, if it is not possible, one should stop trying: "The question is not whether we should take sides, since we inevitably will, but rather whose side we are on" (1967: 234). Know-ing something about the field is to have a perspective, which, in turn, is to be positioned in the world. As long as you are writing about a prison, you are either taking a critical position about what is happening in it or you are not. This is a political choice, writes Becker, and therefore neutrality is practically impossible. The best we can hope for is to show the readers of our research results what having chosen a position means, so that they can decide whether or not it influences the results in an unacceptable manner.

But does the fact that you inevitably have to choose sides mean that you have to choose only one side? What if your sympathies lie in more than one place? Liebling (2001) discusses Becker's problem based on her feelings of loyalty to both prisoners and officers. In her experience it is possible to side with *both* prisoners and officers, even with the perpetual conflict between them at the back of your mind. She introduces a fruitful division between theory neutrality and value neutrality. Theory neutrality is about our perception of what is, about describing reality and the gateway to the truth, which can never be neutral (even if there are more and less neutral approaches). You can, however, bracket your normative stance, the perception of what *ought* to be, at least during data collection: "We can – to some extent – describe what 'is' without always making explicit what 'ought to be'" (Liebling 2001: 474).

Two related questions are being discussed here. One is whether or not it is right to try to be neutral as a methodological and analytical starting point. The other is about whether or not this is, from an epistemological perspective, even possible. In my opinion, these questions can actually be answered independently of each other – you can arrive at the conclusion that, from an epistemological perspective, it is impossible in an absolute sense, but that it is nonetheless worth trying. The fact that a neutral vantage point cannot exist in a complete and perfect sense does not mean that all vantage points are equally biased. I agree with Collins' Weber-inspired challenge:

> We need to distinguish between the politics and the methodology of our work. That is, while as analyst we can understand that all science is in a broad sense "political," as researchers we need to keep this knowledge in a separate compartment.... We need, then, to distinguish between how we do our work and its impact.
>
> (1991: 249–250)

Facts are interpreted, and as interpretation they are inevitably intertwined with values. The Weberian ideal of trying to differentiate between empirical observations, the analysis of these and evaluations based on these analyses is, from my perspective, impossible to achieve in a perfect sense. They are always hovering above each other in some sense. However, the fact that it is not possible to achieve total perfection does not mean that there may not be good reasons for trying to achieve as good a result as possible. My point of departure is that prison research does not *by necessity* have to, at the same time, be a political statement about prison.

Anonymisation

The prisoners' names are, of course, pseudonyms. It may seem odd and theoretically inconsistent to give the prisoners names in light of the project's goals. As I have mentioned, the goal is not to follow individuals and describe their development, but to describe the ongoing interplay of forms of power and resistance; a relational network. On the other hand, text without names would undoubtedly be less readable. Simply using names like "prisoner 1" hardly invites empathy. However, the stylistic argument is not sufficient to balance the theoretical problems inherent in naming the prisoners. I have nonetheless chosen to do this because the names are also intended to indicate ethnic origin and affiliation. In other words, using pseudonyms provides extra information. In practice, I have used Wikipedia's excellent overview of the players in all the national football teams in the world as a source of names. Complete lists of even the Chechen and Kurdish national teams are available here. I have, as far as possible, chosen names that are repeated in the list multiple times. This strategy should also be suitable for assigning prisoners pseudonyms that to a relatively large extent reflect their ages, even if the average prisoner is somewhat older than the average football player. I am less certain about whether the names reflect other forms of cultural affiliation. It is possible that here, thanks to a lack of cultural knowledge, I may have missed the mark.

The officers have not been given names. This is because there are far fewer of them than prisoners, because they are linked to the wings via their employment in a more permanent way than the prisoners, and because any pseudonyms would only have provided a very limited amount of extra information. Sometimes I specify that I am speaking to a "female officer". I only do this where I think that it is particularly relevant from an analytical perspective.

2
The Forms of Power in Prison

A prisoner aged around 50 comes over to me and asks, nicely but commandingly: "Yes, so who are you then?" I explain my project and he presents himself and tells me his first impression of me:

Brede: We are sceptical about people like you who come in with that sort of card hanging round their neck. It reeks of police.

But Brede quickly warms up. He is interested in hearing more. We move to his cell so he can smoke while we talk.

Brede is a mature man with short hair, laughter lines and a cotton tracksuit. He talks enthusiastically, a bit erratically, but nonetheless very intensely. His look glues you to the spot. He is a veteran on the wing. He has done a long stretch in prison before as well, many years ago.

Brede: I have always loved smoking cannabis. That's been my problem.

He sees a big difference between the prison experience then and now. Prison is harder for him this time. Last time he was young, he had lots of energy, was pissed off at the System and worked actively against it. He had had what he calls his daily studies, which largely consisted of writing complaints to the prison or the correctional services on behalf of himself or others. "What should I complain about today then?" became a sort of motto. It's completely different this time.

Brede: I have become a model prisoner; it's embarrassing to say it, but it's true. This period on remand, it's broken me, I have no resistance left. I wish I had all the energy I used to have, but I'm just tired now. [. . .] Everything was better before, you know? We used to be able to smoke a bit of cannabis inside; the lads would sit in the cell and share what we had, you know? We preserved a bit of our privacy, we had something that was ours, sitting and having a good time together. We sort of had a say, us too. It's not like that anymore. Those days are well and truly over, you know? We're run ragged. The police are in charge in here now. The prison and the police are working together, they tell each other everything. They are in complete control. I've had to stop smoking [cannabis]. So in that way I have succumbed to the System. They have managed to make me toe the line.

[Brede's narrative was about the steadily more powerful System that had finally managed to subdue him. I took up this thread again later during an interview with him:]

TU: "Do you notice the police's influence on the wing?"

Brede: "Yes, everything is reported and monitored here and so on. You know how it is, all phone calls are recorded and all letters are written down, and I think everybody has a file here in prison in which they write down who you spend time with, and that you are controlled based on this. They are thinking about it systematically for the future now and want to record as much information as possible about each person."

TU: "They are on their guard for the future as well?"

Brede: "Yes."

[...]

TU: "But they monitor, and at the same time they are meant to manage, you say?"

Brede: "Manage with the other hand, sort of. So the System is very powerful. They hold the middle and both ends."

TU: "And by the System you mean ... the prison, the police ... "

Brede: "The police, yeah, it's the same thing now, you know? Nowadays we see the prison officers more as an extension of the police, to an even greater degree. Even though that's the way it has always been, it's stronger now."

TU: "But the cooperation was there before as well?"

Brede: "Oh yes, definitely. Definitely. But it was different before, the prisoners were just locked in, except for yard time."

TU: "So, in that sense, it is somewhat freer than it was?"

Brede: "Yes, it is somewhat freer. But bans on letters and visits, right, are just being misused, in most cases. They don't serve any practical purpose and everyone who works in the prison knows that. They know it is being misused. Say someone refuses to make a statement, for example, what they do is slap a year's ban on letters and visits, maybe, to put pressure on them."

TU: "Yes, okay. So you think the strain of remand is being used as a tool?"

Brede: "Yes, and they have unlimited time as well, apparently. There are cases of people spending years on remand; it's unbelievable how long they take and often nothing new at all comes out in the case. Six months could maybe pass and the person is just sitting there twiddling their thumbs. Without anything new coming out."

TU: "So even though you are locked in less now, it was fairer before?"

Brede: "You have more power ranged against you, the system of power they have is more visible. What is also more visible is how the prison, prosecuting authority and police, all of them, are like a single power factor, all of them. They are

state employees right, and now they are more and more together, right, in lots
of ways."
TU: *"Together against you?"*
Brede: *"Yeah, you could put it like that."*

* * *

You can roughly distinguish between two levels of power in Oslo Prison. On the one hand, you have the everyday forms of control and administration the prison uses as part of its daily operations, and which are perceived as a necessary basis for ensuring that the institution is able to achieve its more overarching goals. On the other hand, the prison is, as a social technology, designed to change people for the better; the prison forms part of a larger welfare state system aimed at creating a good society. The difference is, in a way, analytical; the various forms of power all play out in and through specific practices in everyday prison life. As Brede alludes to in the extract above, the various forms of power are perceived as a single system, not individual parts.

In this section I will describe the prison's various forms of power. The idea is that the prison as a power technology understands and objectifies the prisoners *as prisoners* in ways that it is difficult for them to accept. I will first provide a brief account of the official objective of imprisonment. I will then show how this plays out in specific power techniques in everyday prison life and point out some of the consequences these have for those who have thus become prisoners.

Defining power and resistance

Prisoners' resistance and counter-power have long been important topics for prison research (McCorkle and Korn, 1954; Sykes, 1958; Mathiesen, 1965; Sparks, Bottoms and Hay, 1996; Bosworth, 1999; Crewe, 2009). Sykes, for example, in his classic study of prison society, describes an institution in a permanent pendulous motion between crisis and equilibrium, where the predictable prison revolt is understood as a periodic result of a number of accumulated small crises (1958: 110). From a Norwegian (or even Nordic) vantage point, one would have to say that Sykes' description is somewhat off the mark on this point. It is easier to agree with the description of Sparks, Bottoms and Hay (1996), who, following Cressey, claim that, given the institution in question, it is the day-to-day balance that must be explained, not the extraordinary eruptions of disorder. As Cressey writes, "One of the most amazing things about prisons is that they 'work' at all" (quoted in Sparks, Bottoms and Hay, 1996: 2).

This book stands out from the classic texts on resistance and counter-power in prison in that it takes Foucault's concept of power as its starting point. From Foucault's perspective, power is per definition an action directed at forming people's actions or space for action; power is *action on action* or *conduct of conduct*. As a minimum, there must, in order to talk about power, be a relationship between (1) an action and (2) another action (concrete or potential, your own or that of others) that this will affect. A relationship of power and resistance between (1) and (2) is the central defining characteristic that must be present in order to talk about power in a Foucauldian sense (Foucault, 2000c; Kelly, 2009).

Power is everywhere associated with forms of resistance. What is resistance? Bosworth and Carrabine (2001) argue that a number of practices, from everyday informal conversations to the unique and dramatic events around which prison legends are based, can be read as parts of resistance strategies. The relationship between power and resistance is fluid and dynamic, even in an environment and in relation to a power relationship between prisoners and officers that may, at first glance, appear highly monolithic. Bosworth and Carrabine describe how power relationships are negotiated in and through the details of everyday life. In practice, any action could be an example of resistance as long as it is part of a concrete power/resistance relationship in which one party attempts to act on another's actions. Forms of resistance are just as diverse as the techniques of power.

One problem with this is that the boundaries of what is and is not resistance become unclear; you risk turning "everything" into resistance. What is it exactly that makes more creative, covert and informal forms of resistance *resistance*, and not just the prisoners' small attempts to cope as best they can?

> Resistance and coping exist on the same spectrum, but should not be confused.... If resistance is defined as any expression of agency or identity, the danger is that all acts are flattened out into the same thing, whatever their aims, scope, and consequences, and regardless of their context.
> (Crewe, 2009: 97)[1]

Common to everything that could be called resistance from this perspective is the fact that resistance practices, in order to be resistance practices, must be connected to specific forms of power. The power side of the power/resistance relationship must be explained, and the ways in which a given practice functions as resistance in relation to a specific form of power must be clarified. The entire relationship as it unfolds in practice must be described. For example, one of the most important forms of resistance Crewe (2005, 2009) describes is drug dealing and drug use in prison. Using drugs does not represent resistance against anything *in itself*, but, in a context like prison, getting high can, according to Crewe, result in a feeling of achieving something that is difficult and of triumphing over a system that has forbidden this sort of thing.[2] At the same time, as the mirror image of resistance, bans and urine tests only have meaning in a context where someone is actually interested in using drugs while they are in prison, even if it is not allowed. In this way, power and resistance can, from a Foucauldian perspective, be described as a continuous game in which forces affect each other.

Resistance does not have to be actualised all the time, though. Locking a cell door is a form of power in practice, even if the person on the inside could not imagine opening the door *right at the moment*. Even if he did not want the door opened until later, for example after the football match on TV had ended, turning the key is an act of power, *conduct of conduct*, as soon as it happens because the prisoner's *room* for action has thus been curtailed. And, as most prisoners quickly learn, there is no point in touching the door when you know it is locked. The locked door has curtailed the condition of possibility, even if the action – lying on bed watching football – may be the same as it would have been if the door had been open. So, although prisoners seldom stand there hammering on the inside of the cell door, the locked door may perhaps constitute the most important form of power over prisoners. In other words, resistance to power is not necessarily actualised, but the potential must exist in order for power to exist.

If there is no prisoner on the inside of the cell door, then no power can exist. It would be difficult to describe locking an empty cell as the exercise of power (unless someone, contrary to expectation, wanted to go inside).[3] If there is no potential for resistance, no prisoner on the inside who wants out and may check whether or not the door is locked, then there is no exercising of power. The above definition of power is expanded such that a relationship must be entered into between someone who is acting and someone whose actions are being acted against, *and who is still an acting subject*. The subject whose actions are going to be affected must have a range of options that are both available to him and possible, and which encompass several forms of action and ways of reacting. If this is not the case, then we are, instead, talking about what he calls "the pure and simple force of violence":

> A chained and abused person is subject to the force one exercises over him. He is not subjected to power. However, his very last way out could be to remain silent and choose death, and if one nonetheless manages to make him talk, one has driven him to act in a specific manner. His freedom has been subjected to power ... Where no ability to refuse or rebel exists, no power exists.
>
> (Foucault, 2000b: 113–114)[4]

Rhodes (2004; cf. Shalev, 2009) describes a prison regime that aims to achieve the almost total neutralisation of all resistance, total control that will make any form of resistance impossible. In the American high security prison she has studied, the mesh of the network of control is so fine that the prisoners' condition of possibility and freedom of movement are so curtailed that the situation appears to be close to one where no resistance is possible. Rhodes shows how the attempt fails in practice. The tiny part of the potential for resistance that remains is utilised. Prisoners who have been deprived of all other possibilities throw excrement or blood, or they harm themselves as best they can, which can function as resistance in an institution that is also formally responsible for the prisoners' health and safety. The specific constellations of the forms of power have their specific forms of resistance, which in turn result in the power adapting; the officers change their patrol patterns to avoid being hit by thrown excrement, and they remove any object from the cells that is small enough to be ingested. The power is shaped by its forms of resistance, which in turn always makes new forms of resistance possible and so on.

In an imaginary situation where any counter-move is impossible or unthinkable, we are not talking about power. The ability to change, modify or destroy a *thing* is something other than forms of power that are put into play in relationships between people. When people and human bodies are exclusively treated as things, which of course does happen in the world, although seldom in Norwegian prisons, this is an instance of a form of capacity to use an object, not power over a person.

Nevertheless, it is clear that the prison has, as a last resort, the right and ability to subjugate prisoners' bodies "in the old fashioned way" when it finds it necessary. This does not happen often, but at the same time it is part of everything that does happen; it is the potential sanction that structures every interaction between prisoners and officers. The officers *can* put prisoners on the ground, carry them down into the cellar and strap them to a bed. The fact that there are, at the same time, alternative and more indirect forms of power at play in the institution does not mean that the power cannot also subjugate the body openly and plainly. The daily jangling of keys, on the one hand, and the bed with restraints in the cellar, the ultimate expression of power disparity in the prison institution, on the other, are from this perspective not the same, but they are definitely related.

Having said all this, I want to further expand the concept of resistance in two ways. First, Foucauldian power is everywhere, and it is everywhere intertwined with forms of knowledge and subjectification processes. This will be examined more thoroughly below. It is sufficient to say for now that, by extension, I also regard attempts to change, oppose or influence the power's associated gaze and categorisations as resistance. In other words, this is resistance not as an attempt to oppose the power's *conduct of conduct* directly, but as more of an indirect attempt to influence or evade the forms of objectification the power necessarily has as a by-product.

Second, the forms of resistance may be directed at the prison as an everyday control and administrative system in itself, but they can also be directed at the routines and the monotony the control entails. This is the form of resistance that is most similar to "coping" in the sense used by Crewe.

Cohen and Taylor (1976) describe the resources most people use to break the monotony of everyday life: holidays, evening board games, drug use, daydreaming and swinger clubs can all serve as means of escape. Holidays have a special function because they create a situation of voluntary, temporary, relatively risk-free alienation; a deliberate break from everyday life. In prison the everyday monotony, predictability and regularity are on a different level from the lives of most people on the outside, and the means of escape are fewer and less accessible. By extension, breaks from the monotony and boredom can function as resistance in that prisoners can "escape" from the tedious repetitiveness of everyday life that follows directly from the way remand imprisonment is designed and implemented.

With these two theoretical expansions it becomes clear that the ultimate objective of resistance is not necessarily to successfully evade control. The goal may, instead, be to face that control in a satisfactory way, preferably by making it more liveable and at the same time making yourself more than someone who is being controlled by the process. Even small, covert practices can weigh heavily in such a project. Take, for example, the ironic laughter and gallows humour that follow when a new prisoner discovers that the fire service has actually posted plans of the building around the prison, complete with colourful arrows and the helpful legend "emergency escape plan".

Producing security, managing risk

Three signs were posted outside the open door of the officers' work and break room in wing four in *Bayern*. All three were meant for prisoners on their way into the officers' room, and all of them were intended to administer the prisoners' entrance into the officers' territory. But that is where the similarities ended. The tones of the signs differed and, as communication, they each provided a very different portrayal of the role of the sender in relation to the receiver.

The first sign (assuming the Western tradition where you start at the upper left and work your way to the right and down) was a red, landscape-oriented sheet of A4 that said, in Norwegian and in a large font that almost filled the page, "KNOCK AND WAIT." The instruction could not be misunderstood; the large letters made up for the lack of an exclamation mark. This was an order expressed by those who decide to those who must simply comply, the sort of commandment one might find on stone tablets. At the same time, the order allowed for the possibility that prisoners could actually come in, as long as they knocked and waited first.

The message on the second sign, hung immediately below the first, was written on a white sheet of paper. The font was smaller and normal orthographic rules had been followed with respect to lower case letters. The message, again in Norwegian, was that "Inmates do not have access to the officers' room." Here the request was made in the form of general information that was not aimed at anyone in particular. Just in case a prisoner did not know or might have forgotten, the sign told him that he should not go through this door. That is the rule; this is for your information. The sender does not order and decide, but is someone who knows and could inform those who did not know this information.

The third sign was perhaps the most interesting. Its location meant that it would probably be read after the two others, and it had the smallest font of all. Here, too, the message was written on a white sheet of paper. The request, also in Norwegian, said: "Please help us maintain order and remember the rule that inmates do not have access to the officers' room." The sign was written by an "us" who want to maintain order, even though it is difficult. They need help to achieve this and hope that members of the group "inmates" can lend a hand. After all, they would not want to be difficult or unreasonable, would they? Perhaps "us" and "inmates" can together achieve what "us" cannot achieve alone? Obviously, there is a rule that states that inmates do not have access. Where this rule came from is unknown, but "us" wants to do their best to comply with it. "Inmates" who move into the room are not just rule breakers; they also represent mess and disorder.

One lunch break I asked an officer what they hoped to achieve with the three different signs:

> Well, this is what happens. First you put the red one up and that doesn't work. So you hang up another one and that doesn't work either. So in the end you try another that is more persuasive. But that doesn't work either. So what do you do then?

Not long after, the last poster was taken down and replaced by a physical barrier. A rope was hung horizontally across the door opening at neck height. A yellow sign hung from the middle of the rope saying "No Entry." The sign could be raised or lowered as necessary. Thus, a difference was created between when prisoners were not allowed to enter and when they were *really* not allowed to enter. From this perspective, might not the yellow sign have been counterproductive, since it cancelled out the other two?

Who was the last sign aimed at? Not me. Even though I almost mowed the sign down a couple of times, I could duck under it and go in when I wanted. Nor were any of the prison staff affected. The yellow note was exclusively directed at the prisoners, which all the parties involved immediately understood. It was not the barrier that separated officers and prisoners; this separation was already a reality for everyone in the prison. It was assumed, and was implemented by the barrier without it having to be made explicit. The message was in English, with the shortest, least flowery wording of all: No Entry (for prisoners). More information is probably superfluous when explanations are replaced by physical barriers. It was the unruly bodies of the foreign (non-Norwegian) prisoners that had to be stopped. The use of this solution was a subject of controversy among the officers. It was only used when a few specific officers were on duty.

Four different voices of power were talking over each other outside the door to the officers' room. The first was authoritarian and commanding; the second was explanatory, informative and focused on formal norms; the third was questioning, inclusive (but not in a sense that would transgress categories – it still differentiated between "inmates" and "us"), persuasive and focused on the relationship between prisoners and officers; while the last had just given up and fallen back on physical barriers in order to organise and control the prisoners' behaviour. First, absolute authority; next, the dry application of rules; then, encouragement to be reasonable and decent; and, finally, direct control of the prisoners' bodies. All four were power techniques used to achieve the same result: an officers' room without prisoners. Together they can be read as a picture of the good old prison paradox: the prison is an institution with self-contradictory goals and means, which in the final instance often falls back on and resorts to walls and keys (Drake, 2012). One may, of course, ask oneself: why did the officers not just close the door and lock it? After all, the officers are the only ones with keys, are they not? The answer, of course, is that the pros and cons of the open door go both ways. If the officers had locked themselves in, and given up the wing's entire common area, the prisoners would not have minded. The open door is a necessary control measure.

This is an example of how prisoners in Oslo Prison are positioned in a series of different power relationships where the goal is, in very different ways, to act on their actions. As an overarching technology, the prison adopts widely differing, more specific power techniques, and these in turn have very different effects on everyday life in the prison. I will explain this in more detail below, but by way of introduction one can roughly differentiate between forms of power in the prison on two different levels.

On the one hand, one finds the everyday forms of control and administration that the prison uses as part of its daily operations, and which are perceived as necessary in order for the institution to achieve its more overarching goals. These are continuous practices and are such a common and well-integrated part of everyday life in the prison that it is easy to forget them as long as they are carried out within the informal everyday norms that have emerged in the prison. Doors are locked, cells are searched, the prisoners are counted and recorded, the bars in front of cell windows are checked, applications for leave are refused, troublemakers are transferred, prisoners are called in from the prison yard, and the wing is always kept clean and tidy. All of these are part of the prison officers' routine duties. As long as nothing deviates from "the way things should be", the power being described here does not readily catch the eye. This does not necessarily mean that the prisoners' forms of resistance are difficult to see. The prisoners, almost as routinely, do an extra couple of laps around the prison yard even though yard time is over, or they jokingly hide behind the sofa in the common area so that the officer who is supposed to lock them in cannot find them straight away. This is also resistance, even though it is done with a twinkle in the eye and fully conscious of the fact that it will end with you being locked in. The act of locking in is a practice of power: if the officers stopped locking the doors, the prisoners would, from the perspective of the officers, definitely go where they are not meant to go. And, just as clearly, if the prisoners had, instead of these informal and to some extent acceptable forms of resistance, chosen to say a loud and clear no, the power status of the routine practices would suddenly become much more obvious. I witnessed prisoners refusing to come in from the prison yard once during my fieldwork. These were tense minutes, while resigned and slightly surprised officers assessed the situation. Just before the big, formal apparatus of power ground into motion – which would undoubtedly have resulted in the prisoners, after having been physically forced inside, having to do without yard time for the foreseeable future – the situation was resolved in a manner that allowed both parties to put it down to one of those regrettable misunderstandings.

On the other hand, the prisoners have, often against their will, been positioned in the broadly constructed welfare-oriented social technology for changing people for the better. The prison as a whole is a power technology that is, in turn, part of a greater welfare state apparatus in which the prisoners are supposed to be changed so that they do not commit criminal acts in the future. The rehabilitation machine utilises a number of different techniques. In practice, the prison collects information about the prisoners, divides them into groups based on this information, makes various services available to them based on what they know about their shortcomings and needs, and works to facilitate and coordinate this work with the welfare state's other agencies, all in order to change prisoners from offenders into law-abiding citizens. In other words, concrete power techniques are not merely supposed to affect the prisoners' actions during the daily life of the prison; the effects are also intended to solidify and attach themselves to the prisoner in a way that makes them more permanent. Even though it makes sense to say that this is a form of power on a different level from that in everyday routine duties, they are also all practices that are experienced as tangible and in their specificity, and which are thus intertwined with specific, concrete forms of resistance.

Norwegian prisons are grouped into different security categories. High security prisons, like Oslo Prison, are what most people imagine when they think of a prison. They have high concrete walls, security gates at entrances, CCTV, barbed wire, a relatively large number of officers per prisoner, and locked cell doors with lockable metal hatches in them. As a rule, lower security prisons are smaller, with fewer places, fewer officers per prisoner, and a generally more open regime. The prisoners are only locked in their cells at night and they have greater freedom of movement around the prison's grounds. Finally, there are what are called halfway houses, where prisoners often have permission to leave the prison unattended during the day to go to work or attend school.[5]

Correctional services policy documents differentiate between three different kinds of security measures (St. Meld, 27, 2007–2008). Static security consists of substantive, physical measures such as cell doors, surrounding walls, bars, CCTV and alarm systems, and control routines like monitoring the prison yard, checking bars, searches and the constant counting of prisoners. As far as security categorisation is concerned, high security prisons will have a high degree of static security. Organisational security is the security that results from how the institution organises its work. Examples of this include staffing plans, training, handling deviations and crisis management plans, which must all be designed and implemented in concert to achieve a secure prison. Finally, dynamic security means the security that is a product of the interpersonal relationships and systematic work of creating security-enhancing interaction between officers, and between officers and prisoners.

It is worth making a few extra comments about dynamic security. For example, the current correctional services white paper emphasises that

> [The] regulations [state] that staff should be present during all social situations in high security prisons. This is primarily to maintain peace and order. This is best achieved, insofar as it is possible, by their presence being based on *natural interaction and genuine tasks in the social situation*, and the control element being exercised with respect without its purpose being lost .... This method reduces the level of conflict and results in the more effective performance of duties.
>
> (St. Meld, 27, 2007–2008: 8.2, my emphasis)

The day-to-day relationships between officers and prisoners are therefore shot through with instrumental purpose. Every cup of coffee shared by an officer and prisoner can *also* represent the exercising of an interpersonal control technique. The idea is that the "natural interaction" and "genuine tasks" (presumably tasks that are not inherently control-based) will partly function as an informal, day-to-day version of a risk identification and controlling optic and partly help to create relationships and ties between officers and prisoners that make it less likely that the prisoners will do something unwanted. The interaction over a cup of coffee is also intended to function as a "softer" form of control and power in contrast to the "harder" static techniques (Crewe, 2009, 2011). In certain situations it may be unclear whether the cup of coffee is an example of "natural interaction" or whether it is also part of the dynamic security work. After all, any situation can potentially be useful in the context of dynamic security. Theoretically, the space for non-instrumental interaction has been narrowed so much as to be almost non-existent. From this perspective, the purpose of dynamic security can be understood as a modification of the Panopticon principle (Foucault, 1977a; Bentham, 1995), in which the idea was to create a situation where the prisoners controlled themselves at all times because they never knew when they were being watched. The difference here is that in this Neo-Panopticon the disciplinary effect is no longer expected to come from the prisoners not knowing when they are being watched, but from them not knowing what the person obviously watching them wants or what the person concerned attaches importance to in specific situations.

Crewe (2009) describes a resulting change in tone, a new relationship between officers and prisoners. The tone may well have been harsher before, the material conditions poorer and the regime in some ways "stricter", but the rules were clearer. There was a clear and predictable line in the sand and you knew full well what the consequences would be were you to cross it. In a context characterised by neo-paternalism, prisoners no longer know how they should behave. In what circumstances will the prison trust you to exercise self-control? And when will it react in the traditional way? As previously described, the underlying truth behind all interactions between prisoners and officers is that officers *can* put prisoners on the ground and haul them down the stairs if the prisoners prove unable to control themselves. The softness and hardness of the power are therefore intertwined, and in a way that makes it unclear where the boundaries lie; where the velvet glove ends and the iron fist starts.

The three forms of security are regarded as complementary. All three are important in creating optimum security in relation to the concrete conditions that apply in a specific institution. Walls and locks, routines and systems, and interpersonal relationships constitute three parallel families of power techniques that must be organised and coordinated optimally in relation to the relevant group of prisoners such that they all pull in the same direction and help achieve the prison technology's subsidiary goal of having the right person behind the right door at the right time. The wall is an obstacle, but not an impassable obstacle. Almost anyone could get over it given sufficient preparation and creativity. The wall is, therefore, instead regarded as the final part of a comprehensive network of defences. Combating escapes is a continuous part of everyday prison life. Regular cell searches, the checking of bars, periodic relocations and so on are, not least, motivated by the aim of uncovering and thwarting possible escape plans. The threat of losing a possible parole or transfer that can be glimpsed somewhere in the distance is another means.

Everyday power and untrustworthy bodies

On the level of day-to-day interaction, the prison's control over the prisoners is largely about controlling the prisoners' bodies. It should be said that detailed control over the prisoners' every movement, as Foucault (1977a) describes, is neither a goal nor a reality in today's Oslo Prison. Nor are bodies marked and colour-coded for the purposes of control, as described by Rhodes (2004) and Wacquant (2002), or made the object of control with the aid of technologies that utilise the body's specific shape, such as, for example, through the use of so-called biometric data. Nonetheless, imprisonment is very much still a physical punishment which cannot be executed without the use of prisoners' bodies, by keeping bodies locked in rooms designed for that purpose. One of Foucault's main points is that the changes that resulted in the prison should not be described as though some new, non-physical imprisonment were taking the place of outdated, bestial corporal punishment. Instead of destroying the body, prison life today is about the administration of bodies in time and space with the aim of producing effects in the present and future. This type of administration of bodies would be impossible to carry out without a certain addition to the punishment, an add-on that concerns the body itself: sexual want, eyes watering thanks to tear gas, or something as basic as being shut in behind a locked door, are all by-products of an overarching goal of administering and controlling the prisoners' bodies. In some contexts this will be an unintentional but unavoidable consequence of being locked up. Other times, this physical add-on will not be explicit and will perhaps go unacknowledged. The point is that it would be hard for prison as an institution to exist without it. If the institution is going to keep the right person behind the right door at the right time, the person's body has to be involved. This goal is the foundation on which is based the relationship between prisoners and officers, or between what, from the perspective of the institution, appear to be *untrustworthy bodies* and *trustworthy bodies*.

The professional officer's gaze is always scanning for untrustworthy bodies: first and foremost, for bodies that are somewhere they should not be; bodies that are resisting their correct placement in space. This is, of course, due to the obvious fact that most of the prisoners would disappear if the officers did not prevent it. It is key to understanding the entire institution that the vast majority of prisoners do not want to be there and would walk out of the institution given the opportunity and, equally important, if there were no consequences for them. But it also applies to the more routine control over the prisoners' bodies in time and space that the officers are continuously trying to maintain. Doors are locked and unlocked again and again, the right body must be behind the right door at the right time, all the time; it must be possible to account for the overall dispersion of the bodies in space at all times. Day-to-day control on the wings involves continuously gathering data about the location of bodies, dividing time and arranging space (Shalev, 2009) into permitted and forbidden zones, and continually controlling the location of bodies in the various forms of space at different times. Bodies that do not want to be where they are supposed to be, or which simply disappear, frustrate the prison's ability to achieve its most fundamental goal. Following Douglas (1970), one might say that the officer's gaze is always looking for prisoners' bodies out of place.

In other words, the prisoner's body could disappear and evade control in time and space. Second, prisoners' bodies can also be perceived as threatening, especially in two ways. They can be bodies that could physically attack officers with punches and kicks, or they can be contagious bodies the officers have to watch out for and interact with in ways that reduce or eliminate the risk of infection. Finally, prisoners' bodies can lie and conceal the truth. Bodies that are searched in the hunt for drugs or which are forced to give urine samples are examples of attempts to exact secrets from untrustworthy bodies.

The officer's gaze thus focuses on four subcategories of untrustworthy bodies. These are misplaced bodies, violent bodies, contagious bodies and secretive bodies. The officers have to implement various specific forms of control and power in their everyday encounters with these four different types of risky bodies. The institution's and the officers' understanding of the prisoners is marked by a fundamental and institutionalised lack of trust. Meanwhile, from the point of view of officers, the potential risk is not evenly distributed between prisoners. Despite the officers' insistence that all the prisoners are equal in their eyes and that everyone should be treated the same, they see a variety of types of prisoner. Some prisoners go from being part of the general risk group to being considered particularly dangerous. The dangerous prisoner is a prisoner one has to be careful around, who can *see red*, who can *lose it* or *go nuts*. Risk is more or less explicitly present in a large proportion of the officers' conversations about prisoners – whether they are about prisoners in general, individual prisoners on the wing, or the many "war stories" about (often named) legendary prisoners who repeatedly crop up in anecdotes about the hard, demanding, important but also fun profession of prison officer.

First, then, you have named, specific risks in the form of individuals who may have a "short fuse". One officer who manages work parties described his mindset when he is planning the day for himself and the prisoners in his work party:

I have to have these four [prisoners] with me all day. Four of them for one person, that's a lot. Here [on the wing] there are cells, you know? So if someone goes off on one, you can just lock him in and call the principal prison officer. Where we are, there are no cells. I have to watch them all the time. When they are chatting nicely and everyone is content, I relax. If someone is a bit quiet and sort of withdrawn, I have to keep an eye open. He may be planning to escape. He may be having a hard time and intend to cause trouble. You never know. When someone is quiet,

I have to keep an eye on them. Or I have to be smart. They have their ways of doing things; they prefer to work at their own pace. If I want to control that, I have to be smart. I have to find the perfect time to tell them something so that they do not have time to get irritated, so that it matches their rhythm. If I do, then they are content when I lock them in. That is the goal, right, that they are not thinking "fuck what a jerk" as I lock them in. I have to manage them continuously, so that they are in the best possible mood in the morning. After all, it's my safety on the line.

Next, there is a more general, unnamed, unidentified risk that can appear at any time from anywhere. Working on a prison wing means working in the midst of an omnipresent threat. After all, you never know. This institutionalised mistrust has numerous consequences for life in the prison (Lindberg, 2005). One example of this is how the officers have, as part of their everyday routine for opening cell doors, developed a physical habit of having one foot against the door in case of sudden force from inside. A prison officer opens and locks hundreds of cell doors every week, always with a protective foot in place. Very few have actually experienced a situation where this was necessary, but, then again, that is not the point. The general risk the prisoners represent is the reason for a number of different minor and major (assumed) safety-producing practices. The prison values and reproduces being "better safe than sorry". Everything is *basically* dangerous from this perspective. The workday is structured, down to the smallest detail, by the fact that one group, the prisoners, is potentially dangerous for the other, the officers. The safety mindset has become a professionalised physical routine. The prison is a place whose design is based on the worst case scenario. And, from the officers' perspective, safety, *our* safety, must come first.

Rubber gloves, stab-proof leather gloves and boots with steel toecaps are, therefore, important everyday work tools. This is another consequence of the prison paradox: here there are many widely different objectives running in parallel that in practice could perhaps be said to be contradictory. How do steel toecaps and care go together? Tear gas and rehabilitation work? The safety equipment is more than a necessary tool, more than safety measures determined by health and safety regulations. This is also equipment that helps to define the prison as a symbolic space. The prison is fundamentally understood as a place where such things are needed.[6] Moving about in a prison always entails a certain level of risk. And the nature of this risk differs from that which, for example, can be found on a building site. Prisoners are inevitably symbolically positioned by such security instruments as dangerous people. It is important for the officers that risks are discovered as early as possible. They have, therefore, developed a prison-contextual hermeneutics of suspicion with the goal of discovering potentially dangerous people and situations before the danger arises. This mindset becomes apparent when two officers discuss a prisoner who is known to be difficult:

> Officer 1: I popped in and had a chat with [prisoner X] and he was suddenly very nice and polite.
> Officer 2: What? Hasn't he been a real pain? This is not good [shakes his head grinning]. You'd almost think he'd done ART,[7] heh heh. We'll have to watch him carefully...

This was said with a certain glint in their eyes, but still, change, even for the better, is suspicious. Any change can be dangerous or indicate potential risk. Simply put, every activity involving prisoners will entail some degree or other of (unknown) risk for officers. When the prisoners are active, the officers have to be on their guard. When they are locked in, inactive, the officers can relax. The doors are locked and peace descends. A peaceful wing is a wing without visible prisoners. The officers have tidied away the dangerously heavy pool balls and stacked the magazines and newspapers in a neat pile on the table in the common area. Not because the pool balls are a dangerous weapon (although officers occasionally remind themselves that they actually *are*), but mostly because they want it to look neat and tidy should one of the governors happen to pop by. Mess, disorder and noise are all results of the prisoners' temporary release from their cells.

The officers' semiotics of risk, the system of signals that can be understood as indicators of risk, has a special relationship to sounds. The prison is a place with many different sounds and a lot of noise. For example, there are numerous different beeping sounds that communicate a variety of distinct meanings. The telephone rings, sometimes uninterrupted. Five minutes before the officers' break is over, the intercom system begins to buzz. Some prisoners call in the middle of a break because they do not know the routine, they forget, or they want to annoy the officers. The lift beeps when it stops at the floor. Prisoners who want to enter or leave by the door on the first floor call the officers' room on the third floor. Sometimes assault alarms sound, either just one, because it has a bad battery, or all of them in concert when the alarm goes. The metal detector gate beeps when someone passes through it carrying metal or when the metal door next to the gate gets too close. The radios carried by the officers regularly crackle. The TV in the common area is also almost always on, usually with the volume turned up. On top of all this is the omnipresent jangling of keys and key chains. Unlike the eerie silence in the American supermax prisons described by Shalev (2009), even when the prisoners in Oslo Prison are locked in and it is quiet, it is not particularly quiet.

When one group of prisoners is let out for a social, the noise starts: the sound of eight to ten lads and men talking, laughing, chatting and shouting. The sound of pool balls hitting each other, rolling across the worn, green felt and hitting the cushions on their way to the corner pocket, accompanied by a happy cheer or a resigned sigh. The crisp impact of a table tennis ball hitting the table before it curves past the opponent's racket and ends up at the other end of the long room so they have to call for someone to throw it back. The metallic clang of the heavy weights in the gym area rhythmically hitting each other. Sometimes they hit each other hard, accompanied by the concentrated heaving and breathing in and out of sweaty bodies. The trolley being wheeled along with today's food, cell doors being locked and opened again. Shoes against the hard floor make one noise; slippers make a peculiar slapping noise. All the sounds bounce off the smooth walls and door surfaces and echo down the corridors and between floors.

All of these make up the sound of a normal, well-functioning prison wing. They are, therefore, also the sound of an abstract, potential risk, the sound of a wing that is calm right now, but could blow at any time. The sound of life when the prisoners are unlocked is, for the officers, the sound of work and bother, but also of potential danger and death. This is the normal situation. All deviations from this are a sign of danger that is far more concrete and acute. Like when the lunch break in the officers' room was suddenly interrupted by a deep, heavy crash:

> While we sit there and chat a noise from far away still reverberates through the entire building and is sort of felt deep in your gut. It is not the first time I have heard such sounds. One of the officers smiles and simply says:
>
> Officer: Cell smashing.
>
> The noise is heard again two or three times. We sit quietly and listen. No one does anything in particular. After a few seconds a message comes over the radio from wing one to the operations centre:
>
> Officer wing one: Could you pop down here when you have some free time?
> Officer operations centre: We have some time now, we'll be right down.
>
> Everyone round the table has already understood what is going on in wing one. They grin at their colleague's playing down of the situation and deliberate choice of words:
>
> Officer: Heh heh, it's funny when he is at work, he doesn't use the big words, does he.
> The operations centre also knew at once what he was talking about. You cannot mistake the sound of a cell being smashed up.

Gullestad (2002) shows how in a Norwegian cultural context tension exists between "peace and quiet" and "hustle and bustle". Both parts are desirable, even if the first may perhaps have more positive connotations in a Norwegian context. These are examples of categories that initially appear to be mutually exclusive, although they do not need to be. From the prison officers' perspective, both "peace and quiet" and "hustle and bustle" are associated with the prisoners' activities. "Peace and quiet" describes a quiet, orderly wing with prisoners behind locked cell doors. "Hustle and bustle" describes the prisoners' activities, which can quickly tip over into "noise and mess", which in turn can entail, in a security context, a potential for danger and death. A prison wing with prisoners locked in their cells is a peaceful place that can give the impression of an empty space where nothing is happening. However, there are many people behind the closed doors with closed hatches. But they cannot be seen and, as a rule, they cannot be heard either.

If all the prisoners are locked in, the quiet is not dangerous. But quiet represents danger when there should be noise. Too much sound is a sign of danger when noise levels should be normal. The wrong sounds at the wrong time can mean the same. Therefore, in prison, sound does not always mean life while peace and quiet mean death, as can be the case in other contexts. In prison both different sounds and the absence of sound can signal danger, as long as the prisoners might be involved. An unexpected sound is suspicious and will result in a *Shush! What was that? I had better go and check.* In the vast majority of cases the unfamiliar sound is not a sign of danger. But it *can* be as long as you do not *know*. Therefore, it is best to check. And sometimes it is serious; the sounds *are* a sign that danger really is present:

The officers are sitting around the break table discussing the cell fire the previous Easter. A young prisoner, about a week into his time on the wing, set fire to his rubbish bin and mattress. After a while, brownish yellow smoke poured out into wing five. The mood round the table is quite relaxed; this is the sharing of a "war story". The anecdote is not about the tragic accident that almost happened, about a life that could have been lost. The whole episode is related with a slight shake of the head in a slightly baffled manner while leaning back on the sofa.

Officer 1: He had buzzed first, but he was screaming into the intercom, he was probably right up against it, so we couldn't understand anything that he was saying. But when we went out there, there was all this smoke coming out of the door, the closed door, so of course we knew what was happening.

Officer 2: I think he thought he would be let out quicker, heh heh.

TU: So you don't open the door at once, just because smoke is coming out?

Officer 1: No, we don't open at once, no. After all, he could come out with a knife or a table leg or something. We don't open until we have full control of the situation and of him. The principal prison officer gave permission to open it up after a bit. So we went in and got him, put him on the ground, got the handcuffs on, and shipped him off to the hospital. It was hard; he had a cast on his hand, around the wrist, so it was bloody difficult getting the handcuffs on him. I was standing there trying to get them on. Then the fire service turns up, we let them in, they put it out in a couple of minutes and then the water had to be hoovered up. That's the worst thing about fires, having to clean up afterwards. The fire service poured three or four hundred litres in there. It was running down to the fourth floor while it was on. When he came out, he wouldn't lie down. He just wouldn't get down, so we just had to use the good old out with the leg and on the floor you go. I had my short sleeved shirt on; I wasn't going to let him puke blood on me, no way.

The officers are discussing a situation where they made a risk assessment on the fly during the incident. Potential dangers were being assessed continuously: the prisoner in the burning cell could come out with a knife and stab me; once out he could go nuts and hit me; if he stays calm, he could still vomit blood on me, which could be infectious. Some prisoners in some situations represent multiple forms of risk simultaneously. Good officers never let themselves forget this.

In other words, each of the four subcategories of untrustworthy bodies gives rise to specific forms of power and control. A number of different power relationships, forms of power and power techniques both exist in parallel and intersect in the prison. To sum up, it can be said that a power of law exists (Foucault, 2007), an administrative power which puts up barriers, which constrains, which controls the prisoners' bodies and keeps them on the right side of the right door at the right time. This is a power that wears a blue uniform shirt, that locks in and lets out, controls doors, monitors and records where bodies are located, and impacts the freedom of the bodies' movement with the aid of walls and barbed wire. In practice, it is a power that isolates, that erects barriers, that forces you into loneliness, cut off from others. But there is also a more overarching power that, for lack of a better word, can be called political. This power affects, controls, guides and administers; it collects data, knowledge and information about the individual and uses it to create effects on a wider level. And there is a form of day-to-day disciplinary power that attempts to change, influence and improve, a pedagogical and psychological power that knows what can be done to shape and reshape prisoners and their actions. This is a form of power that knows how others *ought* to behave, a paternalistic power that says "Listen to me and it will be fine." This sort of paternalistic power is, frequently but not always, associated with an idealistic desire to help others who are disadvantaged. Finally, there is a form of power that is brought into play as a supplement where the other, legitimate, forms of power are misused – as when normal rules and routines are practised in ways that are more invasive than necessary or envisaged. A naked prisoner's body can be searched considerately and respectfully, or brutally and ruthlessly. When the latter happens, the legitimate purpose of the control is associated with an illegitimate desire to degrade and subjugate. Conversely, the forms of power can also be exercised in less invasive and more humane ways than normal. A smile, a look, a chat, a cup of coffee make the walls, locks, keys and uniforms more bearable.

Being a prison officer

What do the forms of power look like from the officers' perspective? The Norwegian correctional services is a bureaucracy in a Weberian sense, designed to control many people. It has an administrative staff with a specific set of rules, a well-defined framework for expertise and responsibility, impersonal relationships with those over whom they preside and so on. The bureaucratic rationality means that the officers lack the characteristics of tyranny: not having to take responsibility for one's actions.[8] The officers are bound, they allow themselves to be bound, by rules, laws, circulars and action plans.

> A police officer on the street, a judge in the courtroom, a teacher in school – all have powers that they can choose to exercise over others, but only by virtue of a context of meanings and subject positions that they share with those who are subordinate to them and only by virtue of a sense of discipline that underpins the entire situation.
>
> (Widder, 2004: 423)

The officers' world is a world of endless piles of documents, forms, regular meetings, meaningful abbreviations, regulations, management tools and everything else that characterises these types of systems. Oslo Prison has for several years used the "balanced scorecard" management tool, which was developed for use in private business and which is based on regular, standardised measurements of user satisfaction. The importation model, where the prison "buys in" services such as health care, education and social services from the ordinary external systems, can result in contact with similar parallel management tools. This control rationality has grown in strength in recent times – in prison as in public administration in general. This development can be seen in the context of the trend towards the professionalisation of the estate and the ongoing development of a knowledge and science-based Norwegian correctional services.

The bureaucratic rationality exists in parallel in the prison with a traditional paramilitary structure of superiors and subordinates. There are a lot of officers and fewer governors who constitute the career path from the wing to the director's office. The uniform positions the officers as officers and turns them into pieces of a large system, like all the other pieces on the same level, functionally speaking. At the same time, officers are positioned in a hierarchy where distinctions on their shoulders are symbolic of their position in relation to others. Extra officers and temps have no badges, they just have empty epaulettes. Trainees on their compulsory year of practice wear a simple black cloth sleeve without extra badges. Qualified officers get a yellow stripe. Thereafter one follows the military pattern. The purpose of the badges is to distinguish, to make differences clear. The uniforms standardise and make the officers alike, part of a unit, while the badges maintain and clarify the hierarchy between them.

By virtue of their position, officers have a number of techniques available to them. Officers always have, as described, the ability to exercise total physical power over their subjects. They are the representatives of the state and have thus been tasked with exercising the criminal law's power over individuals who have broken the social contract. Similarly, there is an advanced disciplinary control regime consisting of searches, prisoner counts, lists of who is where and so on. The officers are both architects and organisers; they have to facilitate, organise, administer and construct the system that is intended to produce controlled untrustworthy bodies. At the same time, the officers' gaze (as well as their hearing) is largely focused on uncovering risks in everyday prison life. A key part of their working conditions is the omnipresent potential crisis: situations that occur very rarely, but that can, of course, occur at any time. The officers' goal is to organise things in such a way that the chance of anything happening remains small. Always prepared, is their credo. Good prison officers must be able to tackle and thrive on suitable doses of chaos, and at the same time know what must be done when a line is crossed. The officer is, both in his or her own and the prisoners' eyes, a bureaucrat with a gun, as described by Sykes (1958: xiv–xv). Or, perhaps better put, a bureaucrat with a telescopic baton.

The institution's guiding principle – keeping the right body behind the right door at the right time – depends on the day-to-day continuing maintenance of order. It is only when one has a wing with order and control over the bodies for whom one is responsible that the institution's other objectives can become relevant. It is pointless to highlight successful behaviour modification programmes as a response to having forgotten to lock the main gate. For officers, the maintenance of an (apparently) orderly wing is a key duty. Professional officers maintain order. They are tested on it – the prison regularly organises drills that could just as easily have been called tests of the officers' ability to restore order on a wing; an orderly wing understood as a wing in which all the prisoners are locked in. The officers' gaze also focuses on potential newspaper headlines and tries to avoid them. When the prison ends up as the subject of such headlines because they have failed in their primary duty, it is embarrassing and awkward. During my fieldwork, a prisoner who was subject to a court-ordered telephone ban received permission to use the phone by mistake, which found its way into the columns of some newspapers. The fact that this was a regrettable mistake by a young, inexperienced colleague did not prevent the officers from thinking it was a huge embarrassment.

Some relationships can arise between the prison officers and prisoners, which is probably not as common within other welfare state systems. Sykes finds that officers are often "compromised" and provide prisoners with information that they should not have. The officers have at their disposal few of the possible mechanisms that controllers often use to mark the distance between them and the controlled, writes Sykes, given that they are around each other day in and day out. In practice, this can be a difficult balancing act; one is supposed to be friendly, you learn as a prison officer in training, but not a friend. Unsurprisingly, officers can end up in conflicts of loyalty. On the one hand, the officers have leaders they seldom see and, even more distant, their big employer "society". On the other hand, they have the prisoners whom they know and meet daily. Prison officers, therefore, routinely face a sort of middle-manager's dilemma. The officers are, despite all the power techniques they have at their disposal, not at the top of the hierarchy. They do what others decide should be done (Sparks, Bottoms and Hay, 1996). According to Sykes, the result of this is that one of the rewards officers often dole out is that they look the other way, are more flexible, and are not as diligent as they ought to be (Ibsen, 2012). Therefore, another of the prison's many paradoxes is that the officers can only maintain their power by allowing themselves to be compromised. Only by allowing small things to pass unmentioned can the officers be sure that the major things work as they should, writes Sykes, which does not exclude the possibility that the officers' breaches of the rules may also be due to a rationality of caring, as described by Basberg (1999).

Since the prisoners and officers are each other's most important topic of conversation, a large part of the officers' conversations will at any time centre around the prisoners on the wing – who they are, what they have done or said lately, how they are doing, if anything new is happening in someone's case and so on. Below I describe two frequent topics that regularly pop up and which I regard as illustrative of the officers' relationship to the prisoners.

First, the officers are preoccupied with the prisoners' poor self-control. While the officers are suitably frugal and healthy on a day-to-day basis, the prisoners largely subsist on coke and crisps:

> It is Monday and the articles they have bought have arrived on the wing. The floor of the officers' room is full of tied plastic bags with cell numbers written on them in black marker pen. Every other small surface is full of egg boxes, bags of fruit and melting ice cream cakes. Every spare inch has been turned into a messy shop shelf. The officers sigh.

Officer: It's unbelievable how much time is spent on this every week. Sure, today it's okay, but think what happens when there are only two of us here. It takes hours.

Then everyone gets to work on ripping open the tied bags and checking everyone has got what they ordered according to the order notes the prisoners have filled in. The notes consist of the original and two carbon copies. Any phone cards are stapled to the notes. The officers tick that everything is there, shove it all back into the ruined bag and carry it to the individual cell. Some people only do a bit of shopping. A pack of tobacco, snuff and liquorice pastilles. Others spend hundreds of Norwegian kroner. As well as the almost ubiquitous cigarettes, they buy barbecued chicken, cakes, mineral water, magazines, the lot.

Officer: Look at him now will you, look!

Triumphantly one of the officers starts to put his "catch" on the table. Six 20-packs of Camel cigarettes, a yellow pack of rolling tobacco, three boxes of snuff, rolling papers, three large bars of milk chocolate, a packet of crisps, five litre and a half bottles of coke.

Officer: He's going to have a healthy week. I can't believe it … [He shakes his head.]

The people around the table grin at the contents of the bag.

Officer: Then again, all he does is sit on his backside and smoke the whole time, so it's not surprising he gets through a few cigarettes.

The officer's comments can be read as a moral condemnation of the gluttony, the prisoners' lack of self-control, which is a characteristic officers often ascribe to prisoners more generally. Having "a short fuse", "lacking impulse control" or being a person it is "difficult to figure out" are all common phrases officers use when describing prisoners. Their lack of power to resist the temptation of cigarettes and comfort foods is thus connected to a broader narrative about prisoners who are unable to control themselves, a narrative that is ultimately used as an explanation for why many of them have ended up where they have ended up.

Second, the officers often relate anecdotes about "the crazy prisoner". These are part of a larger narrative about all the strange and crazy things that the most disturbed prisoners can get up to.

The lunch break arrives fast today. I'm hanging out on the sofa with the officers. Once again much of the time is spent sharing stories about freaks. Today they're about people who eat all sorts of things.

Officer: We had one guy where I used to work [another prison]; he used to eat absolutely everything. Razor blades, for example, two of them. He had to go to hospital for an operation to get them out. His cell was totally stripped before he came back so he wouldn't find anything to swallow. But, he'd been locked in for about 15 minutes when we heard a noise. He had chucked the TV on the floor and started to eat all the loose components in it. Including the antenna, a sort of telescopic thing you pull out of a hole [indicating its length of 10–15 cm with his fingers]. He just swallowed the whole thing, as long as it was [everyone around the table laughs, we shake our heads]. So it was straight back to hospital. But when he gets there they just shake their heads and say: sorry, you have been operated on so many times that we won't risk it. This time it'll have to come out the way nature intended. It'll take five to eight weeks. Goodbye. He was so surprised; he didn't expect that. So he was walking around, right, with a TV antenna inside him making its way through his body. After a while it became a joke; he laughed about it too. When he got near the TV we told him he had to move because he was interfering with the signal. We had a lot of fun with that. There he is, the one with an antenna up his arse, you know.

Such anecdotes about *the crazy prisoner* can be used to create and sustain a radical difference between prisoners (freaks) and officers (normal people). What cannot be explicitly expressed because it would breach the official core values of the profession of prison officer (prisoners are people of a different (rank) kind, they are sick, crazy, they make me sick) can be expressed by relating an anecdote. Such anecdotes sustain and continue the important division between the two main groups in the prison. *The crazy prisoner* is in this way regarded as a figure who confirms the distance between the officers and prisoners, and who therefore helps to underscore what an important job the officers do. In the case above, sharing the anecdote about the man "with an antenna up his arse" becomes part of a broader sharing of "war stories" that creates a sense of camaraderie between officers who do a dirty, difficult and hard job on behalf of society, without receiving the recognition (in the form of pay or in other ways) they feel they deserve. The anecdote about *the crazy prisoner* is also an anecdote about the prison officer as a totally necessary, but under-appreciated, part of society's foundations.

The relationship between officers and prisoners is characterised by jokes and quips. This has a number of functions, according to Mathiesen (1965): it reduces aggression among prisoners, it resolves conflicts, it makes the job easier to bear for the officers, and it underscores that officers avoid entering into heavy, difficult, emotional relationships with prisoners. Viewed from the outside, it is a very special mixture of humour and seriousness. The prison could be such fun that I did not want to leave. At the same time, a prison is a terribly sad place, which is not really alleviated by all the fun there. In other contexts it would be unnatural to listen to suicide plans or feel an arm full of shrapnel only to laugh at the next moment – heartily and with gusto – at a gallows humour joke. This is all part of the working day in the prison. Humour and seriousness are not mutually exclusive here, and they are not even incompatible. The humour underscores the seriousness. This is not prison-specific: surprising pain can often trigger laughter. This is social laughter, laughter that tells both you and your surroundings that everything will probably be alright.

Despite all the crazy prisoners, it is largely prisoners from other wings that anecdotes are told about. "Our prisoners" are usually okay enough. Therefore, the anecdotes can also be understood in relation to the officers' negotiation between a desire for excitement and the fear of risk in a job where things "can kick off at any time", even though most days on the job are pretty boring. That which happens very rarely, but which, of course, can occur at any time, must be understood in relation to a desire for more "action".

All in all, the prison is a diverse workplace. Being a prison officer means having to settle into a paradoxical position. The various areas of responsibility and their accompanying forms of power must be adapted and balanced. One must be engaged, but not *too* engaged, be flexible, but not *too* flexible, steadfast and strict, but not *too* steadfast and strict. Living the officer role in practice means trying to walk on several intersecting tightropes at the same time. It seems to me that appreciating this job over time depends on one of two things: either a pretty outstanding social capacity and flexibility or very well-functioning blinkers. Or, which is probably the most common solution, a combination of the two.

The subject and power

The forms of power exercised by the prison have consequences. A power technology must have its objects. One absolutely key by-product in this context is that the prison's power results in the prisoners *being understood as prisoners*, even if this is in slightly different ways, which, in turn, is part of the context in which prisoners continuously have to understand themselves. What is being a prisoner in a high security prison like? As objects of a punishment and rehabilitation technology, the prisoners are understood in specific ways (Warnier, 2009). The daily locking of doors contributes to prisoners being understood as people who have to be locked in, who cannot be trusted, and whom it is best to protect society from by locking them up. The modification system understands prisoners as people who are unable to control themselves, who cannot be trusted, and who need help to help themselves, so that we can all sleep safer at night. If one looks at the policy documents, a prisoner is described as a complex biographical unit composed of various personal deficiencies, risks and potentials. The average prisoner is more likely than others to have little schooling, no (legal) job, no fixed address, no stable social network, physical and psychological problems and illnesses, and so on. The prison technology's goal is also to change the prisoners' situation in order to change how they act in the future, thereby preventing future crime in society as a whole. When specific people are placed in the welfare state's punishment and rehabilitation machine, the prison becomes a system that separates out and creates an identifiable group of people – *the prisoners* – and makes them manageable as a political problem in the broadest sense of the term (Foucault, 1977a). In this sense at least, the prison is a system that produces prisoners. The forms of power are in this way connected to forms of knowledge and subjectification practices. The prisoners must, in their daily work of understanding themselves and their situation, relate to the situation they are in. Again, a specific concept of power allows us here to study how forms of power and subjectification processes are closely bound together, how some of what happens when life encounters power makes us who and what we are. The question below is: how can this work be conceptualised more concretely?

A man walks down the street. Some way behind him a police officer is tailing him with purposeful strides. The police officer has speeded up, but she is still some way behind. Afraid the man will disappear into the crowd, she hails him: "Hey! You there! Stop!" The man freezes, he already knows the hail was meant for him. He turns and meets the police officer's gaze.

This example is from Althusser's (1971) discussion of what can be said to be the fundamental problem in social science: what is the relationship between social structures and individuals? How can one visualise and observe the process in which the social structure enters and becomes part of people's imaginary world and system of concepts? In short, and formulated within the Marxist framework in which he wrote, how does ideology enter and form people? The situation in which the police officer hails the man on the street becomes for Althusser an example of relationships that are continuously re-created between society and individuals more generally. His point of departure for the theoretical answer he gives to the fundamental problem is, therefore, that ideology hails us and we answer, and thereby enter into it as specific subjects connected to a system of subject positions situated in relation to each other.

For Althusser, ideology is not about a freedom/prisoner dynamic, as in traditional Marxist theory, where people who are initially free are caught by an ideology and are thereby made unfree. No non-ideological freedom is possible for Althusser. On the contrary, it is through their (always ideological) relationship to the rest of society that individuals can become free citizens. The individual is always already a subject; it is precisely because they have a social position that it is possible for the subject to think, feel and act at all. The question above (how does ideology enter people?) is in a way poorly worded, since ideology is always already under our skin.

Althusser makes use here of an ambiguous concept of subject. On the one hand, the concept of subject indicates a capacity for action, initiative and autonomy (as we use it in sentence analysis, where the subject, as one learns at school, is the thing that *does*, the thing that is responsible for the verbal action). On the other hand, the subject is subordinate to a higher authoritative power, like a king who has his subjects, understood as people who have submitted their freedom or parts of it to an external agent. On the one hand, submission, and, on the other, the capacity to act and, perhaps less immediately understandable, a connection between them: a capacity to act only through submission. Learning technical jargon and terminology is part of the process of acquiring abilities, which in turn consists of the production of the individual as an ideological subject. The more immersed, the more proficient, the greater the submission. You become better through training and mastering, but you also become immersed in a structure and the view of the world associated with it. Perceptions, beliefs, knowledge and how you view your surroundings are all associated with practices, actions and the doing of something. The better something is mastered, the more the subject becomes immersed in the practice in question and the entire field in which the practice takes place. The paradox of subjectivity is that it is only by being positioned as a subject, in relation to all the rules, constraints and limitations that apply to positioned subjects, that people can be free. It is as a subject, situated and positioned with a subject's rights and obligations, that one is or can be free to do what one wants, or, in fact, even to want; free to take responsibility for obeying the law, for example, to turn and face the law, and thereby make ourselves into a law-abiding subject.

An individual is, therefore, not the same as a subject. Ideology changes or transforms individuals into subjects. For Althusser, a subject is an individual as they are positioned in relation to ideology. The subject position, therefore, becomes a key concept for understanding the relationships between social structures and individuals. The process, which can be described as hailing, is called "interpellation" by Althusser. An individual becomes a subject by being interpellated into an ideological context, while a subject position can only be said to exist to the extent that it is supported and continued by specific individuals.

Althusser introduces repetition as the motor that drives the whole process onwards. A key point here is that subject positions always already exist. They are cultural and social public goods. "Connecting to" or *doing* such a subject position is simultaneously always both a unique event and a retelling of the cultural public good, and, in some sense, of the entire social and cultural context. The main idea is that, when the guilty man in the example above turns 180 degrees and meets the police officer's gaze, this is a physical recognition that the hailing of the police officer and social structure has achieved its goal, and that the man is, therefore, relating to and entering into the subject position the police officer intended for him, a position that is thereby acknowledged and continued. This is something more than a relationship between two individuals; it is a retelling of a social order with specific ideas about the relationship between individuals and the state and of cultural perceptions, meaning categories, crime and punishment clichés, and so on. When the individual is hailed and turns around as a subject interpellated by the police officer, the offender-subject and the police officer-subject are positioned in relation to each other, and both are positioned in relation to the state system, whose legitimacy is thereby re-created.

What sort of subject should I be? How should I relate to power's objectifying hail? Althusser is not particularly specific when it comes to these more practical questions, and the subject-creating encounter between the individual and structure is described in fairly generic terms. He has been criticised (Andersen, 1999; Laclau and Mouffe, 2001) for making this question into a sort of (structuralist and modernist) closed system that "balances", where the relationship between individual and ideology becomes too simplistic and one-to-one. Butler (1997) believes his choice of examples is misleading, since the interpellation (hailing) appears almost impossible to resist. What she calls the Law's imperative (society's abstract Law, which is represented by the police officer in this specific situation) is (almost) just as impossible to resist as the voice of God hailing someone by name, another one of Althusser's interpellation examples. Of course, it is the acceptance and coercive outcome that Butler is trying to problematise here:

> How and why does the subject turn, anticipating the conferral of identity through the self-ascription of guilt? What kind of relation already binds these two such that the subject knows to turn, knows that something is to be gained from such a turn?
>
> (Butler, 1995: 7)

Alternatives and choices are key in Butler's rewriting of Althusser's argument. It is all the continuous situated choices made against the backdrop of such hails that are constructive for the subject. In other words, in her reading, the Law does not just simply command and the subject must simply obey. The Law's voice and the subject who (potentially) obeys are mutually responsible for the outcome. In her version of Althusser's example, the attributing of guilt and a bad conscience inherent in the Law's hail interpellate the individual as a social subject bound to his social surroundings. But what sort of subject becomes, in practice, the result of this is nonetheless far from a given, because a bad conscience can manifest itself in many ways. In the example, the police officer's hail resulted in the man turning. The question is: is this the only thing he could have done? To remain in Althusser's world, it could be said that the form of power's interpellating hail is rarely completely unambiguous. Typically, you do not hear only one clear voice either. It is difficult to imagine circumstances where there are, at the least, no competing voices that are associated with alternative positions to which it is possible to connect. Sometimes there are few alternatives and the interpellating voice is relatively monologic. At other times there are several competing hails fighting for attention, and sometimes one is faced with a choir of commanding voices that, depending on the ear doing the listening, can be described as productively dissonant or a conflict-filled, quarrelling cacophony. In any case, the point is that alternative whispered voices can usually be heard behind or in parallel with an interpellating hail. Acknowledging the police officer's and society's hail, assuming the subject position of *offender on the run*, does not, therefore, mean that everything that can be said has been said. On the contrary, this is a theoretical starting point for observing something that could go in any direction, which must be played out as a concrete practice with all this involves with regard to opportunities for variations on a theme. Turning and meeting the law, face-to-face, is not a *necessary* result of the law's hail. The hailed subject has been positioned in a field of options. Interpellation is, thus, not the opposite of agency; the continuous practical subjectification game is, on the contrary, the necessary arena or stage for agency. It is precisely through such processes, with the aid of the opportunities and limitations the processes set, that agency becomes possible. Individual players can always enter into and play out subject positions in different ways. One clear advantage of such a perspective is that it acknowledges the surroundings' constitutive and creative power, while the individual's ability to perform an activity and make choices does not disappear.

At the same time, it is important to underscore that here "choice" is meant in its broadest possible sense – the choice between alternatives is not a "choice" in the sense of rational choice. It is a situational choice, a choice that must make sense there and then. The idea of "choice" is not meant to indicate a prior conscious process; it is simply meant to underscore that individuals on their way to becoming subjects have options. It is about a form of choice that is always, simultaneously, a product of the subject position the individual is already in. How does one relate to competing hailing voices and conflict-filled positions? This nascent conceptual development can take as its starting point the concepts of identification, counter-identification and disidentification (Neumann, 2001).

Identification involves entering the subject position relatively loyally, faithful to the discursive framework that applies. But it must be noted that, at the same time, identification does not entail a mechanical repetition of a memorised position. Any connection between individual and position, any instance of a subject position being articulated in practice, is played out in a concrete context with the opportunities and limitations that apply within it. This is why identification is not incompatible with creativity either. Counter-identification entails the individual resisting available subject positions as they are basically defined in the relevant discourses and entering into a diametrically opposed position. This is not a qualitatively new position; rather, it is the negation of the positively defined subject position. Disidentification involves a more creative form of protest. One does not assume the relevant position without friction, but pulls it in a new direction. Here you will find hybrid forms, resistance practices, transgressive solutions and genuinely innovative ways of relating to one's surroundings.

After all, it is not the case that the man's only option in the example, when he realised that the voice was directed at him, was to turn and acknowledge the police officer's and state system's legitimacy (and, in some sense, the entire prevailing social order). The law's subject who turns and meets the law's enforcer could, for example, be an agreeable, law-abiding subject, but also a resigned, reluctant subject. But he did not have to turn around. He could have turned himself into a resisting subject. He could have pretended nothing had happened, tried to make the police officer unsure about whether she really had the right man in front of her, and tried to disappear into the crowd at the first opportunity. Or he could have started running, believing he could shake her off. He could even have turned and attacked her, to mention just some of the more obvious options that far from cover the almost infinite range of creative expressions of resistance that are available to subjects in various power relationships and constellations. Note that all three alternatives are fully compatible with the man immediately recognising the hailing voice as being precisely directed at him. The various responses to the attempt at interpellation all involve a positioning of the subject in relation to the state power, but in completely different ways and with variations of the subject position "wanted offender" as the result.

From a Foucauldian perspective, becoming a subject is about believing that specific things about you are true; it is about experiencing yourself in a certain way through having arrived at specific forms of knowledge about yourself. In a Western context it is key that the modern desire for the truth, as described by Foucault (2003), has attempted to define, identify and point out various forms of deviation and rule breaking as a tool in creating normality. The subject is the product of a meeting between an individual and discourses, institutions, power relationships and knowledge practices that produce the truth. The abnormal individual is identified in the encounter with such practices, while everyone else is pushed in the direction of normality. It is also key in this process that the subject is not determined, a simple result: the subject reacts and adapts to the interpellations. The subject works on himself and actively changes himself within the opportunities afforded by the context and the subject's position. Participating in the ongoing subject-producing power–resistance game of hailing and reactions to hailing is both an individual and a social necessity for a member of a society.

As part of the renegotiation of his previous works, Foucault (2000c) describes how he has, through his books, analysed subjectification processes as being related to three forms of objectification. First, he describes the forms of examination that are given and give themselves the status of "knowledge", and how producing knowledge simultaneously creates knowledge objects in ways that can have a subjectifying effect on those being made into objects. Then he describes the objectification of subjects inherent in the discriminatory or categorising practices associated with normalisation systems and their associated classification principles (Foucault, 1977a, 1990b); what he calls "dividing practices" (2000c: 326), that is, practices that objectify the subject as either the same or different in relation to something else and which can thereby become of significance for subjectification processes. One example he constantly returns to is the subject's connection to a norm, how "normality" and "normalisation" have an impact on both those who are viewed as normal and those who are thus understood as abnormal. Finally, he has worked on how people turn themselves into objects for themselves; they can work on themselves and their relationship to themselves as specific forms of subjects with a view to controlling their own behaviour and relationship to other people (Foucault, 1990a, 1990b, 1992).

There are obvious connections between the various forms of objectification. Deviants who become the object of knowledge extraction and production processes turn this into part of their knowledge about themselves. Individuals who receive a diagnosis must, in any case, deal with this, even if the work on themselves pulls in a direction of resistance to the diagnosis and alternative truths about themselves. Both perspectives must be present: individualising knowledge is established about the individual that connects him to a larger regime of knowledge and places him in a position (as deviant, criminal, etc.), while adapting to or resisting the attempted interpellation could contribute to the individual experiencing himself in a new way.

The common denominator in all of Foucault's texts that deal with this is that, in the encounter between individuals, practices and technologies for extracting (powerful) knowledge about the individual, the subject is shaped by the fact that the individual is connected to and must relate to himself in various "truth games". Common to all forms of power is that they are connected to a desire to acquire specific forms of knowledge and that through their knowledge-producing effects they see specific objects, a relationship that can be described using Foucault's neologism "power/knowledge". Power technologies, forms of knowledge and the resulting subjects are all intertwined.

How is a subject positioned as a specific subject in relation to a specific power/knowledge regime according to Foucault? A knowledge regime is a way of looking at the world. Different regimes have different subject-interpellating optics. For example, the clinical gaze creates healthy and sick subjects (Foucault, 1976), disciplinary techniques control and observe subjects with cooperative bodies that are thereby made effective (Foucault, 1977a), the law sees subjects that are positioned in a specific relationship to the (legal) truth (Foucault, 2000d), while the state's attempt to collect knowledge about and control its population creates a subject that wants to self-control as a member of the population (Foucault, 2007), to mention just some of the many possible examples. The clinical gaze sees the world in one way; the statistical gaze that systematises the population in another. The various forms of power, therefore, constitute different subjects. Foucault's debt to Althusser is clear here. Power bound up with everyday life that categorises and objectifies the individual, which marks a person's individuality and then connects him to his future social position, is a form of power that turns individuals into subjects. From this perspective, the subject is an effect of power. Note that, by extension, if the prison can be understood as a suitable place to study power and resistance, a connection between the power and the subject (Foucault, 2000c) will also make the prison a good place to study subjectification processes.

The subject is created when individuals are immersed in society, when the power impacts individuals and creates subjects. A Foucauldian rewriting of Althusser's thematics is that the individual becomes a subject in the encounter with the power, the power which is everywhere, and which everywhere is set in relation to subjects. It should immediately be stated that writing *the* power, using the definite article, singular, is problematic in a Foucauldian framework. There are an infinite number of different forms of power and relationships that operate in relation to different logics. Subjectification processes are therefore complex, intersect each other, and are diverse. When one lives out one's sexual freedom in the field of sexuality and when one exercises one's political freedom to participate in democratic elections in a political field, it has no meaning from this perspective to say that one is "the same", even if in both cases one becomes a subject in relation to forms of power. The subject is again contextual and relational.

The prisoner status as challenge

Taking this as the starting point, being put in prison (and thus being hailed as a "prisoner") could involve a series of challenges at the level of the subject. Seen in relation to the diversity of the forms of power in prison, one could say that many different, apparently contradictory, subject positions are available to prisoners. Prisoners are in part understood as people who have chosen to do the wrong thing, who are morally inferior, and who must therefore be punished. They are also partly understood as having an inner inclination to do the wrong thing, and they must therefore be normalised and made responsible. In this way, prisoners find themselves put under administration, where the goal is to teach them to control and manage themselves with the aid of techniques designed to produce responsible subjects. The individual should come to see himself as a risk subject and learn to act accordingly in relation to himself. A good citizen is a citizen with self-control and a citizen who has proven, through his day-to-day practices, that he is ready to assume responsibility for himself.

As a cultural starting point, "the prisoner" alternates between being sick, dangerous, abnormal and irresponsible. The prisoner is a person who should have a poor conscience, someone who ought to understand the wrong he has done, someone who is incapable of seeing the consequences of his actions. He is an unethical or morally inferior person, a defective and dangerous person, someone who has done something so terrible, or at least wrong, that he must be locked up, who cannot be trusted, a member of a population that must be administered, controlled and rehabilitated before they can live among us again. Someone who is serving a sentence in prison is probably there for good reason. "Lock them up and throw away the key!" is an oft-heard cry in public debates about criminals, prisoners and imprisonment. Prison, therefore, loudly expresses the idea that productive work on oneself is expected, that there is a power that expects an individual to pull himself together, contribute, and make use of what he is being offered. Being hailed as a prisoner means having to relate to the truth about yourself as a prisoner, as immoral, pacified, evil, stupid, and so on.

The ascribed position also has a gendered dimension. Seen through a cultural gender-sensitive lens, the status of prisoner entails, which Sykes (1958) already touches on, that male prisoners are removed from that which is perceived as good, important and right to do and be for men. Conversely, the prison and the resulting status of prisoner basically have an emasculating function (Messerschmidt, 2001; Jewkes, 2005). Prisoners are people who have had much of the control over their own lives taken from them and who have only a limited capacity to intervene in and change their surroundings. Achieving something, mastering something, showing that you are capable are key cultural expectations for men, at least in a Western context (Whitehead, 2002; Kimmel, 2006). The opportunities to live up to these expectations are limited in a prison. There are no cars to fix or floors to lay here. Prisoners are also understood as morally inferior, as people you cannot trust. They are unable to make enough money to support their families and they are largely prevented from being there when they are needed. The institution makes almost all decisions for them; they must ask for permission to shower and often have to eat what they are served by a prison that controls them. As in other institutions, this is part of a more general trend in which prisoners are deprived of many of the privileges usually associated with being an adult man (Ericsson and Jon, 2006). If "real man", whatever one means by that, is the name of a collective, negotiated cultural objective for men, a yardstick, then prisoners are deprived, as prisoners, of most of the conventional tools for achieving the position of real men. From this perspective, the status of prisoner will put male prisoners in what Kolnar (2005a, 2006) has called a "peripetal movement"; a movement away from masculinity's cultural centre and out into peripheries of unmanliness.

Traditional masculine values include that the man – the *real* man, the man with a capital M – is trustworthy, he is safe and good, a supporter, and one who will catch you when you fall. A real man does the right thing, even if it is unpopular, and even if he is subjected to peer pressure and persuasion.

The man with a capital M has morals; he is responsible and rational. Many of the challenges a prisoner faces as a result of being hailed as a prisoner can be described as challenges to the prisoner's masculinity (Newton, 1994; Carrabine and Longhurst, 1998; Levit, 2001; Sabo, 2001; Jewkes, 2005). The status of prisoner also basically breaches masculinity markers such as having the ability and competence to act. Prisoners are pacified and largely in no position to influence themselves and their surroundings. Mastering, achieving and succeeding are masculine goals to strive for. Agency, the capacity to act, the ability to intervene in and influence one's surroundings – all of these also form part of what can be called general masculine values in our civilisation, and all of them are made difficult or impossible for prisoners. Taking away a prisoner's capacity to decide, not giving good reasons for what is happening, and taking decisions into which they have no insight, all puts them in the subject position of child, a process that is referred to as infantilisation (Lindberg, 2005; Ericsson and Jon, 2006). That's just the way it is, little one. Don't worry your little head about that. Thus, being interpellated into a position on the peripheries of masculinity is perceived as a challenge. This is what Kolnar (2006) calls "the centripetal invitation". For men who are at risk of sliding out to the margins of masculinity by being positioned as a prisoner, it is usually necessary to try and counter this movement in order to once again move towards the centre of masculinity.

Because the individual has room for action, being hailed as a prisoner is viewed as a challenge by many prisoners. It is, of course, possible to start resisting the power's interpellative calls. Although it is difficult for a person put in a cell to avoid acknowledging their status of prisoner at some level, this does not mean that there are not many ways of "doing" the position of prisoner. There are variations on the theme within what must be understood as identification with the position, as well as counter-identification and disidentification: no power without resistance, no ascribed position without the opportunity for concrete conversion on a micro level in and through day-to-day interactions. The prison's forms of power and the resulting status of prisoner entail a subject-related challenge that must be responded to if one wants to be something other, or more, than "a prisoner". Given this, the prison, the institution created to implement the deprivation of liberty, is probably our society's best arena for studying freedom. It is precisely in such institutions, where the network of power technologies is so diverse, so finely meshed and so overarching, that forms of resistance are most complex. It is precisely because one is, as a prisoner in prison, so immersed in the institution's power relationships that resistance becomes so important and so common. It is because of all the limits on freedom that escape attempts become so important and so easy to implement, since it does not take much before one bumps into some boundary or other that can be crossed. The more walls that are built, the more often you will be able to find someone trying to climb one.

It is the prisoners' freedom-creating actions when faced with the prison's many different forms of power and the resulting changes in the status of prisoner that are the topic of the rest of this book. It is the transformed prisoner subject, as a real man, as free, as active, as morally superior and responsible – in short, as a *non-prisoner,* or at least as not *just* a prisoner – who is continuously created in the tension between the power's attempts to influence and the resistance's practices when it comes to forms of adaptation and escape attempts the book will now explore.

3
Taking Liberties

Yard time is over; the prisoners who have been outside walk up the stairs and into wing four. Tarik, sweaty after playing football, asks if I want to join him in his cell for a chat, and I do. Tarik was recently sentenced to 16 years in prison for drug smuggling. He is one of the few on the wing who say they are innocent – the only thing he has done is to have the wrong friends, friends who smuggle drugs and earn lots of money.

Tarik: *I'm a car mechanic, me, not a rich man. I have a perfect life, drive a nice car, eat every day, and have a flat, a perfectly normal life. I don't make my living as a drug smuggler. And no one testified against me either. No one has seen me do anything. It's all circumstantial evidence. Nonetheless, one got six years, the other got 15 years. I got 16 years. But if you ask me if everything is okay, I would say yes, everything is okay. You have to smile, always smile. It's for my own good; I couldn't stand it otherwise, that's why I smile. I don't say that I'm innocent out there [pointing to the common area]. They wouldn't believe me anyway. That's not how we talk in here; "yeah, yeah, we're all innocent in here" they say. So I can't talk about it. So I say I'm doing time for drugs. Fifty kilos of cannabis and 30 kilos of heroin and cocaine. But, I'm innocent. It happens; it happened to Fritz Moen and it happened to Liland [famous examples of wrongly convicted people in Norway]. And it's happening to me. There are a lot who talk big out there, but when they are alone in their cell, they cry. Being here destroys you; you become brainwashed. Just imagine, 17 or 18 months of pure routine. Lock-up, social, hanging out, lock-up, social, hanging out. It completely does your head in. Do you think we hang out because we are such good friends? We aren't; we hang out because we are allowed to have that little hatch in the door open. I'm not kidding Thomas, that's why.*

TU: *I've spoken to prisoners who say you can forget that you can open doors yourself. When you come out, you end up standing outside shops waiting for someone to open the door for you.*

Tarik: Yes! And it's the same for officers as well; being here really changes them too. It's the same for both sides. A temp who was here last year said to me: "Tarik, I'm not kidding, I've started knocking on doors before I open them at home." You can become really brainwashed. But that box there [pointing to the TV] at least makes it a little better. If it hadn't been for that, I swear, they would find someone hanging here every day. Every day; I'm not kidding. At least it's some company. There are two types of people here, two types of inmate. When the prison squeezes them, squeeze, squeeze, squeeze [he gestures as if squeezing an orange in his hand]; either they kill themselves or they begin to fight. Either they break, or they get even. And this makes new problems for them. They end up back here again and again. I've got a new book I'm reading; it's straight from Morocco. It's about how one should think positively, always think positively. Remember that there is always someone who is worse off than you, much worse off. I am healthy, I have food, a toilet, clothes on my body; I have everything. I can study what I want; it costs a lot of money to go to school on the outside. Here it's free; I pay nothing. You have to think positively. There is a saying in Arabic "even after the darkest night there will be light in the morning".

TU: Yes, we say, there is light at the end of the tunnel.

Tarik: Yes, it is the same thing. And it is true. After I found out that I was going to be a dad, everything has changed 180 degrees. Life is completely different. I see everything differently. I can't wait; I just walk around smiling all the time. The future is bright.

* * *

Those who are put in prison become prisoners, with all this entails. The rest of this book is based on the idea that many prisoners do not wish to remain prisoners. What follows are five juxtaposed sections that each, from a different perspective, look at how prisoners, within the framework set by the prison institution, and in and through day-to-day practices, adopt various tools and strategies to resolve the challenges inherent in being ascribed the status of prisoner. The five sections should be read as descriptions of five different aspects of the prisoners' repetitive work of doing freedom or taking liberties, and thus, simultaneously, making themselves into something other than a prisoner, which is the main theme of this book. By (1) positioning themselves in relation and contrast to various so-called constitutive others; by (2) transforming space, for example by converting an impersonal cell into a unique home; by (3) food and mealtime-related resistance to the prison's control regime and Norwegian society outside; by (4) renegotiating the opportunities for untrustworthy bodies and symbolic liberation of the prisoner's body; and by (5) renegotiating their own moral position and positioning themselves as morally superior, the prisoners put their status as prisoners into play and turn themselves into something else.

Relationships and constitutive others

What is a prisoner? A possible answer to this question is to assume that subject positions (like "prisoner") acquire content, meaning and qualities through comparisons with the content, meaning and qualities ascribed to other positions in the relevant discursive field in a never-ending game where similarities and differences are collectively negotiated. From such a perspective, any position's meaning is always partly a result of everything this position is, in a specific context, not. This has a number of consequences. Derrida's term *différance* may be instructive. *Différance* describes a specific, productive negative relationship where the part defined as negative on the one side is a necessary part of the positive part's positivity on the other side. Self-understanding as a specific subject requires that which is left out, that is, what one is not or that which falls on the outside (Derrida, 2006). Ambivalence and instability are thus placed at the core of the formation of meaning: everything that is, is also (simultaneously) that which it is not. Conversely, that which is, is what it is by virtue of that which it is missing, that which is called "the constitutive other". This has been a fundamental leitmotif in post-structuralist theory (Derrida, 1981, 1988; Norton, 1988; Laclau and Mouffe, 2001; Søndergaard, 2002): That which is pushed out, that which is placed on the outside as a boundary marker to make the inside stand out and become visible, is, at the same time, an essential part of the inside's necessary conditions. This also applies at the level of local subjectification processes: "[T]he subject is constituted through the force of exclusion and abjection, one which produces a constitutive outside to the subject, an abjected outside, which is, after all, 'inside' the subject as its own founding repudiation", writes Butler (1993: 72), with explicit reference to Derrida's term *différance*.

Subjectivity construction based on the exclusion of something else often simultaneously establishes a hierarchy between the two resulting poles, where that which I am is, as a rule, perceived to be better than that which I am not (Connolly, 1991). In more traditional sociological terms, identification with an in-group instead of an out-group results, as a rule, in prioritisation of the in-group and often also, simultaneously, in devaluation and suspicion of the out-group. Identification with one position entails a parallel exclusion process whereby those who, or that which, are used as a meaning-creating reference become identified and excluded as outside, an outside which in most or all cases (albeit in many different ways) is devalued.

Seen from inside the prison and from the individual's vantage point, this, in practice, largely has to do with relationships. Some forms of relationships are due to, and are derived from, the special situation the prisoner is in as a prisoner. Other relationships already existed before the status of prisoner was assigned, but are reshaped by the new situation. From the individual prisoner's perspective, nothing is left untouched by his new life and by the prison's everyday decisions. The prison structures or directs relationships in specific ways; not that this means that all prisoners are alike or that they experience everyday prison life in the same way. This section will examine the key constitutive "other categories" prisoners use in their daily self-positioning work, with particular emphasis on showing the benefits the various other categories can provide. What attributes are ascribed to the inside, given that the outside is populated in precisely this manner?

Prisoners and the System

When the prisoners talk about the System, they mean something that from the vantage point of an outsider may appear to be a messy alliance of agencies at various levels. First and foremost, they mean the criminal justice system's various actors: the police, prosecuting authorities, courts and the Norwegian correctional services. However, they often also mean the lawyers, a group that in other circumstances are highlighted as their allies in the struggle against the same System. In any case, these are actors who are important in their everyday lives and whom they must deal with during their entire time as remand prisoners. But the System can also include associated, cooperating welfare state partners like the health and social services, or even the state system in general. Sometimes one even gets the impression that (especially) foreign prisoners are talking about Norwegian civil society when they use the term.

Seen from outside, the unity the term is supposed to denote seems fluid and messy, as if its use does not "add up". From an inside perspective the logic is clearer. When the prisoners talk about the System, they are talking about an adversary they have experienced as having, collectively and in many intersecting and often hidden ways, a negative effect on their everyday lives. The System is often more concretely a collective term for actors who are behind, or are assumed to be behind, the developments that put the prisoner in prison or who are contributing to them still being there. From the prisoner's perspective, the System has investigated your case, taken it to court, and often defended you poorly on the wrong basis, before it has sentenced you to serve the sentence you are serving. The System now controls you and ensures that you behave as you should, at the same time as, for some reason or another, it is not doing its job so that you can be released.

Moreover, the current situation is often only the last in a long line of encounters the individual has had with the System. The System is active in schools, it runs child welfare institutions, it sits and waits at social welfare offices, and it guards the country's borders. The term is thus used to create order in a chaotic mixture of public, semi-public and even private actors at various levels, who for various reasons have affected the prisoners, or are assumed to have affected them, in ways that they experience as not being to their advantage. Seen from outside, one could say that the term probably overestimates the willingness and ability to work together of the various actors it includes. Seen from inside, the term has meaning as a collective term that in one word sums up the entire, massive system that prisoners perceive they are facing. In the following I will primarily concentrate on the prisoners' perception of, and relationship with, the various actors in the criminal justice process. I begin with conceptions of the System as a whole, before looking more closely at the individual actors.

One typical perception among the prisoners is that the System cheats. Cheating, and the accompanying feeling of unfairness, is a major source of "disorder" and problems, as others have already found (Mathiesen, 1965; Sparks, Bottoms and Hay, 1996). The refrain is that it would be okay to be imprisoned if it had been done in a fair way, if the mighty System had only played fairly and by its own rules. However, prisoners believe that they are part of a game in which the adversary has a one-sided ability to twist the rules of the game to its own advantage. Note that the problem for the prisoners is not the System itself. The prisoners acknowledge that a system is required, that a state governed by the rule of law is necessary to maintain law and order in society. The problem is that the System does not play by its own rules, at least not any more. The game has become corrupt and dirty. As Tom put it:

> We don't have a state governed by the rule of law in Norway anymore. They use all types of means against us, and they get away with it. Any means are permitted against us criminals, aren't they?

Scott (1990) describes how the dominated, in a context where the dominant power is broadly perceived as socially legitimate and the dominant party has a safe historical and cultural basis for its dominance, need a counter-ideology, a negation of the dominant power's basis for its superior position. Small acts of resistance in day-to-day life are not enough; you have to frame the resistance and frustration in a more general and comprehensive understanding of the dominant power's illegitimacy. This can be a useful perspective for understanding the prisoners' disappointment with regard to the System that breaks its own rules. The side that should be most interested in the rules, which created the rules, which owns the interpretation of the rules, does not follow the rules itself. Therefore, its dominance is not legitimate either. The frustration with the police who cheat, the deputy judges who lack their own will, and the arbitrariness of everyday prison life can be understood within the framework of such a broader transformation of core values. The prisoners do not disagree per se that the police exist, that the courts must do their job, and that the prison incarcerates those who need to be under lock and key. In most cases, their resistance can, therefore, not be understood as being a result of any notion of social revolution in any real sense. But, on the other hand, they cannot completely accept their dominated position. This is resolved through the narrative of the System that does not abide by its own rules, the System that cheats, that is bent, and that cannot be trusted. At the same time, acts of resistance by extension become, in some sense, legitimate. Most prisoners do not want to be revolutionary radicals. They like the current state of things, in theory. But the way it is practised is unfair.

Mathiesen (1965) describes the result as "censoriousness", a sort of critical finger pointing from below at the powerful who do not comply with their own rules. Unlike key American references, Mathiesen did not find that the prisoners participated in a common prisoner culture to alleviate (the perception of) the pain created by prison. Instead, prisoners positioned themselves as the System's critics: they accused the System's representatives of not managing to abide by their own rules and fulfil their own goals, of being inconsistent or of complying with rules *too* literally.

Questioning the System's legitimacy provides benefits at the level of freedom-creating subjectivity work. This understanding of the world allows the prisoners to partly position themselves in a narrative where they are the little man under the heel of the big system, and partly to position themselves as the elegant, street-smart player who is fighting the bent System as well as he can – and who is coping, despite all the cheating from above. The resistance is, therefore, not just legitimate; those who resist create positions they can enjoy. Without such an overarching counter-ideology, the everyday acts of resistance could be interpreted as banal, boyish pranks – or, at best, creative adaptation tricks. Based on the notion of the System that cheats, however, everyday acts of resistance can instead be used to position oneself as "the legitimate fighter", he who is resisting against all the odds. The notion of the mighty but illegitimate System transposes many prisoners to a position where they are almost a form of political prisoner. From this perspective, the narrative of the System that cheats frames all other forms of resistance.

The main point when the term *the System* is highlighted in the prisoners' anecdotes is to underscore the wide-ranging and massive system with all of its resources that are the prisoners' adversaries. Prisoners who talk about the System are, as a rule, positioning themselves as victims of the System's mistakes or abuse. Even though it is the police who are perceived as the main adversary, a common narrative exists in which all the actors under the umbrella of the System are really one and the same, where the police, prosecuting authorities, courts, prison and, sometimes, the lawyers too are working together against the prisoners. It is an impersonal, well-run, public machine that does what it can to run over and crush individuals. Robert is representative of such a view after a day in court:

Robert: So what can I do Thomas? The prosecutor, police and judges are standing there arm in arm. After all, there's just me.

Robert kicks the door and punches the wall. He is frustrated, fed up and angry.

Robert: They are exaggerating everything, interpreting everything in the worst possible way. And they put everything they have into getting you. That's all they're interested in, getting you. My lawyer is okay; he puts his tie on and goes to court and tries, but he is not getting anywhere with them. So it's no use.

He shakes his head and throws his arms up, frustrated. He is the little man against the big system.

Many foreign prisoners perceive this all-against-one situation as peculiar to Norway. In the countries they come from, or in other countries in which they have been arrested before, the system has more integrity. In Norway, the System has set aside traditional legal safeguards and guarantees for human rights in its pursuit of criminals. It is a pursuit in which any means are now permitted. One prisoner shared his frustration about his case with me as follows:

[Prisoner X]: There are no witnesses, no evidence, no DNA, no finger-prints, no wiretaps, nothing that links me to the drugs. [...] Nonetheless, the prosecutor wants to put me in prison like them [the others in the same case] for 14 years.

TU: Why? If they don't have any evidence against you?

[Prisoner X]: Why? Because I am a criminal. That's what they've decided. The prosecutor looks at me and says: "Hmm ... Fourteen years in prison, I think that's appropriate for you." In Norway, the prosecutor, defence lawyer, and judge are all one and the same. They play on the same team. My defence lawyer says to me: "You must confess so you can get a discount from the judge." I say: "Never! I will never confess to something I haven't done to get a discount." I sleep well at night, like a baby, because I am innocent. And if I get 14 years, I will do the time. That's okay. I know I'm innocent. But if they do that, that will make me dangerous. When I do get out, then I will be dangerous. Then I'll find that bitch who put me in prison for 14 years [the prosecutor], and I'll kill her. I swear I will.

The latter was said with a half-smile and a glint in his eye. I perceived it as more of a way of underscoring the injustice it would be if he were actually to receive a sentence of 14 years than a genuine death threat. As a problem-solving tool, violence has a gendered dimension. In this case, I would say that the more or less seriously meant potential for violence primarily had existential effects. Every man, in order to be a man, must have a cause for which he is willing to fight. If the cause is important enough, a man should be willing to go to some lengths in that fight. The prisoner in the extract above turned himself into a man willing to fight a superior force with all the means at his disposal.

It is the work of the police that has the most immediate, tangible consequences for the prisoners. It is, therefore, not that surprising that the police are regarded as the main adversary. The police are their most active counterpart. It is the police who are in control of the work against the remand prisoner; it is they whom one must avoid coming into contact with in order to avoid the intervention of the System. Amin described his situation as follows:

> It's like a game of chess between me and the police, as I see it. The problem is that it is like a game of chess where the police have a 90 per cent chance of winning; I have 10 per cent. They have all the pieces, while I'm sitting here with a single pawn. Damn, given that I'm sitting here in prison, I wish it was for something I had actually done.

The police cheat. They break the rules, their own rules. This was a recurring theme; many prisoners shared Amin's perception of the situation. The feeling of powerlessness he expressed was echoed down the rows of cells in wings four and five. It could be heard from Tom, who had recently received his case file from the police:

> When prisoners get their case documents from the police it means that the court case is approaching. Tom stares at the six large, blue ring binders full of papers in front of him. The result of months of work. His entire financial history from the last few years fills one binder; all the transactions from his various accounts are exhaustively documented. It contrasts greatly with Tom's preparations for the court case. He is working on a small pile of handwritten notes in a single notepad. He shakes his head, his gaze wandering:

> Tom: What should I do, Thomas? What can I do?

This imbalance in relation to resources is a source of great frustration. Tom had a defence lawyer, but he had far too much to do. For their part, the police are numerous, they have massive resources and, thanks to the spineless judges (to which I will return), all the time they need.

As far as the division of resources is concerned, the game is already perceived as being skewed in the police's favour. In the experience of many head-shaking prisoners, the police cheat when it comes to the evidence in their cases as well. They manipulate photographic evidence and misunderstand witness statements in ways that benefit them. The above-mentioned Tom believed the police were railroading him, that they had decided to get him, and that it had become personal. Vincent describes the breadth of the feeling of powerlessness he felt in his encounter with the System:

> Sitting here on remand really does your head in. Every time my remand is reviewed the police get their way, four more weeks. When can they conclude the investigation so that the case can come up? They don't know; they believe by the end of the year. So then the year ends and they say that it will probably take a bit longer, it will be the first of March. So the first of March arrives, then it becomes the summer. In the meantime, the police get four more weeks, four more weeks, four more weeks. And then the judge starts to get fed up; that happened in my case in the end. They see the police aren't doing anything. After all, they are presenting almost nothing new, no new evidence; they are doing nothing and the months are passing. So the judge says to them, no, sorry, that won't work any more, you cannot keep him on remand for ever if you are not going to do a better job. You can have two weeks. My prosecutor, he got so angry; shit, his face turned completely red! But we'll see you in two weeks, he says to me. And two weeks later, what did they do? They suddenly expanded my charges; they introduced lots of new things, things that had nothing to do with me at all, just so they could keep me, keep me on remand for longer. Four more weeks. I was so pissed off; I told my lawyer, fuck, the police KNOW that I had nothing to do with this. And they still do it; they are so fucking slippery! Yes, my lawyer said, the police do this sort of thing, that's true; they do it just to keep you here. Shit, fucking sly police! It's not strange you get so pissed off. But what can you do? What can you do, Thomas? The problem is, you know, that we see the police always getting their way. They decide everything. The judge doesn't resist; they get their way. Fuck, they kill people during arrests, yeah, and nothing happens! SEFO [Norwegian Bureau for the Investigation of Police Affairs] just shelve the case! They can do what they want; there is no one to stop them. There is no one who can stop them. So what can we do? We who are in here, we have no chance. It's not easy.

The System is a source of great frustration. On the other hand, anecdotes about the battle between the police and prisoners are a popular topic of conversation. The prisoners become enthusiastic; they talk over each other, support each other, and try to outdo each other's stories, whether it is an anecdote where the prisoner wins or stories about the police's many tricks, as in Morten's anecdote:

> Morten: I've just been released after a long sentence, right? I was out for
>   11 hours before the police came and arrested me for something they say
>   I did while I was inside. Can you believe it? I didn't even get to give the

missus one! I was having a little release party and then planned to go home with my missus, and then they arrived.

TU: Why did they wait until you have been released?

Morten: It was pure strategy that. I would have to start a new sentence from the start, right? Earn new leaves and so on. It was just to do me over that little bit more. They say it happened three months before I was released and so they wait and arrest me 11 hours after release, so it was right back to remand after 11 hours of freedom. They told me, just cooperate and you will avoid this sort of thing. But I will never cooperate with the police. Cooperating with the police means having to forget about your mates. And I won't do that.

Traditionally, and in popular exchanges, the fight between the police and criminals is the fight between good and bad. For kids who play cops and robbers, this is obvious. The various anecdotes in the prison about the police's practices can be read as a complex attempt to nuance and disprove this traditional moral narrative. It is difficult to discern who is good and who is bad in anecdotes like the following:

When I was imprisoned in Spain, I had quite a bit of money on me, about 15,000 euros. And a mobile phone of course. When I came up in front of the judge, for the first review of my remand, I said "What will happen with my money, when will I get it back?" "What money?" the judge asked. That's the way it is. There's no point even getting angry. It my own fault for walking around with sums like that. You're asking for it to disappear. But that's not just a bad thing, that, it can be quite good as well. When I arrived in Norway, the police here asked me: "Do you mean that we are supposed to believe someone who does what you do travels around Europe without any money or a mobile phone?" I could only smile and shrug my shoulders. Of course they wanted my phone so they could get information off it, right? But, of course some stupid Spanish copper had given that phone to his wife, heh heh. So corruption is fine. It's always important to have a nice, expensive phone so you can be sure it will disappear. It's always the same with drugs as well. You get caught with ten kilos. And then you arrive in court and learn that you are charged with possession of three kilos. You have a questioning look on your face, but your lawyer just whispers "Shut up! This is good for you!" Police officers with sticky fingers are, as a rule, to your advantage, heh heh.

In the prisoners' anecdotes about the police, the fight between good and evil is transformed into a fight between actors who are equally bad but where one team has the most advantages.

Compared with the police, the courts are a more passive and indirect part of the System. The main problem with the courts is that they are not objective, they are not neutral; they are team players on the police's team. This happens for a number of reasons. Sometimes the judge is too young, ignorant and inexperienced to be capable of standing up to experienced police detectives, as below, where Erol talks about his experience of the monthly remand reviews:

> Remand reviews, they are pathetic. A 25-year-old deputy judge sits there and doesn't dare do anything other than exactly what the police say. Twenty-five years old, straight from secondary school to law school. Wouldn't it be a good idea to choose people who have lived a bit as judges, who know a bit about what they are talking about? It feels a bit strange to be judged by children who don't dare do anything other than what the police say.

Or you can, and this is worse, come up before judges who decide to work against you more actively and support the police. Youssuf has just finished in the court of appeal, where his case was up before the high court. He experienced the judges in the lower court and the court of appeal as radically different. He found the differences between the two judges so striking that they coloured how he described the two court cases. He had a lot of positive things to say about his encounter with the lower court judge, who made him feel understood and respected:

> It was good. You feel seen. I sent a picture to the judge afterwards, as a gift. I wrote on it "Thank you for describing me as a man of honour." On the other hand, in the court of appeals, it was as if I didn't need to be there. He [the judge] exaggerated the injuries so much! He writes [in the judgement] that the knife came dangerously close to the main artery; I haven't seen that anywhere. The expert, the doctor who examined her [the victim], wrote something completely different. But does the judge listen to the doctor? That's when you think that this is personal. What has he got against me? What have I done that to make him want to do me over like this? It's like he knows the injured person, like he is her brother, you know what I'm saying? It is dangerous. It is very dangerous. [...] We expect the police to cheat, but not the judge. For Muslims, the judge is the man who stands closest to God. The judge represents God on earth. When that man lies and says such things, I find it really surprising!

Youssuf felt neither seen nor heard in the court of appeal. In the city court he had been a person with more sides to him than those that were relevant to just this case; in the court of appeal he was just a criminal whom they wanted to get. The story fits snugly into a bigger narrative about judges who are no longer the servants of justice. They have allied themselves with the police and become part of the System, and the classic guarantees of the rule of law no longer apply. The undermining of the jury system is another example. What is supposed to be a guarantee that the courts cannot simply do as they want has, for many prisoners, lost all credibility:

> Just look at the jury system! It's mad, I mean, it just doesn't work. Recently there have been three cases where the jury found the defendant not guilty, and the judge just pisses on the jury and sets the judgement aside! Look at Thomas Thendrup [high-profile convict in the so-called NOKAS case]! First he was acquitted. But that wasn't good enough, no, after all, he's a criminal. So he gets 14 years instead. That fits better, eh? So what's the point? There is no point in having the whole jury thing; they might as well just get rid of the entire thing. In fact, things are better even in the USA – at least there you have to have multiple, clear pieces of forensic evidence in order to convict someone. There are a lot of things wrong with the American system, but I'll give them that. Here just a few, minor pieces of circumstantial evidence are enough, and the fact that you are a recognised criminal, and you get convicted. Here it is just mis-carriage of justice after miscarriage of justice, and that's meant to be okay, because if you haven't done it, you've certainly done something else. The whole thing is rotten to the core. If you are a criminal, then you are a criminal, and that means you'll stay a criminal.

In the prisoners' anecdotes about the role of the courts, Lady Justice has thrown off her blindfold, put down her book of laws and sharpened her sword. Behind her is often her boss, a more experienced police officer point-ing the way. There are exceptions. Good judges do not allow themselves to be pushed around by the police and have enough courage to make their own (correct) decisions. But in the prisoners' anecdotes, they are exceptions. Whether it is as a result of a lack of experience or bad will, the majority are the servants of the police. Lacking in objectivity or neutrality, they enable the corrupt police, who cheat, to do their job of getting criminals, whatever the cost, as efficiently as possible.

The lawyers play an even more dubious role in the prisoners' anecdotes. On the one hand, a lawyer is an important supporter and ally, someone you must trust and who can mean the difference between continuing your life behind bars and freedom. Good lawyers are worth their weight in gold. On the other hand, in the experience of many prisoners, lawyers also end up doing the System's bidding because of a lack of experience, too little time, or a generally low level of commitment to the job. If you get a bad lawyer, then you are in trouble.

Prisoners are deprived of much of the control and autonomy over their lives. Facing the mighty System, in a court populated by actors who know all the codes and where you are the one with both the most to lose and the least influence, the lack of control can feel perilous. In such situations it becomes particularly important to retain and cultivate the forms of control over your surroundings that you still have. One of the options the prisoners still have is to take advantage of their right to freely choose their legal representative. A number of copies of a thick list of lawyers who work on criminal cases in the Oslo area can be found on the wing. Switching lawyer is as easy as getting the officers to send a fax. But whom should you choose? And why? How can you know in advance who will do a good job? And what characterises a good job? This is a dilemma many prisoners struggle with, a decision on which they perceive their future freedom stands or falls.

The choice of defence lawyer allows the prisoners to control, or at least influence, the outcome of their pending case. Tom had recently decided to change lawyer and was tense about the impact the change would have:

> You could say that the "paragraph riders" are those prosecutors who are obsessed with the wording of statute, that things should be like this and like that. They are not flexible; they go by the book. Put it this way, if you get a paragraph rider you have been unlucky. As you have if you get a paragraph wanker; they are defence lawyers who in some way or other enter into a relationship with the paragraph rider and, sort of, cooperate with him. And then you are in trouble. I have just switched; I'm going a slightly different way than most others. My defence lawyer used to be a paragraph rider, right? But then he discovered there's more money to be made on the other side. So he switched. Have you seen the TV series "Shark"? My lawyer is just like that. He knows all the tricks of the trade; he can't be fooled. Put it this way, he has let me see papers that I shouldn't really be allowed to see. So that I know what is coming, so that I can answer properly and avoid preventive detention. Other lawyers don't do that, you know? If you have a famous lawyer, let's say Staff [high-profile Oslo-based defence lawyer], then you know the prosecutor will prepare his case extra well, because he knows who is coming. There is prestige at play. So, even if he is good, it can always go either way.

Tom had the impression that his new lawyer, partly because of his background as a "paragraph rider" on the side of the System, had many of the attributes that characterise a good lawyer. He knew how the other party thinks; he knew all the tricks of their trade. He was knowledgeable and could provide good, concrete advice before, during and after the case. At the same time he was willing to operate outside the rules so that Tom would be as well prepared as possible. And nor was he the type to which the other party would allocate extra resources to "beat", which they would with one of the celebrity lawyers.

Such conversations about what characterises good and bad lawyers, who is good, whom you should avoid, and so on, are common on the wings.

Tips and recommendations are often a part of it, as when Amir was later discussing with a satisfied Tom:

> Amir: Who's your lawyer?
> Tom: I have [X].
> Amir: [X], yeah? Are you happy?
> Tom: Hell yes! He is so incredibly aggressive in court; he never hesitates. You never hear him stutter or stammer. He just takes it to them. Who do you have?
> Amir: I actually have a woman right now, [Y]. She's pretty good.
> Tom: Switch to [X]. Just do it, at once. He just rules!

Tom was over the moon with his switch. Robert was equally dissatisfied with his choice after having been in court:

> It is unbelievable! I'm so disappointed with my lawyer; I can hardly stand to look at him. They were supposed to have 40 minutes each, but the prosecutor took over an hour, while my lawyer spent 20 minutes. What is that all about? The judge just stood up while my lawyer was talking and said it was time for a break. He was after my lawyer from the start. My lawyer was completely put out, poor thing, he never came back; he was just so passive. No, I have to switch lawyer and appeal. I really don't have a choice.

Good lawyers are aggressive and do not let themselves be picked on. Good lawyers also make time, they come and talk to you long before the case starts, and they let you know what might and should come up. He or she is there for you, they set aside good time for your case, and turn up to remand reviews in person. Those lawyers who are far too busy send a proxy. Or perhaps there may be a reason why they are so busy? Is little time the price one has to pay for a top lawyer? Once again the dilemma is: whom should you choose? And why?

The number of conversations about lawyers increased during the weeks the NOKAS case – a high-profile case of armed robbery where a police officer was shot and killed – was before the Norwegian Supreme Court. The hearing was broadcast live on TV. All of the prisoners followed the broadcast. The performances of the lawyers involved were discussed as if it were a sports event:

> Look at [Y], he's at least a couple of notches better than all the others! He's impressed the judges, you can tell. [Z], you know, the earlier one, he turned the judges against him. He did really badly; he was interrupted by the judges all the time. That's not good. But he tried to place the blame on all the other defendants to save his own client. That's not good. But

that [Y], he's just unbelievably good in court, man! I had [Y] before, but I replaced him.

Why did you do that?

[...] He's not very good before the cases come up. He just sends a proxy all the time; he never has time himself. He takes on far too many cases; he loves money, you know? But now I've seen him in court, I'm really regretting replacing him; he's a bloody genius.

The conversation continues with comments on how the various lawyers look and act in court: who looks tired, who looks to be having a good day, who always does a solid job and so on. A good lawyer has a natural self-confidence in court; his whole demeanour shows that his description of reality is the right one. A poor lawyer stutters and stammers, he appears uncertain, and is defensive. Viewed as something midway between a sports event, soap opera and advert, the broadcast from the Supreme Court was very popular, and many switched lawyers as a direct result of someone having made a good or bad impression on TV.

A good lawyer is experienced and driven, has plenty of time and turns up in person, is aggressive and self-confident, is a sly fox who knows and is willing to use all the smart tricks and so on. The problem is just that no single person possesses all these qualities simultaneously. The ability to choose a lawyer makes the prisoners feel that they can exercise at least some degree of influence over their cases, and thus their own fates in their struggle against the System. If things go poorly in court, you can blame the wrong choice, switch lawyer and hope that the new one does better in the second court.

Finally, the prison is also part of the System. When the prisoners talk about the prison, as a rule they mean something somewhere between the prison institution as a whole and the prison leadership and its decisions. In other words, the term is used as a concretisation of a system that is perceived as pretty abstract; the faceless level that controls the prison institution, that lays down guidelines for, and affects, how the prisoners are regulated and administered every day, and that takes far too long to respond to the prisoners' applications and complaints. In other words, "the prison" refers in some way or another to the institution as a whole: as it is part of, and intertwined with, the overarching System and, as the System's tentacles, intervenes in and impacts on everyday prison life. The officers, specific individuals who work on the wing, do not necessarily have anything to do with it. The prison is a system with a head office somewhere else, but which determines, and has a concrete impact on, the prisoners' everyday lives.

Perhaps the most common interaction between the prisoners and the prison, as part of the System, concerns the prisoners' complaints and applications. The prisoners must apply for transfers to other wings and prisons;

they must apply for release after serving two-thirds of their time, for longer phone time and conjugal visits, and for leave and escorted leave. They complain in writing about all the different forms of decisions the prison makes, as well as everything else they think they can complain about. Depending on the type of complaint, it is sent to Oslo Prison's administration, the regional correctional services, or the Norwegian Correctional Services Central Administration. All of these are covered by the term "the prison" as the prisoners use it.

The prisoners generally think that it takes a long time to process complaints and applications and get an answer, that the answer is usually, or as a rule, negative, and that reasons are rarely given. Adam's description serves as one example:

> Adam: What makes being in here so tiring is that everything takes such an incredibly long time, that it is impossible to get a clear answer, that you almost always get a no, and that no reasons are given. That's just the way it is, like. Before, when I was in wing nine, I got longer phone calls so I could talk to my son. Forty minutes of calls a week, instead of the usual 20. So, now that I've been transferred they suddenly take that away from me. When I asked why, I was just told that a memo had been issued that said that they should try and cut down on that sort of thing. So I apply for longer phone calls again – a written application. I get a verbal reply from the principal prisoner officer – no. I ask for a written reply. I don't get one. Aren't I entitled to that?
>
> TU: Yes, I think you are entitled to that when you have applied in writing.
>
> Adam: Yeah, well I didn't get one, just a no, like. So 20 minutes a week is all the time I get to talk to my son. The only thing they said was that 40 minutes was very long, that it is really unusual to get that. That it's unfair to the others if I get that. I have complained to the region. They said it was a total waste of time complaining, but I did anyway. So we'll see if I get a written reply this time.

Another example can be found in Naveed's anecdote about what happened in the wake of an incident where he was disciplined for attacking an officer with the triangle used to set up the pool balls at the start of a game, an anecdote he related as an example of how incomprehensible and unreasonable "the prison" can be. He had given the triangle to the officer concerned at the end of a social and had gone up to his cell without any drama. Nothing more was said at the time. Later he learned that the officer had felt threatened by the way he did it. She thought that he had tried to pull the triangle over her head; she regarded it as an attack and had written an incident report. Naveed said that at the time he was bewildered, but it would get worse.

After a while he received a written reaction from the prison: ten days' exclusion from socials. Naveed was very surprised – after all, first, he did not think he had done anything wrong, and, second, a ten-day disciplinary action was a very strong reaction. However, as he read the letter he realised that there must have been some mistake. It described another incident as the reason for the reaction, an incident that had nothing to do with Naveed. The lawyer who had written the decision had misunderstood and credited him with that incident as well. He made the officer aware of the mistake and she immediately agreed that it was a mistake. Everyone remembered the relevant episode and knew that he was innocent. All he had to do was write a complaint and it would probably be sorted out.

Naveed prepared a complaint – another officer helped him to write it – and he took this as a sign that a number of the officers agreed that this was an overreaction on the part of the prison. The complaint was sent to the regional office, which is the appeals body for such matters. After a while he received a reply. His appeal had not been upheld. Incident number two, the one in which he was innocent, was no longer mentioned in the decision, but the new result was 14 days' exclusion from socials. The letter gave no reason for the stricter punishment. Naveed was fed up when he told the news to Adnan and me:

Naveed: There must be a reason though, that's the way society is; they can't just do things like this without giving any reason! They just quote the *Execution of Sentences Act*, and that's it, like?

Adnan: Hey bro, we are criminals, what do you expect? They just do whatever they want. And you can't fucking complain. [. . .]

Naveed: This is impossible to understand this is. You just have to laugh. It's a joke. [. . .] Being in here is fine by me; things are not so bad in here. But these sorts of things that you haven't done, that you don't understand, they follow you, you know? It will continue to bug me; I won't get past it. Quite a few officers have popped in and said that they think it was overly strict. But what can they do? It's the regional office that decides.

TU: Did you tell your lawyer about this?

Naveed: No, I didn't. I didn't think there was any point bothering him with it.

Adnan: No, you would probably have been moved to another wing at once.

Naveed: Do you think so?

Adnan: Yes, they would definitely have moved you. They would have had to come up with an official reason and to avoid that they would have moved you.

Naveed: Now I've kinda been tagged as a troublemaker, haven't I? And I've noticed that some officers are thinking that, that they try to wind me up, like; that they try to get me angry. That they come up to me and sort of expect me to cause problems.

In Naveed's anecdote it did not matter what he did, it was always wrong. And complaining was no use at all because "the prison", like the System more generally, did exactly what it wanted. Naveed and Adnan became members of a criminal class without rights and who were victims of a prison that did not comply with the normal guarantees of the rule of law, a prison that put itself above the law. At the same time, some distance was established between the prison, the abstract point where the institution meets the System, and the officers, individuals Naveed and Adnan meet every day, who could not understand why what had happened had happened. The prison's arbitrariness and unreasonableness were thus further underscored.

In relation to the "the prison" as an abstraction, a specific prison wing constitutes a peripheral area. Decisions are taken somewhere else. In the same way, a specific cell is a peripheral area in relation to the officers' office and break room. Alone, locked behind cell doors, the prisoners are far from where things are decided, whichever yardstick you use. And above the whole things hovers that omnipresent threat of being transferred. The prisoners have a bifurcated relationship to being moved. On the one hand, everyone wants to be somewhere else, on better wings with more open conditions and perhaps access to a kitchen. On the other hand, everyone is aware that there are worse places to be than wings four and five. And those who do not behave as the prison wants are moved down the floors, to wings with longer lock-in periods and more obstinate officers, as the story goes. The threat of transfer is always on the prisoners' minds, but so too is the hope of a transfer. Wings four and five become a waiting room where you stay temporarily until you are transferred to something better or worse.

Prisoners and officers

The most fundamental and meaningful difference in a prison is the one between prisoners and officers. There are, of course, other important groups in the prison whom prisoners use as references and to contrast themselves with, such as teachers in the school and work officers who lead work teams, but, by comparison to the meaning-creating dynamic between prisoners and officers, all the other groups are mere extras. There are also, as I shall show, various ways of dividing up the prisoner group and officer group into subgroups, but the relationship between prisoners and officers is a fundamental distinction that cancels out and equalises all other internal differences. Even if one prisoner dislikes another, he will, with a few exceptions (e.g. rapists and snitches, to whom I will return), defend him in front of, or in relation to, the officers. It is as if a thick, red, symbolic line runs right through the prison separating the two groups from each other. Even if sometimes one can sense that members of both groups are approaching the line, it is never, with few exceptions, crossed. The need for internal solidarity within the group and the various ways of distancing themselves with respect to the other group are equally important on each side of this symbolic line.

The relationship between prisoners and officers is a relationship between individuals who have got to know each other over time and who meet many times a week, sometimes over a period of several years. The officers' world and the prisoners' world are different, but parallel and to some degree intertwined. The prisoners and officers share a sort of common fate, given that they are positioned in the same time and space. To some extent they also share some common interests in relation to the prison as an administrative system (Crewe, 2009). Both prisoners and officers must live with the decisions and directives that come "from above" and affect the lives of both groups. The officers' group sometimes, usually out of the hearing of the prisoners, express the same level of frustration as the prisoners at the prison's new, incomprehensible ideas. Nonetheless, nothing that happens on a prison wing is untouched by the fundamental power inequality in the relationship between prisoners and officers, and the continuous game of everyday power and resistance practices that exists between them.

The prisoners often relate anecdotes, based on their daily encounters with the officers on the wing, about how the officers are incapable of complying with their own rules or achieving their objectives. Such anecdotes are, at least partly, about retelling the relationship between officers and prisoners in a way that repositions the prisoners. In a context where the status of prisoner entails prisoners being understood as sick, evil, unsuccessful and/or stupid people who must be watched, the prisoners often adopt a strategy aimed at creating a new position for themselves, as people who are not as bad as everyone believes, through productive comparisons with the officers where one of the main points is to show that *they* are no better than *us*.

One common example of this is the narrative in which the officers are simply unable to perform their duties, due to a lack of either willingness or ability. These types of anecdote are often about how the day-to-day decisions the officers make as part of their routines on the wing are characterised by arbitrariness, ineffectiveness and a lack of logic. As in, for example, the anecdote below where Christian describes what you have to do to get a shower:

> If you want a shower, you have to write a note saying so and hand it in in the morning. But that is not enough. You also have to go and tell them as well. If you only tell them, they say that you can't shower because you haven't written a note. If you only write a note, they forget the whole thing. Both parts are required. Can you imagine? But often nothing happens anyway. So then I think that I should call and remind them about it, but then I think that I shouldn't nag them. If I nag them, they will get irritated. If they get irritated, it's definitely going to take a long time. Then it will take a long time tomorrow as well. But if I don't ring, I won't

get to shower. You know? I have worked out, so I have to shower. What am I supposed to do? All that for a shower, man! That sort of thing does your head in.

Christian's anecdote can be read as the completely normal sort of sigh one emits when confronted with a Catch 22 situation: if he does not remind the officers that he wants to shower, they will forget, but if he does remind them, they will get irritated and sabotage him showering. In either case there will be no shower. However, it can also be read as a productive renegotiation of the narrative about the officers and their duties in relation to the prisoners. In this, the officers are ineffective, they are not interested in fairness, and the routines do not work. In short, there is no equality before the law. By extension, the anecdote can be read as a criticism of the entire prison as an institution, because what sort of rehabilitation and control can there be when the officers cannot even manage to ensure the prisoners get their showers?

The profession of prison officer is complex (Sykes, 1958; Basberg, 1999; Nylander, Lindberg and Bruhn, 2011). If one leaves aside the control duties, which make prison officers look a lot like police officers, and the rehabilitation duties, which are reminiscent of the kind of things social workers and psychologists do, the profession of prison officer is similar to a pure service job. This service function that officers have can also be cultivated in anecdotes about the officers, such that the other two types of duty become almost invisible:

It's true Thomas. They work for me. I ring and ask for something; they bring it. They bring food when I'm hungry. I swear, even if I'm on the loo and I ring, they bring me toilet paper. Into the cell, while I'm on sitting on the loo. It is unbelievable. They are my servants; they do my bidding.

Here Arfan is describing the officers as occupying a position that is somewhere between a domestic help, a caretaker and a slave. This is repositioning work whereby the officers become someone who is at the beck and call of the prisoners all day long. These types of anecdotes are based on the idea that it is the prisoners who are *really* in charge; the officers come across as the prisoners' employees. All they do all day is ensure that the prisoners are as comfortable as possible.

A third common type of anecdote concerns the illusory nature of the officers' control and power over the prisoners. There are so few officers in relation to prisoners that peace and order in the prison can only exist insofar as the prisoners wish it to.

Come on, look at them. After all, they are just little girls who weigh 60 kilos. What could they do? Nothing. We could just throw them over our shoulders and carry them off wherever we wanted. But I don't want to screw things up for myself. I have to think of my boys, of getting out for them. But, I mean, the police, they bring us here with a helicopter and four or five cars, and all that malarkey. Everything they do is done as if we are really dangerous. And then we are let out onto the wing here, 50 of us, where three small girls are meant to watch us. Three small, blonde girls. They wouldn't have a chance; we are the ones who really decide here, heh heh heh.

Each day that a major prison riot does not break out and the prisoners do not take control of the prison is a day that the prisoners have decided they do not want to riot. In this narrative it is the prisoners who *really* have the power and control – they could at any time, if they wanted to, take over the prison and the officers would not have a chance of stopping them.

From this perspective, the officers' control is control at the mercy of the prisoners. Brede touched upon the same subject when he told me about how he had had to intervene and do the job of perplexed officers who did not know how to react when they discovered a suicide attempt:

The officers don't do anything when that sort of thing happens. They always wait until there are 20 men; then and only then will they dare go in. So, we are the ones in control here, really. How many are they? And how many are we? If we wanted to, we could take over the whole place in five minutes, at any time, no problem.

Such anecdotes have the double effect of constructing prisoners as reasonable and rational people, despite everything, and at the same time underscoring the prisoner group's strength and potential. Once again: the officers do not control the prisoners, not *really*.

A fourth common type of anecdote concerns the officers *only* being officers, that they have had to choose the profession of prison officer due to a lack of better options and that as officers it is fair to say that they are more or less unsuccessful people (Cohen and Taylor, 1981). Ilir thought that many of the officers on the wing were okay, as far as it goes, but he was not very impressed by the standard of their job:

I guess there is a reason that they are officers, right? I don't suppose there is much else they could have been, is there? If they could have done something else, they probably would have. It's not exactly like working for NASA, is it? There are people in here who are really smart. You often notice that the officers can't really keep up with the conversation.

Such narratives about unsuccessful officers are often linked to the far more successful life the prisoners had before they were imprisoned:

Sabri: Well we have experienced a lot, fast living and excitement, you know? I mean, the officers haven't experienced a fraction of what we have; I don't think all the officers [collectively] have experienced what just I have experienced even. I have, at 27, experienced as much as many experience their whole lives. That can't be healthy, heh heh.

[...]

Vincent: I spoke with my detective. He said he had worked for 25 years and that he had finally saved enough for a watch that cost 40 grand.

Sabri: Forty thousand? That's a month's income isn't it? No, fuck, a week's.

Vincent: Yeah, he had said to me how is it possible that you, who are in your twenties, have a watch worth 180,000; it must come from some monkey business? But it didn't actually; I inherited that particular watch.

Sabri: Twenty-five years for a watch...that's just so sad. But what do they get for working for 25 years here [in the prison]? A lousy gold watch?

Vincent: Heh heh, I'm earning more than them even while I'm in here [grins]. That is sad, man. They are pretty sad.

Sabri: Yes, like that [officer X], for example, he's one of those people, I can tell, he leaves here and goes home, sits in his chair, in uniform, watches TV, drinks beer and waits for the next shift, sleeps in the chair, is ready, doesn't even change his uniform; it's always on. He's on his own. I don't know for sure, but he strikes me as the type.

Vincent: Or like he's married, I don't know whether he is married, but he's married, right, and the wife decides everything at home, is always giving him an earful, decides everything for him, so that he has to come here and boss us about, heh heh heh, show that he has a bit of, what's it called...

Sabri: Power.

Vincent: Yeah, a bit of power. He needs a bit of power too and we are the ones who get it in the neck. That's why he strolls around and is so fucking tough and wants to decide everything. Do that! Go there! Shut up!

The officers are pitiable people who are a bit simple and lead sad, boring lives. The prisoners use this caricature of an officer in the same way as the working-class boys who had lived the good life described the boring, but academically successful, middle-class boys in Willis's (1977) classic study. The prisoners are captivated by the notion that working in the prison affords the officers the only opportunity they have to decide anything in their otherwise low-income, powerless lives. By contrast, Tarik and Vincent have lived richer, more exciting lives, and, even though their lives are a bit boring while they are inside, it was all worth it. If you want to live a good, fast life, you have to be prepared to pay the price.

A fifth key topic of discussion between the prisoners is the poor, useless extra officers who cannot do their job. These narratives, naturally enough, peaked in the summer when the wing was full of nervous summer temps in oversized blue shirts:

> Nadir: They know nothing; they don't have a clue. The prison shouldn't do this sort of thing; they should organise things better. They're just children, yes, children with a need to assert themselves.
> Adnan: [About an officer who passes the open door] Can't you go and change that officer's nappy, eh? She doesn't have a clue.
> Nadir: They're just a bunch of brats, brats who can't do their job.

The extra officers are children who do not know the routines and do not know what the normal atmosphere is and should be on the wing. The "full-time ones" are more flexible; the "new ones" feel the need to assert themselves because they are insecure and afraid of making mistakes.

At the same time, you can have a lot of fun with extra officers who have yet to learn the ropes. Like when an extra officer dropped his alarm from the fifth floor landing down onto the fourth, where it clattered across the floor, naturally to the great amusement of all. Tarik took it upon himself to run up with it again, laughing. Few things are funnier than being able to help a hapless extra officer who, blushing, had to accept the alarm from a smirking prisoner. Or, even better, when they forget to lock a door. Ilir had to call a stressed extra officer back as he was about to leave for the evening so that someone could lock his cell door. Haughtily teaching the extra officers their job is brilliant. The result of the laughter is a sort of carnival-like reversal of hierarchies in the sense used by Bakhtin (2003), a laughter that comes from the king momentarily having become the fool.

So far this has all been about the prisoners' perceptions of the officers' mistakes and deficiencies. There were, of course, also officers who were well liked, who personified exceptions from the officers as a group, and who definitely represented something other than the abstract prison and the System of which it is a part. A good officer is effective, proficient and trustworthy. If the person concerned says that he or she will do something, then it will happen. However, the way it is done is even more important. Ilir had a contact officer who was okay as far as it went, but who was bossy:

> Ilir: He is okay. He does what he says he will. It's just that he's so fucking bossy to everyone. And you know there are some here who can't deal with that, the fact that he bosses them about. Me and him, we manage, but you have to live with the fact that he thinks he knows what's best for you. That's the way he is; he suddenly just decides something for you, you know? That's the way he is.

A good officer is polite, respectful, has a twinkle in the eye, and shows that he is thinking and cares about the prisoners. This last figure – the empathetic officer – is perceived to be rare:

> The good officers, well, let's say your house is on fire [...] the good officers would, at least, feel the heat a bit. But most aren't like that; it is a job for most of them, then they finish for the day and don't give it a second thought. I'm in solitary confinement and when you go home you won't think about me any more before you return. But, in the meantime, I've been sitting in solitary the whole time! Most of the officers don't care, not really. Quite simply, they couldn't give a fuck.

Good officers care and they show that they care. Good officers want to do more than just lock you in as efficiently as possible:

> Click, click, click, [demonstrates the locking of a cell door] and then "goodbye". He [a new officer] scurries around here just worrying about the locks. I said to him, "chill out! You are being trained by the Best Officer in Oslo, chill out." She [the Best Officer] does everything she should; it's not that, she does her job. But it's the way she does it. She is the most respected of all of them here, just because she is a bit nice. It really doesn't take that much.

Sometimes it is not what you do, it is the way you do it that is important. Good officers acknowledge you and see you as an individual, not as an impersonal number in a row. The difference between good officers and bad officers lies in how they do their job. Good ones have empathy and a good sense of humour. The bad ones are sour and do not care. In other words, the bad officers are not those who abuse their power, who are violent or sadistic. Rather, they are not very sympathetic, or, to be more precise, they communicate sympathy to a lesser degree. One can, therefore, say that, as far as the prisoners are concerned, the good officers are those who acknowledge the prisoners' self-positioning and who can, therefore, be used as tools to transform yourself into something other than another example of a criminal prisoner. Bad officers have little time, are impolite and not very nice. They are also lock-fixated rule fetishists who regard you simply as part of a grey throng of prisoners who are pretty much alike.

The Norwegian and the liminal prisoners

Although the difference between the prisoners and officers is the most fundamental one in the game of similarities and differences on a prison wing, this does not mean that many other similarity and difference relationships are not also important. In the Introduction I describe how remand wings are very complex as far as ethnic and national affiliations are concerned. This section looks at how the tensions between the Norwegians and non-Norwegians manifest themselves on the prison wing. Are the prisoners Norwegian? When someone says "I am Norwegian", what does he mean?

"Norway" and "Norwegians" as categories would not have been what they are had it not been for the long, historic tradition of interaction with our Nordic neighbours that has resulted in today's love/hate relationship of largely friendly and, sometimes, very childish competition between sibling nations. The constitutive exteriors are generally important in such processes. Barth (1996) demonstrated how ethnic groups are reproduced through the maintenance of borders that separate them from other people who are understood as "other people" because of their lack of some characteristic or other. He suggests that the game of similarities and differences should be studied on the basis of the boundary markers that are used; so-called *diacritics*. Language has always been an important example, but basically anything can be given such exclusive and exclusionary meaning and used to draw boundaries. Which diacritics are actually used, and in which ways, is an empirical question. I.B. Neumann (1998) used this perspective to study how the relationship between the Eastern neighbours Russia and Turkey has been important in the emergence of the idea of Europe, while Edward Said (1979) made a similar point about the relationship between the West and the "Orient".

Below I will look primarily at the subgroup of prisoners who are, basically, unable to adopt a clear position in relation to "Norway" and "the Norwegian": those who are, in various ways, "in-between". As Norton (1988) describes, they can be said to be *liminal* in relation to the field's available positions. A liminal position evades categorisation. It is both within and outside at the same time; it treads a path between positions and can switch back and forth depending on the context. Every structured order includes such groups with an unclear status who do not fully fit into a single category or who cannot fully fit. Prisoners can generally, to some extent, be understood as being liminally positioned; they are both part of the society on the other side of the walls and positioned, at least temporarily, as outsiders. The prisoners discussed here are also liminally positioned in another way; as both Norwegians and non-Norwegians, they contribute to the collective renarration of the history of Norwegianness. The liminal prisoners have ties to Norway to some extent or other, but whether or not they are "Norwegian", and what this would actually mean, is unclear.

Seen from outside the walls, these liminal prisoners are what are often referred to as "criminal immigrants". They are used as constitutive exteriors to construct normal, moral Norwegianness. A nation is also a moral community. The continuous production of this moral community depends on immoral outsiders, among whom the criminal immigrant has taken centre stage. The law is a system for constituting truth in our society (Foucault,

2000d). Some people who, through the law's truth, are hailed as criminal immigrants feel a need to reposition themselves both in relation to Norwegian law, which knows the truth, and in relation to Norwegianness and "the Norwegian" more generally.

These are prisoners who speak Norwegian, have lived in Norway for a number of years, and have established families in Norway. Most of them are Norwegian citizens, but they are not perceived as and do not perceive themselves as Norwegian merely on that basis, at least not without problems. How do you navigate between socially active variables like "Norway", "Norwegians" and "the Norwegian"? What discursive relationships are set up in and through their use of such categories in their self-positioning as subjects imprisoned by the Norwegian state? Anderson's (1983) point that nations are imagined communities is just one place you can start. The question becomes: what sort of "Norway" is being utilised and with which social consequences in the prisoner community? Take Fariz, for example; in the following he explains his situation to me:

> Well, I was on the run before I turned myself in. That's why they are afraid I will go on the run again. After all, I could just have left; they would never have found me if I hadn't come voluntarily. But I was born and grew up in Norway, so I could never have run off to Pakistan where I really come from. Come on, I don't even speak the language! What are they thinking?

What does it mean when the prisoners say they *have* a Norwegian passport but that "really" they *are* something else? Even though he grew up entirely in Norway, and has no other linguistic affiliation, Fariz perceived that he *really* comes from Pakistan. Notwithstanding this, the status of this "really" is somewhat unclear; he simultaneously meant that the Norwegian state, paradoxically enough, was wrong when it ascribed to him any particular affiliation to the country. The relationship between being born in and growing up in Norway and really coming from Pakistan is unclear in Fariz's narrative. To understand why this is so, one must look at the construction and shaping of a sense of national affiliation. What characterises those who experienced the bond that unifies all Norwegians and separates them from all non-Norwegians? There are markers such as skin colour, language, history, territory, religion and so on. But, obviously, it is neither necessary nor sufficient to speak Norwegian, have white skin, live in Norway and have a relaxed relationship to a state religion, and childhood beliefs that only come to the fore in festive seasons, in order to be perceived as and perceive oneself as a Norwegian. No matter how many one adds to one's account, "objective" markers do not tell the whole story.

Connor (1996) differentiates between nationalism and patriotism as two different, but in many cases intertwined and mutually reinforcing, loyalties. Nationalism is loyalty to a perceived national community between

people, while patriotism is loyalty to the political unit the state constitutes and its organisations. Does "I am Norwegian" refer to a relationship
between an individual and the Norwegian state, and, if so, does the sentence describe citizenship? Or is it a relationship to a national and ethnic
community?

In a Norwegian context, this split does not necessarily mean that
much. The Norwegian situation has been that the state's and the nation's
borders have pretty much overlapped, at least since the dissolution of the
union with Sweden in 1905. The difference between Norway the state and
the nation of Norwegians has not been clear. Norway has, of course, been
home to ethnic minorities before, such as the indigenous Sámi people, but
they have been relatively few in number. The fact that nationalism and
patriotism can be two different things has, therefore, not been immediately
visible to the average Norwegian; the state–nation–territory trinity has normally been pretty unproblematic. Norway is, therefore, an example of what
Øverland (2003) has called an "ethnic state". This is not the most common
situation: globally speaking there are thousands of so-called ethno-national
groups, while there are only around 200 states. For "most people" in the
world, any feelings of loyalty to state and nation overlap only a little. They
can often also be in conflict with each other.

Most of the liminally positioned prisoners are Norwegian citizens. Given
this, they are obviously Norwegian state subjects in a literal sense. The few
in this group who are not citizens are married to a Norwegian citizen and/or
have children who are Norwegian citizens. As prisoners in a Norwegian
prison, they are also positioned in a specific formal relationship with the
Norwegian state. They are also Norwegian in the sense that they see themselves as Norwegian subjects with legal rights and duties. The question is
whether this rights relationship is enough for them to feel a form of affiliation or loyalty to the Norwegian state which has locked them up, and, if so,
what sort of loyalty and how strong it is.

Norwegians have displayed a relatively large degree of trust in the welfare
state's willingness and ability to organise everything in their best interests,
a relationship that Pratt (2008a, b) highlights as one of the reasons for the
relatively low level of Norwegian penalties and the relatively humane conditions in Norwegian prisons. As the shepherd, the welfare state wants the
best for its flock, and it is generally true that Norwegians trust the state and
feel that they are citizens of a well-functioning state with a well-functioning
state apparatus, with some important exceptions, such as, for example, issues
concerning tax levels, which it must be admitted are controversial. One
expression of Norwegian trust and pride in the state can be seen every
year when the UN publishes its so-called *Human Development Report*. Since
2003, Norway has reigned at the top of the ranking of the world's countries, which means that the report predictably gets a lot of press. Newspaper
headlines such as "Norway still the best"[1] and non-ironic blog headlines like

"Congratulations! You are Norwegian"[2] follow. The ranking is controversial in Oslo Prison, to say the least. Tarik reacted as follows:

> I heard on TV that Norway is the best country to live in? I had to laugh! Morocco, where I come from, is not the best. But it's much better than Norway! In Morocco they cannot just put you in prison for 17 months without your case coming up. They might beat you up. But, they can't just put you in prison when they want. It's also nice and warm, as well. Look [pointing out of the window at the Norwegian summer], not like here, heh heh heh.

I have shown how many remand prisoners are likely to regard their specific cases as examples of the state cheating and breaking the rules. Youssuf is an example of including the myth of "the best country in the world to live in" in such a context:

> I'm ashamed of my Norwegian passport; I'm going to change back. As quickly as possible. What's happening is a very dangerous trend. Very dangerous, Thomas. I used to be proud of being Norwegian. When I've been abroad travelling, for example in the USA once, I have told people about my country and shown them pictures of my wife and children. And they have said, Nadir, you are so lucky to live in Norway with the world's best social system, with fantastic nature and nice people, with a beautiful wife and great children, and I've been so proud of being Norwegian. But not now. Now I feel more ashamed about that red passport. Everyone abroad is now talking about Norway, about how they treat people here, foreigners they don't want, and about how they lock up people on remand for far too long. Norway is not a good country any more.

The frustration Youssuf feels about being unfairly treated is transferred to and laid on top of his view of the Norwegian state as a whole. Norwegians are a servile people in the hands of state authorities who do whatever they want. It is this servility that is the hardest to understand for Tarik:

> It's good in Norway, but the best country to live in? There are many who say that. Norway is rich. But Norway is also poor. What about all the old people? They are even more Norwegian than you [TU]; they have experienced war. Nonetheless, everyone goes to Spain. Why? Can Norway be the best country to live in then?
>
> [...]
>
> In Norway everyone says "yes, yes, yes". Higher prices for petrol? "Yes". More tax? "Yes". Ordinary people like you and me have no money left. But nobody says no. In England, for example, they would have said no. They tried to increase tax on sugar by 1 per cent, there were almost

riots. But in Norway, everyone says "yes, yes, yes". You have to say "no" occasionally!

It is clear that being positioned in relation to the Norwegian state in the way Tarik is does not immediately foster feelings of patriotism and loyalty. Here he is attacking Norwegian trust in the state. Norwegians trust the state too much, while prisoners see it for what it is. For remand prisoners the refrain is, rather, that the state cheats, that it cannot be trusted. Their relationship to "the Norwegian" is a relationship to the Norwegian state in relation to which they perceive they have rights, rights that are not worth the paper they are written on. The prisoners articulate, to a varying degree, but sometimes to a very great degree, such a rights relationship in their subjectification work. The focus, then, is on the broken promises, the rights that remain on paper only.

If it is right that a nation only exists when someone is willing to die for it, then the liminal prisoners are not Norwegian national subjects. When Erol, with his red Norwegian passport, described such feelings of fellowship with new prisoners who arrived on the wing, it was the Albanian nation he had in mind:

Erol: Some of them [new Albanians] who are here, I know from before, and we have been out together, we have partied together, like, have hung out together out there, but you can say that 70 per cent of them are people that I haven't met before, but as soon as they speak Albanian, I hear he is an Albanian, and that is everything to me.

TU: That's when you are on your home turf?

Erol: That's when you are on your home turf straight away. That's when it is life or death for that person, like.

TU: So in practice it is the language that decides it.

Erol: In practice it is the language. That's when I know where he is from and that's how it should be for everyone, like. The Pakistanis should also stand up for their own and their people, Norwegians should stand up for their own; I mean come on, why do we go to war and who do we fight for if there is a war? I mean, I have been to war for the Albanians, for my people, and should there be any of them in here, I'll stand up for them too. No running away or hiding under the bed or trying to be invisible. That won't happen.

Erol, a refugee from Kosovo and a Norwegian citizen for many years, feels a strong national sense of solidarity with other Albanians in the prison. He is proud of their strong ties and does not believe other similar ties can compete. Some of the same pride comes to the surface when Tarik, who has a Moroccan background, describes a conversation with a fellow prisoner with a Pakistani heritage. He is irritated because his fellow prisoner thought he had grown up in a mud hut just because he is from Africa:

Tarik: He's asking me if the houses have indoor toilets? Fuck me. He is 18 and driving around in a Ferrari in Oslo city centre and thinks he owns the world and what does he believe? That the houses in Morocco don't have indoor toilets? What does he think? What can I say, Thomas? It is a catastrophe; there is nothing you can do about such stupidity. You can only smile and shake your head; no, there aren't indoor toilets in Morocco, there aren't. Fucking ignorance, what the fuck do they think, just because it is in Africa, they think there are fucking monkeys and fucking zebras and giraffes, and that's it?

Tarik describes Morocco, Tangier, fantastic cities and a rich cultural heritage. He shows pictures, both from a Tangier newspaper he has lying around and private pictures of him with good friends. We talk about the food. I want to go there.

Tarik: What you can eat? You can eat whatever you want Thomas, whatever you want. Fish, beef, lamb, chicken, tajine, just not pork, heh heh, not pork. Morocco is a very nice country, a very nice country. You have to visit it Thomas. Take your wife, eat well, walk on the beach, visit a museum, rent a car, drive around a bit, hike in the mountains, it is very nice.

The liminal prisoners do not regard themselves as full members of the Norwegian nation; they are not "Norwegians", and feel they are to some extent outsiders in relation to Norway. Nonetheless, "the Norwegian" is still important in their subjectification work, but as a meaning-creating contrast to themselves.

One important boundary marker the liminal prisoners set up is how (the "real") Norwegians are feeble, weak and cowardly, and, by extension, deficient as men. This is not always a clearly negative thing – Erol wanted his children to also master what he called soft Norwegian society – but there is no doubt that there is a hierarchy in which the prisoners' "home culture" is presented as superior.

Later, on the sofa, with Amir, Naveed and others. Amir is kidding with Bassim, who is sitting opposite me.

Amir: You know, that one there is no good [smiles at Bassim]. The doctor said that it's not good to talk to him.

TU: Is it dangerous?

Amir: Yeah, he's nuts you know. He's been on remand for two years.

TU: Two years! Bloody hell...

Naveed: Yeah, but it's alright [shrugs]. The police say you foreigners, you must be on remand. You can take it better than Norwegians, heh heh. Norwegians can't take it. That's right; those of us who have experienced a bit of a harder life, we can take it better.

Amir: [smiles] That's why there are only foreigners here. Look around, how many Norwegians do you see? Two or three? Foreigners have to be here because the police think we'll do a runner. The Norwegians get out.

Naveed: But why would we do a runner? We've lived here many years, speak the language, have jobs here, homes. We aren't going to do a runner.

Amir: [more serious] We are both Norwegian, man. He has a Norwegian passport, I have a Norwegian passport and yet we still have to be in here.

Naveed: [leaning back] But it's alright. We can take it. We are strong. One day we'll get out and then there'll be hell to pay, heh heh.

Amir: Revenge can be very sweet, they should think about that [shakes his head]. There are different cultures. In our culture [Pakistan] we only think that revenge will be very sweet.

Both Amir and Naveed have Norwegian passports, but they are not like the weak, wimpy Norwegians. As non-Norwegians, they won't let themselves be broken by a long time on remand. Erol touches on much of the same when he explains to me how it is much easier to trick a Norwegian than a foreigner:

TU: Yeah? Why? Or, perhaps, how?

Erol: Well, it may be because we have had a difficult upbringing and we are used to it, the hard stuff, almost all the time, from the day we are born, and that's why it is difficult. You have to use stronger methods to get to us than your ordinary Norwegian who was born in a hospital surrounded by flowers, and is surrounded by flowers from day one, right up until he starts to get some sense. And, as a rule, they make the wrong choices, right, some of them, but again they don't have enough, I don't know, don't have enough honour, have enough things that make them strong people, to stand up for what's theirs, regardless of which course they choose, whether they go the right way or the wrong way.

Norwegians' protective and weak culture means that they lack the strength and sense of honour necessary to take responsibility for what one has done. This can also be seen in anecdotes about the extremely poor relationships most Norwegians have with their families:

Nadir: I can't understand it. I will never ever understand how it is possible to act the way you do to your family in Norway! Why are you like that? I was speaking to a Norwegian, I asked him: "When did you last see your parents?" "Not long ago, at Christmas," he said. This was in May! I don't understand it, what a boring life! I mean, you have to see each other.
[...]

My mother will never be in an old people's home. I'll die before that happens. Either she will die, or I will die. Until then I will look after her. That's the way it is.

This poor family life may, of course, be a result of Norwegians' generally deficient sense of honour, but it may also have something to do with their repressed, cold and unsociable nature. The Norwegian culture hinders a sense of community; most Norwegians would rather be at their cottage alone. Because of this, Mehmet, also a Norwegian citizen and who has a Norwegian girlfriend, is struggling a bit with the idea that his children might grow up in Norway:

TU: What about your children, where do you want them to grow up?
Mehmet: ...I'll be straight with you, and you mustn't think I'm being rude now, but I don't want my children to grow up here. I want them to be sociable people. They won't become that in Norway. If you see a neighbour on the street, you should say hello to him. And him to you. If you see an old man who needs help, then you help him. It's a given! The Qur'an says that [quoting the Qur'an in Arabic], that means "if you go to bed at night with a full stomach while your neighbour is hungry, you will be punished". That's the way it is. It's wrong. But that's not how children become in Norway. I don't want my children to grow up in Norway. They should be sociable; they won't become that here. And that doesn't mean that you have to go all the way to Morocco either. You don't have to go any further than Sweden before you notice people are more sociable; people look at each other in the street, they smile and greet each other. You notice it.

Norwegians do not take responsibility, have no honour, are not men. They are cold, reserved and unsociable. In addition to these familiar, almost routine forms of criticism of the Norwegians' nature and habits, some of the liminal prisoners bring up Norway's role as part of a Western imperial, military power:

Youssuf: You must think why are you there [Afghanistan]? What have those people done to you? Have they come here and bombed the Norwegian parliament? No. Have they bombed the SAS hotel? No. Have they killed your children? No. That's it. Be neutral. Those people have never hurt us. If we count how many Afghans are in Norway, there are more than 800 of them here. Asylum, poor things, they don't have shoes. Those people have not hurt this country at all. And they say they are sending soldiers for peace. You never send a person with a gun for peace, heh heh, that's just stupid. Some bloke walking around your house with a gun, and he's a soldier for peace? It's unbelievable! Never. He can be a soldier for peace if he goes to a school and teaches Afghan children English. That's it. Volunteer, civilian. Then you can say he is a soldier for peace. Civilian. Or work at a hospital, doctor, that's good. But walking around with a gun, conducting your own exercises in the desert there; that is not peace, that is just misusing the theatre of war for your own training. You don't have any desert here, you want to train there. That's sly. It is not good; leave those people in peace. Help them. It's very dangerous. I have met people here who are very angry with Norway now. It is dangerous. The police have destroyed, unfortunately, they have destroyed Norway's old reputation.

TU: So there is a lot of frustration and anger directed at Norway here [in the prison]?

Youssuf: Yes. There is a lot in the world now. A lot. You'll see. You'll see Norwegian tourists being bombed. Different places now. Soon.

TU: You think so?

Youssuf: Yes, it is your turn now. It's our turn. It's completely true. It's going to happen to us.

Note how the Norwegian citizen Youssuf switched between being and not being part of the Norwegian community in the paragraph above. Many of the liminal prisoners have a similar fluctuating and conflict-filled relationship with Norway. According to Connor (1996), when nationalism and patriotism come into conflict with each other, nationalism will as a rule draw the longest straw; one example he gives is how Bosnian, Croatian and Serbian nationalism were more potent than Yugoslavian patriotism. Loyalty to the nation generally trumps loyalty to the state and its organisations. For the liminal prisoners in Norwegian prisons, positioned as enemies of the state, a negative relationship with the state is infectious and makes identification with Norway in general difficult. In a situation where the difference between a state and a nation can be difficult to identify, the negative assessment flows over and covers the national symbols generally. The liminal prisoners may, therefore, view themselves as Norwegian in relation to the Norwegian state, but they largely perceive themselves as non-Norwegian in relation to a nation of normal (weak, boring, cold) Norwegians.

Fellow prisoners and other prisoners

A prisoner is not a prisoner. Similarity and difference relationships come into play even inside the prisoners' group. The law is supposed to apply regardless of social status, gender and so on. At this level all prisoners are equal. In one sense, the prisoners also perceive each other as equal, as part of a group of equals who must stand together against the officers. The fundamental difference between prisoners and officers helps to reduce and conceal the differences within the two groups. On the other hand, and as a direct result of the prison's generalising optics, the prisoners utilise a number of different distinguishing techniques and categories to show that they are different from the other prisoners, that they are unique. This view is to some degree supported and reinforced by day-to-day operations inside the walls. All of the prisoners' cells are the same, everyone gets the same food and the rules apply equally to everyone. At the same time, the officers clearly see some differences between types of prisoners and individual prisoners. This is a form of subtler categorisation that they must guard well against applying or articulating in front of the prisoners. In many ways, the institution also tries to smooth over and wipe out differences between the prisoners. The officers' use of cell numbers instead of names when discussing individuals is one example of the prisoners' experience of being turned into a number in a series of equal units.

The prisoners also greatly contribute to this tendency. An attitude emphasising that "we prisoners must stand together against the System" is effective in other contexts, but it helps to mask differences between prisoners in day-to-day prison life. The permanent conflict in the prison between the two groups means that the members perhaps view themselves as group members to a greater degree than they would in other arenas. Both prisoners and officers seek to maintain a unified front against the other group. This fundamental attitude is understood as necessary, but it helps to maintain and sustain the difference between units such as the *System/officers and prisoners* in everyday forms of interaction, while internal differences within the units disappear. At the same time, the prisoners resist the officers' generalising gaze, which concludes that *you are all the same to us*.

Of course, there have to be boundaries. The purpose behind the reproduction of the group's most important product, internal solidarity in the prisoners' group, cannot rub out every difference between prisoners. Some absolutes must be maintained; some deviant figures among the prisoners must be shunned. I will describe three such figures who, in various ways and with varying results for those who are positioned in one of the groups, are used to split the prisoners' group in two. On the one hand, there are the prisoners who are positioned, from the perspective of the prisoners, as what can be called *real* or *proper* prisoners, proper people who stick to their principles and are not as bad as their situation would suggest. On the other hand, there are the categories of prisoners who are shunned because any equation between *them* and *me* would not be very flattering, or would simply be painful. There are three main reasons why these figures, and, by extension, individuals who are perceived as representatives of these, are shunned. The first has to do with morality. They must distance themselves from prisoners who breach a basic moral code, who really *are* evil and dangerous. The second has to do with how you tackle life's day-to-day challenges, whether you are inside or outside the prison. Here the problem is that you tackle life poorly, that you are weak and pitiful. The third and final element is about age and the position of *junior*. The youngest prisoners are restless and immature, and not yet ready for the realities of life. They have not quite managed to find their place. Through exclusion based on these differentiation axes, *real prisoners* become those who are admitted to the "we" that is constituted in and through prisoner solidarity, to adult, proper men who are not evil, not weak and not immature. Below I shall show how the prisoners make use of weakness and the junior position in their subjectification work. The final form of distancing tool, the one that involves morally inferior fellow prisoners, is examined in the later section about moral men.

There are several ways in which one can be positioned as weak among the prisoners. The most common form of weakness is represented by those in the group "drug addicts". A drug addict is weak because he is a slave to the drugs he uses. In other words, this does not simply refer to someone who gets high on narcotics. A drug addict is someone who does it in a special way and who also fits under the heading "drug addict" more generally; the characteristics of this category include life situation and appearance. Telling stories about your experiences of getting high can be used as a tool in competitions between prisoners who are showing off, where the goal is to outdo each other's experiences. Having tried most types of drugs has masculine connotations. The stronger and more dangerous, the better. The drug addict's problem is that they have been caught by the drug, that they are controlled and cannot manage to regain control. The more affected by drug use you appear to be in the prisoner environment, in relation to markers such as choice of clothes, posture and general health, the more likely it is that you will qualify for the title "junkie", a description that is almost spat out with contempt and describes a group whom ordinary, proper prisoners barely tolerate, but never acknowledge. Erol explains the characteristics he judges important when deciding which prisoners he will get to know and which prisoners he does not want anywhere near him:

> Erol: You know the whole thing, all the wings here, everywhere I have been, you do see differences because everyone finds themselves in others, in a way. I mean they find their own group of friends they want to be with and divide up the good and the bad. It's not, to put it this way, there are 52 here now and I know maybe six–seven, eight, let's say ten, who I talk to. The rest, I don't know where they live, their cell numbers, I don't know anything.
>
> TU: You just say hello to them?
>
> Erol: No, not even that. I say hello to few of them. That's just the way it is; they are here. They are probably here for their reasons and I don't know. Because, that's how it is, the junkies hang out with the junkies. People who are a little better off, they hang out with people who are better off.

Birds of a feather flock together, and Erol wants to distance himself from those he thinks of as trash and riff-raff. He has done well in life and wants to fraternise with others who have also done well. The losers can do want they want. This can be understood as an example of resistance to what he perceives as the general narratives of the prison and its inhabitants. Seen from outside the walls, those who live in the prison may look like losers, prisoners with all sorts of problems, the sort who own little and have to steal to survive or sustain their substance abuse. Erol is not like that; you do not have to feel sorry for him. On the contrary, Erol prides himself on being a good businessman who can grasp those opportunities that come his way. He values independence, not least financial independence, and does not want to be a slave to anything or anyone.

Another type of weakness is the mark of the prisoner who, for various reasons, is not tackling being in prison very well; someone who, in the jargon of the Norwegian Correctional Services, is "serving time difficultly". This is a person who, in some ways like the snitch, who will be described in depth later, has succumbed to the pressure of being on remand and the accompanying isolation this entails. However, he has not entered into the service of the enemy and he is therefore tolerated, and occasionally also the subject of care mixed with pity. At the same time, a person who is serving time difficultly has completely succumbed in relation to dominant masculine values such as strength, independence, and the capacity and ability to endure. Where, for example, the snitch is *also* a tragic figure, those serving time difficultly are *completely* tragic; they do not evoke anger, just sadness.

Jassim was one of those, who was coping very badly with remand. The following extract is from a conversation around the long table in the common area where the prisoners were updating each other on the status of their cases.

Jassim comes over and sits down. He is quiet, mutters, and is a bit difficult to relate to. The others tease him a bit, but I notice they are treading carefully. They hope he will laugh, as if they are trying to cheer up someone they know is having a hard time. And he laughs, but his eyes are darting around; he won't look anyone in the eye.

Jassim: I have forgotten my name now. I'm just called Remand. I have now been on remand for 17 months. I'm going to tell the judge that at the next remand review. Hi, my name is Remand, heh heh.

We laugh around the table. Then we joke that he should instead choose a Norwegian name, like Vebjørn Hansen, a real Norwegian name, and then perhaps he would be released from remand. But he is more interested in being called Remand, while all the time he is grinning and his eyes are darting about. Later on, another prisoner tells me that he is having a really hard time. Jassim is, quite simply, broken, he says, and will never be the same again; there is nothing left.

For the prisoners around the table, Jassim represented the prisoner who had given up: he was the result of a system that has won, that has pushed him over the line, and that has forced him to give up all autonomy and power to resist. He was understood as an example of what can happen if you cannot withstand the pressure that comes with the status of prisoner. It was difficult for the other prisoners to deal with someone like Jassim. On the one hand, they felt legitimately sorry for him and he was the object of care and attempts to cheer him up. On the other hand, he reminded everyone of how bad things can get. The most common way of dealing with this tension appears to be not letting yourself get too involved – after all, everyone has their own things to worry and think about without having to think about him as well. Jassim was therefore largely ignored, except when he was used as an example of how hard and difficult it is being on remand.

However, sometimes those who are understood as being a member of this group are also made the objects of humour. The prisoner who is not all "there", who has "lost it", is a figure who is often the butt of more or less amusing jokes. Like this one Torstein told me:

> An officer opens the cell door of a prisoner, Ole. He's sitting in the middle of the floor on a chair with his arms out in front "driving a car": "Brrrrrrmmm-brrrrrmmm." "Er, what are you doing?" "I'm going to Bergen to meet some mates." "Okay. [Raises his eyes]. Have a good trip then." He closes the door. Later the same officer opens his cell door again. Ole is still sitting on the chair and driving the car. But suddenly he changes gear, pulls into the side and puts on the handbrake before taking the key out of the ignition. "In Bergen now?" asks the officer. "Yes, just got here. Bloody hell, this will be great." "Yeah, well have a good time," says the officer and closes the door again. He moves on to the next cell and opens the door. The next prisoner is sitting in the middle of the floor, wanking. "And what are you doing?" asks the officer irritated. "I'm just taking the chance to shag Ole's wife while he is in Bergen," answers the prisoner.

The prisoner who cannot cope with imprisonment, who has *lost it* and *is not quite right in the head any more*, is a tragic and amusing figure, often at the same time. The fact that being in prison is difficult, especially a remand prison, is something that all of the prisoners have experienced. The isolation and uncertainty drain your humour and make every day a challenge. Those poor people who are serving time difficultly remind everyone of what the tragic outcome can be. Incidents like suicide and cell fires are viewed in this context and read as reminders to all the others of where they are. At the same time, those serving time difficultly represent a figure who can be used to throw your own performance into relief. Tackling a heavy, difficult period on remand is an achievement that becomes even greater when someone else succumbs.

Finally, there is a third category of prisoner whom the majority position as unlike themselves. These are *the immature youngsters*, often the youngest prisoners on the wing, although the status of immature youngster is not necessarily associated with age. You can be young without being one of the kids on the wing. This status also has to do with being perceived as immature and ignorant. These are the group of prisoners who are inexperienced, and who also, thanks to their habits and noisiness, often represent a source of chaos that those around them find tiring. In the extract below, Espen, Tom and I are sitting on the sofa in the common area. Espen was the youngest; he was new on the wing and had not got to grips with all the important terms:

> Espen: Hey, I have to ask you, what does doing section 12 time mean?
> TU: That's when you are doing time in a form of institution other than a prison, a treatment institution for example.
> Espen: Yes! I got a one year sentence and that section 12 time. That's a good sentence, isn't it?
> Tom: Are you kidding? That's going bowling and swimming all the time. Total waffle prison.
> Espen: Yes, ok, so that means I'm done being in prison?
> Tom: Done for now, yeah, heh heh, come back in ten years, when you're a real criminal.
> Espen: Hey, I've actually been in prison three times and I'm only 18. Not a lot of people have done that.

Those who have been locked up for a petty crime are not taken completely seriously. Being young also means not having yet accumulated the abilities and routines necessary to be regarded as a professional criminal. You have to cross a line to be taken seriously. Belmonte found the same line in his work in the poor neighbourhood of Naples he studied:

> In the local scale of values, if a man were sent to prison for a petty crime, he became an object of ridicule and contempt. But if he were sentenced for a more serious offence, especially a shooting, he was heroised by the local youths as a paragon of sorts, a *guappo*, deserving admiration and respect.
>
> (1989: 131)

In the extract above, Espen demanded respect for everything he had done despite his young age. He did not want to hear that he was an inexperienced kid who was messing around. With his comments, Tom joined the ranks of those with a more general tendency to position themselves at the expense of those who are still wet behind the ears.

Erol, who was preoccupied with his own professionalism in contrast to most of the other prisoners' amateur status, differentiated between businessmen and small fry when he talked about the criminal environment he was part of on the outside. He was himself an example of the businessman, and the differences between him and the small fry included the fact that they loved to brag.

> Bragging in here about the length of your sentence, how much drugs you have sold, it is just so stupid! If you are so fucking good, what are you doing in here then? My motto has always been to do as much as possible and be seen as little as possible, that's what makes you good. In the beginning, I often told people who asked, as a bit of a joke, that I was in for stealing bikes. That startled them! On remand for bike theft, like, heh heh. I said yes, but they were expensive bikes, heh heh. [...] But there is a lot of that in here, asking others what has he done, what is he in for? That whispering. It is so fucking stupid; if you have something to say to me, something you're wondering about, you should come to me.

Businessmen are professional and discreet; they know what it is all about. They keep a cool head in difficult situations; they are calculating and strategic. They control themselves and do not let their feelings and uncertainty run away with them. On the other hand, the immature youngsters are quick-tempered and have a need to show off. They are perceived as breaking the commandment about not trying to be something other and someone more than what you are. They are not authentic; they do not take responsibility for who they are and what they do; they try to make themselves bigger. Trying to outdo each other in stories about everything you have been part of is childish and immature; you do not brag, you *do*. The immature youngsters bark far louder than they bite, thought Erol.

At the same time, the youngest, with all their ignorance, provided an opportunity to show off his experience and expertise, like when the aforementioned Erol and Henning joined forces to teach the young Adem a bit about business:

> Erol: I have a question for you, then; you who have some experience and have done a lot of things. If you have one kilo of 100 per cent pure cocaine and you're going cut it so it is 80 per cent, how much should you mix in then?
>
> Henning: Two hundred and fifty grams.
>
> Erol: Correct! Many people think the answer is 200 grams, you know, but that is wrong. Many people would have overdosed! It's the difference between life and death that, being able to do maths, Adem.
>
> Adem: ...I can't do anything like that, me.

Erol: No that's quite right, that, you shouldn't be able to do things like that, you are far too young for it, you know?

Henning: I fucking wish I had never learnt to do that as well, that stuff has ruined so fucking much for me [speaking to Adem].

The sermon was combined with expertise in the lesson Erol and Henning gave Adem. Unlike the 18-year-old Espen above, who tried to demand respect for his experience, Adem submitted and freely admitted that he was not particularly good when it came to such things. The two adult prisoners showed him that he had a lot to learn before he could be like them. At the same time, Henning threw Adem a lifeline by emphasising that being like him was not necessarily something to which he should aspire.

Overall, the prisoners use several different resources in their work of positioning themselves by establishing similarity and difference relationships. They use narrative reconstruction to respond to many of the subjectivity challenges that come with the status of prisoner. Their relationship with the officers is reformulated to provide prisoners with the capacity for action and so that they are not morally inferior. By resisting "the Norwegian", the liminal prisoners avoid the negative feeling of being interpellated as "dangerous immigrants". By distancing themselves from the weak and immature, they insert new values and attributes in exchange for what basically links them to the position of *prisoner*. The prisoners feel and perceive a generally stigmatising hail from outside the walls that equates all prisoners *as prisoners*. Everyone in prison is equally good (or equally bad); they are there for good reason, they are dangerous, and society must protect itself from them.

I am not like the other prisoners, you know? This is a common theme in conversations with prisoners. The difference between "me" and "the other prisoners" is established in various ways with the aid of different forms of distinguishing tools. The prisoners distance themselves from "the junkies", even if they have lived hard and, of course, taken their share of drugs. Or they want to study alone at school since there are people in the class who cannot concentrate, who are fools and make a racket. Or they raise themselves above the feeble who cannot handle life. They are older, more experienced, more professional, more practical or more creative. *I am not like the other prisoners*. None of them are.

Transforming space

I went to the viewing of a flat in Åkerbergveien during my fieldwork. It was on the first floor and faced onto the prison wall. The view from the living room in this run-down, one-bedroom flat was dominated by the grey concrete surface opposite: smooth, impersonal and solid. There is a large space hidden from public view in the middle of Oslo. But, although the boundary between city and prison appears absolute from the outside, this is not always the case seen from the inside (Baer and Ravneberg, 2008). From inside the walls it quickly becomes clear that the city seeps into the prison in various, important ways. On 1 May, true to tradition, Blitz, a group of (usually) young political activists, were outside giving a concert for the prisoners. This situation was interesting as an exception to the rule, where the people on the outside were trying to speak directly to the people on the inside without going via the correct channels. As an exception, it was treated like an exception. The officers locked the prisoners in their cells and readied the riot gear, waiting expectantly on the inside for the first independent hooligan to run wild over the wall. However, similar communication also takes place on a daily basis.

The prisoners spend most of the hours of the day locked alone in their cells. Being locked in, however, is not always synonymous with being alone. In some places in Oslo Prison it is possible to speak to each other from cell to cell. The cells are connected by the ventilation system; the windows are also old, single glazed and many of the panes are broken. For the lucky ones, the conditions for conversations are good and their neighbours are pleasant. At the same time, it is possible for those with cells facing into the prison to have conversations with prisoners on other wings. When the prison is in night mode and most of the officers have left for the day, multiple conversations can sometimes be taking place at the same time between the buildings facing each other. Those with cells that face out into the world have, instead, an opportunity to talk to friends and family in the park outside in the evenings. How many times have I walked through the Sculpture Park at night and observed conversations between park and prison cell? Stories also circulated among the prisoners about the woman who lived in a flat right across from the prison yard and who liked to show her breasts to the prisoners on days when the weather was fine. A new father in the prison could even see the building where his wife and child were waiting from his cell window. Sun or rain – the weather – also communicates that there is a world outside. Fine weather is a sign of everything you are missing. Rain is a sign that everyone else is also inside now, which makes things better.

The prison is, in a material sense, history manifested. The walls of the Botsfengsel are permeated with generations of different lines of argument in favour of some goal or other behind locking people up. Rhodes (2004) believes that the prison, therefore, has phantoms – shadows of initiatives, discourses and mindsets that are no longer regarded as relevant in modern, evidence-based and knowledge-based correctional services, but which haunt the same corridors they once helped realise (Schaanning, 2007b). Behind the heavy cell doors in Oslo Prison's wings four and five are 7–8-square metre rooms that are basically the same as far as design and furnishings are concerned. The small rooms are dark and exhibit varying degrees of wear. The walls are whitewashed, plastered brick; the floors have either old or new linoleum flooring. There are horizontal bars in front of the windows. Each cell is equipped with a bed, a writing desk with a small TV, a small fridge, a bookshelf above the desk, a chair, a stool, a shelf for clothes with space for hangers, a toilet, a sink and an intercom system by the door. The wooden furniture is made in the workshop down in unit A and, as a rule, suits the rest of the room because it is well worn.

On the shelf above the desk you will usually see some food, such as chocolate, sandwich toppings like Sunda and Banos, freeze-dried coffee not in its original container (coffee is doled out by the officers from big bags), salt, pepper, sugar, chocolate biscuits, muesli, tins of tuna (probably the most common food), spices, bottles of squash, teabags and orange packets of five-minute rice that becomes edible after being soaked in hot water. The fridge will contain margarine, slices of cheese, eggs, coke and tins of mackerel in tomato sauce. On the shelf you may find a handful of books; crime fiction is common, but I also saw romance novels, fantasy literature and true crime literature. Men's outdoor magazines and pornographic magazines of the type found on sale in newsagents are also common. Sometimes the porn is just lying around. Other times the magazines are piled, half-hidden, under a bed or on top of a shelf. On the shelves there will be some, but not too many, items of clothing, usually quite nicely folded. On a cork noticeboard by the door hang pictures of children, wives and naked women, sometimes side by side. You will find a thermos of hot water, a dish, a glass, a cup, all made of plastic, a butter knife and a fork. Finally, there will be shaving soap, shampoo, aftershave and deodorant.

Outside, in the wing's common area, the ventilation system's metal pipes wind the whole length of the wing with ducts into each cell. The ventilation system is meant to replace stale air with fresh, but it is a common complaint that it is not working properly. Many prisoners break some of the small glass panes in the windows to let in more fresh air from outside. They regret it when winter comes. It is generally pretty cold in the cells then, including in the cells with intact windows. But in the summer it is hot, especially in the cells on the side of the building that gets the sun all day.

For Mauss (2006), patterns of movement, surroundings and subjectivity are inter-related. Being a prisoner means having a prisoner's body, being forced to remain in the prison, in the surroundings the prison can offer its occupants. The material surroundings, the patterns of movement they invite and the objects that are available as tools and opportunities are intertwined in the encounter between individual, power relationships and surroundings where subjects are constructed. This process is the focus of this section.

What is a cell? What characterises this special type of room and what differentiates it from other rooms in the prison and elsewhere? Many prisoners do not use the word "cell"; they simply use "room" instead: *Shall we go to my room?* Others are angered by what they perceive as embellishment and demand of their fellow prisoners that they use "cell", which, after all, describes what they are *really* talking about:

> TU: You also make a point of, a language point, that you oppose what you see as prison euphemisms, calling a cell a room, for instance.
>
> Mark: Yes, to this day, it pisses me off! After all these years, hearing not only prison guards, but other prisoners, they say, let's go to your room. Every time, and I say, it's not a room, it's a bloody cell. It's like softening the environment, you know, no, it's a bloody cell, it's a prison. I don't want to, it's like they're almost in denial.

A body that is locked in a cell has limited opportunities for movement. The way the items of furniture are arranged in relation to each other and the TV, which is on the writing desk across from the bed, means a lot of the time is spent horizontal. You rest, wait, relax and sleep in the same position. You read, pluck or play guitar, and watch football matches or a film from the same bed. And you lie there lounging and eating. Sometimes you may sit at the desk to work on your English homework. Or get up to stare out of the window. Those who want to work out a bit also have space to do a few push-ups or sit-ups on the floor. The rest of your time is spent on the bed. A prison cell is a static room for waiting bodies, a room that signals stagnation and boredom, which are characteristic of prison life more generally. Thus, as a point of departure, prison cells are rooms that help to turn their occupants into passive subjects.

A cell and a home

A cell is not necessarily a cell; a room is never just a room (Baer, 2005). The uniform cell, an impersonal room intended for anyone, is transformed into a home by the prisoners in various ways, with specific consequences for the ongoing subjectification game of those who inhabit this home. In other words, a home is more than a delineated room one frequents. The word "home" combines in one term both the idea of a place and the idea of a social fellowship associated with this place. In the pair of words "home/outside", home stands for the snug, cosy, safe (and perhaps a bit boring?), according to Gullestad (1989). As a potential "home", a prison cell basically lacks the snug and cosy dimension, while boredom is very well represented. In the vast majority of cases, the security of the cell is not preferable to the more insecure "outside" beyond the prison walls. Outside there is life; inside the prison there is stagnation. There are two parallel inside/outside opposites in the prison: inside the cell and out in the common area on the one hand, and inside the prison and outside in freedom on the other. In both cases, outside is clearly preferable to inside. There are some curious exceptions to this that simply underscore the rule. The anecdotes about prisoners who *want* to be inside again are anecdotes about crazy prisoners, prisoners who are "not quite right". In the same way, prisoners who suddenly do not want to go out into the prison yard are associated with danger. When prisoners suddenly prefer their cell, something is wrong. In any case, this process of turning a cell into a home is not an easy one to begin with.

On a material level, the buildings and objects, which can never be separated from the symbolic values ascribed to them, are important components of the continuous subjectification work. Regardless of any material similarities, and to contradict an oft-repeated criticism about luxurious (and therefore not very effective) Norwegian prisons, there *is* from this perspective a difference between a newly built prison cell and a cheap hotel room or a cabin on a "booze cruise" ferry. The rooms may at first glance appear similar, but, at the very least, they position their occupants as very different subjects with very different symbolic connotations and totally different ties to different power relationships. The cell refers to the status of prisoner in the same way as a nice, expensive hotel room will refer to a guest's financial status.

According to Young (2005a), a room becomes *my* room by me taking residence in it. The feeling of the space belonging to me is thus a practical question. A home is supposed to be a personal space, a statement about those who live in it, an extension of the resident's body. Objects and furniture are arranged to suit ordinary movement, colours and patterns are chosen as an expression of personal taste, everything is tied to my personal biography and carries with it meaning (for me) that differentiates the home from anywhere else. At home one's patterns of movement are automatic; they flow without resistance. You can walk from your bed to pick up the morning paper from the steps almost without opening your eyes, even if you are really still asleep. Body, subjectivity and the home are thus linked to each other organically; I *am* in some sense what I regard as my home. Because the home is understood as an expression of those who live there, it becomes a symbol and has expressive meaning; a home becomes understood as an "expression of a creative effort" (Gullestad, 1989: 56). From this perspective, the home is an arrangement of things in a space that reflects those who live there, their perceptions, habits and practices.

A home will be filled with objects that position the occupants as parts of a continuum, that position them in time in relation to ancestors and descendants. An old sideboard bought by the grandparents that grandchildren will inherit is not something that you walk around thinking about every day, but such objects link the *here and now* to *that time when* and *perhaps sometime*. From this vantage point, such signal objects tie the individual to a family fellowship that has existed and remains constant over time.

The objects in a prison cell link the occupant to a different fellowship. The chessboard carved out of the seat of a stool and coloured with ink from a broken pen refers to an earlier prisoner who did the work, who lived here, in this cell, who was bored, and who wanted to pass time by playing chess. Thus, cells often retain traces after real, flesh and blood prisoners have met the open space and adopted different strategies to make it their space. A room in a hotel should, preferably, refer as little as possible to earlier guests. Hotel guests who find clear traces of a previous guest will generally complain and demand to switch to a new, "clean" room. The cells in Oslo Prison, however, do not achieve this anonymising effect as perfectly as successful hotel rooms. Marks from previous use, be they inscriptions, burn marks from cigarettes or general wear and tear, are in most cases pervasive and difficult to erase.

The pronoun "my" in "my cell" and "my room" does not reflect any real ownership; that much is clear. The prison staff can decide to move a prisoner without warning or to go through the entire cell and all its contents hunting for infringements (the cell is "searched"). However, a lot of effort is put into creating the illusion of ownership, the feeling of a private life (Moran, Pallot and Piacentini, 2013). The uninhabited cell is, in some sense, a clean slate, although, of course, the opportunities are limited. The cells are alike and are supposed to be alike. What the prisoners are allowed to have in their cell is regulated in detail down to the number of t-shirts, jumpers and trousers. But the cells *are made* different in order to underscore individuality (Baer, 2005).

In the work on personalising the cell you have to work with the resources that are available. The resources in a prison cell are limited. The prisoners are not allowed to rearrange the furniture; the table must stay where the table is. In this way, the cell as a room, with its specific atmosphere, its odour and rules concerning the position of its furniture, is another expression of the institution's power over the individual. You may well live there, but you only have a little leeway when it comes to deciding how it will look. Again, this is about generalisation: the prison cell is a room that tells the prisoner who lives in it that "you are all the same to us". It is, therefore, not that surprising that prisoners often want to respond with various individualisation practices. On two occasions I observed two prisoners creating better conditions for a meal together by placing the desk in the middle of the floor while hanging out together for a shared cell-made dinner. The desk was transformed into a dinner table since they had made it possible to sit opposite each other, one on the chair and the other on the bed. At the end of the hanging out and the meal, the furniture had to be put back where it belonged.

How is an individualised and individualising *home* created within the prison cell's four walls? First, the official framework that surrounds the room is reduced by the prisoners trying to turn the cell into their own private sphere (Baer, 2005). This is done through the utilisation of domestic patterns of movement – the prisoners lie back on the bed; they are *laid-back*. This position emphasises, as described above, passivity and stagnation, but also comfort and domestic laziness. None of them would sit like this on the sofa in the common area; here you sit erect in a more active position. In the cell, the body is off duty. The position that most clearly signifies home and leisure is half-lying in front of the TV with a cigarette[3] dangling from the corner of your mouth and a glass of fizzy drink within reach.

However, there are also other strategies. Luca literally papered his cell with drawings, some done with a pen, most done with a pencil. He was strongly inspired by comics and regularly borrowed from series such as Frank Miller's *300* and *Sin City*, the gangster-conspiracy epic *100 Bullets*, and the classic *Blueberry* from the prison library. Well-known characters, with small changes and messages that had meaning in the specific prison context, often turned up on his walls. One of his drawings was of a heavy prison door bearing the legend "Please give me the keys to this cell", which he hung on the inside of his door. The other topics Luca focused on were: ladies (often naked), tough men, cool animals, derogatory semi-racist messages to various ethnic groups, weapons, scenes of violence, suicide and the situation in the prison. The other prisoners regularly came over to his cell to have a look at the "gallery" and called him "da Vinci". Luca's cell was transformed into an art gallery, he into a smiling artist.

In Youssuf's homely room, it was clear that the occupant was a religious, home-loving man. He set the tone with a tablecloth on the desk, lots of photos of family members printed out on the prison's black-and-white printer, the Qur'an clearly on display on the window ledge, and his rolled-up prayer rug.

Religious affiliation was also clear in Sugath's cell. The room was decorated with religious motifs, largely depicting Jesus. The imagery was familiar, but the choice of colours was definitely "garish" in my eyes. Religious motifs with very strong colours and glossy finishes are common in Sri Lanka, according to Sugath. Several beautiful posters in strong, explosive colours portrayed images of Jesus and his disciples. Leonardo da Vinci's famous painting of the Last Supper was decorated with a thick border of gold foil. There were also a lot of drawings on display in his cell: largely nudes in pencil, but also a drawing of his mother copied from a photograph. The drawing hung next to the original photograph; the likeness was good. Both of his parents were in the photograph, but Sugath had so far only got around to drawing his mother.

In contrast to Youssuf's and Sugath's references to religion and families, there was the younger Adem's room. "Allahu Akbar" written in Arabic text did hang above his bed, but the rest of his cell was decorated according to different principles. The walls were plastered with posters of naked and semi-naked women. Even his thermos was decorated with a glamour model with slightly parted moist lips. His clothes lay around the floor in heaps. As one of the youngest on the wing, Adem had clearly turned the cell into a "boy's room".

Another important opportunity for transforming the cell into a home comes when one introduces a foreign element in the form of a guest. A home with a guest needs a host, and the person playing the role of host is thus underscoring that the room one is in is precisely that, *his* home. As Brede said the first time I visited his cell: *I have always liked having guests. There's always someone or other staying at my house. That's how I like it, so you are heartily welcome here.* I became the guest, he became the host and the room we were in became his home, with all the rights and obligations that apply for those entertaining guests at home. Once the guest is in place, the prisoner body can no longer be *lying* inside. You are sitting, together. The number of places it is possible to sit in a cell is limited. There is only one chair, one stool, which is not particularly comfortable, and the bed. When a guest like me visits, these seating possibilities constitute a hierarchy, with the chair at the top and the stool at the bottom. The hierarchy was clear when Mark told me about how during another period of imprisonment he experienced a humble prison governor who came to his cell to apologise on behalf of the institution: *He didn't even want the chair; he sat on my bed and let me have the chair!*[4]

The most common thing to do is emphasise the guest's role by giving him the chair and sitting on the bed yourself. Now and then we both sat on the bed. This underscored intimacy and equality. In this way, good friends hanging out together sit across from each other on the bed. Besides the bed's symbolic role, this results in physical proximity; you sit so close to each other that you could touch each other at any time. On rare occasions I got the bed, while the cell's occupant took the chair himself. I experienced these as acts of my subordination, plus the design of the bed made it difficult to find a completely comfortable position, unless I had put the role of guest to one side and lay down on it.

Another way of underlining the relative positions of guest and host was to serve me food and drink. Døving (2003) describes how in the Norwegian context being able to offer coffee is to be at home, to take the duties of being at home seriously.[5] The coffee cup given to the guest refers to the home he or she is visiting. It simultaneously positions the giver as the host and the recipient as the guest in relation to each other. The first time I visited Erol in his cell he gave me the chair and placed a glass of pretzel sticks and a plate of chocolate biscuits on the stool between us. He also offered me both coffee and coke.

Erol: I don't walk round eating this all day; this is what I put out when I have guests. It's important to us; we have grown up with it. When guests visit in Kosovo, you put the best you have on the table.

Later he starts the evening's cooking. He has bought two bags of fried chicken legs and is making a feast for seven, me included. I try to say that he doesn't need to make food for me, but that doesn't wash. A guest is a guest. Erol will, of course, take the smallest portion. I insist on the opposite, but it falls on deaf ears. He takes the plate with easily the smallest piece of chicken for himself, and says smiling:

Erol: Come on, Thomas. You are a guest. Shut up and eat.

The coffee cup, pretzel sticks and the relative placement of the bodies help to construct a cell as a home and position the occupants as hosts. Re-creating a home by assuming the role of homemaker can be read as an attempt to turn yourself into something other than a prisoner. A prisoner is in his cell. A man in his own home is free.

Private life and public spaces

Gullestad (1989) describes "the home" as a key symbol in a Norwegian context. She shows how the home as a social category is associated with, and nuanced by, opposite pairs like private/public and child/parent. In a prison context, the opposite pair private/public is, as I shall show, extremely important. The prison is a (pseudo) public space without any genuine private counterpart. In the prison you are on show: "One of the most degrading aspects of penal confinement is this denial of any 'backstage', of any 'territory of intimacy'", as Wacquant writes (2002: 378).

A prison cell is a diverse room with many functions. The prisoners eat, work on homework or studies, sleep, watch TV, lie and think, receive guests, go to the toilet and have sex (with themselves) in the same small room. From this perspective, a prison cell is a private sphere, an intimate sphere. In the world outside, the home's front door is the most important boundary between the private and the public spheres. However, the home's rooms can also be placed on a public–private axis. The living room is the most public room in a home, a room furnished with guests in mind. The parents' bedroom is the most private. In prison, prisoners simultaneously invite guests into the bathroom, living room and bedroom. This, therefore, upsets the normal order of public and private rooms. The cell has to function as a kitchen, dining room, TV room, bedroom, laundry room, hall, toilet and home office. Within the four walls the prisoners must simulate all the rooms in a home on the outside, from the most public, such as the hall and dining room, to the most intimate and private, such as the toilet and bedroom.

What is a private life? Young (2005b) discusses the concept in relation to how the experience of a private life is created and challenged in an old people's home; a public–private arena which is, in this regard, reminiscent of a prison. The essential, tangible starting point for experiencing a private life is, according to Young, a separate room to which you can refuse or grant others entry, a room you control. A home is not a home if everyone has access to it. Access to a specific home is an exclusive benefit; a person who breaks in and makes himself at home without permission is a burglar.

It is in the nature of prisons (and old people's homes?) that the occupants cannot fully exclude those who work there from their rooms. The ownership and control of the prison's various rooms must be administered and negotiated in some manner or other. As a researcher in a prison, I have often felt that I was intruding when I entered an occupied cell. This is generally not true for officers; they, like nurses or cleaners, are professionals who work in other people's private spheres. The apparently private room can, at any time and without warning, be invaded from without. A cell is similar to a boy's room where the parents can pop their heads in to make sure that all hands are above the duvet. Once again, the officers are positioned as the adults while the prisoners are infantilised, a trait that is not prison-specific, but which has been described in closed institutions more generally (Ericsson and Jon, 2006).

At the same time, it is also true that some rooms in the prison are more private than others. According to an unwritten rule, both officers and prisoners one does not know very well should knock loudly and, ideally, politely ask for permission to come in before entering a cell. Some officers observe this rule better than others. And sometimes private and public spheres collide despite the best of intentions, as when the smell in a cell clearly communicates that it has recently been used as a toilet, and the equally uncomfortable occupant and visitor try to ignore it as well as they can (cf. Weinberg and Williams, 2005). Entrance procedures vary, of course, depending on the relationship between the person entering and the person occupying the cell. Good friends may perhaps enter and have a cigarette whenever they want, even when the cell's owner is absent, while it is best for new extra officers to tread carefully and watch their manners. One needs to be very familiar with the rules. Those who do not observe the entrance rules can cause agitation and anger:

Ayhan has entered the cell of his fellow trustee, Tom, and borrowed his workout gloves without asking first. On the way to the toilet, Tom walks past the gym equipment where Ayhan is standing with his gloves on. He is, to put it mildly, pissed off. It is difficult to hear the details from where I am standing, but Ayhan gets a real tongue-lashing. Tom is so angry that he is shaking and pointing his index finger right in Ayhan's face. Ayhan stands there taking it, but his stare is wavering. Everyone else who happens to be in the common area is watching. The atmosphere is tense. Tom then marches back, clearly furious, and finishes his game of pool.

Tom: I'm so fucking pissed off! You don't do that. You're just stupid if you do. For fuck's sake, we are not that good friends.

[...]

Later the two colleagues are on their water round together. This duty requires cooperation; one person fills the thermos bottles with hot water and the other carries them to and from the cells. The two are working together, but not nearly as well as they usually do. It is awkward; they look away, won't look each other in the eye, and will not talk to each other. After a while, Tom has had enough; he tries to breach the distance with Ayhan again with a few jokes. Slowly but surely the situation normalises during the water round.

The locked cell door shuts you in, but is also necessary for the prisoners' experience of security and a private life. On the inside you are free. No one can see you; you are not on show as you are outside in the public common area. Behind the closed cell door you can, to some extent, relax. That is why there are rules about how to behave in this public–private room, invisible boundaries whose meaningfulness is clear when they are crossed without the right application of "shock absorbers" or "entrance procedures". When the doorway is suddenly and without warning filled by a uniformed body it breaches the prisoners' carefully constructed experience of the cell as a private room. Someone can knock quickly (two or three knocks) and come in at any time. In a prison cell, the experience of a private life can be fleeting and fragile.

> Erol: I have lost it with several officers, you know? Two different ones just recently. One of them was asking me to get back in my cell because I had talked to someone who was on a social. I went back in and he followed me, just waltzed in here into the cell, stood here in the middle of floor and was going to give me what for. "Get the hell out of here before you go flying down to the third head first!" I said to him, I was so fucking angry, he was so fucking close. He left, heh heh. Afterwards he came in and said that he was sorry, he apologised. No report, nothing. [...] Another officer, one who doesn't usually work here, an okay officer really, he walked in and out several times, just right in, no knocking, nothing. "Listen here," I said, "this little room, this is what you have given me. And it's mine. So you can bloody well knock if you want to come in." "I can come in here when I want", he said. "No, you fucking can't!" I said, pissed off. "Is that how it's going to be?" he said. "Yes, it bloody well is! Get the hell out!" He didn't write me up on report either, heh heh.

Home is a place that is re-created by acting as if you were the man of the house with the same rights and obligations as someone at home playing the role of host (with food and gifts) or the indignation that results from some-one "taking liberties". My home is my castle. The symbolic moat around the castle must be respected. Officers who just stroll right in, without knocking and politely asking for permission, breach the code.

The informal boundaries between more private and more public spaces in the prison can come under pressure, especially when the officers are pressed for time. For example, when hectic officers are struggling to lock all the prisoners in fast enough during a drill:

> The message comes, full lock down, red lamp. Next to the red lamp in the middle of the wing there is a notice: "If the red lamp lights, go directly to your cell for lock down." The whole thing runs relatively efficiently.

The prisoners who are out smile and shrug their shoulders – and move towards their respective cells. In two minutes everyone is inside. But then more prisoners arrive – a group has been to spinning class and comes up good and sweaty. They have to be locked in. Then some people who really should be in classes turn up; they have to be locked in. At the same time, the switchboard starts to ring for confirmation that everyone is locked in; the officers hurry back and forth, spending too much time on this is embarrassing. A female officer who does not work on the wing full-time thinks things are moving too slowly and puts her arm around a prisoner and tries to push him gently but firmly into the cell. The prisoner spins around and stares furiously at the officer:

Prisoner: Hey, don't you push me!

He holds the door so she can't close it, but she pushes back. For a moment, there is static warfare over threshold.

Officer: Get in, get in, it's a drill!

Prisoner: Well next time, don't you push me like that!

He stands for a second longer before acquiescing and stepping into the cell, making it possible to close the door. The officer locks it, shaking her head. Seconds later a hard blow strikes the inside of the door and reverberates down the wing.

The officer wanted to demonstrate her ability to regain control of the common area as quickly as possible. The prisoner's problem was that a room someone tries to shove you into by force is not your home. An officer who tries to push a prisoner into their own cell, an action that transforms the space within from the symbolic position of "home" to "cell", is an officer who will hear about it. This is an example of a conflict between prisoners, who reserve the right to control their own private sphere, and officers, who have a professional ownership relationship with all the rooms in the prison. Officers' attempts to act as if it is a cell that is involved (a practice which, at the same time, makes the prisoner a prisoner, not, for instance, a host) can cause conflicts.

Nadir felt that his experience of having a private life was also under attack when he wanted to "report" a theft from his cell:

Officers' room at break time. Nadir is on the intercom. We are all sitting around the lunch table listening. He is upset and wants to "report" the theft of the TV remote from his cell.

Nadir: Someone has taken it, I'm sure they have, I've looked everywhere, through all my clothes.

Officer: Then you will get a new one, you know?

Nadir: Yeah, but it must be one that works.

Officer: You can choose it yourself from those we have in the drawer here, okay? [Hangs up]

Nadir immediately calls back. The officer hasn't had time to move and, somewhat exasperated, answers the call.

Officer: Yes?

Nadir: Yes, but you have to understand; I'm not worried about the remote, I'm worried that someone has been in here messing with my things. We have to sort it out, it's important.

Officer: Yes, er, I'm not really sure what we can do, but it isn't good, no it's not.

Nadir: No, but we can't have a situation where things are going missing, where people are stealing; that's not good.

Officer: In any case, you will get a new one afterwards Nadir. We're on a break right now, okay? [Hangs up again.] [To those having lunch:] Okay... you could use your brain a bit; I mean, you're inside here with 50 or so criminals, might it not be a good idea to close your door? If you leave your room with the door open, well... [Smiling, shaking his head].

Like the cells, the wing's common room is divided up into different functions. Visitors to the wing first arrive in the gym area. Here there are a small number of pieces of gym equipment and a spinning bike. If some prisoners have been unlocked for a social, some of them will be in the middle of a workout, focused, sweating and panting. A bit further in you cross into the "basement sitting room" with (in order from the lift) a table tennis table, a foosball table and a pool table. Finally you arrive in the lounge where the wing's big TV is. Two sofas stand opposite each other with a low coffee table between them. On the table is a selection of magazines and a couple of days-old newspapers. The TV is almost always on, but sometimes the sound is turned down. If you look up, it is not unlikely that you will catch the eye of someone hanging out on the landing. Both prisoners and officers can assume a relaxed posture, literally hanging over the railing. The height provides a perfect overview; one can rise above the situation down there and comment on what is happening from a bird's eye view. The rectangular common area has two floors of cell doors along both long sides. The flooring is blue linoleum with luminous strips that point the way to the emergency exits. The walls are again whitewashed plaster. The two wings are colour coded – there is blue detailing downstairs and green upstairs. In contrast to many of the cells, the common area is newly decorated and shows little sign of wear.

If the cells are rooms that people have tried to privatise, this has also been done in contrast to the public common area outside. As a room everyone shares, a room for everyone, the common area is a necessary condition for the constitution of the cells as private and homely. If the cell is like a home, the common areas are like the world outside the home. There is no private property here. Those who leave something behind here, like a newspaper or a hunting magazine, surrender it to the community. Each time the prisoners are locked in, the officers tidy up, move the furniture back to "where it should be" and gather the magazines and newspapers into neat piles. When the prisoners are locked in their private rooms, the officers transform the common area back into a neutral status, untouched by prisoners' hands. Individuals and their habits, movements and perceptions are wiped out; what is left is the generalised prisoner, the prisoner collective the officers mean when they say that "you are all the same to us".

The cells may be a bit worn, but they are often very clean. Many of the prisoners take their time and wash their cells often because it passes the time, and not least because the person doing the washing can have the cell door open and can go in and out to collect clean water and soap. The cleanliness of the common area is the responsibility of the trustees. According to Døving (2003), outside the prison, housework is associated with female love and a sense of duty to one's family. The housework in the prison common area is associated with a different register. When Tom explodes at a fellow prisoner who gets in the way of the floor polishing – *Hey you! I'm not your mother, right!* – it is not about housework motivated by love between related people. He is the professional cleaner irritated by ignorant civilians who should stay out of the way, a role that the skilful handling of a large floor polisher and industrial cleaning agents only reinforces. The trustees professionalise the housework and simultaneously turn the common area into a public space where professionals are working.

In addition to the large common area on the wing, there is another room that, in an interesting way, brings the prisoners' experience of a private life in the public sphere into play. When the family comes to visit, the homely private life outside the walls must be re-created and simulated down in the prison's visiting area. The large, common visiting room is a big, L-shaped yellow-beige room. Six tables have been placed around the room, each with four stools, all made of well-worn, white wood and heavily inscribed. In one corner there is a bookshelf with some games and children's books. A heavy metal door leads out and up to the wings, complete with the usual illuminated emergency exit signs stuck to the flooring. Another metal door on the other side leads to the world outside, and through this door families, friends and girlfriends – the next of kin – enter. Five or six prisoners at a time can receive visits from their loved ones. The room is monitored constantly by officers behind a large one-way mirror. The officers can sit with a cup of coffee in a small group of seats and keep an eye on everything that is happening. As well as the large common room, there are a number of so-called lawyer rooms, small meeting rooms with a desk and two chairs for visits from lawyers; a room for visits, separated by a glass wall with a small white intercom handset on each side of thick plate glass; and a private room intended for conjugal visits.

This little "love room", as the officers jokingly call it, has a single sofa bed with a wooden frame and a removable backrest. There is a small sink and paper towel dispenser fixed to the wall, a small shelf with a transparent plastic box (like a lunch box) containing condoms, and a change of bedclothes, crumpled but clean and ready for use. The walls are the same yellow-beige colour as outside. No attempt has even been made to make this a more pleasant place; it would, in any case, have been doomed to fail. There is no mistaking that the room for private visits is a room in a prison. Those who wish to maintain a sex life have to put up with their sex life being made public through other people having a professional relationship to it. Adem relates:

> Now, last time, as we are lying there, someone suddenly knocked loudly on the door: "Visiting time is over!" Then, less than a minute later, he [the officer] was on his way in, I mean, you should have time to get bloody dressed! I asked him on his way out, are you in a bad mood today or what? He said: no I do that to everyone. I guess he is used to people not hearing very well while they are shagging, heh heh.

The "love room" is a public room for a private life: a room with a well-used, shared bed that, unlike a successful hotel room, cannot avoid referring to all those who have used it over the years. It is a room that is only good for one thing, and which does not try to appear to be anything else. An honest room. As Brede said: *Even if it does look awful, it is still the room I like best in the entire prison.*

Referring to the home outside

The prisoners also strive not to show how hard they are missing their loved ones on the outside. Mentioning family members or telling a mate that you are missing your wife and children are okay. However, it is not okay to talk about missing them all the time or to cry openly. This balancing act is demanding for many people. Your wife or girlfriend and children are at the forefront of your mind, and missing them is painful; at the same time, it is not *comme il faut* to "go on" about such things. Here the prisoners are subscribing to the general gendered expectations of men: it is about taking it like a man. It is well known that big boys do not cry in Oslo Prison.

Food can play a part as an effective prop here. Comfort (2002) describes how female next of kin bring the home with them when they visit their men in San Quentin State Prison. By transforming the prison as well as they can into a satellite of the home, they try to invest their prisoner men in the life that continues on the outside. One of the important ways they do this is to bring with them food, lots of food. For the most privileged prisoners, who have access to the prison's apartments or trailers for family visits, these provide an opportunity for the women to cook for their men. Women who visit prisoners without access to the apartments or trailers instead smuggle in their own home-made food wrapped in plastic and attached to their body. The traditional route to the man's heart is thus reopened, at least for a while. Women use food as props to turn the prison into a home for themselves and their men. The women's food smuggling makes the wall between prison and family life porous, according to Comfort.

In the same way as the women transform the apartments and trailers in San Quentin into satellites of the home, the men in Oslo Prison put a lot of effort into using food to refer to the family meals they are missing. The food functions as an escape route; the prisoners "do home" to get over the wall, if only for a little while.

Food's ability to evoke memories is a well-known theme – for example, Proust's use of the madeleine in the opening of his series of novels *In Search of Lost Time*. For Erol, the whole process of cooking is a reminder that connects him to his friends and family outside, and, by extension, the whole Albanian community:

> Erol: This is a really common traditional Albanian meal so we have to listen to traditional Albanian music. It might sound stupid saying it, but it's lovely to put this music on and shed a tear now and then. It's better that I cry in here than that someone sees me break down out there, that they see they can do whatever they want because, you know, he's completely broken. In here, in peace, it can be okay just to let it out. And it's nice to know that we can celebrate a bit in here too, like friends and family are celebrating out there.

> First he makes a salad. Initially, I was surprised by the knife he conjured up – a small, 7–8-centimetre long blade with a black plastic handle; far more effective than the ordinary butter knives most prisoners use to cut onions. And, of course, completely prohibited. Erol just laughs at my surprise. He had borrowed it from the officers and "forgotten" to give it back. He left it lying in plain sight so that he couldn't be accused of concealing anything. They could take it if they wanted to. He also turned on some music on his "system" – a discman connected to the TV (this is also prohibited) – and traditional Albanian music streams out into the room. It is the day after Kosovo's Independence Day; the TV pictures were still showing red flags with black eagles sticking out of hooting cars, but the tunes are now Albanian songs about unhappy love. Erol dances while he works and sings along out loud, complaining, but smiling. The food, flags, music, dance – everything merges into a greater whole.

Erol's Albanian salad deliberately functioned like Proust's madeleine. Unlike the prisoner Godderis (2006) interviewed, who changed the channel to avoid television commercials that reminded him of the meals he missed, Erol added music and dance and let the memories flow.

Lupton (2005) argues that there is a strong connection between food habits, emotions and subjectivity. Food is an essential part of the world that absorbs and organises our relationship with the past. According to her, the relationship between food habits and memory can be seen as symbiotic.[6] Sutton (2005) describes how the power inherent in day-to-day objects or practices can be used as a tool in the work of remembering experiences that can be useful in subjectification work. According to Sutton, food can be used to rectify the feeling of being a part that has been removed from a whole; the food is used as a tool for (temporarily) finding your way back to the whole. Such moments of reunion with the whole are fleeting and therefore bitter-sweet. The ability to symbolically reintroduce family and loved ones in a new, difficult situation can, from such a perspective, be understood as vital to functioning in everyday prison life.

Some prisoners are lucky enough to be allowed to taste home-made food regularly, literally. The monthly remand reviews are one such opportunity for remand prisoners with family in the Oslo region. The court sessions are public and, therefore, present a welcome opportunity for many prisoners to meet friends and family among the spectators. Remand reviews usually do not attract very many spectators, so, as a rule, the court is populated by the prisoner, his defender, the prosecutor, the judge and the prisoner's friends and family. The meeting with the family in the court house's waiting room provides a welcome breathing space in the everyday life of remand:

Adil: The only time I eat Indian food is at the remand reviews [grins].
Thomas: Oh yes? Down in the waiting cell?
Adil: No, in the lower court, in the room next to the court or anywhere at all. My family brings real home-made food; my favourite is a type of meatball with sauce, or chicken with sauce, rice and dessert, real food. Mum's food, heh heh. It's fantastic! I sit down and enjoy, you know, real home-made Indian food; it is so bloody delicious. It's the only reason I go to the remand reviews.

The food thus becomes a way of sort of getting over the prison wall for Adil; it connects him with life on the outside and reminds him of a community there of which he is still a part. With home-like food as the home's props, the cell is transformed into a home, at the same time as the home outside is referred to and drawn into the prison. The food makes the cell homely. But food and meals, as will become apparent soon, also refer to other registers.

Food, resistance and masculinity

Based on his fieldwork in a psychiatric institution, Goffman (1961) describes the common threats to the self that characterise what he calls "total institutions". The clients feel that they are subject to a process of violation due to things such as the fact that bodily functions like sleep, hygiene and defecation are no longer private matters. The prisoners' relationship to the food they are offered in prison can also be understood from such a perspective; the prison food becomes an expression of their deprivation of the status of adult men who can decide what they will and will not eat for themselves. The feeling of violation gradually transforms into adaptation to the institution's regime, and Goffman describes how the clients try to create free areas where the institution's supervision and control can be evaded: where they, in one way or another, can exist on their "own terms". In other words, Goffman's clients find their way back to "themselves" through small, subtle forms of resistance to the institution's regime of control.

In Schaanning's (2007a) historic analysis of the role food played in disciplining prisoners in Norwegian prisons, he shows how access to food in prisons was controlled and utilised in the management of prisoners as early as the 1700s. One of the most important means of controlling prisoners throughout the 1800s was restricting their food; it was part of the system and stipulated by statute. The Criminal Act of 1842 made it abundantly clear that bread and water were meant to function as an independent sanction. Food, therefore, was part of the normal, professional operation of the institution and a key tool in the effective control of the prisoners. It was used as both a punishment and a reward. Additional food for good behaviour was part of the institution's system of progression. The administration of meals functioned as a power technology and therefore formed part of a broader disciplinary strategy, as described by Foucault (1977a).

Today, prisoners can no longer be punished by depriving them of, or changing, their food: a fact Pratt (1999) places in the context of the civilisation of prisons, in the sense used by Elias (1994). Meals are now regarded as a fundamental right. Food is one of the few things prisoners are entitled to and, therefore, they cannot be deprived of it for the purpose of punishment.[7] (The most serious threat of punishment of this type today is the threat of having your TV taken away.)

Godderis (2006) uses food as an analytical means of studying subtle daily power and resistance practices in prison. Her point of departure is that prisoners in prison are placed in a situation where they are deprived of a large proportion of their capacity for action and autonomy. They are able to take few decisions that affect their day-to-day lives; the prison makes these for them. This also applies to food; in prison you largely have to accept the food you are served (Valentine and Longstaff, 1998). For example, sticking to a special diet or choosing especially healthy, organic or ecological products is difficult. Religious preferences are respected to some degree, but are not always a priority. The food prisoners are served, therefore, forms part of the institution's more general system of prisoner control and care – most prisoners would call it an essential part – while Godderis describes how food-related practices are central to the prisoners' work on creating space for action and the associated feeling of autonomy. She describes a form of food-based resistance to the System whereby prisoners seize the opportunity to challenge and shape their rigid surroundings through the procurement, preparation and consumption of food, and thereby affect their own position in relation to these surroundings.

Even though the era of doing time on "bread and water" has ended, food is still part of the prison's system of discipline, albeit in a less direct manner than that described by Schaanning. As previously mentioned, Foucault (1977a) underscored that imprisonment has never functioned without a certain addition to the punishment, an addition that concerns the physical body. For a prisoner, the scope of punishment is felt as an encroachment on all aspects of life. Foucault highlights food and restricted food rations, as well as sexual longing and incarceration. The administration of meals in time and space represents some of the power over the body that, according to Foucault, flows through all of the prison's practices.

A version of the meticulous division of the day into periods of time and the related administration of space in relation to the day's periods, which Foucault describes as a key disciplinary tool, also applies in Oslo Prison. And the day's periods of time are marked, as they are outside the walls, by meals. The food is distributed and prisoners locked in for lunch and dinner at set times. From this perspective, food and meals are, therefore, integral parts of the prison's system of discipline, even though food has become a fundamental right that prisoners cannot be deprived of as punishment. Every meal can, therefore, be understood as a tiny movement of a cog in the prison machine. However, it should be stressed that this applies to ordinary food, not some extraordinary, outmoded sanction whereby the prisoners are put on bread and water.

Godderis (2006) differentiates between four distinct forms of resistance associated with food. "Individual adaptations and adjustments" include, for example, so-called cognitive tricks that prisoners employ to make coping with prison life easier. One of her examples is the prisoner I briefly referred to earlier, who avoided watching television commercials depicting meal situations with tablecloths and lit candles: images that made him think of romantic meals with his beloved. Examples of "individual displays of opposition" include confrontations with authority figures like kitchen staff, as well as more subtle forms of resistance like starting a rumour about prison cooks urinating in the officers' food. "Legitimate group activities" include, for example, forming groups based on ethnicity and celebrating a national holiday with a traditional meal. Finally, Godderis describes various forms of "illegitimate group activities" that are much like Goffman's (1961) adaptation strategies; food practices whereby prisoners collectively break the institution's rules, and can thus be said to be challenging the entire regime, and, by extension, the entire prison system in which the rules are practised.

Food in prison is a complicated phenomenon, since food is simultaneously part of both the prison's control regime and the prisoners' resistance to it:

> [I]n prison, where control is taken away as the prisoner and her body become the object of external forces, food is experienced not only as part of the disciplinary machinery, but also as a powerful source of pleasure, resistance and rebellion.
>
> (Smith, 2002: 197)

Clearly, food must be understood as involving far more than just nutrition in this context. Food habits and etiquette are cultural variables; the food you eat communicates something about who you are and to which community you belong: what you could, following Barthes (1961), call the place a particular dish has in food's cultural system of signs. The fact that food is a sign means that food can be understood as functional units in a cultural communication structure. This is true for all food. Even the most ordinary and seemingly banal portion of porridge communicates something about the person who is eating it and connects them to a larger context, for example, in the case of porridge,[8] to "the Norwegian", healthy and unaffected:

> A vitamin pill has as many meanings as a portion of foie gras. A slice of brown bread just as many as an entrecôte of Japanese Kobe beef from oxen fed on beer, massaged to be soft and tender, and brushed with sake. It is not that we do not just live by bread alone, but that the bread is already more than bread. Not to mention the wine.
>
> (Stene-Johansen, 2007: 11, my translation)

The heavy symbolic weight of food means that it can be used as markers of difference and community. The ways in which groups of people eat, how they get and prepare their food, and how they structure a meal provide opportunities to create internal similarities and external differences; in short, group identity. The individual can be part of a large unit, and the larger unit can distinguish itself from other larger units (Fischler, 1988). In other words, food practices are not simply a result of biological necessity; food marks boundaries between social classes, geographical areas, nations, cultures, genders, life phases and religions. Food also marks the division between ordinary days and celebrations, the passing of the seasons, and thus the months, and what time of the day it is. Food habits are used to establish and symbolise control over your own body. Therefore, a simple meal conveys meaning on a number of different levels (Lupton, 2005; Brownlie and Hewer, 2007).

Food practices are also described as important to our self-understanding and perception of *being in the world* as a body (Smith, 2002). Food helps to tie the perception of being a subject to the perception of having a body. The relationship to food can, therefore, also be understood from a gender perspective. Various food practices are often associated with femininity in Western cultures. In her study from a women's prison, Smith (2002) views food as a lost opportunity to do femininity. Given that food shopping and preparation have traditionally been women's work, and since female prisoners usually do not have an opportunity to make their own food, they lose the opportunity to practise this traditional women's work, which is experienced as an extra *pain of imprisonment* on top of what Sykes describes.

This corresponds with what we know about the gender division of labour in Norwegian homes. According to Døving (2003), the reports of the Norwegian man's entrance into the kitchen are exaggerated. Olsen and Aarseth (2006) come to the same conclusion. Although this appears to be changing, making food is still one of the more gender-divided duties in the home, along with maintenance/decorating and clothes washing. In other words, cooking (at least everyday food) is, now as before, albeit to a smaller degree than previously, the woman's responsibility. What may perhaps have changed is that more people accept that it does not have to be this way. In those families who are most equal in this area, food is used as part of a strategy to "get the family to sit down together" – the shared daily meal is a shared project for both the mother and the father. In such a context, cooking can be used to position yourself as "the good, equal husband/partner" and "the good father". The problem is time: when fathers are also partly responsible for meals, the time crunch also impacts them that bit harder. Therefore, a number of Olsen and Aarseth's informants associated cooking with a bad conscience.

Fürst (1993, 1997) takes the responsibility for making and serving food within the family as her starting point for discussing what characterises a distinctive female rationality. The woman's role in the family's division of labour, involving (primary) responsibility for buying, cooking and serving food, contributes to a distinctive female rationality that focuses on care and responsibility for the health and enjoyment of the members of the family. At the heart of this is the experience of being a mother and the relationship between mother and child. This relationship is communicated by and constructed through food: first through breastfeeding and then through packed lunches and making dinner for the nuclear family. The female rationality that springs from cooking is, therefore, associated with a physical experience of being a mother that is exclusive to women. The traditional female role's responsibility for cooking combines two sources of human vitality: food and love. The fact that the relationship with the mother who cooks is also a form of power relationship is one of Døving's main points.

The question, then, is: what does it take to make it possible for "traditional woman's duties" to be used to do masculinity in a man's prison? Can what Fürst discusses as "authentic female practice" be used in male prisoners' resistance work? What contextual adaptations are required in these circumstances to position the apparently "equal" practices in a "male ratio-nality"? The goal below is to try to analyse the prisoners' food practices as a tool in the male prisoners' work on resisting, and renegotiating their position in relation to, the challenge the status of prisoner entails.

The official prison food

The rules concerning prisoners' diets are described in very brief terms in the *Regulations to the Execution of Sentences Act.*[9] They contain one prohibition and one right. The use and storage of dietary supplements are not permitted, except when such supplements are prescribed by a medical practitioner. And the prisoners shall have an opportunity to purchase food and drink and toilet articles at least once a week (section 3–23). Otherwise they refer to the current regulations at any given time.

This is gone into in more detail in the guidelines.[10] These state that "Every prisoner in Norwegian prisons shall be able to eat their fill of ordinary, good, nutritionally correct food. [...] It is up to the people responsible for the kitchen to present a diet that satisfies these requirements" (2.2). The daily fare is defined as "ordinary fare that corresponds to the fare the population eats every day". This is not specified in more detail, other than that dinner shall consist of a main course as well as a starter or dessert, that the main course shall, for nutritional reasons, be fish at least twice a week, that there shall be access to several types of bread and grain combinations in connec-tion with sandwich meals (which are breakfast, lunch and supper), and that prisoners shall, insofar as it is possible, be able to choose their fillings them-selves. Where this is not possible, the chef is responsible for ensuring the prisoners eat a varied diet. In addition to the *daily fare*, it is possible to have a *special diet* for health reasons and an *alternative diet* due to your beliefs. These must be identical in terms of nutritional content, portion size and variation.

What constitutes nutritionally correct food is described in some detail. Based on the nutrition policy recommended by the Norwegian National Nutrition Council, the guidelines describe the recommended total daily energy intake (12 MJ) and the diet's composition (10–15 per cent protein, 30 per cent fat and 55–60 per cent carbohydrates).

The guidelines are addressed primarily to kitchen staff in the country's prisons (as well as external suppliers who deliver the food). These are pro-fessional chefs who are assumed to have a good understanding of food tables, food hygiene and energy content measures in MJ. The focus is on the health aspect: the food offered should be healthy and nutritious. Healthiness constitutes quality; other dimensions that are often used to describe food like taste and aesthetics are absent, apart from the vague term "god kost". "God" literally translates as good, but in the context it means something between real and regular. "Kost" means fare. Prison fare, then, is supposed to be regular, in contrast to gourmet food, and real, in contrast to junk food. The choice of words also underlines the fact that the food is supposed to be "good enough", a kind of food suitable for a prison, not a hotel or restaurant.[11]

The main goal of the guidelines appears to be to make the kitchen staff responsible in relation to the effect they have on the prisoners' health situation as far as diet is concerned. The Norwegian Correctional Services Central Administration has thus delegated some of the responsibility for the prisoners' health to the prison chef, and at the same time covered its back: if the professional chef does as the guidelines prescribe, the prisoners should have nothing to complain about; they will be served a generally good, nutritious diet. The need for food in a nutritional sense is thus acknowledged, as are special medical needs. The prison will also take account of religion and ethical views. Otherwise, the food's non-nutritional aspects are not a priority.

Since Oslo Prison does not have a kitchen, all the food is produced by a local hospital kitchen and delivered daily to the prison. Once here, it is distributed to the individual wings by prisoners who are assigned to work "in the kitchen". Dinner arrives on the wing, via the lift, in stainless steel food containers; each element of the meal (usually potatoes, meat/fish, vegetables and sauce) is in separate containers. The trustees on each wing are then responsible for placing the containers in specially constructed steel counters on wheels that keep the food warm, dishing up the food for each prisoner, and delivering the plates to the individual cells. Dinner is served at 2.30. The sandwiches have by then already been distributed to the cells in the morning. The trustees load another trolley with bread, milk, hot water and sandwich fillings. Each prisoner is given a sliced brown or white loaf, today's fillings and half a litre of semi-skimmed milk. He also gets a thermos filled with hot water at the same time.

Apart from wanting a special or alternative diet, as described in the guidelines, the prisoners have no influence over the food they receive. You get the dinner or fillings you get, without advance notice. There are no facilities for the prisoners to make their own food and they basically eat every meal alone in their cell.

Given that the prisoners have no form of influence concerning what they are served or what fillings they get, the all too predictable result is that large quantities of food are thrown away. Some eat half of the dinners they are served. A small number eat (almost) all of the meals and think the food is okay. However, the common line is that the food is disgusting and many throw all the dinner and most of the fillings they receive straight into the rubbish. The prison administration is aware of this problem, but cannot see how anything can be done about it. As one of the officers said: *After all, we have to ensure that everyone gets a minimum, the same. Everyone is going to get what they are entitled to.* And if everyone is going to get what they are entitled to, you have to live with a lot being thrown away.

The food's role as a general fundamental right, *the only thing they cannot take away from us*, helps to emphasise that the prisoners are a uniform group. The food is the same for everyone; the prison cannot make exceptions. In relation to the official food, the prisoners are positioned precisely as just that, prisoners, with no autonomy, people who have to accept what they get, what the trustees give them, with no right of appeal. Being able to decide what you eat and when, being able to decide not to eat up, is part of being an adult. Thus, the food is part of the general tendency to infantilise the prisoners, with the prison as the guardian who feeds you at specific times and who decides what is on the menu.

However, those who want some say over their diet have, as the regulations also stipulate, an opportunity to purchase their own food from the prison store once a week. Every Sunday the prisoners have to give the officers a list of what they want. The store has placed lists in every cell of all the goods available; the product range is reminiscent of a small Norwegian grocery store. The goods arrive on the wing on Monday in a large number of white plastic bags, each with a cell number written on it in black marker pen. The officers go through the bags and check the contents match the orders before delivering the bags to the cells. Remand prisoners usually have access to their own money while they are on remand. Nonetheless, a shopping limit of NOK 850 (or roughly £85) per week has been set for practical reasons. As well as food, drinks and toiletries, this is also meant to cover phone cards for the prison phone and cigarettes, two major items of expenditure for most prisoners. Goods that are not available through the shop include, naturally enough, beer, sugar and yeast. The latter two could be used to produce alcoholic beverages in the cells. There are restrictions on alcohol-containing aftershave for the same reason.

It is no exaggeration to say that the official food is massively unpopular with the prisoners. When you ask the prisoners what they think of the prison, what they would change, or what they most look forward to about being transferred or released, the first thing they mention, almost without exception, is the poor food. Even though better food is not officially one of the institution's rewards upon progression to a better prison regime for good behaviour, the opportunity to cook your own food is the first thing the prisoners highlight when they are going to be transferred. As in the extract when Sabri had just learned that his application for a transfer from Oslo Prison to Ullersmo Prison had been granted:

> Finally, Thomas! I'm finally moving to Ullersmo! I'm really looking forward to it. Fuck, it will be brilliant! I've got loads of mates who I know are doing their time there. They have told me loads about Ullersmo. I can't wait to see them again. Whichever wing I end up on, I have old friends up there. I can finally start my sentence! I'm having steak tonight. I've

really missed being able to cook my own food. Fuck, a bloody steak will be really good!

In other words, food as a "reward" lives on in some sense; looking forward to moving to another prison also means looking forward to being able to cook your own food.

The prisoner officers' food

When the prisoners are locked in their cells in the middle of the day it is time for the officers' lunch. As at any other workplace, the officers gather on the sofas and chairs around the coffee table at the back of the officers' room on the third floor. Against one wall is a kitchenette with a fridge, cooker, and shelves and drawers with everything you would expect in a kitchen. On another wall hang thank you cards from staff who have got married, postcards from colleagues on holiday, and photos from the last summer party, as well as the coffee list. The officers' room is divided in two. The front part, closest to the rest of the wing, is for work and has a PC, phones, a board containing information about all the prisoners and so on; the inner part, where lunch is eaten, is for breaks. Officers from both wings, other staff, like those who work on the so-called youth team assigned to the wing, and staff from other wings who are visiting all gather round the table. There are usually 10–15 people around the table at lunch, sharing a daily meal. The prisoners do not have access to this gathering.

True to tradition, most of the officers bring food from home. Døving (2003) describes how the packed lunch is a central element of the Norwegian national narrative. This is also the case in Oslo Prison; the packed lunch still holds a strong position, as in most Norwegian workplaces. Lunch can also be bought from the prison's canteen. Most return from here with rolls and portion packets of sandwich fillings. Even though the food is bought on site and not packed in sandwich paper, it would be true to say that for most officers their daily lunch consists of fairly healthy, simple, tasty and filling sandwiches.

As the week goes by, this sometimes changes. It is not unusual for the officers to indulge in a little taste of the weekend towards the end of the week. The officers pool their resources before lunch and send someone to the nearest shop outside the prison to buy for everyone. She (as a rule is it is a female officer who assumes/is given responsibility for the practical aspects of shared lunches) returns with fresh rolls, beef burgers and bacon and egg for everyone, and gets to work in the kitchenette. These shared meals create a good, easy-going atmosphere; you are allowed to indulge yourself a little sometimes, are you not? The aroma of freshly fried burgers fills the wing while the rest of the officers lock the prisoners in as they arrive back from school or work.

When the weekend finally arrives in the prison, the officers' menu changes radically. Gone are the sensible packed lunches; a completely different set of rules applies from Friday to Sunday. The officers are divided into weekend teams who regularly work the weekends together. The weekend teams often have set dishes for the different days. When Friday arrives, the designated person brings a bag of ready-to-cook dough in their backpack and the pizza is on its way. Typical weekend dishes include, besides pizza, tacos and lasagne – according to Døving (2007), the typical working-class indulgences in Norway. The range of tasty dishes helps to mimic the weekend outside. They are dishes that at some point in the 1970s and 1980s earned the label "exotic", but which have now become popular indulgences and been transformed in the Norwegian context in a way that long ago removed any distinctive power from the dishes. The pizza in prison is the Norwegian type: a thick crust, roasting pan pizza; the sort that has so many toppings you have to eat it with a knife and fork. The wafer-thin, Italian, stone oven-baked type with the characteristic aftertaste of burned flour is not to be found in Oslo Prison. The following extract from my fieldwork diary serves to illustrate the mood on Saturdays:

> Arrive on Saturday; the officers are nearing the end of their big Saturday dinner. A half full ovenproof dish with burritos reigns in the middle of the table, flanked by various taco sauces, sour cream and a big bowl of salad. Everyone is leaning back, stuffed, full of food. They offer me some, but I decline. There is loads of food left. Otherwise the wing is quiet; the prisoners are locked in. The mood is good.

According to Roos and Wandel (2005), while weekday food is positioned in a context of routine and the necessary intake of energy, without wasting time, different rules apply when the weekend arrives. At the weekend you are allowed to indulge yourself a bit, in this case eat more unhealthy "weekend food", assuming that you deserve it, of course. This is absolutely typical; for most people Friday represents the transition between moderation during the week and the weekend's (controlled) excesses (Døving, 2003). Weekend food becomes the inversion of weekday food, marking that the weekend has finally arrived. And when the weekend arrives, it is time to "indulge ourselves". Showing restraint means torpedoing the weekend and the associated festivities; withdrawing from the "we" that is constituted by the indulgence. Abundance and comfort are keywords for working-class meals, writes Fürst (1993) with reference to Bourdieu, and especially in the case of men's meals, in contrast to the bourgeoisie's more controlled and stylised food. Weekend food forms part of a morality of pleasure – where the weekend, the time for enjoyment, *will* be enjoyed – in contrast to a morality of duty with greater contrast between the good and the pleasurable. The officers, who work every third weekend, make a big effort not to miss this indulgence, and by extension the weekend feeling, even if they have to re-create it at work in the prison. From this perspective, this re-creation of the weekend at work helps to connect the officers with life outside; working while others are off is made a little less painful if, insofar as it is possible, you mimic having time off.

The prisoners are not particularly thrilled about the officers' regular weekend parties. For those who have just been served porridge or fish pudding by a trustee, the aroma of Friday pizza is perceived as a direct provocation:

> I am sitting with Erol chatting over a cup of coffee in his cell. The delicious aroma of food wafts into us through the half-open cell door. Erol shakes his head.
>
> Erol: They don't think about the fact that there is a life after death, that there is a God. They don't think about the fact that they will have to take responsibility for everything they've done at some point. They sit there, gorging themselves, and we have to make do with the smell and slices of dry bread. Oh, well. I have lived well; I have eaten out a lot, at restaurants no officers can afford to go to. But they will have to take responsibility for that one day. That's the way it is. Well, Thomas. Life is good!

Erol took the opportunity to rewrite the problem in religious terms. At the same time, it was clear yet again that prison officers are just that, prisoner officers, people who can never have tasted the good life, given the poor wages they earn. This narrative is about the notion that, while the prisoners have lived lives of excitement and luxury, the officers did poorly at school; they tried, but failed, to get into the Norwegian Police University College and, therefore, had to settle for being prison officers. They are just "ordinary people", while the prisoners are extraordinary, criminal adventurers.

For Adem, the delightful aroma of food coming from the officers' room was not about God's righteous anger on judgement day; it was about people's unfairness in the here and now. He became so irritated that he went into the officers' room to say so:

> Adem: Are you really allowed to cook food in here?
>
> Officer: What?
>
> Adem: It smells so good, waffles and that, you make lots of food here, it makes us crave waffles.
>
> Officer: You should have thought of that before! Of course we are allowed to, after all, we work here. It's not me that is in prison, Adem, heh heh.

Later, in the cell, when we were far out of the range of the officers' hearing, he complained to me:

> Fuck, they are so horrible, I mean, the whole wing smells of pizza and stuff. Every weekend, every Friday! And we get nothing! It just pisses you right off! They are so fucking stingy!

Erol and Adem were not the only ones who complained. Towards the end of my fieldwork one of the prisoners, "on behalf of many", went to the wing's managers to discuss the problem of the tantalising aroma of food. An officer later told me the outcome:

> Officer: Yeah, heh heh, he tried that one on. […] But he might as well just forget about it; the employees' working environment takes precedence over the inmates' wishes, that's how it has to be. He will just have to live with the smell of the food. A 12 hour weekend shift and you're not supposed to be able to make yourself some food?
>
> TU: But, I mean, the aroma of delicious food must be frustrating?
>
> Officer: Of course. But he will just have to live with it. In other places inmates are able to make their own food; can't do that here, we don't have the room. There are too many of them. That's just the way it has to be.

Other prisons, and also other wings in Oslo Prison, often have a shared kitchen and long table for shared meals. However, this is not the case in wings four and five. There are a number of reasons for this, some of them due to the building itself and staffing levels. There are so many prisoners in wings four and five that the prison, from a control and security perspective, would have to have far more officers at work than normal in order to let everyone out at the same time. Nevertheless, this has consequences for the interaction on the wing.

What the prisoners, who have to make do with their ordinary, good fare, find frustrating is, for the officers, simply part of the natural order of things. The "food apartheid" that plays out on the wing when the weekend comes around therefore helps to mark the boundary between frustrated prisoners, who see it as yet another sign of the unfair System, and officers, who view the prisoners' protests as yet another sign either that the prisoners are attempting to manipulate them or that they lack a fundamental understanding of the world around them. From this perspective, the officers' food underscores the difference between those who work in the prison and those who live there. When the prisoners point out the perceived injustice, the officers shake their heads at being held to the same standard as the prisoners: *Come on, they have to understand that there is a difference between inmates and staff.* Because there is, and there will be, not least through different access to weekend delicacies.

Secret prison food

Holm and Smidt (1993) describe, in their analysis of food practices in a children's cancer ward, a reality that in some areas is reminiscent of prison. Meals were eaten in the individual's room, in isolation. Holm and Smidt believe the hospital's architects may simply have completely forgotten about meals, since there was no special room for eating. The patients' meals are not a priority; meals must be eaten wherever possible. They describe how mothers despaired when they saw that their children would not eat the food the hospital had to offer. For a while. They soon began to cook their own food for their children instead, either at home or in one of the small kitchenettes in the hospital. The situation is similar in Oslo Prison.

The prisoners' alternative, secret cooking can be described as falling into one of three categories: (1) cooking the prison's rules allow prisoners to do (i.e. practices that do not break the rules), (2) a grey zone where officers would probably intervene if they became aware of specific instances, but which they do not regard as serious and therefore does not entail a particularly big risk for the prisoners or (3) a more serious breach of the culinary rules, which, were it to be discovered, would result in the prisoner being disciplined, moved to a more restrictive wing, and a report going into their file that would follow them throughout their imprisonment.

The first category involves adapting and modifying the official food to make it more edible. Most prisoners use the shopping scheme to build up an abundant selection of different seasonings that they can use to improve the official food (or parts of it) to make it more like the meals with which they are familiar. The shelves above the cell's desk will be full of bottles of olive oil and vinegar, jars of olives in brine, various spices, such as cumin, ginger and garlic, the ubiquitous tins of tuna, and often a jar of Vegeta.[12] On the window sill will be a bag of the week's purchased fruit and vegetables, such as onion, cucumber, tomatoes and oranges for freshly squeezed juice. On the bottom shelf of the cupboard will stand jars of different Uncle Ben's sauces; even though they are, of course, viewed as cheap imitations, they at least have a certain familial likeness to mum's curry. In the fridge there will be margarine, as a rule far too much, since few prisoners manage to eat all they are given, as well as slices of Norvegia (a common Norwegian yellow cheese), eggs, coke and mackerel in tomato sauce. The standard equipment in a cell includes a thermos of hot water, one plate, one glass, one cup, all made of plastic, a butter knife, a spoon and a fork. These are the resources the prisoners have at their disposal for their project of changing the Norwegian food they are served into something that is closer to what they are used to and which is, therefore, more edible.

I am hanging out with Florin from Romania. It is pleasant, as always. While we chat he starts preparing his evening meal. On the desk there is a paper bowl containing the cooked pieces of carrot from the day's dinner. He smiles and nods towards the rubbish bin where the rest of dinner is. He opens a box of tuna in water, drains the water off into the sink, and breaks the tuna into pieces over the carrots. Next he generously seasons with ground cumin, chopped garlic in oil from the fridge, and salt and pepper. Finally the dish is topped with a spoonful of tomato purée, which is then mixed in. The tuna salad is left on the desk for a couple of hours so the tastes can marinate. Later, when he dishes up a plate for each of us, he smiles, pleased with the result.

Florin: About the food, it's not that I want to break any rules, you know? I just want to survive. You have to do something to survive in this place.

Florin's cooking can be compared to the work of a professional chef in the same way as the bricoleur can be compared to the engineer in Lévi-Strauss' classic work *The Savage Mind* (1966). The bricoleur, a jack of all trades or "trickster of all trades" as a true craftsman would call him, works in untraditional ways with what he has to hand. He does not have access to all the ingredients or tools in the world, but must manage with what is available: a universe of opportunities that is a mixture of many things, since his toolbox is a result of circumstance and his ability to renew and enrich his stock. For the bricoleur, every object may be of use in the future. You never know what jobs will turn up. Armed with creativity, a solution-oriented approach and an arsenal of hoarded gadgets, leftover parts and out-of-date materials, the amateur bricoleur gets to work and finds an improvised solution. From this perspective, the bricoleur puts key masculine values to work. With MacGyver as a role model, he is a bricoleur *man*; always exhibiting the capacity, creativity and ability to transform his surroundings and make the best of the situation has masculine connotations.

It was this bricolage logic Florin put to work when he picked all the filaments out of an old washing up brush and used it as a whisk, and it was the same logic that was being applied when Tarik took a shelf, turned it upside down, put it on his bed and used it as a cutting board. You use what you have; the bricoleur's culinary arts require creativity under difficult circumstances, both when it comes to procuring and preparing ingredients and when it comes to the constant development of new tools. Adil put it like this:

> You have to do something, be creative, make something, otherwise you would starve Thomas. It's impossible; I eat dinner one or two days a week, maybe, the rest is inedible. It's not food. So if you don't want to die, you have to be a bit creative, do something with the awful things you have been given.

At this basic level, cooking is primarily about making the inedible edible and simultaneously being able to assume the position of a creative person who is mastering a difficult situation.

At the next level, food preparation becomes more advanced. The next step is to use heat in your cooking. In this grey zone, vis-à-vis the prison's rules, it is possible to heat food with the desk lamp or ceiling lamp. A 60-watt bulb generates enough warmth to heat up an already fried chicken to something approaching a proper temperature, given enough time. It works far better than warming up chicken in a plastic bag immersed in hot water in the sink, which raises its temperature to just above body temperature, but, of course, the rules do not really permit lamp warming for fire safety reasons. However, if you wait until the officers have left for the day and the prison is in night-time mode, then a lot would have to go wrong for you to be discovered. Many prisoners feel confident enough about using this method that they use it during the day as well.

Lamp-warmed food is warm, but not *very* warm. And a lamp does not enable you to boil or fry. This is difficult to achieve, and prisoners are pro-hibited from doing it. But it is not impossible. The third level of secret cooking involves methods for heating, boiling and frying food in the cells that involve more direct breaches of the rules, with the associated greater risk for the prisoners.

The camping stove variant from the officers' stories about *the crazy prisoner* who fries pigeons does occur, but is uncommon. Naked flames are problem-atic since they trigger the cell's fire alarm. If you use margarine as a fuel, for example, it produces a lot of soot and really smells. The smell easily disperses through the wing, making it difficult to get away with it. Prisoners caught with naked flames are immediately excluded from socials and often eventu-ally transferred to a more restrictive wing. Therefore, the various home-made kettle solutions are more subtle. There are a handful of designs that all, in the best tradition of bricolage, involve transforming freely available tools and resources into electric cooking appliances that can be used to make simple dishes like boiled rice, pasta and casseroles like *chilli con carne*. With further upgrades, the cooking appliance can also produce a surface hot enough to fry on – at least hot enough for a fried egg or an omelette. At this third level the prisoners can achieve most of what you can achieve in an ordi-nary kitchen; one even showed me how he managed to make pasta dishes with an "oven-baked" texture and taste. I cannot, for research ethics reasons, describe in more detail what these appliances consist of or how they are made or concealed. Suffice it to say that such solutions are not particularly uncommon on the wing. The officers are aware that these things happen. Occasionally, they find and confiscate such an appliance, but as a rule they do not find them.

How should one understand the prisoners' distaste for the official food? Are they being picky and difficult, or is the "hospital food" they are served really that bad? Or are there alternative interpretations on levels other than the individual's tastes? And what benefits do all the various forms of more or less secret alternative cooking provide?

Food and resistance to the Norwegian prison

The food guidelines describe the food prisoners should receive as "ordinary fare that corresponds to the fare the population eats every day". In these globalised times with immigration, mass tourism and food programmes on TV from every corner of the world, the "fare the population eats every day" has become more complex than before. It is now more difficult to identify a "pure" Norwegian food culture. The food we eat is heavily and increasingly influenced by a number of different traditions. What were once exotic dishes have transformed into today's popular food in shop freezers everywhere in a way that means the space for what is defined as exotic must constantly be refilled with new dishes in order to maintain its distinction value (Bourdieu, 1984). This is resulting in every food culture being influenced by trends that create complex, previously undreamed-of relationships that cross old boundaries; as part of a global "creolised" food culture (James, 2005), one could say that the food we eat has been hybridised. All the ingredients in the world are available everywhere, year round, in a way that has dislocated what we eat from time and space. What was once reserved for the very richest, such as expensive spices, is now available to everyone.

Nonetheless, from the perspective of a specific food tradition, for example Norwegian cuisine, it would be right to say that some foods seem more "foreign" than others. Using such a scale, the food served in Oslo Prison can be described as very Norwegian and not very hybridised. In relation to Barthes' (1961) ideas about food's system of signs, one can say that the food that is served is largely of the kind that could be used to represent Norway without much difficulty. Porridge and fish balls, meat, sauce and potatoes, smoked haddock and a half litre of milk a day; this is traditional Norwegian food, what parents, grandparents and other ancestors have subsisted on for generations, at least if we are to believe our popular notions of the past.

What identifies Norwegian food as Norwegian? Rozin and Rozin (2005) ask the same question about Mexican food and conclude, unsurprisingly, that the distinguishing Mexican feature is the presence of chillies of every imaginable colour, shape, strength and flavour. The Rozins extrapolate this and conclude that a particular food culture is recognised by the combination of a few characteristic ingredients that leave their mark on an entire food tradition. They call this the food culture's flavour principles. Different flavour principles help to provide a clear, characteristic identity to dishes that belong to a specific cuisine. The Southern Italian use of garlic, basil and olive oil is another example. These three ingredients help to make a specific dish recognisably Southern Italian, even if in reality the specific dish does not exclusively consist of traditional ingredients or has not been prepared in traditional ways. Why have these flavour principles come about? Why do people season their food? One explanation could be that traditional taste combinations may have something of the same effect as traditional folk costumes and traditional religious practices; they help to define and provide self-understanding for a delineated group, to individuals who are members of that group, and to distinguish the group from other groups. Flavour principles, therefore, function as boundary markers.

The traditional Norwegian flavour principle can be described through two typical ingredients; potatoes and milk. Døving (2003) describes "the Norwegian" and the potato as being strongly associated with each other. This association also provides meaning in prison – it is so strong that the word "potato" can actually be used synonymously with "Norwegian". And not without reason: peeled, boiled potatoes are, of course, included in the vast majority of dinners. They are accompanied by boiled, mixed vegetables, as a rule overcooked and soft, a piece of meat or fish, and sauce. Because they are made in a big institutional kitchen, the potatoes are usually steam cooked and then reheated later, which gives them a characteristic chewy surface. The meat or fish, the part of the meal that in a Norwegian context constitutes the central, defining element, is often a mixed product like meat patties or fish pudding.

The daily glass of fresh milk is as ubiquitous as the potato. According to Lyngø (2007), the narrative of Norwegians as a milk-drinking people was created in the interwar period. A large information and promotional campaign presented milk as the healthiest of all foods; each drop was full of health and milk was the "path to a healthy country". From a drink for children or an ingredient, milk was reconstructed as a drink for the entire Norwegian people.[13] The campaign was so successful that, if Barthes (1973) is correct that wine is a French *totem drink* that symbolises and defines "the French", the same can be said about the role of milk in Norway.

James (2005) theorises the relationship between food habits and cultural identity: the construction of the notion that "in our culture this is what we eat". And, conversely, if you do not eat this, then you are not part of our culture. We eat pork, they do not. They eat grasshoppers, we do not. Notions of what counts as food, and what cannot be eaten, create dividing lines between people. However, today things have become a bit more complicated. Increased immigration into Norwegian is bringing with it a people who, for example, are not used to drinking milk. According to Mysterud (2007), adults who drink milk are an exception and can only be found among ethnic Europeans and some African tribes. People of another ethnic origin often have problems digesting lactose and are therefore milk intolerant. This applies to a large proportion of the prisoners in wings four and five at any given time. The role of milk as the Norwegian totem drink can, therefore, be understood as a notion that helps to define a large proportion of Norwegian citizens as being excluded from "the Norwegian". The idea of Norway as the country of milk excludes people in a totally specific, physical way.

We have thereby made room for one interpretation of the prisoners' dissatisfaction with the food. Compared with the hybrid meal patterns outside the walls, the ordinary good food on the inside seems dated. The food being served can be described as a 1950s diet from the country of milk; to the average prisoners this food is cheap, tasteless, watery and unpleasant. As Fariz says when the trustee brings his dinner plate to his cell:

> [Sigh] I never eat potatoes on the outside. And I can't eat them now at all; I'm so sick of them. I'll never eat another fucking potato as long as I live!

Potatoes represent "the Norwegian"; the reluctance to eat potatoes, porridge and fish pudding can be interpreted as disliking boring, tasteless and over-cooked food, but also "the Norwegian" and Norway, and, by extension, dislike of the Norwegian prison that serves them. The prison food positions a very large proportion of the prisoners as *foreigners*, without admittance to "the Norwegian". The food they do not like underscores their ascribed positions as unwanted and far from home. In general, the reaction to unfamiliar food from a foreign food culture will in some way or other balance between curiosity, excitement and aversion. But in prison, of course, more is at risk, since the unfamiliar Norwegian food becomes part of the prisoners' under-standing of the institution that is offering it. Prison food is prison food, representative of the rest of the institution; the result is that any evaluation of the food starts from a position that leans in the direction of unpleasant and inedible.

The 1950s food from the country of milk evokes resistance in most prison-ers. Some feel that giving everyone a carton of semi-skimmed milk every day is almost a form of provocation: *What am I supposed to do with it? Milk is for Norwegians and calves!* In this way, distaste for one group's food is used to dis-tance oneself from the group; food and food habits become distinguishing tools (Bourdieu, 1984). Intolerance and aversion are strong things – the nau-seating milk represents the nauseating Norwegian System. But some know what to do: the bricoleur can transform the Norwegian semi-skimmed milk into yoghurt and fresh cheese:

> I have seen several Eastern Europeans enjoy home-made fresh cheese together in socials. A used Norwegian cheese wrapping filled with home-made cheese is passed around the table; everyone takes a piece with their fingers and enjoys it. They lick their lips and smile. I later ask Erol how they do it. He tells me. You heat up the milk to boiling point and cool it down. Then you let the milk stand at room temperature for a while (about a week). During that time, you skim off the water that collects above the cheese mass and season with salt. Finally, you strain the cheese mass using a clean t-shirt. The cheese mass is then allowed to stand for a bit longer, and the cheese is ready.
>
> Erol: It's not as good with semi-skimmed milk, but it's okay. After all, the most important thing is to have a project. It's almost like a hobby because it takes several days and involves lots of small tasks.

The surplus milk that many do not like or cannot drink, therefore, becomes instead an opportunity, a chance to *do* a disidentification position whereby one's own abilities and own food culture step into the foreground in front of the status of prisoner. "The Norwegian", sturdy and boring are thus made familiar and understandable in relation to one's own flavour principles, and at the same time, yet again, one has an opportunity to prove that one can master the difficult conditions the prison throws up. Food preparation becomes a form of resistance to the Norwegian food that is served to them in the Norwegian prison and, by extension, resistance to "the Norwegian" more generally.

Food-related constitution of camaraderie and differences

Simmel (1997) assigns the sense of taste and eating a special position in relation to the senses and human activities in general because they are based on the person as an individual, separate from all other people. What I can see I can point out to others; what I think I can (try to) communicate to others; what I eat, *precisely* what I eat, no one else is able to eat. Simmel believes that people's relationship with food is, therefore, fundamentally self-centred. A meal's social and socialising power fools us into overlooking this. Eating together allows us to ignore the fact that we are not eating "the same things". Meals create solidarity and a sense of immediacy. Ochs and Taylor (1993) view meals as a social arena for problem solving and constructing a sense of family. "The family", as experienced camaraderie, is created around the table by eating, drinking and talking together.

The prisoners in wings four and five have basically lost the opportunity to create such mealtime camaraderie. The prison appears to want individuals who eat, who consume nutrition, not a group of prisoners who share a meal. For their part, the prisoners try, as best they can, to reinstitute mealtime camaraderie with their more or less secret, alternative food. Every second day, when the prisoners can hang out together, they can visit each other in their cells, two at a time, for an hour. It is not unusual for a group of prisoners to buy a little extra evening food on such occasions. One is responsible for preparing the food, which is then shared when they are let out and allowed to hang out together. The two prisoners hanging out together can therefore enjoy the food together in the closest they get to mealtime camaraderie.

First, this creates a group feeling. The prisoners get together as prisoners who can achieve despite the restrictions: *We are not like the other prisoners, just look at what we can achieve. Things aren't that bad for us after all.* This camaraderie can also be associated with a hierarchy among the participants. For example, some are better at preparing food than others, and this, therefore, creates relationships between experts and novices, as when Youssuf is visited by a younger fellow prisoner who wants to learn the art of making food in your cell:

> Youssuf scurries around in the limited space, cutting vegetables with prac-
> tised movements, grinning, humming, whistling, and enjoying being at
> the centre of events. Being able to prepare a good meal in these surround-
> ings is obviously an asset. His younger fellow prisoner can't do it, but he
> wants to learn. Youssuf regularly turns and demonstrates what he is doing;
> we are the two apprentices observing the master.
> Youssuf: A bit of this [stock] in the rice. But just a bit! It's quite salty, you
>   mustn't add too much.
> Like the TV chefs, he wants to make it easy to follow each part of the
> process. We sit quietly and follow what he's doing as best we can.

Such mealtime camaraderie can also be intertwined with other experienced
camaraderie in prison; for example, food can be a way of *doing religion and
culture*. The mealtime camaraderie thus simultaneously becomes a shared
religious and cultural experience. Food and food habits may play central
roles in situations involving migration and minority status (Beyers, 2008).
There are examples of food habits being sustained and used as identity markers long after a group's original language has disappeared. When the eater
incorporates a food by eating, he simultaneously incorporates himself into a
culture and, thus, a community of people who eat this. But, if food can create
feelings of equality and camaraderie, it can also create differences. In order
to be inclusive, a thing must at the same time exclude those who will not be
included. One example of this is the difference between the smart prisoners
who manage to influence their difficult situation and the others, the weak
prisoners, who are under the power of the prison and unable to do anything
about it. As Erol says: "There are not many others who could have managed
this under these difficult conditions. I am not like the other prisoners, you
know?" Anyone can complain about the food, but only a few will manage
to do something about it, and Erol is one of them.

Sharing the benefits, which above was placed in the context of constituting a community, also has (often simultaneously) a difference-creating
component, as when Erol, responding to my resistance to getting the largest
piece of chicken, told me to shut up and eat. This generous attitude can
be read in the context of a narrative about the honour associated with the
position of *giver*. Giving away food is a practice that positions the giver as
someone who is able to give. Conversely, being unable to serve your guests
anything is embarrassing. This is a duty that Døving primarily describes as
feminine, but being unable to serve something can also be a challenge to
masculinity. Mauss (1954) views the relationship between gift giving and
honour as absolutely key. A clan chief's personal prestige and the prestige
of his entire clan are dependent on the gifts he gives. In some contexts this

involves being the most unrestrained spendthrift. The chief must give to remain on top, not to lose face. Giving means manifesting your superiority, being more, higher; to accept without giving anything in return is to submit, to become small, of lower rank (Mauss, 1954). Note how Daniel emphasises the value of being able to treat someone and condemns concealing food in the anecdote below:

> Daniel and I are sitting in his cell. The subject turns to the trustee upstairs, but I notice that Daniel is reluctant to talk about him.
>
> Daniel: I don't talk to him any more.
>
> TU: Why not?
>
> Daniel: Because he held back food so he would get more. He doesn't give people equal amounts; he makes sure there is always some left over. If you go to him and ask if there are more potatoes, for example, he says there aren't any more. But there are more, in his cell. It's the same with milk; one lad went and asked for more, he said there wasn't any. Later I saw him carrying two cartons into his cell. He is a bad trustee. I share what I have; when I cook, everyone gets a taste. I've shared with him. I bought the stuff with my own money. If I can do it, why can't he share out the prison food fairly? It's not right. That's why I've stopped talking to him. Nothing, not hello, nothing. That's the way I am. If you are stingy then I will have nothing more to do with you. That doesn't mean I'll go to the officers. I won't tell everyone either. If you want to be a jerk, be a jerk. That's your choice. But I won't tell everyone about it – we're not women! That's a saying where I come from: after all we are not women! You know how women are, they gossip about everything.

Treating others (either fellow prisoners or visiting researchers) can also be understood as creating a difference. The generous person creates a difference between those who can afford to treat someone and those who can only receive. At the same time, gift giving can be understood as an opportunity to position yourself as a real man, while not giving, or, even worse, acquiring something illegitimately, can be dishonourable, at least when it is fellow prisoners one is depriving and not the prison. The extract above is also about the fact that men do not snitch on each other. *Real* men do not talk behind each other's backs, but nor do they tolerate people breaking unwritten codes about camaraderie between prisoners in the same situation; they do something about it. After all, a real man does not put up with just anything.

Food, everyday resistance and the smart prisoner

In his influential theoretical treatment of everyday forms of resistance, Scott (1990) takes as his starting point situations characterised by a lack of social equality and asymmetry, where a superior group has power over and dominates a subordinate group. The examples he employs include the peasant's role in feudal societies, the slave's relationship with his or her owner, and the prisoner's relationship with prison guards. In such situations, where the dominated and the dominating regularly interact, a *public script* is generated that dominates public situations and spaces, and helps to legitimise the hierarchical relationship between the two groups. At the same time, two alternative *hidden scripts* are also generated, one for each of the parties and which are exactly that, hidden from the other party.[14] Every hidden script will be characterised by the mutual loyalty between group members and the need to keep quiet in relation to the other group and in the public script. The public script comes into effect when the parties interact and is largely based on the terms of the dominant party and the relationship's asymmetry.

A hidden script comes about through negotiations that are hidden from the other party. The boundaries between the hidden and public scripts are subject to continuous struggles between the groups, although, of course, these struggles are on different terms. As a rule, the public script will be very similar to the dominant party's view of what the world *should* look like. It is designed to impress, conceal and euphemise away the problems and weak points of the dominance. Both group's hidden scripts contain requirements to stand together in public contexts and show solidarity with others in the same group.

In most of Scott's examples there is basic agreement on the public script because of the dominant party's fear of the reactions that would follow open, public resistance. This provides good conditions for hidden forms of resistance. While it absolutely makes sense to call it a total institution in the sense used by Goffman, Oslo Prison is, compared with the types of situations Scott describes, characterised by a greater degree of open disagreement in the public script. For example, the prison is more expressly politicised and also more tolerant of criticism than the Malay peasant society Scott (1985) describes. Open criticism from prisoners is not uncommon and is normally tolerated, as long as it is presented in a "civilised" and non-threatening manner. Sometimes it is even welcomed, although it is seldom heeded. Of course, this is only true up to a point. Practices have, over time, resulted in the emergence of genre conventions and limits with respect to what the officers can and will tolerate when it comes to public expressions of resistance. If the prisoners cross this boundary, they will be moved to a more restrictive wing. This is a threat that most prisoners take seriously. One of the conventions that structures public prisoner criticism is that explicit criticism is tolerated as long as it is formulated in a well-intended, constructive manner, and (usually) as long as it results in the more or less dissatisfied person having to give up in the end. Scott's division of public and hidden scripts, therefore, also applies in prison; expressions of resistance that would cross the boundary must be reserved for the hidden script between the prisoners, out of sight of the officers.

For the officers and in the public script, there are basically two alternatives: either one is a prisoner who *gets the message*, who does what the officers says and stays within the unspoken boundaries, or one is a prisoner who does not get it. The boundary is crossed and the prisoner moved. In such a situation, it is in both parties' interests to avoid expressions of resistance going too far in the public script. The prisoners do not want to be moved, while the officers want peace and order. Meanwhile, a third, absolutely key, alternative opens up for the prisoners and in the hidden script: doing approximately what the officers say without crossing their boundaries, but at the same time marking their resistance and capacity without the officers wanting, or being forced, to intervene. Somewhere between the officers' "good prisoner" or "bad prisoner" there is the "smart prisoner's" hidden resistance that operates within what the officers can accept on a daily basis, but which nonetheless serves as resistance in relation to the prisoners' subject-positioning work. Where the difficult prisoners are moved down into the cellar, and the easy prisoners risk looking fawning and spineless, the smart prisoners will carry out their resistance without the officers knowing it, or without them having an opportunity, or seeing a need, to intervene. Assuming and doing the "smart prisoner" position means doing autonomy, courage and social smartness in the very restrictive environment the prison constitutes.

Food preparation can be understood in relation to two of the characteristics the prisoners ascribe to *the smart prisoner*: the prisoner who tackles everyday prison life, who does not let himself be broken by the regime's demand for submission, who is not visibly depressed, but who can do the time, and who always maintains his sense of humour. In relation to resistance to the prison and its positioning of the prisoners, the food preparation can in these circumstances be used to assume a disidentification position, a position where one does not simply assume a position of opposition, but where one creatively changes the framework and one's position in relation to it.

Florin spoke about how he used cooking to pass the time. Every Monday, when his shopping arrived, he spent the evening chopping garlic. He bought four or five whole garlic bulbs every week, peeled them, crushed the cloves and finely chopped them with his butter knife. This process deliberately took time. Afterwards he put the garlic into an empty fizzy drink bottle, stirred in a couple of teaspoons of Vegeta, and drizzled over some sunflower oil. He then had garlic for the entire week, while at the same time it was nearly Tuesday already:

> When I prepare the garlic, I want it to take as long as possible. I do it slowly; I really concentrate on the task. Suddenly, an hour has passed. It's like therapy or meditation. If it hadn't been for the cooking, I would just lie on the bed, watching TV. Now I make a small meal, just a few eggs, or some rice. And I take my time, work nice and slowly. I eat slowly as well, as slowly as I can. I try to do everything slowly, actually, heh heh.

For him, food preparation functioned as a pastime in the literal sense of passing the time (Moran, 2012). *The smart prisoner*, the prisoner who does not allow himself to be broken by the prison, who copes despite his surroundings, is the prisoner who manages to find ways of passing the time. For Florin, food represented a key part of his positioning work in relation to what he thinks of as *the smart prisoner*.

There is no doubt that food preparation can form part of a masculine register. Just look at Jamie Oliver's studied urban laddism in his early books, which has gradually transformed into a playful, yet confident, provider role in his later works (Brownlie and Hewer, 2007). Or, even more clearly, take Anthony Bourdain's construction of a chef persona that is somewhere between a rock star and pirate captain. The ability to do resistance, the capacity to position yourself as a smart prisoner, has masculine connotations. The prisoners who feel and communicate that they are mastering their situation can be said to be *doing masculinity through resistance*. In other words, managing to make successful food-bricolage in difficult circumstances, often despite the prison's express prohibitions and the risk of being sent to a more restrictive wing or worse, provides an opportunity to do masculinity.

The ultimate food-related form of resistance would be to go on hunger strike. The problem with going on hunger strike is that it is, by necessity, expressive: it does not work unless a responsible party learns about it and is forced to take responsibility. And, as soon as one announces a hunger strike (which happened once during my fieldwork and, in that case, lasted two hours), one moves the conflict over to the public script, the health department becomes involved, and the entire official power and control system at the prison's disposal grinds into action. Ultimately, prisoners who go on hunger strike will be force-fed with a tube. This, therefore, is an example of where prisoners who play hardball will probably lose in the end. Hunger strikes are, therefore, not very common, and thus do not form part of what can be called everyday, hidden resistance work.

The more everyday, hidden forms of resistance are, despite their somewhat subtler symbolic power, superior in a number of ways. They are not public and therefore do not force the superior party to act. However, at the same time, this resistance is sufficient for the subordinate party to position himself as someone who does resistance. As part of the ongoing subjectification work, the hidden forms of resistance have the added benefit of providing an opportunity to assume the position of "the smart prisoner", the one who is not stupid enough to attack the prison on its own half of the pitch, but who instead masters his surroundings well enough to be able to resist without the officers knowing what is going on. A public, physical attack on an officer is regarded as a ridiculous, childish idea by someone who cannot control himself. On the other hand, the secret food's forms of resistance are regarded as smart and elegant.

This form of resistance can be expressed through something as ordinary as managing to make a really good cup of coffee. Tarik has a system in which he puts filter coffee into an empty beetroot jar, pours hot water over it and allows it to brew for five or six minutes. He then strains the coffee into a cup with a tea strainer he procured with the aid of the recreation department. When the aroma of real coffee, unlike the freeze-dried variety the prison offers, fills the room, he smiles broadly and nods:

> Just because we're in prison, it doesn't mean we can't live a little. It is important to be creative, to use the resources you have. Then, all will be well. The circumstances are poor, we have to improvise, we have to be creative. Then, all will be well anyway.

Real coffee is different from prison coffee. And a person who can make real coffee is a person who does not let the prison alone determine his life. Tarik has regained control of a small part of his life. He refuses to accept the prison coffee, he discovers another possibility, and he masters the situation. Or, to repeat Thompson's (2003) resistance concept: refuse, uncover, master. The real cup of coffee, therefore, becomes a symbol of creativity and self-determination. In Tarik's case, everyday resistance functions as freedom in practice that gives him back a feeling of autonomy and capacity.

The mechanism here would appear to be: the greater the risk, the greater the potential gain. The extract below is from a description of hanging out with a prisoner who takes things much further than Tarik's cup of coffee:

> To help with the research, as he says, he really wants to show me how the cooking appliance he has made works. He will make us a fried egg if I stay in his cell at lunchtime. Given my curiosity, I am easily persuaded. During the process the cell door has been ajar. I glance at it nervously, afraid that an officer will stick his head in to check that I am okay, which they do every now and then, before going to lunch. I have that slightly horrible feeling you get from apple scrumping; I can feel it in my gut and my clammy hands. After all, I don't want my presence ruining this. And I would rather not be caught with a prohibited fried egg on my lap. For his part, the prisoner is a picture of stoic calm. He is completely certain they won't check his cell, and that if they do, they won't notice anything wrong. He tells me about the time he made a perfect omelette, put it nicely on a plate and took it with him to another cell to eat it there. He had passed an officer on the way and taken the opportunity to "tempt" him, to show him the delicacy he had. The officer had licked his lips at the tempting sight. But it had not occurred to him that the existence of the omelette was an impossibility without breaking the prison's rules.
>
> Prisoner: After all, the poor guards know nothing. What sort of upbringing have they had? Come on, they know nothing about cooking?

We both laugh at the story about the easily fooled, stupid officers.

The eggs are done; the chef serves me a fried egg on a slice of bread with a light drizzle of salt and pepper. It really is very good. The whole process has taken 20 minutes. The eggs are almost more steam baked than fried, in some weird way or other. The yolk is completely dark yellow, but cooked through, not soft. I eat while the chef watches. He is still full after having three eggs for breakfast. Afterwards, the air in the cell is thick with the aroma of food. But the chef is not concerned about curious noses. I am thinking that, hey, this must arouse some suspicions? But he calms me down.

Prisoner: Just relax. If they come in, you can just say you brought it with you from home. It'll be fine.

In this situation I was included in the mealtime and resistance camaraderie. Together we laughed at the anecdote of how he, at the risk of being discovered, chose to make a diversion via the officer to show him the omelette he had made. And, again, his anecdote is about the poor officers, and their sad lives, who know nothing about making food. He calmed me down when I was nervous he/we would be caught; he clearly showed that he was master of the situation. At the same time, it is implicit from what he said that he expected me to lie to the officers if they stuck their heads in. For a moment, and for this one time only, I was part of a *we* who had managed the impossible under difficult conditions and who had tricked the officers at the same time.

Food, taste and meals cannot be understood independent of food's character as a cultural myth, writes Barthes (1979). From this perspective, the prisoners' distaste for the official food can be understood by imagining that food synecdochally stands for the prison as a whole. Therefore, eating the food the prison offers means "swallowing" the entire prison, making the prison part of yourself. At the same time, not liking what is served, simply transforming the meal into rubbish, constitutes resistance to the entire prison and the prison's general positioning of the prisoners. From this perspective, throwing the food away is an act of freedom. Turning the prison's provision into rubbish becomes remaining an individual, not one of *the inmates*. Refusing to eat the prison food, or eating as little of it as possible, is thus like saying: *You can watch me and administer my body, but that's where I draw the line. You can put me in chains and drag me down to the cellar. You decide when I wake up, what I do when, who I can meet and what sort of contact I can have with my loved ones. But you do not decide what I eat. I will not relinquish that control.* Fundamentally, therefore, resistance to the food can be interpreted as resistance to the institution and a struggle to retain some basic form of autonomy and recapture mastery over one's own body.

The nature of the everyday forms of resistance means they do not threaten the day-to-day interaction between officer and prisoner on the wing, while at the same time prisoners feel they are doing resistance and the officers feel that they are in control. The serious deviations (remember the stories about the crazy prisoner) occur on other wings, we do not have that sort of inmate here, and at the same time we manage to maintain control. The prisoners avoid having to "swallow" the prison; they can at the same time do resistance work that is relevant to the game of subjectification and simultaneously not risk being moved. This is about doing resistance work on a suitable level, a "terror balance" or a power/resistance balance that is precisely that, *in balance*, where both parties can win without any great risk. The prisoners become creative, autonomous and resourceful, the officers flexible and good, humane officers. In other words, this is an example of the situation Scott (1990) describes in which both parties in an asymmetric relationship benefit from not challenging the public script, but let the resistance remain on the hidden script level, below the surface.

By making food in the grey zone, the prisoners go from being someone who has lost and had to submit to being a *creative bricoleur* who can make the best of a bad situation. By breaking large and small rules in different ways in daily life, the prisoners create the position of a subject who is resisting and countering the prison's attempts at influence rather than an object for the prison's (know-all) influence. If one, like Foucault, views every meal the prisoners are served as a tiny movement of a cog in the prison machine, every meal the prisoners make themselves in their cell would be a tiny grain of sand in that machine.

Holm and Smidt (1993) viewed the food in the children's hospital as a free area in the sense that it can represent a way that the family and life outside the hospital can be made relevant and present within the institutional framework of the hospital – home permeates and is evident in the hospital. The good food you make yourself pulls life outside into the institution and therefore helps to tear down the walls. Cooking your own food can underscore that you are not disappearing and allowing yourself to be swallowed up by the institution, that you are sustaining yourself and resisting the institution's attempt to peddle its wares. The alternative food represents the fact that there is still a world outside the prison (and outside Norway). The notion that the official food symbolically extends the prison walls means that a space opens up in which the prisoners have the power to tear the walls down – again, if only in a symbolic sense. They might not be able to stroll out through the gates as they wish, but they can at least eat a little better if they want to.

Capable bodies

In his essay about body techniques, Mauss (2006, originally 1935) was one of the first to point out the link between body shape, patterns of movement and an individual's social and cultural positioning. Using a long list of examples, such as the fact that the trench-digging techniques French and British soldiers learn are so different that they cannot use each other's shovels, he examined how patterns of movement are social and cultural variables that are not simply determined by an individual body's biology. Movements, such as gait and swimming style, are society specific. From Mauss's perspective, an adult has no "natural" movements, at least when it comes to how "natural" is often understood, as the opposite of society and culture.

Mauss's starting point is that actions are goal-oriented; they are designed to achieve something. Children and adolescents learn body techniques by imitating actions with which people they trust and want to emulate have been successful. The social element lies in precisely the fact that the action, in specific social contexts, has been authorised as successful and worth aspiring to. Prestigious and successful actions are incorporated into a person's repertoire of body techniques through imitation and repetition, which in turn helps to sustain them as prestigious and successful. The body's physiology, the individual's psychological dispositions and a specific social context are, therefore, continually intertwined in and through people's actions.

You interact with your surroundings via your body. You *are* your body and cannot avoid the social meanings ascribed to this body by others with the aid of or more or less established cultural frameworks for interpretation. Bodies communicate; my body tells a story about me. At the same time, therefore, bodies are positioned in a social space and specific positions will be ascribed to specific bodies in the relevant discursive context, positions that the subject can, of course, react to and try to change, but which he or she cannot ignore. Bodies become objects for various regimes of knowledge about the body, different gazes intertwined with different normative systems that observe attractive and ugly bodies, large and small bodies, lazy and fit bodies, and useless and capable bodies. This is what Butler (1993) is pointing out when she writes that the body's materiality cannot be separated from the regulating norm that steers its materialisation and the visibility of its material effects as signs. What does the material body become observable as? What distinctions are put to work?

The bodies' experienced abilities and limitations vis-à-vis movement in the space position them as specific types of bodies. Social bodies are created through a process of alienation whereby one is made to see oneself from the outside, turn oneself into an object for oneself through being an object for the gaze of others. This also entails entering into similarity and difference relationships; knowing what you are means also knowing what you are not, and bodies are positioned in distinction systems structured by dichotomies such as man/woman, fat/slim, white/black, tall/short and so on (Bourdieu, 1984). Therefore, the body is both an object for the gaze of others and a tool in the subject's work of responding and adapting to this gaze.

From this perspective, the body is a medium for the surroundings' positioning and the individual's adaptation and negotiations in their encounter with these. For Foucault, it is, by the extension of such a view, fruitful to view the body as the focal point for the meeting between people and society (Foucault, 1977b, 2000c). We are categorised and understand ourselves as bodies, through the body and through being seen as a body, for example, as a type of body. From a Foucauldian perspective, it is, therefore, not the body itself that is important, but how it is always connected to power relationships and subjectification processes, and the fact that it (therefore) is also always a potential arena for physical subversion and resistance to the power. From such a perspective, Mauss's body techniques can function like Foucauldian techniques of the self (Warnier, 2001).

Sometimes attempts to influence using physical power techniques are pretty direct and clear, as in Foucault's (1977a) description of disciplinary techniques aimed at influencing the criminal soul through a physical regime in which patterns of movement are regulated down to the smallest detail. The detailed control of the prisoners' movements is, according to Foucault, a disciplinary technique aimed at influencing the criminals via their bodies. The body, which used to be the object of regimes that employed destructive corporal punishments, would through the discipline's new movement regimes be turned into a productive tool for the work on the prisoner's criminal soul. Bodies made compliant would result in an "in-depth" change; compliant bodies would be transformed into law-abiding subjects. The endless drilling of new recruits aimed at getting them to march in time is another example of this. In a world where soldiers no longer march to war (they use airplanes or drive vehicles), continuously practising extremely regulated and standardised patterns of movement has as much effect as anything else when it comes to turning individuals into soldier subjects. The collective drilling weaves the soldiers' bodies into a single unit (Theweleit, 1998).

Foucault's ideas about disciplining cooperative bodies must not be read as an empirical description of a perfect process whereby bodies are turned into obedient automatons. On the contrary, the body the power is attempting to control is provided with a series of opportunities to challenge and confront the power and its attempts at positioning. In other words, the subjects are not a simple effect of the disciplinary techniques. Nor are cooperative bodies ever just that. What Foucault calls the soul is produced around, on, in and with the body, through a body that is an object for a power technology. "Subjects are creating themselves like pearls around the foreign particles of power", writes Kelly (2009: 89) about that which therefore, bearing in mind an understanding of power as being the conduct of conduct, must also be a physical process.

Such a perspective on the relationship between surroundings, body and subjectivity is a multi-level construct. Here is another example: someone who frequently jogs long distances will acquire a new body technique; they will become good at running. Over time this person will develop a body shape that is different from that of someone who only moves to and from a car; the body is shaped by what it does. Bourdieu's (1990) debt to Mauss is clear when he points to the fact that the body's shape and build are linked to working conditions and habits of consumption, which, in turn, together contribute to the production of specific, class-related, elevated ways of acting and conducting yourself. In parallel, the jogger will be perceived by their surroundings as someone who jogs, and will therefore be defined in a cultural system of categorisations as a healthy, fit and successful person with sufficient self-control to subject themselves to regular, productive self-torture (to mention a few possible connotations of a well-used pair of running shoes). This, in turn, will result in the person seeing themselves as a jogger; the acquired body technique becomes efficacious for the self's understanding of, and work on, itself. In social contexts that ascribe prestige to this, it will, at the same time, make the person's neighbour want to start jogging. In other words, the repetition of the jogging action produces effects on different levels; the body's physiological level, the individual psychological level and a social prestige level. Mauss understands these three corners of the body techniques' triangle as being intertwined.

The powerful motor that keeps the subject-creating game of positioning and reactions to positioning going is repetition, and the same is true on the tangible, physical level. Repeated actions will, within certain limits, affect the body and shape it according to what is being done, but the repetitions will also influence the subject's work on himself. The surroundings' interpellation attempts have a physical dimension. Althusser (1971) uses religious practices as an example. By rewriting Pascal's believer who kneels as an integral part of his self-constitution as a believing person ("kneel, and you will believe"), he points out how one walks to church, stands when the priest says one should, kneels and opens one's mouth to accept communion, closes one's eyes to pray, sings together and so on; all of which are practices that help turn the actor into a Christian person. The person who believes does all this as part of, and seamlessly intertwined with, the reproduction of their belief.

Althusser's example also illustrates the power relationship's role in body-based subjectification processes. When individuals are positioned as religious subjects in the church, they also physically enter into a power relationship in which rights and obligations are assigned to the various positions. What individuals make out of the meeting with body-based positioning attempts in practice is an empirical question. The following focuses on how the body in prison functions as part of this subjectification game, both as a resource and (simultaneously) as an object for influence and power. Following Caputo-Levine (2012), I will describe the complex social construction of the "carceral habitus".

Being an untrustworthy body

Being a prisoner means wanting to be somewhere else. This fundamentally structures how the institution is designed and organised; if no prisoners wanted to open their doors, there would be no point in installing locks. What, then, is the minimum material starting point necessary to enable a prison to function as a prison, as a space that can keep the prisoners' untrustworthy bodies under lock and key? One place to start is a building with walls, a floor and a ceiling, all of which must be quite solid and form a sealed box. The problem with walls is that they need holes in them in order to be useful for something (at least something other than surrounding a tomb). But if you make a hole then anything or anyone can enter or exit. This is the problem with walls, or, rather, the problem with openings, according to Latour (1992). This is why the door was invented. Doors require hinges in order to be opened and closed. A door with hinges can be temporarily opened and then closed again without the wall being destroyed. Doors also make it possible to temporarily close the opening and control who and what enters and exits. If such control needs to be maintained over time, you have two choices. You can post a person you trust (a trustworthy body) to guard the door, although, in order for this person to want to do this job over time, they will probably have to be paid. Therefore, this is an expensive solution. Or you can install a lock and have the keys to it. The lock is cheap; if it is solid it can take over from the guard so that they do not have to be present the entire time. Both solutions are used in prisons, but the first, the expensive one, is reserved for a few very special "doors", such as the main gate.

Notwithstanding this, the most important material starting point that makes a prison a prison is having a least one body that, for a specified period of time, must be kept within the four walls. No prisoner's body, no prison. In order to successfully guard prisoners' bodies, one, as I have already touched on, is dependent on other people one can trust, people with views that make it possible to trust them. At the same time, one must, from a material perspective, differentiate between people with access to keys and people without keys. This division between people with different relationships to the keys is absolutely fundamental for a prison to be a prison. If everyone had keys, we would be talking about something else, such as sheltered housing, for example. If no one had keys, you might as well not have bothered with the door. The keys demonstrate that someone is *persona grata* in relation to the specific door and, more generally, a trustworthy body. Therefore, ownership of the keys is also important in a prison; it is part of what makes an officer an officer, while a prisoner who wants to step over a threshold is always reminded that he is someone who does not have keys. For prisoners, the sound of jangling keys can have a metonymical function as a reminder of their situation, and their position as a prisoner in the prison. It is also a metaphor for the power and the legitimate potential for violence that is the reason for the system, which is expressed by the fact that some people have keys and others do not. The state's relationship to its subjects (in the sense of citizens) is, and has been, linked to the state's right to exercise legitimate violence against its subjects in certain situations. In the prisoners' situation, the state's power over individuals is no abstraction; the state's influence is concrete and tangible; it is felt physically. Life in the prison is thus organised by keys and doors, by locking in and letting out. Let out, lock in, let out, lock in. Let out. Lock in. The institution is run as a constantly renegotiated compromise between freedom and force, space for movement and locking in.

One day towards the end of my fieldwork, Erol was going to collect a package of new clothes his wife had sent him in the post. He wondered if I wanted to accompany him down to the personal property storeroom to see what moving around the prison is like for a prisoner, and, after a brief pause for thought, the officers gave me permission to accompany him:

Erol: Did you see him hesitate when you wanted to do down [to the personal effects storage] with me, eh? Did he think I was going to have a go at you or what, heh heh? What do they think I am?

From Erol's cell on the fourth floor we walk down the stairs between the floors, along the common area, through the metal detector gate and to the door to the stairs that run further down. A smiling officer opens the heavy metal door and we enter. The door is closed and locked behind us. We are now in a space that the officers rarely use. This is for safety reasons – the stairwell is a relatively long way from colleagues who can help and there are no cameras here. We walk down the two floors to the other wing. [...] On the first floor the door is open because the officers on the third have told them we are coming. We walk out and cross the few metres to the right over to the door out of wing two. Erol buzzes the intercom and, after a few seconds, is told by an officer sitting in the operations room (who has also been told to expect us) to state his cell number and destination. After a few seconds the door buzzes and is open. We walk out of wing two, past the operations room, where officers are watching us through safety glass, and to the left, into the beige yellow corridor where the prisoners' numerous art projects are hung. Large, colourful paintings of various animal life adorn the walls. At the other end of the corridor we have to buzz again and state Erol's cell number and destination. Through the door, down some stone steps and we are in the personal property storeroom.

On the way down to the personal property storeroom, Erol's moving untrustworthy body was regularly entrusted to new officers with responsibility for different spaces. The prisoners have no key privileges (not even to their own cell, which is not the case on many other prison wings) and must constantly ask for permission to enter through a door. Communication with the officers, whether they walk over with their key chain or press a button, is necessary to get authorisation to step across the threshold of a door. From this perspective, every movement from one room to another – out of the cell, into the stairwell, out of the wing, down to "personal property" – reminds the prisoners of their status as prisoners.

When the officers let out six to eight prisoners into the common area, they seemingly surrender the room to the prisoners. For an hour they, within certain limits, largely do not interfere in what happens between the prisoners who have been let out. I say "seemingly" because the officers are expected to maintain overall control of the room. This becomes clear when, without warning, a drill starts and the red alarm lamp is lit from the operations room. The officers are then measured, as previously described, with respect to how quickly they can get the untrustworthy bodies back into their respective cells. The experienced officers are calm but serious in such situations. The inexperienced can become nervous and stressed. The officers are expected to be capable of regaining control of the room at short notice or, more specifically, control of the bodies in the room.

As described earlier, untrustworthy bodies are also not trusted in other ways. The prisoners' bodies are dangerous for the officers; they could attack and injure the officer bodies. The officers informally differentiate in various ways between subgroups of prisoners as far as the risk of violent attack is concerned. Some prisoners are recognised as potentially violent, as prisoners you have to watch out for. They are known as being angry or, in some other way, as being easy to predict. You know where you are with those with a short temper. In such cases you simply have to have an extra officer outside the door when you go in to talk to the prisoner. If you know that someone may explode because they have often exploded before, they become predictable and manageable.

In this way, the officers' perception of the potential for violence can be concrete and personified. There may be several reasons why a person is understood as being potentially violent. One example of a prisoner who was perceived as a specific, violent threat during my fieldwork was Adem. Even though at 18 he was one of the youngest on the wing, he exhibited a great deal of physical confidence. He carried his body in a very self-assured manner in the room, puffed out his chest and took up all the space he could, and this showed the surroundings that he had no intention of accepting his ascribed position as one of the youngest prisoners. Given this, he was often tested by older prisoners. He *often ended up in trouble because people were fucking cheeky*, as he put it, and he had to defend himself. And he did it well. From the officers' perspective, he quickly became known as a difficult prisoner, and from when he arrived on the wing it was just a matter of time before he ended up in a fight with someone. It was just a question of when, where and with whom?

> Youth team worker: After all, he notices that people are scared of him, that people pull back a bit when they meet him, and he is a real expert at exploiting that. If he notices that people are scared, that just gets him going even more.

TU: Who is afraid of him?

Youth team worker: Well, yesterday for example, on the way down to [wing] two, he jumps down all the stairs in a couple of leaps and that brings loads of officers from [wing] two running, after all it sounded like someone wanted a fight in there, and then they see him and they are a bit scared of him, and that really fires him up and he gets angry because they are shouting at him, and then it keeps going. It went okay that time, but that sort of thing happens all the time. And I heard all about it, as soon as I started: oh you'll be working with Adem? That'll be a challenge for you, heh heh. Everyone knows who he is of course, and of course he's known for being difficult.

Adem is described as a force of nature, an earthquake lurking beneath the surface that could go off at any time, and God help you when it did.

Other times there is a specific situation in which the officers think there is a possibility that a prisoner will become violent.

I lock myself out of the school and onto the landing on wing five. Something is wrong. Further down the landing are six or seven sturdy "unfamiliar" officers [who don't work on the wing]: all wearing black leather clothes, all with at least one stripe on their shoulders. They are in position outside an open cell door, focused on the inside of the cell. I wander carefully along the landing above, past and down to the third floor. The extra officers who are at work on the wing are standing around, watching what is going on.

Extra officer: He's being moved. And he just got a very tough sentence, 18 years preventive custody. Plus he won't get to see his son. So we don't really know what he'll do; best to be safe.

Here, the logic is that the relevant prisoner has received such bad news that he *should* be unstable. However, the move went without problems. *Well, he took it really well*, said a smiling (relieved) extra officer, summing up the situation. And, as a rule, such situations do pass off okay. However, this does not mean that any adjustments will be made to practices, since the practices are designed for precisely the extreme exception, for the worst that can happen.

People with short fuses are people you can deal with. A bigger problem is the people whose fuses vary or who have fuses of unknown length. The prisoner who does not seem quite right, who can suddenly "see red" and become furious, without warning, without reason, is more difficult to manage. After suffering an inflamed appendix, an officer was told that she would have to work in the operations rooms for a period instead of on her regular wing. According to the doctor, she would not be able to take a punch to the stomach. A prison wing is generally viewed as a place where one could be punched; the prisoners' untrustworthy bodies could throw a punch. Working on a prison wing is associated with a general risk of violence. Very few officers will become victims of serious, physical violence during their career. These type of violent episodes are relatively rare in Norwegian prisons (Hammerlin and Kristoffersen, 2001; Hammerlin and Strand [Ugelvik], 2005, 2006; Hammerlin and Rokkan, 2007). This does not mean that they are not afforded a lot of attention: the most serious incidents become almost mythical in the Norwegian Correctional Services. The stories are told and retold, both as lessons on good and poor safety practices, and as anecdotes about the important and difficult job officers do. Every violent incident is seen as confirmation that the prison is fulfilling its social duty when it comes to keeping violent people locked up.

Even though very few officers have experienced being floored by a punch, most officers have experienced what they consider scary situations at work. One told me about a prisoner who grabbed her in a chokehold for a few seconds before letting go, another that a prisoner had charged him and only stopped right in front of his face:

Officer 1: That's when I thought I'm really going to get a beating, yeah. But it didn't get that far. He didn't take the last step. I put on my toughest face, and hoped for the best. My ticker was racing like a jack hammer; I wasn't feeling particularly cocky to tell the truth, heh heh.
Officer 2: You never know who will actually take that final step.
Officer 1: No, that's true. You can never know. You can get stung in this job before you know what's happening.

The risk of violence is a form of risk that is also understood through a gender-sensitive filter. One afternoon, male officers around the table were discussing the fear they had felt from being alone with a female colleague in a situation where she had to be protected. Because what if you failed?

Officer 1: It was at Ullersmo, when I worked there. I was a trainee and was together with a small girl on night duty. We had to unlock an inmate who needed to go to the loo; we went to the cell and opened up. An enormous beast of a fellow, he had to really duck down to get through the door, heh heh. No, I must admit I looked at the little, blonde girl who was supposed to be the cavalry who had my back, and thought that: now, if anything happens, it could get really ugly. But then nothing happened, like, he was just really good-natured and funny that guy, gentle as a lamb.
Officer 2: The big ones are as a rule. It is the small ones who are so short-tempered, who get fired up in an instant, like ferrets. They're the ones you have to watch out for.

It is this figure, the hidden danger that lurks behind every prisoner, who is the reason for the institutionalisation of the worst-case-scenario mindset. What do officers mean what they ask each other if anything happened at the weekend? There is a specific part of the officers' work that can be characterised as an "incident". When something "has happened" it has been confirmed by the alarm and the red lamp. Those who are reacting to something that "is happening" wear black, stab-proof, leather gloves. These gloves are not a standard part of the uniform, but are normally bought by full-time officers.[15] They do not wear them all the time, but they are put on when an "incident" is about to happen and they are considered necessary. High, black, steel toe-capped protective boots are also a common investment among full-time officers. Given this starting point, the generalised prisoner becomes a body that could attack at any time, and the basis for social relationships between officers and prisoners becomes, to some extent, an interaction atop a powder keg.

The other form of risk the prisoners can represent for the officers' bodies is a risk of infection. This is also a form of risk that can come from anywhere and lies in wait when you are least expecting it. The main difference is that the risk of violence can suddenly and visibly result in a violent explosion before subsequently receding. When it is over, it is over. The risk of infection can last, gnawing at you because of the uncertainty. It can take months before any infection is confirmed or ruled out.

Whenever the officers are on a break, the tap water used for washing and doing the dishes in the small room adjoining the officers' room is always already warm because someone has just washed their hands. As for professionals in the health and care professions, regularly washing and disinfecting your hands, several times a day, is an important part of the professional prison officer's work routine. The route from the wing (work) to the sofa (break) runs through the cleansing, hot water that is a physical boundary marker defining the difference between the officers' front stage and back stage. The difference and distance between prisoners and officers are reiterated and maintained through this daily repetition of hygiene measures. All of the prisoners are treated like carriers of deadly infections, while colleagues are treated as safe, like friends you can relax with.

However, although the water thus has a symbolic function, this, of course, does not mean that the need to wash is not genuine. Working as a prison officer means coming into close contact with other people's bodies and body fluids, people who, statistically, have a higher rate of many infectious diseases:

> Officer 1: There was that case at the weekend. That one down in one [everyone around the table knows who he means] had cut himself again. He only got a 19-day sentence, and he just has to kill himself? What the hell is that about? Can't he wait a bit? Anyway, I was cleaning up

blood for hours. He had even managed to get some blood into the thermos. It clots after a while, and then it's impossible to get it clean. It's a nightmare.

Officer 2: Those small drops everywhere, they're the worst. There's no point trying to wash everything down, you just have to scrape up everything once it's dried. It takes a while.

TU: What happened to him?

Officer 1: Well, we got there so fast that there was no danger. But he'll probably be on the bed for 19 days [the bed with restraints in the cellar where prisoners who represent an acute risk to themselves can be strapped down]. He'll need to be watched at least.

Officer 3: Once I cleaned up after someone who had killed themselves, him down on [wing X]. Fuck me there was a lot of blood. I was washing for hours. Afterwards someone said to me: "Do you think he had HIV?" We were fully protected, masks and everything, but, still, it was no fun.

As mentioned, in her introduction Rhodes describes shit throwing as the last form of resistance of those who have been deprived of everything except their own body:

> The prisoner who sees himself defined as a piece of shit hurls into the faces of his keepers the very aspect of himself that most intensely represents his contaminated status in their eyes. He spreads to them a kind of contagion, not only by contaminating them with "him" but by making them, at least momentarily, disgusting themselves.
>
> (2004: 45)

Bayern is not a "control unit" in an American high security prison, although the degree of isolation remand prisoners in Oslo are subjected to is comparable to what Rhodes' American prisoners experience. I observed no shit throwing. The prisoners in wings four and five would have regarded this as the work of a madman, something only a loser could have come up with. But the officers were sometimes spat on. And sometimes they came into contact with the prisoners' blood, albeit usually when a prisoner had hurt himself. The use of body fluids, especially blood, as a weapon means several months of uncertainty and a series of appointments and injections before one is finally (hopefully) told that one is not infected with (in the worst case) HIV.

The talk during the lunch break in the officers' room is about an incident on another wing. A prisoner has spat in the face of a female inspector. The inspector was sent to accident and emergency after the spitting episode.

Female officer: I would much rather be punched in the face than be spat on. Fuck. It would be the uncertainty, having to walk around for months not knowing if you have been infected. The danger of infection is always at the back of your mind, especially hepatitis. After all, it can take months to prove that someone has not been infected.

Male officer: He said it was because she was a girl that he spat at her. He was furious and was going to throw a punch, but, you know, he couldn't hit a girl. That's why he spat. I mean, come on, it's completely normal to spit when you're angry. Comm-pleeetly normal. He couldn't understand why she got so angry. Bloody hell [shaking his head].

The prison health service has a duty of confidentiality and that is why the officers do not know which inmates are carriers. Or they should not know. Some prisoners are, for various reasons, regarded as more likely to be carriers than others. Nonetheless, all prisoners are treated as potential carriers. In connection with another earlier research project (Ugelvik, 2006), a member of staff in one of Norway's prisons told me, as a way of demonstrating the good relationship between officers and prisoners on the relevant wing, that he did not suffer from a fear of contact. The officers in Oslo Prison have, at least to some degree, a general fear of contact. From the officers' vantage point, they might touch individual prisoners whom they know, but the generalised prisoner, the grey mass out there on the wing, could infect you. Rubber gloves and disinfectant are necessary and understandable tools, which simultaneously help to characterise the relationship between the officers and prisoners. A prisoner is, once again, an untrustworthy body, a body that constitutes a threat.

A prisoner's body is also a body that may have secrets, which could be concealing something. A body that returns back inside from the prison yard, or from the visiting unit, could be carrying drugs. A body may also exhibit traces of previous drug use, traces that can still be read a relatively long time after the fact. The prison is continually trying to shake secrets out of the prisoners' untrustworthy bodies. On the way back from the visiting unit, disrobing and submitting to a search of your body in the hunt for contraband is obligatory. Some of the prisoners view this as part of daily life, and, even though most would rather not undergo it, it is something they can live with as long as it is necessary in order to get visits from family and friends. Others have, for various reasons, serious problems with the arrangement and do not want to put their naked body on display for the officers. One common problem that arises is that there is a female officer among those carrying out the searches. This can normally be resolved to the satisfaction of both parties by her turning her back for the few seconds the prisoner is totally naked.

Searching naked prisoner bodies is a duty that male officers also find uncomfortable. And as in every encounter between officer and prisoner, there are always different ways of doing things:

Officer: No, hell, searches aren't my favourite thing, no they are not. Peeking up some strange bloke's backside is not my favourite activity. I mean, it's embarrassing, really. You just have to block it out, sort of put brackets around the normal limits for embarrassment, just get the job done, really. I try to strike the right tone with the inmate as quickly as possible so that it is as okay for both parties as it can be. But there are some, there's no point denying it, there are some who try to make it as horrible as possible for the inmate; say, for example, there is an inmate who has got on someone's nerves a bit lately and then that someone wants to really get him back during the search. I've seen that.

TU: What do they do, when they want to pick on someone?

Officer: Well… they just overdo everything completely, demand that he crouches down even lower, for example, make much more out of it than you really need to. You're allowed to use your head a bit, you know? But not everyone does. I usually say that you can cover your privates, although we have to take a look from behind. Put it this way, there's nothing in the front that I have any particular need to look at.

The officers are not health professionals and are not allowed to search prisoners' body cavities. Instead, if there is a need, they can use a so-called Pacto toilet. The prisoner who has aroused suspicion is then put in a small, special cell with a bed, a large glass wall and a special toilet that is not directly linked to the sewage system. The officers have to take turns sitting and observing the prisoner until his body is empty of any drugs. Afterwards, the prisoner's waste can be examined to see if he was actually hiding anything inside himself; whether or not the suspicions were justified.

The use of the Pacto toilet is expensive. The officer sitting outside cannot do anything else; he must watch, possibly for hours or days. It is, therefore, not used very often.[16] Urine tests are far more common. Usually there is some specific degree of suspicion behind the prison demanding a urine sample, since analysing these samples also costs money. Nonetheless, larger actions are sometimes carried out involving the collection of urine samples from groups of prisoners based on a general suspicion.

In the Introduction I wrote about Ilir, who came to me with a problem he had. He had been asked for what he was told was a random urine sample; the request was not based on any suspicions. This was at a time when cannabis had been found on the wing. The drug detection dog had been in and marked a number of cells, but not his. Ilir therefore refused to give a sample. I described how Ilir performed "the small man's" resistance against the unreasonable System. He stood his ground, was a man of principle, and would not let himself be scared into giving up a sample of his urine. But the prison also stood its ground, and therefore it was not required. The result of the refusal to provide a urine sample was that Ilir had to serve a sanction for having given a positive urine sample. The general suspicion of all untrust-worthy bodies was confirmed when Ilir would not place his body at the disposal of the prison's attempt to demand it gave up its secrets. From the prison's perspective, refusing to cooperate is equivalent to admitting drug use. Ilir's body, therefore, became a specific untrustworthy body and he had to accept the consequences.

Gendered bodies in prison

Bodies can be said to be part of social power relationships in ways that hail subjects and which therefore become a starting point for the subject's work on the self (Warnier, 2001). The gaze that sees the body is, in a contemporary Western context, to a large extent trained to assign bodies to one of two gender categories. Drawing once again on Althusser (1971), one can say that the surroundings' cultural gaze that sees gendered bodies hails individuals as gendered subjects.

This happens even if what are usually highlighted as the most important indicators of gender difference are, as a rule, hidden. After all, in day-to-day life the genitals are usually covered by clothes to some extent. Clothes choice, hairstyle, body shape, facial proportions, amount of facial hair and so on are focused by a cultural lens as signs of a gendered body that carries an essential gender inside with gender-specific characteristics (Butler, 1993, 2006). Women's chests are not just practical feeding stations for babies; they are read as a sign of an inner, more fundamental femininity, which, in turn, creates expectations that the person with the breasts will have the opinions of, and behave and think like, a woman. For their part, male bodies are read as a sign of a fundamental and lasting masculinity. Someone who sees a flat-chested, broad-shouldered body in a suit and tie sees, in a specific cultural context, for example, a person who is action-oriented, relatively poor at talk-ing about their feelings, but, then again, better at parallel parking. This is in line with West and Zimmerman (1987), as well as West and Fenstermaker (1995), who describe *doing gender* as risking being held responsible for their actions as a gendered person. You cannot remain standing on the sidelines: in the vast majority of cases one cannot avoid being hailed by, and therefore held responsible by, the surroundings as either a man or a woman. Partici-pating in the body's continuous retelling of gender is something one cannot avoid in day-to-day meetings with other people.

From this perspective, "man" can be understood as the name of an over-arching project in the subjectification game. However, in practice there are many, often very different, competing perceptions of what characterises a real man. The overarching "I am a man" project can, thus, be assigned very different content in practice. Connell (2005) is the person who is per-haps best known for theorising about masculini*ties* in the plural form. His starting point is a critique of what he perceives to be an outdated gender role concept. He accepts that there are many ways of being a man (or a woman), and several different masculinities. Connell's project is to describe different variations and the hierarchical relationship between them. At the top reigns hegemonic masculinity, the socially and culturally elevated form of masculinity, what men (perceive that they) should strive for as men, which simultaneously contributes to the patriarchy's continued existence in Connell's conceptual world. Very few men occupy such a position, at least over time. Notwithstanding this, it is important as a culturally elevated yard-stick. Various forms of complicit masculinity are far more common. These include the broad layer of men who (usually tacitly and impulsively) accept the hegemonic masculinity's hegemony and reap the benefits. Finally, there are various forms of subordinate and marginalised masculinity that are, on the other hand, excluded and positioned as contrary to the hegemony. Over-all, one can say that cultural understanding categories associated with the position "man" and perceptions of masculinity's hegemonic centre, periph-eral extreme points and absolute limits provide opportunities for some and (thereby and simultaneously) mean limitations for others.

While Connell has described various forms of masculinity's hierarchical relationships, Nordic masculinity researchers like Liliequist (1999), Ekenstam (1998, 2006) and Lorentzen (2004, 2005, 2006) have taken as their starting point differences between perceptions of the masculine and the unmanly. In these studies, masculinity work does not primarily appear to be directed towards a centre. The starting point here is, instead, constant challenges to masculinity, the omnipresent fear of falling into unmanliness, and the continuous patching up of constantly appearing new cracks in the façade.

Kolnar's (2005b, 2006; Kollhöj, 2005) concepts of "centripetal and peripetal movements" describe exactly this duality of masculinity. His point of departure is a geographical metaphor in which masculinity has central and peripheral areas. There are forces that move men out towards the periph-ery, interpellations to unmanliness. The man has to counter these in order to manage to move in towards the centre, which can be said to consti-tute various images of an (experienced) hegemonic masculinity. Most men will have a well-tested repertoire of techniques or tools that can be used to re-create temporary stability when they encounter destabilising or emas-culating forces. This does not mean that the beneficial effects of specific centripetal tools are guaranteed to work in a specific situation. It is not a given that one will not end up in situations where the repertoire of tech-niques does not work, where other actors do not share the perception of what should constitute masculinity's centre or have different perceptions of what are effective or legitimate techniques.

Kolnar takes men's use of violence as his starting point. He describes centripetal violence as violence that, in a specific historical, cultural and social context, can help men move in towards what is considered the centre. Peripetal violence is the opposite kind of violence that pushes the man out into the margins. Centripetal violence is not really *violence*, but self-defence, necessary interventions or limited military actions. Peripetal is not just violence, but also cowardly, unworthy, unfair and emasculating.

There will always be conflict about the topography of such a landscape. There will also always be more or less local (subcultural) alternative landscapes – or alternative maps that see and describe the landscape in different ways. What can function as centripetal violence in one (local) context could at the same time function as peripetal violence in other contexts. What in a heated situation may be a legitimate defence of threatened honour (centripetal violence) may afterwards and in other contexts (e.g. a courtroom) prove to result in branding as a criminal assailant (peripetal violence).

In this perspective, gender is something that is re-created when gendered subjects performatively relate to the gendered interpellation call. Claiming this does not mean the same as saying that "gender does not exist", that bodies "are just language", or something similar. Butler's concept of performativity is among the most misunderstood concepts in social theory and philosophy. It is easy to find examples of readings that are based on her meaning that physical bodies are unimportant, that the body is purely a linguistic variable and so on. Butler's point is, rather, a rejection of "pure" bodies, bodies outside and before the social, and, thus, also feminism's classic division between social and biological gender (*gender* and *sex*). The goal is to surpass dualities like nature/culture and body/consciousness, which has also interested Foucault (e.g. 1977b). Bodies obviously exist, but as human bodies they are always already intertwined with cultural categories used to understand the bodies of reflexively oriented social people. This is the physical–social interaction that is meant by "gender" in the following.

What characterises the objectification of the male body? Young (2005c) describes how it is fundamental to understanding the female body that many women perceive their bodies as an object for someone else's gaze, and as a vulnerable "thing" with built-in limitations. Women's self-esteem and gender identity are, according to her, to a large extent a product of experienced encounters with restrictions and limits. When one views oneself as a woman, one at the same time views oneself as vulnerable and breakable. Having a woman's body means having a body that must be protected and that must stay within clear boundaries so that it does not break. Women therefore learn to limit their physical repertoire. For example, according to Young, the male gait is generally more proportional and suited to the body's potential for movement than the female one. Men carry their bodies in a way that is more "open" to the world, while women enclose their bodies to protect them from all the dangers in the world. Most women do not see themselves as capable; their starting point is that they cannot manage.

Whitehead (2002) discusses Young's theses, and concludes that most men do not share such a perception of their bodies. On the contrary, being a man means *not* seeing yourself as vulnerable. According to Whitehead, dominant physical masculinity markers are, instead, *toughness* and *capacity/competence*. Ideally, it should be possible to use the body to represent these two values. A male body should appear to be a capable, hard body that can clearly cope with all situations, and which can take care of itself and its own.

At the same time, the masculine ideal is, to some extent, as Beauvoir (1953) points out, *not* having a body, or at least not allowing yourself to be defined by it. Men should not allow themselves to be held back by physical limitations, but should exceed their body's capabilities. They should only allow themselves to be influenced by the body through pain, and even then the goal is, insofar as it is possible, not to allow themselves to be (visibly) influenced. A man is someone who does not allow himself to be defined, who is himself, fully and completely, without external influence; someone who does not let his own body dictate to him, the master of his own body.

All of these are, despite more or less local variations, broadly acknowledged masculine values. The prestige for individuals who seek to turn themselves into masculine subjects is associated with more general perceptions of masculinity of this type that are performatively reproduced when they are associated with specific men in specific situations. These perceptions can be said to constitute a general, body-based expectation that applies to all men. Jefferson (1998) also underscores the idea that men's bodies are objects for the gaze of others (men and women). This occurs in other ways, and through the use of other registers, than is the case for female bodies, but, nonetheless, it is absolutely fundamental to men's lives and self-perception as beings with bodies. Both men and women regulate their bodies when they encounter the gaze of their surroundings. In such a context men must, by some means or another, deal with the expectations inherent in the gaze of their surroundings in their positioning work in order to be men (West and Zimmerman, 1987). Most men, of course, do not master this completely or all the time. The point is, rather, that all men, in order to be men, must manage to create a seamless relationship between their body, the body's physical surroundings and dominant masculinity discourses. The point here is that they perceive that this is how things should be and that very many men, in some manner or another, to some degree or another, try, with the costs that this entails.

For individual men, this work consists of trying to present an appearance and conduct that overlaps with the expectations the body creates, displaying signs of an inner masculine core that "fits" the body. However, a number of different variations on the theme are possible within the general gendered expectations. After the introductory division into two between the genders, men and women are quickly placed into suitable subgroups based on a finely meshed set of distinction categories to which I will return – *what sort of men* and *what sort of women* are we talking about? The focus is on a continuous intertwining of bodies, practices, power relationships and subject positions, rather than an understanding of gender as a closed, binary system. An individual's meeting with the culture's gendered expectations involves trying to reproduce a readable and culturally understandable whole that is, as closely as possible, associated with socially and culturally elevated values, but which cannot avoid being variations on the same theme. The question, therefore, is not whether or not a man should associate various discourses about masculinity with himself, but how this should be done. The alternatives that are available depend on the context and situation, and options are limited, or are, perhaps, rather directed, in specific situations in relation to a number of other variables such as age, body, health, ethnicity, nationality and, not least, the individual's unique history.

Above I describe Young's (2005c) ideas about the female body, which limits itself in relation to space. Women learn that physical performance is difficult, that they cannot manage. Women's attempts to manage are affected by this starting point; the result, therefore, becomes, according to Young, that in many cases they actually cannot manage. Young further discusses the female body's lack of capacity based on Merleau-Ponty's division between *here* and *yonder*. A body is always a body in space, a body positioned in the structure of opportunities and limitations that a specific space provides. While a body in a space is positioned exactly where it is, contrary to being in another space, the body is also potentially a tool for moving yourself *from here* to *there*. Women's relationship to their body is affected, according to Young, by a breach between *here* and *yonder*:

> The space of the "yonder" is a space in which feminine existence projects possibilities in the sense of the understanding that "someone" could move within it, but not I. Thus the space of the "yonder" exists for feminine existence, but only as that which she is looking into, rather than moving in.
>
> (Young, 2005c: 41)

The female body stands *here* and looks *yonder*, but without perceiving that moving from one to the other under one's own steam is a realistic possibility. These feminine body modalities are not based on anatomy, physiology or a feminine essence. They come, according to Young, from women's social position. Girls learn to limit their movements; they learn that they are vulnerable. Being a woman means living in fear of, in the worst case scenario, your body being invaded by others.

There are several similarities between Young's description of the female body's acquired self-limitation and the physical experience of doing time in prison. First and foremost, there is a clear and distinct breach between *here* and *yonder* for prisoners. The breach is manifested by the four-metre-high concrete wall that separates the prison from the world outside. The view of the world differs depending on which cell you are in. Outside the prison lie Galgeberg, the Sculpture Park, the roofs of buildings in the Gamlebyen area, and the blue mosque's minarets. And in the summer friends gather and play football in the park. Girls study for exams and sunbathe on the grass. On New Year's Eve, the borough celebrates in its best clothes and lets off screaming rockets from the football pitch opposite. All of this is *yonder*, just out of reach.

The fear of the body being invaded and subjugated is also easy to find in the world of the prisoner. I am not thinking about prison rapes here. These have been thoroughly described in the international specialist literature, but are an almost unknown phenomenon in Norway and the rest of Scandinavia. Instead, I am thinking of searches in connection with visits, forced urine tests, being forced to the ground or strapped to a bed. The institution's legitimate subordination of the prisoners always involves subordination of the prisoners' bodies. As a prisoner, one is surrounded on a daily basis by people who, in certain circumstances, are entitled to force upon you physical restrictions, even physical pain, if required. The life of a prisoner entails mixing with people who can restrain you, sit on you or strap you down, and who have power over your body.

One of the keywords Whitehead (2002) uses to describe the expectations regarding men's bodies is "capacity". Men should master and manage; men should be able to influence and change their surroundings according to their wishes and needs. This is a key part of the general, body-based interpellation of men in a Norwegian context. Real men should, for example, be able to repair and fix things in and around the home (2003). According to E. Johansson (2006), the Northern European masculinity ideal is characterised by the high value placed on some forms of manual labour, physical knowledge and technical ability. Even highly educated men are expected to be capable of tiling a bathroom or laying a parquet floor, an expectation that, according to Johansson, does not have clear parallels in Southern Europe, where the emphasis is more likely to be on having a more "elegant" male body dressed in expensive clothes and a physical appearance that symbolically excludes manual labour. Such an appearance could, in a Nordic context, be perceived as unmanly.

Achieving something, mastering something, proving yourself capable; I have mentioned these as key cultural expectations for men. Obviously, the opportunities for demonstrating capacity are basically limited in prison. What opportunities do prisoners have to *do* and *master* in prison? Several forms of practice are relevant. In a situation where the prisoners' bodies are regarded as untrustworthy bodies that must be controlled and organised in time and space, it is not surprising that, for example, prisoners sabotage the officers' prestige-filled attempts to create a wing with bodies shut up in the right place. It is not unusual for prisoners to try and drag out socials or for them to counter the officers' attempts to clear up by placing the prisoners behind their individual cell doors:

> Amir and Naveed are playing pool, I'm "hanging out" and watching. The talk round the table is lively. From the landing above us comes a voice. A large, fit officer (who does not usually work on the wing) explains authoritatively that "We're ending the social now". The way he does it almost demands a reaction.
>
> Amir: What's happening, we've got half an hour left, yeah?
>
> Officer: No, that's only at weekends. Come up, your time is up.
>
> The prisoners ignore the officer's order and keep playing. There are still a lot of balls on the table; the game is far from over. Above them, on the landing, the officer is visibly irritated, perhaps extra irritated because he had me as a spectator of his "lack of control over inmates". It is a power struggle, with an audience. He looks at me with a resigned expression, and wants to include me in his resignedness. He stands there for a long time, a couple of minutes, at least. Then he disappears into the officers' room.
>
> Amir: Heh heh, I love to fuck that one around. [Turns to where the officer is no longer standing] Bitch! Heh heh heh.
>
> Naveed, for his part, is clearly less comfortable about being dragged into Amir's "fucking around". The officer comes out again, this time accompanied by another (female) extra officer. The two of them take up a relaxed position on the landing; arms resting on the railings and upper bodies bent forwards over the room below, signalling that they are in no rush really. Nonetheless, the first officer tries again:
>
> Officer: Come on, it's finished now.
>
> Amir: We'll just finish the game.
>
> Officer: No, we go by the clock here. It's the same for everyone. That's just how it is. Come up now.
>
> Amir [smiling at me]: What's the problem, eh? We're just going to finish the game.
>
> Naveed [has had enough, gives me the cue]: Do you want to play?
>
> Amir [to Naveed]: No, you're finishing the game!
>
> Officer: It's the same for everyone. Now come up.
>
> The last message is said with finality. The last word has been said. There is no room for further negotiation. The officers straighten up and cross their arms over their chests. They are back at work, they are not hanging over the railings, and they have given an ultimatum. If the prisoners do not listen to them, they will be stepping over a line. Thirty very long seconds pass before Amir, irritatedly and demonstratively, throws the pool cue onto the table. Amir and Naveed walk up the stairs to be locked in their respective cells. Naveed nods happily to me on the way up, pleased that it had not escalated.

Several things happened here, simultaneously. Amir tested the extra officers' limits. The officers' ability to ensure that the bodies of Amir and Naveed were where they should be at that precise time was thereby challenged. The fact that I was standing there watching did not make it any less about prestige. Naveed was uncomfortable with the entire situation, but could not go against another prisoner. He tried to lessen the tension in the situation, but was told in no uncertain terms by Amir that cooperating with the officers was out of the question. However, the situation can also be interpreted as something more than just simply testing extra officers. The positioning as an untrustworthy body, which must be cleared away to its prescribed place, was challenged by a prisoner-subject who wanted control of himself and his own body. A person who dares to stand his ground and take up the fight is also positioned as a resistance subject who will not just passively accept being moved around at the whim of the officers, even if he must, of course, concede in the end. After all, there is a difference between doing resistance and being stupid.

A related modification of the prisoner position takes place when prisoners talk about, joke about, discuss and dream about escaping from prison. During my fieldwork I heard many, more or less well thought through, escape plans. For example, allegedly there is a small wire inside some non-reusable lighters that can be used to saw through the bars in front of the windows, as long as you are patient. A toothbrush and razor blade from Gillette can, with the aid of a lighter flame, be made into a bladed weapon, which can then be used to threaten your way out of prison. Many of the prisoners stressed that it is good to know that you could get out if you absolutely had to:

> Knowing that if you had to get out you could get out is okay to know. You would. I don't want to ruin things for myself, but if I had to, then I would just grab one of these small, sweet extra officers and I'd be out in five minutes.

Escape opportunities are an important topic among prisoners. People who have to get out, get out, even if the consequences are serious. That is also why one does not *have* to get out. In this way, the prisoners turn themselves into prisoners who have chosen to stay. Every day you wake up in your cell is a day you have chosen not to run off in the middle of the night. You are responsible enough and rational enough to understand that this sort of thing hurts no one other than yourself in the long term.

Escapes from Norwegian high security prisons are, in practice, very uncommon. There was only one real escape from Oslo Prison (as opposed to not returning from unescorted leave, which is also, as described above, very unusual) in the year I spent in the prison. A prisoner managed to get himself over the wall and into the world outside with the aid of energy, cunning, climbing skills and courage. However, he injured himself during the escape and was caught and returned to the prison after just a few hours. This was, nonetheless, a big story for the prisoners, a "week's material" that obviously garnered prestige for the person who dared to make, and was capable of making, the attempt. As Florin said:

> It was all over the newspapers. They tried to keep us from reading about it; we had no newspapers for two days. But we knew about everything the following day, anyway. It was all over the yard that first day, heh heh.

Adem was also very interested in what had happened. He went into the whole thing in some detail:

> Adem: Yeah, they caught him at the bus station. With a broken knee and that.
> TU: He was limping round with a broken knee the whole time, then?
> Adem: Yeah. He said he used a plank and that, heh heh. He had been out for two hours and then the police call and ask, has anyone run off from you? And the prison has said no, no one. And then they have given them his name, and they have checked, gone down to his cell and the whole window was gone, heh heh.
> TU: Heh heh, that must have been a bit embarrassing then.
> Adem: Yeah, think about it, the prison didn't know he was out! He could have been out and come back and they wouldn't even have known. Bloody hell, heh heh.

For Adem, this was a story about a fellow prisoner who, even though he was returned quickly, managed to trick the prison and make the institution look foolish. He had demonstrated that the institution's control over the bodies that present an escape risk is not perfect and that, on the contrary, it is temporary and always at the mercy of the prisoners. The escape story was, thus, confirmation of who is *really* in control.

Nonetheless, public boundary testing and escape attempts are the exceptions. One of the legitimate arenas where prisoners can fight to prove themselves good and capable in everyday life is the pool table. The table is popular; as long as there are prisoners in the common area, there is usually someone playing pool. A practised eye can quickly tell whether someone is good or not by how he moves around the table. The pool player holds the cue in one hand with the tip up and angled away from the body, simple and effortless, while he moves to the best shot solution, almost before the balls have stopped after the previous shot. He shoots precisely and confidently, with just enough power to achieve what he wants. The beginner's biggest mistake is not knowing his own strength. Using too much power or playing pool according to the chaos method, without a clear plan for each shot, is regarded as amateurish, even when it works. When someone makes a mistake and sends a ball off the table due to the use of too much force, it is funny, and just a bit embarrassing, as when Amir, laughing, tells Timour after one such an unlucky shot involving too much power: *Hey, hey, hey, easy there lad. Do you need to go on an anger management course, or what?*

Meanwhile, there is room for variation within this framework. When he plays, Espen's body language is more aggressive than that of most of the others. He stands and stares at the table as if he really hates the balls. Even when, controlled and carefully, he nudges a ball so that it just rolls in, his body language gives the impression that he wants to destroy the entire table. For his part, Daniel's playing style communicates calm and self-control. With a modest self-ironic grin, he sinks balls after ball as if he is constantly mildly surprised that he is actually managing to do so.

Clearing the table is in itself not enough. The real test of virtuosity is not just sinking your balls, but managing to leave the white ball in position ready for the next shot. Planned movements of the body around the table, planned movements of the white ball, planned potting of the entire rainbow in front of acknowledging looks, all with precisely the right amount of power. The least possible effort, the least possible hesitation. These are the values for which the pool body strives.

In Whyte's (1955) classic study of gang life in "Cornerville", a poor Italian American neighbourhood of Boston, he shows how bowling became a meaningful metaphor for the social hierarchy in the gang, and between the gang and other groups. The members put their social rank to the test through bowling. As a rule, the existing hierarchy was reproduced in and through the game. Activities create general hierarchies. You can be more or less good, and you can ascribe more or less prestige to being good. Some of the same dynamics play out at the pool table in Oslo Prison. The person who does well can, since the winner stands, "own" the pool table throughout an entire hour's social, from beginning to end. Challengers come and go, but the master remains standing. In the end no one expects to win. Every time the master pots the black ball in the right pocket, his opponent just nods with a mixture of recognition and acceptance; it ended as it had to end. It is about a self-confidence that is linked to one's position in the gang. Sometimes one is in the "zone" where everything flows just as it should. The more self-confident you are, the more accessible this zone is, according to Whyte. And it is about the eyes watching; when someone who is considered a good player bowls poorly, he is having a bad day. When someone who is considered average bowls well, it is luck. When someone moves to the end of the table to break, there are already expectations about which of the two players *ought* to win. This man is under pressure. The man not under pressure is the one who is not expected to win.

The players in prison are not subjected to the type of deliberate interference that Whyte's bowlers are expected to put up with. But the pool table often attracts many spectators. As the same person wins more and more matches, the excitement rises. Who will manage to beat the master? At the same time, the spectators become more involved, sitting there with their arms crossed over their chests discussing the players' options, strategies and techniques. There is an informal "list" of good pool players. When prisoners who are not on the list exceed expectations and win a surprising victory over established players, it evokes humour. The same thing happened when a researcher managed, for once, to win a game:

> I'm playing Arfan. We play for a long time. It is going badly for both of us, but mostly for me. Towards the end Arfan suddenly pots the eight ball. He shakes his head and reluctantly walks to the sofa hanging his head and declaring to the others that I won, which evokes much laughter and pointing. And praise for me, even though the only thing I did was to watch him mess up and pot the eight ball too early. It is obviously extra embarrassing to lose to me – a non-prisoner who is known as a poor pool player. The mocking Arfan is subjected to is joking, but real enough.

For Whyte's gang members, bowling was what Geertz (1973a), with reference to cockfights on Bali, called "deep games". The deeper a fight, the more is at stake: masculinity, hierarchy, kinship, conflicts between centre and periphery and so on. Pool games in prison can also be more or less deep affairs, depending on who is playing and the relative position between them. One seldom plays on teams in prison (values such as "everyone should get a go", "the most important thing is to have fun", etc., are not particularly pronounced). But as a player one can, nonetheless, represent "teams" that are put up against each other in and through the pool match. If a prisoner and an officer play each other, the game immediately becomes a deep one. Two groups in conflict can meet via representatives for their groups in a game that thus becomes charged with a heavy subtext. If a status hierarchy based on age is put into play, the game is also deeper. On the other hand, less is at stake in a match between equals and the game becomes shallower, even if more "pure" prestige may also come into play. Pool is obviously a means of passing time, but it is far from *just* a means of passing time. Status is put on the stage and dramatized, or challenged and put to the test. The losing party can blame the equipment – one cue was shorter and was poorer. This can, of course, also be used to further increase prestige. Daniel consistently chose the equipment that was considered poorer in order to show how good he was when he usually won anyway, and to provide a ready-made explanation for any rare losses.

The foosball game is another arena where capacity and skill can be demonstrated. The difference between skilled players and beginners is, if possible, even greater than on the pool table just three metres away. The skilled player does what he wants: he can score at any time, he can pass to himself, and he has full control over the tiny ball. Beginners helplessly try to get the small plastic figures to spin as quickly as possible in the right direction, completely devoid of a plan. One example of this was seen when Erol played Adem. Erol was a skilled foosball player even before he arrived in the prison. After a year on remand, he had had a lot of time to practise. Adem had just arrived on the wing and was a newcomer when it came to foosball as well. Predictably enough, Erol was easily able to put the newcomer in his place by outclassing him:

> Erol is really something when it comes to this game. He can score at will, to Adem's great bewilderment. He can only stand and watch Erol dazzle; there's nothing he can do to stop him. Erol grins as, with a simple twist of his wrist, he yet again hammers the ball past Adem's passive keeper. I attempt to stretch out a hand to a frustrated loser:
> TU: That's just the way it is Adem, he's unbelievable. I played him a while ago; I've never taken a beating like that before in any game or sport. He is good.
> Erol, at least, greatly appreciates my comments. He grins and strolls over to the pool table. He moves with a naturalness and a presence in the room that show he feels completely confident and at home in the situation. He is soon called over to the table tennis table by a frustrated Adem, hunting for revenge. It ends in a loss for the newcomer here too. By the time the social is over, Adem has had enough. He has gone from loss to loss during the hour-long social. He has to prove what he is good for before being locked in. He takes centre stage by walking on his hands on top of the pool table. It does not look completely safe, and an extra officer glances nervously at one of the more experienced full-time officers. She just smiles; her entire posture shows she thinks Adem should be left to get on with it. He ends the show with a backwards somersault from a standing position in the middle of the floor, a feat that Erol, far heavier and more powerfully built, obviously cannot copy. The loser, Adem, has thus reconfirmed that he has a useful body, just in time before the cell door will be locked behind him.

Adem was thoroughly beaten in two different games, both of which are key to the production of physical capacity on the wing. As "pure physique", as a capable body, he well and truly got his own back with his heart-stopping stunt and somersault. On the way up the stairs, the smile and physical confidence were back.

The two officers afterwards commented on the performance, shaking their heads. They had not caught the entire prelude. That is why they instead framed Adem's performance in a narrative about a body that wanted too much, a body with too many things going on. The term ADHD was not used, but it was lurking in the background when one officer, smiling, sighed to the other: *There's a lot he needs to release during the day.* However, it is possible to apply another interpretive framework than just energy that *needs* to be released. Adem would not allow himself to be positioned in his pre-scribed place in the hierarchy. Both the foosball and the table tennis table interpellated him as passive, unfit and incapable. With his backwards som-ersault he had changed the framework and become an athletic body without limits.

What you do is important, but so is what you become. Bordo (1998) has described how in today's (Western) society we live in a culture that perceives the body as a plastic, changeable project. The body is a malleable starting point; shaping the body is each individual's responsibility. The body thus functions as an arena for work on the self, the shaping of a preferred or legitimate body that connotes the right social values, an important project (Heyes, 2007). Again, body techniques can function as techniques of the self (Warnier, 2001).

Bodies are understood and positioned in relation to a series of dichotomies: they can be small (and relatively harmless) or big (and threat-ening), short or tall, soft (lazy) or hard (fit), old or young, immature bodies or mature bodies. Comparable cultural perceptions of successful male bod-ies constitute the dichotomies in a masculine body hierarchy. In a society like ours, tall, hard, fit, young (but mature) male bodies are regarded as better than short, soft, lazy, old or immature bodies. The regulating gaze the surroundings direct at the body means that people regulate their bod-ies. Different men experience different positioning and objectifying gazes with different consequences. For example, brown bodies may be subjected to a different gaze from white ones (Finstad, 2000; Sollund, 2006). In prac-tice, the surroundings' expectations vis-à-vis the observed body will also vary depending on age, ethnicity, social class, sexual orientation, (more or less local) culture, and immediate context (Schwalbe and Wolkomir, 2001: 90). The individual's room for manoeuvre in the construction of the self thus partly depends on how these other variables are read in the male body being observed.

The male bodies in prison are also on display. Several people have described the key position that working out plays in the prisoners' daily lives (Johnsen, 2001; Sabo, 2001; Jewkes, 2005). What is the ideal body, the body that the body sculptors strive for? In prison the body should primarily be well trained, in contrast to slim. The body builder's body is the ideal, rather than the fitness freak's body that has gained hegemony in the rest of soci-ety. The shoulders should be broad, the upper body V-shaped, and the waist narrow. Arms and legs should have large, clearly defined, visible muscles.

The relationship between your body and the socially elevated one is a relationship of conformity or difference (Bourdieu, 1984, 1990). How much energy, time and money do people spend in their attempt to get their more or less plastic bodies to look like the socially legitimate body? In such a system the body, positioned in a hierarchy of more or less good-looking/strong/fit bodies and unlike bodies that are ugly/weak/lazy, can be a valuable difference-creating resource in the production of distance between your body and other, inferior bodies with other shapes. As when Abdi, who has just finished working out, is sweaty and has bulging muscles and wants to show off, sits in the sofa with the older Ricardo, who is not easily impressed:

> Ricardo: Here and here [pointing to Abdi's biceps and chest] it's good, but here [shoulders] you've got nothing. You have to work your shoulders more.
> Abdi: I would like to be much more defined. That's why I work out, to become defined, you know?
> Ricardo: Yes, and that means you have to work on your shoulders. That will accentuate the transition here [points between the shoulder and triceps on Abdi's arm].
> Abdi: Isn't it also true that if you want to bring out the definition then diet is really important?
> Ricardo: Yes, when I work out a lot, I eat six times a day, but only a little. Always a little.

The experienced man is giving the younger man exercise tips, critiquing his muscles, telling him what he should focus on and what he should eat. Ricardo's muscles function as an asset that affords him a position that means that someone like Abdi must listen to him.

The gaze directed at the male body changes as men get older. Age is a threat to the traditional masculine ideal's focus on hard, fit bodies. Where it used to be regarded as legitimate, or at least unavoidable, that the body changes over time, men today are under pressure to counter such change processes, or delay them for as long as possible. Several older prisoners expressed concern that the sedentary prison life was ruining their body projects. As in the following conversation between Tom and Brede, two of the oldest on the wing:

> Brede: This time in prison, I have noticed that I am tired. If you are 20 years old, you can cope with the isolation and sitting still pretty well. But, well, I'm not 20 anymore. At the most, I eat half of what I do on the outside and yet I've still put on seven–eight kilos while I have been in here. You notice you're getting older.
> Tom: Of course you do. I see that you're running a bit. I'm very focused on working out to stay in the best shape I can. It is very important to stretch all your joints properly.

Some prisoners run lap after lap, thereby demonstrating that they are not in as bad shape as their age would suggest, although, of course, they are not in as good shape as they were when they were young.

The wing's weights are also in constant use in the evening. For many, the body is, in line with Bordo's perspective, an expressed project. Daniel was an example of someone who felt that working out helped. He spent a lot of time on it and got noticeably bigger during his time on remand.

> Well, this is the only thing we can do in here. We need projects, you know? Something to focus on. Changing your body, working out and body building, is the only thing the prison facilitates for our recreation.

For Daniel, shaping his body is about passing the time, but also about a sense of mastery, about setting yourself goals and managing to achieve them. Majors (2001) describes how sport and working out can be an arena for masculine physical construction of the self among men with otherwise limited opportunities. The weight training is also sociable. Many have regular workout partners, which makes the working out a shared project. They help each other, support each other, and try to motivate each other to push the weight up one more time.

> After a while Daniel is joined at the weights by Ayhan. I am surprised to see that Daniel is a good deal stronger than the younger and seemingly fitter Ayhan. This means the weights have to be changed and changed back between each set. The equipment's geometric settings also have to be changed, since Ayhan is taller than Daniel. The machinery is old and rattly. Changing the settings is, therefore, a two-man job, or at least a job that is easier when there are two of you. Working out thus becomes a shared project; the two work out together, not after each other. After a while the obligatory "Come on!" and "Two more!" are heard and a supportive finger is placed on the bar when someone has had enough.

A workout session can involve a lot of fellowship and care when, with the sweat pouring, you stand together against the heavy weights. At the same time, both the prisoners and the staff agree that sport is a necessary safety valve for prisoners with a lot of pent-up frustration and that working out has an important mental hygiene function. The puffing and grunting are understood by both groups as audible signs of aggression dripping out of the bodies and accumulating as harmless puddles on the floor.

Hard and heavy bodies' potential for violence

Søndergaard (2006) describes the relationship young people in academia have to their own bodies. The healthy, fit body connotes, with its hard and firm, but not oversized, muscles, control over oneself and one's surroundings, a healthy lifestyle and an appropriate degree of modest interest in one's appearance. It communicates, writes Søndergaard, willpower, discipline, health and a capacity for social progression. The prisoners are interpreted and interpret themselves via another register. I have described how prisoner bodies are perceived by officers as disorder and potential risks, as untrustworthy bodies. How prisoners look at each other is different, but related. Erol explains what he sees when he sees a new prisoner on the wing:

> TU: But what do you look for, like when a new man comes onto the wing? What do you look for when you are deciding if this is someone you want to get to know or not?
>
> Erol: Me, well... first I look at the first impression, the way he walks, the way he is...
>
> TU: Posture?
>
> Erol: Posture, right; their body tells you a lot about each person here. And if you're a junkie, then you can see it straight away; if you are proper, then you can see that; if you are special in some way or other, in some context or profession or other, then you can see straight away what he is good for. I think we criminals, or who are regarded as criminals, we have the knowledge to see... people, based on their posture or body language, at once, faster than most people out there can, like. I mean, I think we recognise ourselves. I don't know, we just know what a person may stand for, kinda. We don't look for any special signs. I mean, I'm not the type who walks around and is interested in getting to know someone either, but, if there is something interesting, I mean, there are some things; if a person is very open, then he is not, right, the dog that barks, it doesn't bite.

A specific subcategory of capable bodies may be associated with the body's potential for violence. The body creates expectations. A body reveals whether its owner, as Erol says, is someone who stands for something, or whether he is a junkie one can ignore. The body, as a sign, promises something about the new prisoner who has arrived on the wing. For those who have a body that signals that you should take them seriously, the challenge becomes to fulfil what the body promises, to have a body that shows you are telling the truth. If you look like someone who stands for something, then you must stand for something. In this context, the body's size and, not least, weight are important. Body mass is read as a sign of capacity: having weight means, in a literal sense, being able to handle difficult situations. At the same time, it is regarded as interesting – either surprising or funny – when the order of things created by the bodies' signs is upset:

> Later on the sofa, Rune and Ayhan describe the last time there was a fight on the wing. Christian had gone over to Bassim and told him that he should watch himself because he, Christian, did kickboxing, whereupon Bassim had just knocked him right down. One punch.

Rune: Ha ha ha, Christian weighs 80 kilos, Bassim weighs 50, ha ha ha!

Ayhan: No, 49, ha ha ha!

Rune: He just knocked him flat. Bang! [Demonstrates by punching the air.]

Ayhan: The little guy. It's just so fucking funny. He was just like "I have been a kickboxer" and Bassim was just like "But I have been in a war". And then bang! Ha ha.

The mood was humorous the whole time. It is quite a laugh that big Christian was knocked down by a 49-kilo Iraqi, even if the Iraqi had actually been in a war and had a body full of shrapnel.

Whitehead's (2002) concept of physical toughness can be understood as a collective term that includes physical strength, but also toughness and courage, both of which are performative variables that must be *done* (1998). The hard male body must be solid. A man should not be afraid of hurting himself, but should be willing to risk his body. Toughness is also about the willingness to take risks. Physical capacity and competence (Connell, 1983) are more about the ability to take risks. The male body does not allow itself to be limited by the space, but conquers its surroundings and crosses boundaries. Male bodies should take on challenges, master their world, and move wherever they want. A hard, fit male body with clear muscle definition communicates willpower, focus, capacity, toughness and an ability to back up words with action, to stand for what one has said, to defend one's points of view if necessary. This is what I *stand* for. I will, in other words, not *lie down*, nor will I *turn* my back and run; I will instead *stand my ground*.

Øygarden (2001) describes, in his study of an amateur boxing scene in Stockholm, how a relationship between physical capacity and a potential for violence exists, and the link between words and actions. Stepping into the boxing ring means, knowingly and willingly, putting yourself in a risky position. If you retreat and leave the ring again, you risk your word, reputation and pride. If you step forward and face your opponent, you risk your body. In this way, boxers are, according to Øygarden, continuously balancing between dishonour and pain. Pride prohibits retreat; pain prohibits stepping forward. Stepping into the ring means stressing that what is said about you is more important than the physical pain. The burden of proof rests with the individual, with their body as the only tool. That is why boxers cultivate a feeling of having their back to the wall. When you feel your back is against the wall, the only choice is to step forward. This is the feeling boxers must produce in themselves before a fight:

> Many of the boys have invested years of training in order to avoid retreating. A physical potential can be reassuring, a freedom, but it can also be a

prison. A wall at your back limits elbow room. It is between those worthy of the duel that the hierarchies are built.

(2001: 233, my translation)

If you are what in German is called *duel-fähig*, and want to remain that, you must deal with the fact that the surroundings could hail you as a dueller. The person who is challenged must prove that he is actually worthy of the duel, that the body is not lying, because when the body does not fulfil its promises, as in the example with Christian and Bassim above, masculinity is threatened. By assuming and dealing with physical risk, the body can become a resource in the work of doing masculinity in relation to its surroundings (Messerschmidt, 2004). It is okay for men to lose, as long as they risked something by participating.

Young (2005c) describes women's existential experience of having a threatened body. For Young, this experience had a constituting effect for women's gendered relationship with their own bodies. This is also true for men; the difference is that, as a man, one perceives and must perceive an obligation to actively take account of such risks. This is the case when Arfan talks about how he thinks twice before he positions his body in the space that is the prison wing's common area:

> Arfan: I always like to sit with my back to the wall, you know? I became like that after the shooting episode. You just never know what is coming up behind you.
> He leans demonstratively against the wall behind him.
> TU: Yeah, you know now.
> Arfan: Yeah, it's fine now. But I always sit with my back to the wall.

A man should actively deal with threatening risks, and he should be able to defend himself and his loved ones should anything occur. This is why the body's weight and heaviness play a special role in the environments Øygarden describes, and in prison. Having weight is often used as a metaphor for experience and the capacity to handle difficult situations. In prison, where the potential for violence is a living part of the male body's repertoire of skills, physical weight is a benefit. This is not the case outside in the rest of society, according to Kolnar (2005a). He uses the example of Pat Bateman, the main character in Bret Easton Ellis's novel *American Psycho*, to discuss the masculine body ideal as the so-called *hard body*. A hard body is, according to Kolnar, a modern version of the hardened male body: "[M]uscular and polished, it stands as the impregnable front against the world. The male body thus becomes its own communicative universe, a reservoir of symbols and masculinity markers" (2005: 13, my translation). In the body semiotics Kolnar describes, obesity is feminising and a sign of poorly developed masculinity in general.

For prisoners, putting weight on is just fine, and something many actively seek to achieve, but preferably by trying to increase the body's muscle mass by lifting weights. However, the passivity of a life with little activity means that many experience their body changing in a negative way. Reduced consumption of illegal drugs and steroids can have the same effect. Aesthetically, Erol feels that he is degenerating. He can sigh heavily when he shows pictures of himself taken by the accident and emergency unit in connection with an episode where he was shot four times:

> I saw the pictures that would be used in court as well, my lawyer showed them to me. Fuck, they made me sick. It looked fucking horrible. But I do miss having that back. The pictures are from behind, with my back to them, and I was a lot bigger then. I used to use steroids and worked out some. I weighed around 130 kilos. Now I'm down to 113. You don't get big taking steroids if you don't work out, you just get fat, and in here I can't work out like I should. So now I've lost almost 20 kilos and at the same time got fat. But he said it to my lawyer, the prosecutor in the case did: "I have seen the pictures and your client does not look like the type one should try it on with." "No," said the lawyer, "they tried it on with the wrong man."

Erol misses the back he can see in the picture, and, of course, it is the muscle definition he means, not the bullet wounds. However, at the same time, having the physical weight that means no one can easily push him around is a key part of his self-understanding, as on another occasion when he talks about a conflict with Ilir that could easily have deteriorated:

> Fuck, Thomas, he was standing there [pointing to the spot] and said that I should shut up and that, completely mad. Fuck, I just said to "calm down little man, if you don't, there could be consequences that you don't like." Bloody hell, he doesn't weigh more than 60 kilos! And that's with the bed he lies on! I mean, he'd have no chance against me. But he just stood there, shouting. He was on his way down to the fourth floor, face first, over the railings, I'm not kidding! Just then he was so fucking close. But I was calm, and said he could just fuck off out of my cell [...] I feel sorry for the lad, right, I think he's one of those psychopaths. I mean, it's not... he could be capable of killing, he could, to prove something, to drag you down to his level; if he can't manage that, then he could injure you, like, if he has something to hand; I mean, I doubt that he could hurt me, but you always have to watch your back with people like that, to put it that way.

Being a lightweight is challenging. The small body basically lacks the potential for violence, even if it can surprise and attack you from behind. The big, heavy body, the body with weight, is a potentially far more dangerous body. In this culture, the male body connotes hardness, the female body softness. However, this is, to some extent, transformed when the softness is coupled with superior size and weight.

Scars as signs of capable bodies

The scars of those who have stood their ground, who have backed up their words with their bodies and paid the price, are borne with pride. Scars and war wounds become trophies as anecdotes of a life lived and former feats. For Erol, the scars on his body are a source of pride:

> Erol is lounging in his workout clothes on the sofa, smiling. He is telling me and Naveed about the bullet wounds in his thigh, knee and arms. One arm bears a long, thick scar that runs almost from his shoulder to his wrist, right through his elbow. I am shaking my head; the mood is filled with restrained laughter as one scar is succeeded by another. He pulls his shorts down a few centimetres and shows the bullet holes in his hip and the small of his back as well.
> TU: Bloody hell!
> Erol: Heh heh. Yeah. But, I mean, I chose a hard life, right. All this and I'm only 23 years old. Think about it!

Scars from stab wounds or bullets that are still in the body are both reminders that you literally carry with you and signs of your career so far. The anecdote about Bassim, who knocked down his far bigger fellow prisoner, had consequences when he got to show off his scars as confirmation of his war experiences and his general hardness.

> Bassim also has his scars. He shows a right arm with 20 or so large and small scars up and down his arm. Pieces of shrapnel from Iraq. Many of them are still in place. We are allowed to feel the shrapnel and nod in acknowledgement. More scars are mentioned and shown. My scars are really not worth mentioning. I remain quietly in the background.

The scars also became visual aids when Erol related what had happened, the events that had left their mark on his body:

> Erol: ... and then they say to me "aren't you going to lie down?" [...] and I say "no, I don't intend lying down", and then they say "you have to lie down" and I say "I'm not going to be gay and turn around for you", in other words turn my arse to you, "what do you want?" "No, lie down, blah blah blah", and so I charge the one wearing the mask, because I'm having him, and he shoots first and hits me in my left knee, but again I don't go down, and then the other one shoots and he hits me in my

right thigh, but again I don't go down and keep fighting, and try to take the gun from the one wearing the mask, and he shoots again, in my left thigh, and then I say "okay, that's enough", because I started losing blood, and of course, I'm also losing energy, and then I say "okay, I'm getting down now, slowly", then I hear handcuffs, one of them is trying to pull some out, so I panic again, and so I resisted again, and then he shot a fourth round into my back.

TU: Bloody hell.

Erol: And that was enough, heh heh. And so I lay down, and they put handcuffs on me.

[...]

Erol: So the Pakistani without the mask started to talk. He said that he wanted three million from me, and so on, so I ask why he should get it and, like, he said that he owned Oslo, and that I was working in their city, and that I have done so well that he thought I owed him three million, so it was a type of fine, right, because I hadn't asked who owned Oslo. So I say, okay, if you own Oslo, then you wouldn't hide your face, so let me see the face of the other one, and then okay, I will pay you. They say no, you will pay us now, and then he starts whipping me with a sort of cable, wire, chain, whatever, cable, for two and half hours; then they hit me, hit me everywhere, right, the worst was when they hit me eight to ten times in the same place on the back, like.

TU: Where you were shot?

Erol: No, like, over my whole back, whole head, I mean, I have marks here on my head from where they pistol-whipped me, with the tip of the gun like, and tried to... they tried everything like, they wanted their three million, and they got some stuff; I had a watch that was worth 240,000 and I had a gold chain that weighed 450 grams...

TU: You must have been a total mess?

Erol: I was a total mess, I was, after all, I had lost a great deal of blood, right, but again right... if one is strong enough mentally, then I think, you can cope with most things. Although, I had started to swell up, right, I had started to get really bad. I started to swell up in my face and my arms and so on, so again I managed to get myself down, and get myself into my car, and drove at 240 kilometres an hour to accident and emergency in Oslo.

The scars were an integral part of Erol's narrative and self-positioning. He stood up and pulled off his t-shirt or pulled down his trousers to show off the visible evidence to illustrate what he was telling us. Erol was kidnapped, but he did not give up voluntarily. He was scared, but had also demonstrated vigour, courage and strength when confronted with a superior, armed force. Real men who have lived real lives should have the scars to prove it. A good scar is added to the capable male body's CV and can be shown when necessary: as when, on another occasion, I asked him whether he was not scared of being caught for some of his "grey zone" cooking and he answered: *Eh? Are you kidding me? I've been shot four times. Do you really think I'm worried about anything they can do to me?* Showing his scars is an opportunity to tell a story about his own courage and vigour. It also works the other way; when one displays courage and vigour in other ways, the scars can be brought up and further confirm the impression.

All in all, the prison wants cooperative prisoner bodies. The prisoners work on not being (just) cooperative bodies; instead, they use their bodies as a resource to turn themselves into something else. The prisoner body is, at the same time, necessary for the prison as a power system and, therefore, a meaningful tool for resistance. When the prison's efforts are directed at dangerous bodies that must be made inactive, waiting, passive bodies, removed from their familiar arenas for mastery, then staying active, not letting yourself be defined by it, and mastering and managing something, can partly be understood as a form of resistance and partly as self-positioning in proximity to normal masculinity markers. In this way, prisoners become capable men who are doing resistance.

Moral men

Edel and Edel's (1959) *Anthropology and Ethics* takes as its starting point the idea that ethics and morality constitute a key part of a society's foundations. Every member of every society, understood in a broad sense, is expected to accept and comply with a bottom line of shared perceptions of goals and benefits in order to be perceived as, and remain, a member of the society. Ethics is understood here as social systems of conduct that deal with what you can or should do and not do. It is said that no man is an island, and shared norms are a key part of what binds a group together as a group, regardless of the depth of the research. This is the background for their attempts to systematise the terminology in the area of norms, ethics and morality.

What is clear from Edel and Edel's systematisation is that human cultures have displayed enormous breadth with respect to what is perceived as good and evil, right and wrong, and honourable and dishonourable in different contexts. The ethical standards of human societies constitute a myriad of different, sometimes completely incompatible, systems. The differences go beyond the simple difference between the formulations of the specific rules: the systems also vary with regard to the norms' choice of sanctions, preferred control system and degree of coercion, to mention just a few of the analytical dimensions Edel and Edel suggest.

Why ethics? Why have people even decided to order their societies in such a way that right and wrong have meaning? There are several possible answers to this question. For Edel and Edel, systems of ethics are different answers to pretty much the same question. They are built up and developed over a long time, but they are all formed by common human biological and psychological needs and processes. Different cultures have developed different answers.

When thought of as practical activities, they bind individuals to a relevant system of ethics and, by extension, to a society or a group that shares, or is perceived as sharing, the same values. From such a perspective, talking about private ethics makes little sense. The question then becomes: who counts, morally speaking? How do people draw the boundaries around their shared morality? Edel and Edel distinguish between having a moral status, in other words being someone or something with intrinsic value in moral assessments, and being a moral participant. The net is cast relatively widely in our society; *all* people currently alive today (including, for example, women, children and old people) have a moral status. So can animals and trees, although rocks basically cannot. As yet unborn people have been afforded a moral status in environmental questions, although they can hardly be expected to participate morally. Therefore, one can act morally in relation to a dog and one's as yet unborn offspring, but not a flagstone or a washing machine. If you choose to dump an old washing machine in a city's drinking water, you are, again, perhaps acting unethically in relation to other people, but not the machine.

It is not difficult to find examples of moral status and moral participation having been organised differently. In the past, for example, some races of people have been denied a moral status, with all the subsequent consequences this has had. Moral participation also changes. When the term "child robbers" takes the place of "boyish pranks" this may, for example, indicate that children are expected to be moral participants in a different way from before. The gendered aspect of morality also becomes visible when the term "boyish pranks" is used, which I will return to below.

Where ethical norms exist, you will find some form and degree of encouragement to comply with the norms, ways of complying with them in practice, and practices that are deemed deviant. These are often associated with some form of sanction, whether it be social disapproval or the death penalty. This is ethics in practice. From this perspective, ethics focuses on what is required to turn yourself into an ethical person and what should happen to unethical people. Anthropology that focuses on ethics can thus study what the world looks like because of this, which categories are put to work, and which dividing lines are constituted and continued in and through a group of individuals performatively making themselves into ethical people.

One feature of norms, in particular, will be highlighted in the following: ethics creates a dividing line between ethical and unethical people. Therefore, ethics functions as a "dividing practice" (Foucault, 2000c). Every good, ethically sound action carries with it, via its reference to the system of ethics that turns it into a correct action, condemnation or, at least, disparagement of the wrong. From this perspective, morality is about membership of a moral collective and the parallel exclusion and condemnation of the unethical. Morality is, in this way, part of the social glue. Moral people come together as carriers of a shared moral perception, unlike, and a safe distance away from, immoral others. It is ethics and morality in practice, as adopted in the continuous subjectification work, that are in focus here. This means that I will not be describing people's actions and choices in themselves; I will be describing how they articulate moral categories in specific contexts in order to position themselves as moral people, with all this entails, and in contrast to various forms of immorality (Davidson, 1986; Laidlaw, 2002).

Individuals have long been expected to behave as ethical people. In *The Care of the Self* (1990a) Foucault describes how a fundamental change took place in the first two centuries of our era when care for the self became an obligation for everyone, of all ages, and also a goal in itself, rather than something you should do for the sake of the city state, as was the case before. The subject is expected to have an active relationship with himself, to actively participate in controlling himself and producing himself as an ethical person. The self's relationship with itself is, therefore, a power relationship, because it represents a way of relating to yourself, working on yourself, mastering yourself, and achieving power over yourself and, therefore, becoming yourself in a specific way. This has become something that is expected of all subjects who want to maintain their moral status in our society, although the specific techniques that the individual is expected to use may vary. Foucault analyses several of these techniques – first and foremost through examples taken from antiquity – associated with everything from the correct enjoyment of food and drink and how best one should relate to a desire for young boys in the context of antiquity, to admission and confession in early Christian tradition. The unfinished five-volume work *The History of Sexuality* (Foucault, 1990a, 1990b, 1992) is not really a history of sexuality; it is a history of practices that have been used to constitute ethical people. This has, from and including the advent of Christianity, largely been done through sexuality. The area of sexuality is, therefore, a privileged example, and that is why antiquity is so interesting by contrast, since no "sexuality", in the modern sense, existed then as an underlying collective attribute that could tell the truth about a subject. Moderation in the area of sexual intercourse was just one of several forms of desirable moderation, one of the areas where individuals had to work on themselves in order to overcome temptation and master themselves.

Freedom and responsibility are key concepts. An ethical action presupposes that it is possible to freely make an ethical choice. Without this possibility, no one can be made responsible for acting correctly. This is why Foucault describes techniques of the self as freedom practices. Doing freedom simultaneously produces free individuals, just as doing ethics produces ethical individuals. From such a perspective, freedom and its benefits are produced together through doing. Freedom does not mean being able to act according to your *real* or *true* will, nor is freedom the name given to the total absence of restrictions. Foucault's concept of freedom, as described above, is situational and performative, and always directly coupled to the limits of freedom. The subject makes himself both free and ethically conscious by positioning himself as a subject in relation to the forms of freedom and ethics.[17] This is a self-constituting freedom, which, of course, also includes the possibility of wanting to live out a desire to be an unethical person; without such a potential possibility the "free" choice would be of limited value. At the same time, this entails, in some sense, limiting one's own freedom. Those who simply do whatever occurs to them are slaves to their own impulses. Those who restrain themselves and manage to exercise a form of self-control are free in relation to their impulses and inclinations.

Ethical actions and neutralisation

Through a particular form of behaviour that is perceived as compliance with a set of rules, the acting subject becomes the ethical subject. Althusser's example of the encounter in the street also describes a situation in which an ethics-based hailing applies. The criminal on the street: who should he be? Should he be the repentant sinner, the criminal with a bad conscience? Or the street-smart criminal who tries to slip away? Or the uncompromising criminal who will not let himself be caught without a fight (a fight that, in this example, could even entail a risk of ending up in the emasculating, unethical position of being the man who is willing to hit a female police officer)? The choice between these alternatives is not a "choice" in a rational sense of the word "choice". It is a situational choice, a choice that must have beneficial effects there and then. Can he outrun the female police officer? Can men hurt women? Is the police officer even a "woman"? How can you explain that you hurt someone to get away? In a specific context, one may be faced with a choice between options that are perceived as more or less correct from an ethical perspective. An unethical choice must be defensible, or at least understandable. Reacting to an interpellating hail entails associating oneself with, or positioning oneself in relation to, society's dominant values. How do actors position themselves as ethical individuals in such an ongoing process? Is snitching an option to avoid criminal prosecution? And what does that make you?

Where do "immoral acts" come from? Why do people breach the norms they believe in and perceive as important? This is the question Sykes and Matza (1957) discuss in their classic essay on neutralisation techniques. The authors take as their starting point a critique of Cohen (1955), among others, who writes about a deviant subculture in which the values have been turned on their head. The subculture has a set of values that are the absolute opposite of those of the law-abiding majority, a reversal of values. This results in deviant behaviour. The main point Sykes and Matza make is that this is not about "morals turned on their head", but society's "normal" set of values combined with a number of neutralisation techniques. In other words, they find that juvenile offenders have the same values and norms, and feel the same pressure to conform, as ordinary, law-abiding people, but that with the aid of these techniques they manage to combine deviant actions and non-deviant values. Deviants share the dominant values in society, but use techniques to turn their specific histories into exceptions.[18]

Norms are generally flexible, not absolute. That means that they do not apply regardless of context; they are not binding in all contexts. One example of this could be the norm: "thou shalt not kill". In war, for example, it is permissible to kill the enemy. This is also true in criminal law. Punishment is only applicable when no mitigating circumstances exist. The neutralisation techniques, say Sykes and Matza, function as such mitigating circumstances that are not widely recognised as such by the general public; indeed, they may only be recognised as such by the actor. Sykes and Matza discuss five techniques. *Denial of responsibility* involves the offender viewing himself as being moved by external forces, not as someone acting on his own. A person who does not act voluntarily cannot be held responsible for his acts and has thus not really transgressed any norms. *Denial of injury* involves no real harm or damage having been caused by the act. If no harm or damage has occurred, then there really is nothing to discuss. It is not unethical to steal from those who are well insured. *Denial of the victim* involves changing the victim's status to someone who deserved what happened. The offender becomes, through "subtle alchemy", an avenger or a defender, not an illegitimate assailant. *Condemnation of the condemners* doubts the motives and actions of those who regard the offender as a deviant. The many errors and deficiencies of the police or the System are highlighted and explain why things turned out as they did. Finally, an *appeal to higher loyalties* can work by the offender recognising that what happened was wrong, but that he had no choice because he had to be true to a higher, more important rule. Examples of statements based on the five neutralisation techniques could be: "I didn't mean it", "I haven't really hurt anyone", "they got what they deserved", "everyone is after me" and "it was illegal, but not wrong".

The neutralisation techniques make it possible to position yourself as an ethically aware subject, even in the face of widespread ethical condemnation and stigmatisation by your surroundings (Cavanagh et al., 2001; Presser, 2004). In this sense, the neutralisation techniques can function as part of a broader ethical technique of the self. From Foucault's perspective, ethics as a practice is necessarily a relational exercise; becoming an ethical subject in and through everyday life's ongoing subjectification game means making yourself observable (to others as well as yourself) as an ethical subject. Success in the game means necessarily having to relate to one or more ethical others. It is on such ethical relationships, as they apply in prison, that the rest of the section focuses: through relationships with their families, the prisoners turn themselves into responsible men; through their relationship to rapists, the prisoners turn themselves into rational, professional criminals; through their relationship to snitches, they become men who can be trusted; and through transforming the victims' status, they become harmless and understandable.

The good prison father

A boy of three or four runs across a lawn to a group of adults who are sitting and talking. He shouts "Dad, Dad!" One of the adults, a man, looks towards him, answers "Yes?" and gets up. From Althusser's perspective, this is more than just a local exchange between two related people. It can, for example, be read as an articulation of the relationship that a specific social and cultural community envisages between a parent and child, of a legal institution created to order and organise familial relationships, of discourses about gendered differences between fathers and mothers, of cultural perceptions of what a child is and so on. All this meshes and is articulated in and through the concrete relationship between two people, who are thus positioned on a local level in relation to each other as the subjects "dad" and "son".

What is a "good father" in a contemporary Scandinavian context? With a small historical detour (based on Sweden of the 1800s), one can say that the father's position in the family was connected to his status as the head of the family, which in turn was connected to and supported by the father's work that provided the family with access to material goods, his role as the physical guarantor of safety, and his status as the educated or experienced guide; "father knows best" (Johansson, 1998). Father may not, perhaps, have been particularly talkative (being interested in talking was a female thing), but, when he spoke, he did it with the weight of the person who decided. Father's voice was law, a voice that could differentiate between right and wrong, and punish the wrong. "Your father will hear about this" was synonymous with saying "you will be punished for this". On the other hand, father was pretty worthless in some more down-to-earth areas. Men have been viewed as incompetent carers. The helpless father, who tries to do things in areas he basically does not master, such as practical childcare, has long been a comic figure. Lorentzen (2006) describes three historical areas of responsibility: providing for the family, cooperating with the mother in forming a child's moral character, and equipping a child, especially a son, with the attributes necessary for them to do well in life. A good father, therefore, was a father who put food on the table, who owned the moral truth and was able to transmit this to his child, and who taught (male) children what they needed to know in order to tackle life outside the family, a life with which the mother was unfamiliar. It was a polarised gender culture in which men and women, as men and women, faced different expectations, were assumed to have different attributes and were ascribed totally different psyches (Johansson, 2001: 164).

Although this may be perceived as old-fashioned, a traditional perception of a father's rights and obligations similar to this still resonates in a Norwegian context; it has what T. Johansson calls social evidence (2001: 164). The content of the positions and the differences between them have, of course, changed to some extent, but even today we live in a polarised gender culture where fathers and mothers have different rights, obligations, strengths and weaknesses. For example, it is easy to find notions about such differences in debates about paternity leave and fathers' rights when couples separate (e.g. fathers as inferior or at least poorly trained carers). At the same time, the middle-class, patriarchal stereotype's attributes and duties are sustained in the positions "father" and "good father". The difference is that the *pater familias* figure faces greater competition than before. Various other institutions were given a greater say in a child's upbringing during the 1800s. Today, much of the father's traditional power base has been replaced by various public institutions and systems. At the same time, the power centre that was previously dominated by men has been given to, or at least been partly populated by, women. The father is no longer the indisputable head of the family; authority in family life is shared between more people, while the role of parent has been thoroughly regulated. The patriarchal father has thus been, and is being, challenged and has been joined by alternative discourses that offer alternative positions for fathers. The result is that the father's powerful position as the head of the family has, at least partly, been replaced by a demand for activity, presence, involvement and participation. The notion that a mother should participate in her child's upbringing has been a given. The notion that a father should also participate, and even on an equal basis (if not in exactly the same way), has become an expectation for the modern Scandinavian father. One could say that the involved and present father has become a hegemonic ideal in a Scandinavian context (Brandth and Kvande, 2003; Forsberg, 2007). And, on the level of practice, it seems that fathers are actually more present in their children's upbringing than before (Holter, Svare and Egeland, 2008), even if some research results indicate that there may be some disparity between real life and surveys (Olsen and Aarseth, 2006; Forsberg, 2007). The use of time is an important measure of a good father within this discursive context. Spending time with the family, at least so-called "quality time", helps to bind the family together and is in the best interests of all involved. This equal use of time is a central value in the Scandinavian, equal middle-class family's view of the world: modern, equal parents are supposed to alternate with respect to duties and tasks in everyday life (Forsberg, 2007).

In parallel with this, a father's absence from the everyday life of his family has been redefined as a social problem. Absent, invisible and, in the worst case scenario, irresponsible fathers are a common concern (Johansson, 2001). The father who does not see the importance of such a participatory father's role has been clearly marginalised. A father's allocation of time to family life has become a question of values; the bad father is a father who prioritises wrongly, who does not take responsibility, who is not there, and who is an unethical father.

By extension, based on this rough historical outline, the term *father* cannot be understood as an unchanging constant; instead, it is the name given to a subject position that can be linked to different discourses, with various consequences for the definition of the role of "father" in practice. Nor is an individual simply a father; he can vary between different father positions, even within a single conversation (Forsberg, 2007: 112). The family is the central arena for this subjectification game in which good and bad fathers are positioned.

In Edel and Edel's (1959) ethics anthropology, the starting point for the analytical part of the book is a moral norm linked to what they call humanity's perhaps most basic need and moral feeling; the norm that a mother should look after her child. This is about as close as one can get to a universal moral imperative across cultures; it is, according to Edel and Edel, even more widespread than the prohibition against incest, which they also discuss. Having said that, the terms "mother", "child" and "care for" are obviously filled with different content in different contexts. How this norm is administered, sanctioned and formed in specific contexts is and has been very different. What specifically defines figures such as "the good mother" and "the good father" may vary between cultures: "The actual behaviour of a 'good mother' in one culture may horrify and shock the mother in another culture, equally concerned with child welfare" (Edel and Edel, 1959: 38).

Being a moral *man* is not necessarily the same as being a moral *person*. Some ethics-based interpellation hails can be general, while others can, to varying degrees, be gendered. Mothers *must* care for their children; that is a fundamental ethical requirement. Thus, ethical standards often involve different roles and expectations for men and women. If a man and a woman fight, this is a situation where the woman is basically understood as the (moral) victim, while the man is positioned as the (immoral) culprit. Men are subject to some specific expectations that women are not (and vice versa, of course); being a "man of honour" means precisely that, being a *man*, not a woman. Men and women experience different moral expectations.

Bosworth (1999) finds that the imprisoned women in her study gain strength, the energy to resist, agency and self-esteem from the roles of mother, wife, girlfriend and daughter. They feel that they "are treated like children", while the officers forget that they have children themselves on the outside, which becomes a source they can draw on to achieve the status of adult. They turn themselves into adult, competent people through their relationship with their children, a relationship that simultaneously positions them as *mothers*.

[T]he prisoners' images of themselves as active, reasoning agents is constantly under assault from institutional constraints which encourage them to exhibit traditional, passive, feminine behaviour at the same time as denying them independent identities and responsibilities as real mothers, wives, girlfriends, and sisters. They must, therefore, negotiate discourses which valorise traditional, passive forms of femininity – epitomised by the work and education typically offered by establishments – as well as those which encourage autonomy, agency, responsibility – found, for instance in the valorisation of motherhood.

(Bosworth, 1999: 218)

Positioning oneself as a mother is not the same as positioning oneself as a father. The women in Bosworth's data highlight housework, cooking and making the home "work" in day-to-day life. So, what about fathers? What should and can men do as part of the rights and obligations associated with the position of *father*? Is there such a thing as specific father ethics? In a context like this one, the answer clearly appears to be positive. Taking care of the family, providing food, clothes and safety for those for whom you are responsible, and taking responsibility on behalf of the family, in everyone's best interests, are moral and ethical obligations men have felt and still feel. The fact that the equal society has changed some of the concrete expressions of such obligations does not mean that they do not still apply. From this perspective, being a good father means acting within the ethical requirements for good fathers.

Living conditions surveys indicate that more than half of prisoners in Norwegian prisons have children, and that most of these children are under 18 years old. Most of the prison parents were responsible for the daily care of their children or had visiting rights at the time of their imprisonment, and eight out of ten maintain at least weekly contact during their time in prison (Skardhamar, 2002; Friestad and Hansen, 2004). Apart from this, as in society on the outside, there is a great deal of variation between the various family constellations and familial relationships of which the prisoners are a part. Some have children abroad whom they do not see very often, with women with whom they are no longer together. Some have children with more than one woman, with whom they have sometimes very different relationships. Some are married with children who come and visit them every week. Some experience conception, the entire pregnancy and the subsequent birth from inside the prison. *Made in Oslo Prison*, responded a prisoner with a broad grin when I congratulated him on his new baby.

Given the requirements for participation and empathy to which *the good father* is subject, imprisonment in itself may propel a prisoner towards the position of *bad father*. After all, in a certain practical sense it is obvious that a prison sentence will entail dad being relatively absent for a period. As far as the subject position *good father* is concerned in today's Norwegian gender equality discourse, where good fathers are present fathers who are involved in their child's life on a detailed level, being absent is in itself an expression of a man being a bad father. Prison fathers are positioned outside the family's day-to-day life, most of them unable to provide for their loved ones and spend time with them every day. There are three main ways of communicating with family and friends on the outside when you are in prison: telephone calls, letters and visits. The wing has a small telephone room adjoining the officers' room. Officers can open a curtain and lift a handset from their desk to monitor phone calls from the small telephone room. Phone calls must be booked via a booking form that is handed out in the morning so that the officers can organise their working day as efficiently as possible. Prisoners are basically allowed 20 minutes of phone time a week. This is not a fixed rule, but a way of administering a benefit that ensures everyone has a fairly equal share. If, when the end of the week nears, the phone queue is fairly short, it is possible to get a few extra minutes more than the 20 minutes. It is also possible for prisoners with children to apply for extended phone privileges of up to 40 minutes per week.

Post to and from the prison generally works as it does on the outside, with the obvious difference that letters in both directions must pass via officers who open them and read the contents. The only exception to this rule is communications between lawyers and clients. On the other hand, letters between fathers and children are read by a third party looking for more or less concealed messages and information.

People who want to visit someone in prison must contact the visiting unit to book a visit. Prisoners are basically allowed two hours of visits per week, but, again, it is possible to sign up for more if there are vacant spots. The visiting unit is also flexible when next of kin have travelled a long way. The Norwegian Correctional Services conduct a basic background check of visitors, who, if everything is okay, are then assigned a visiting time. The person arrives at the prison, signs in, passes through the metal detector gate, and meets "their" prisoner in "visiting". I have already described the L-shaped, yellow-beige room where up to six prisoners can meet their families at the same time. In other words, every meeting between father and child takes place with other prisoners and other prisoners' children present, and officers behind a mirror observing them. This situation affects the interaction between father and child. For Erol, this meant never being able to totally relax as long as he was in an official prison context:

> I have no opportunity to be with the kids alone in a room, to experience playing with them, being stupid, making faces, doing what the hell I want; like with games, throwing myself on the floor and doing exactly what suits me. Like, I'm being watched all the time.

The visiting room is not a private room; it is a room in the prison. The meeting between father and child is, therefore, characterised by the fact that it takes place in a prison, by the prison's meaning-bearing categories. In this official room you have to be careful about how people will view you. Even though the idea of putting games and toys in the corner naturally makes the room as unlike a prison as possible, it is not enough for the fathers to forget where they are.

Many experience their situation in relation to their family as desperate. Being unable to support their family, a duty that has always been one of the cornerstones of the role of father, is painful. Erol reflected on this while we stood bent over the package of new clothes we had been down to reception to fetch:

> Erol: Is it any wonder that I love my wife?
> He unpacks the new clothes and lays them out on the bed, smiling, pleased that everything looks like it will fit.
> Erol: It is strange though; I've thought about it. In a way I've now become my wife's wife. Like, she buys things for me now. It doesn't feel quite right.

Imprisonment has deprived Erol of his status as the family breadwinner, the one who puts food on the table. It does not really feel right, he said, which can only be understood as an understatement, given his subsequent description of the allocation of responsibilities in his home:

> Erol: After all, our [Albanian] women don't say anything. Not a word. As long as I continue to put food on the table and pay the bills, she doesn't say a word. As soon as that disappears, then she'll say something, but until then, not a word. That's like the natural way of dividing up responsibilities for us. Both are happy with it. After all, not every wife gets a car from their husband. And when my son turned one, I bought him a flat. So, she has nothing to complain about, really. My brothers, all their wives are envious. They see her driving round in a brand new Mercedes. My brother is a bus driver. He can't do that sort of thing for his wife.

Erol's role as a father is linked to his ability to provide for his family. The fact that he proudly describes extravagant gifts simply underscores the point: a family man is a man who provides for his family, who has and takes responsibility for ensuring the family has everything it needs, and perhaps a bit more.

So much for fathers as providers. It is not only money that good fathers should contribute; they should, as previously mentioned, also give of their time. Someone who is not present during their child's upbringing, someone who cannot share quality time with their young ones, is not a good father either. Investing time in your child's upbringing is also necessary in order for a father to perform his traditional duty of preparing a child to tackle life outside the family. Not being able to see your children is painful. The fact that you are letting them down, the fact that by being absent you cannot give of your time (which is something you now have more than enough of), and are thus being a bad father, is just as painful. For many, the feeling of missing life on the outside primarily means missing those they love the most. The pain imprisonment entails is even more intense when it comes to children. The starting point for many prisoners' desperation is them imagining life on the outside. Out there life continues without them, a day-to-day life that in some ways may have been made more difficult for the family because they are locked up. The family suffers financially and it must, in many cases, live with the stigma associated with dad being in prison. Because what should you tell them? How much do children understand and how can they relate to the fact that dad is a prisoner? This is something Erol thinks about a lot:

> Erol: After all, he understands everything! He wants to go to papa, where's papa? No, papa's at school. That's what my wife has said, right; papa has gone off to finish school.
>
> TU: Well, it is true [Erol is a pupil at the school]?
>
> Erol: Yes, well, it is true, but, heh heh, I didn't exactly leave voluntarily, to put it like that.
>
> TU: That works, he buys that?
>
> Erol: Yes, he buys that. He misses me so fucking much though, he talks about me every day, picks up the phone at home, my wife says, and pretends he is talking to me, and...
>
> TU: And pretends that you are on the phone?
>
> Erol: Yes, sort of. I mean, I'm not sure he has actually felt that dad is coming, dad is coming; he has said that loads the whole time, sort of pretends that he is talking to me on the phone, and says to my parents and my wife that dad is coming. They say that perhaps it is an omen that you are coming out on leave, heh heh, but, well, I don't know. I don't want to claim that victory in advance.
>
> TU: That's tough, eh?
>
> Erol: Yeah, kids are tough, but, seriously, I don't know if everyone feels as strongly, has the feelings for their family that I do, but those who do have some feelings, well, it is very hard being in here when you have family, you know? It's why you don't... it's why you should have thought before you did anything out there. And by that I mean think things through properly, because it isn't worth it.

Erol's son was supposed to be spared from knowing that his father was in prison, but it is difficult, given how smart he is. It was especially difficult, given that he missed his father so much, a sense of expressed loss that was reciprocated by Erol, and which was a source of pride; he himself emphasised that he was one of those who particularly missed their families.

Brede has accepted the consequences of his children possibly having to experience the negative consequences of having a father in prison in a different way. He has sent his two youngest children to their mother abroad:

> Brede: I don't want them to experience ending up at the bottom of the social ladder.
> TU: What do you mean?
> Brede: You know, with a dad in prison and everything that comes with that; that isn't easy for a little kid. They went to [school in Oslo's west end]. It's not easy having a dad in Botsen there. Down there [abroad] it's different. Down there it's like, if you have a bit of money and are a nice guy, then you are on top. Everyone likes you. It's not like that here [in Norway]; it's more closed in a way. Everyone is more interested in status, so when your dad is in prison you are really at the bottom. I don't want my kids to have to experience that.

The painful feeling of missing their closest loved ones is often associated with the prison institution in more general terms. The prison's inability to facilitate the fathers' lives as fathers is used as one example of an institution that generally does not function as it should, as when a prisoner receives a rejection to his application for escorted leave in connection with his son's operation:

> [Prisoner X]: It's all going to hell now, Thomas.
> TU: Is there something new that's going to hell, or is it the same old stuff that's going to hell?
> [Prisoner X]: No, something new. My escorted leave has been rejected.
> He thrusts the rejection letter at me, clearly upset, angry and morose. The prison case officer has briefly written that the prison does not have the resources to allow him escorted leave on that day.
> [Prisoner X]: Look at the dates! It's so I don't have time to appeal, that's how they do it; they are so fucking slippery. They misunderstand every-thing. They write that there's no point me being there because my wife will be there, that it isn't necessary. But I don't want escorted leave to support my wife; it's to be there for my son.
> [...]
> [Prisoner X]: Operations are serious; things can go wrong. My wife speaks neither Norwegian nor English. She is scared and there's no one who can tell her what is going to happen there. I had to call her yesterday and tell her that I can't be there. Not now, when it counts. Birthdays, you can get escorted leave for that; buying clothes, you can get escorted leave for that, it's true, there are people on the wing who have got it, [prisoner]

has got it, but you can't get escorted leave for this. It's so fucking bad! What makes them think they can treat people like this? I don't feel like a person now, I don't.

[...]

[Prisoner X]: I hope for God's sake it goes alright. If everything doesn't go like it should, I swear to God that I will find the person who signed this letter [the rejection], and I will ruin that person's life. He will wish he was never born; I swear it, on my life! Fuck. That I can't be there for him [his son] tomorrow; it's horrible. They need me. It's like I'm not a person; they can't treat people like this. Who do they think they are that they can treat someone like this?

The prisoner feels powerless in relation to the moral obligations he feels. The prison has refused to let him take on the responsibility he feels he must take on in order for him to see himself as a good father and a good man. He must be there for his son, to care for and support him because he is going into hospital. He feels a clear ethical challenge. He experienced that the prison made it impossible for him to be a good father, and, even worse, they manipulated the dates on the letter in order to achieve this. The prison that cheats, that breaks the rules to ruin things for him, is the prison that kept him away from his wife and son who needed him, and which thereby did not let him make himself into a good father. For him, this was part of a long history. As part of the case against him, his heavily pregnant wife was also imprisoned on remand. His son was, therefore, taken into care for a while by the child welfare services.

[Prisoner X]: And so they took my wife, and as if that wasn't enough, they took my son. My family wasn't allowed to take care of my son, but one of those step-in families from the child welfare services was, which had to come in and get my son, and that was all just to make it difficult for my wife, because, you know, pregnant women are very emotional, especially when they are in their ninth month. So...they came to me, I mean they spoke to me, blah, blah, blah, and then they say, now we have to have a court hearing, so I say, okay, with whom? No with your wife, not with you. So I say, fine, I mean, they want a court hearing with her, without me being present, so I got it into my head that I had to be there, and then they decide that, yes, second week, two days before the whole week had ended, which she had got remand in, they had chosen to let her out, why? Yes, because two days after she got out she had to be in the hospital to have the baby. So, I had a daughter, and that was really...it's really good that I have got a daughter, but it was really stupid, because my son had had a birthday and we were both under arrest, and...

TU: He was with child welfare services at the time?

[Prisoner X]: He was in care at the time, together with child welfare services, because I had been arrested in February, so we were both arrested, and my son had his birthday, and then I get a daughter. I didn't get escorted leave, I can't meet anyone, I get nothing, I can't meet my kid, I was in [prison X]. I talk to my lawyer all the time, I'm just, what is happening, like, after all, I have to be able see the kid? Come on, I can have escorted leave, if they have spent so much money on guarding me all the time, couldn't they spend a little more so I could see my kid?

He related how the police, as part of their investigations into him, used his heavily pregnant wife as a hostage in order to get him to talk. Here he wrote himself into the broader censorious narrative about the unethical System that does not hesitate to use any means to get prisoners convicted; innocent women and children are fair game in the pursuit of remand prisoners. The result of the poor or malicious prioritising of the prison and the police was that he, against his will, was positioned as an irresponsible father who could not be there for his son, and who was thus also a bad husband to his wife. The difficult relationship with wife and child was mixed in with the relationship with a system that he perceived as trying to get something on him and keep him locked up at any price. From such a perspective, the threat to his case officer can be read as more of a translation into a familiar language that enabled him to regain control over the situation and decide a few things too, rather than a genuine threat to find the case officer and avenge himself. Someone who is willing to sacrifice himself for his child (*I swear on my life!*) is a good father, an ethical father who would walk through fire and water for his loved ones, who takes responsibility and puts the welfare of his child before his own.

Relationships with children are the source of many frustrations, but they also become a symbol of life on the outside and the release that will eventually come. It is extremely important for many prisoners that they try to stay up to date and participate in life on the outside, insofar as this is possible, despite great geographical distances and difficult communication.

Erol and Daniel are standing and chatting outside Erol's cell. Daniel's daughter is turning three and he wants to send her a card he has made. The picture is of a little girl on a swing and is surrounded by an elegant border. Otherwise the card is full of flowers and feminine sweetness. He has been helped by Luca, who is good at drawing, but has done much of the decoration himself, all the colouring and the borders. He wants to make sure he gets the postage right; it would be terrible if this card was returned in the post. He smiles and puts two stamps on it just to be on the safe side.

Children's birthdays are occasions that must be marked. New photos of children constantly fill up the cork noticeboards on the cell walls. Children thus function as specific points of light in an existence that seems grey. As Arfan said:

> I live for those two kids now. It's all I have left, all that gives me hope. They are my only hope for the future. Everything else has been taken from me. They give me hope; without them I have no hope.

This hope is often also associated with a desire to make life changes so one does not end up in a similar situation in the future. Daniel, who has for many years made a living from credit card fraud, hoped to find something else to do after his sentence, although he did not really believe he would:

> I really want to quit. Right up until I drink a bottle of wine, then it's off the rails again [grins]. I'm never going to get caught, that's my problem. I know it. The only reason I got caught this time was that someone snitched on me. So if you know what you are doing and are a bit careful about whom you hang round with, you won't get caught. Ever. But I want to stop for the sake of my daughter; I want to be a good father for her, a good role model. But it's not easy! We'll see. If I do manage to quit, it will be because of her. Not the prison. There's nothing in here that's teaching me that it's wrong to steal from others anyway.

Daniel's heavy sigh shows that there is much that is uncertain. On one level he wanted to find something else to do, but did not really believe that it would work out, since he has got used to a lifestyle that he would probably never be able to finance by legal means. He wanted to be a good, law-abiding role model for his daughter. As a father, he felt a father's responsibility for his child's moral character, as Lorentzen (2006) describes, and he regarded himself as a bad example. But what was he supposed to do? After all, he had to be able to provide for her as well, didn't he?

The fact that relationships with children are in this way bitter-sweet and insecure is a recurring theme. Alban had received advance notice of his deportation from Norway. His children are Norwegian nationals and will, in any case, remain in Norway with their mother, even though the Norwegian immigration authorities are throwing him out of the country.

> He says that if he is deported, then he will just treat it like a paid trip home to Kosovo, have a few beers with some mates and then jump on the first flight back. He smiles, but his expression is serious as he sits there leaning towards me in the cell, coffee cup in one hand and a roll-up in the other. After all, he has four identities ready with passports, bank cards,

everything; four to choose between. It is not like returning to Norway will be a problem. He thinks a bit.

Alban: But if it does become a problem, if it looks like they will manage to throw me out and keep me out, then I will kill two prison officers in [another prison]. And I know who they will be. That will get me 21 years in Norway and I can see my boys twice a week. What more can they do then? I can do time. It's not a problem. They can't do anything they haven't done before.

This is another example of a prisoner threatening specific representatives of the System that intervenes in their lives and helps to keep them from their children. Again, I would argue for a reading that stresses the symbolic power of what is being said. The situation was already difficult, but, despite everything, Alban's children got to visit him twice a week in the prison. If he was expelled from the country, he would be totally absent from the children's lives, a memory of a father far away. The threat positions him as a father who is willing to go far – very far – to see his children grow up. Doing time in a prison close by becomes the best alternative. In the process he regained power over his own situation. Alban still had possible alternative courses of action. No *good* alternatives perhaps, but he could also choose the least bad. The good family father does not let anything come between him and his children, regardless. He will sacrifice himself to get to see them, and let the chips fall where they may.

Lorentzen (2006) describes the father's responsibility for the child's moral upbringing and the job of equipping the child with the qualities necessary for them to do well in life. These are duties the prisoners constantly return to when talking about their children, duties they are afraid of not fulfilling well enough. For many of the fathers, this problem is exacerbated by the fact that their children will grow up in a Norwegian culture, with all the risks this can entail. What they perceive as a Norwegian upbringing is problematic in a number of ways. Tarik, for example, believes Norwegian children go through their entire upbringing without hearing the word "no":

Tarik: When children do something wrong in Norway, they are told "please don't do things like that, blah, blah, blah." When children in Morocco do something wrong, you say "No!" [shows with a pointed finger and strict expression that he is serious]. No. Simple. The child stops doing it. There is no negotiation; it's the adult who decides.

TU: It is the way you say it, then?

Tarik: Yes, you have to say it properly. Then they get it at once. Then they stop doing it. They don't do it again. In Morocco you don't watch kids that much when they are small. A "no" every now and then when the kids cross a line, that's enough. But children are largely out on their own, playing. In Norway, the parents mostly watch the children while they are small and then they let go bit by bit as they start getting a bit older. When the children are 16 they are completely free, like adults, and go to the Med and get drunk and have sex, total chaos. That's just stupid! In Morocco it's the complete opposite; small kids can play and run around on their own, the older the children the more you have to watch them. After all, that's when they can do dangerous things. From the age of ten, that's when you have to watch them. That's when they start to get interested in clothes, in the other children, in what they think, everything like that. The parents become less important. That's when you have to watch them. I want children who start off being completely wild and who become calmer and more adult over time. Norwegian children start off calm and get wilder and wilder. After all, they are completely wild when they are 16! That's the complete opposite of how things should be.

The relaxed, non-authoritarian Norwegian approach to bringing up children is associated with the moral decay of Norwegian youth. Different child-rearing philosophies have very different results. Johansson (2001) differentiates between a strong and a weak version of the patriarchal father in contemporary father discourses. The strong version, exemplified by the Christian men's organisation Promise Keepers, is reminiscent of our notions of the strict father of the 1800s as described by Lorentzen; he wants total control over the family and does not acknowledge contemporary gender equality discourses. The weak version, the one that can be used to assume the position of an equal and modern father, is a father who cares and creates an atmosphere of security and respect, but who simultaneously must be understood as being historically connected to the strong version, according to Johansson. Child rearing in a cross-cultural context presents particular problems. Tarik wants his children to have the best of both worlds. While he is sceptical about the Nordic model with its weak paternalism and focus on equality, he realises that his children must be equipped to function in today's Norwegian society.

Ilir also struggles with such problems. He is afraid of the influence Norway may have on his child and is planning to go far to ensure the conditions are right for them to receive what he believes is a good upbringing:

Ilir: I hope that in the future I can home school her, teach her at home, so that she doesn't have to go to a state school. Children are so vulnerable. I want to protect her until she is old enough to make independent choices. Youngsters are so naive, right? They want to be tough and cool; they want to do what everyone else does. Between perhaps 12 and 17, or 18, they are very vulnerable. It's a very vulnerable period. Look at me: my mates wanted to smoke, so I started smoking. My mates wanted to be tough, so I was tough. Skived off school, started doing crime. You are just so unbelievably stupid at that age. I want to spare her all that.

TU: But, perhaps girls avoid a lot of that anyway?

Ilir: Yes, that's true, but then you have the boys. They want to hang out with the boys, do as they say, be popular. That's not good. I get so angry when I see things like the "Playboy Girls" on TV [programme on TV3] – what sort of role models are they? Should we reward that sort of bimbo factor, should we look up to them? Are they the heroes? We reward stupidity, don't we? Or look at Røkke [famous Norwegian wealthy industrialist]; is he, like, the idol? He is a criminal who has never read a book, are those the sort of people who should be our idols? But of course, she won't be completely isolated either; the whole family will take care of her, be together with her. There are a lot of us. It's important to have social antenna; she will also work on that. I just don't want her to do anything stupid. Therefore, I will try to watch out for her until she is old enough to make her own decisions. […] I have missed out on so much, missed so much, which I regret now. That won't happen with her. I hope I won't be in here too long, so I can get out and get started. I think about this a lot, you know?

Ilir grew up in Norway and includes himself in the "we" when he talks about Norwegian society. At the same time, he wants to protect his daughter against the dangers Norwegian society and a Norwegian education entail. He hopes that he can get out soon so that he can take responsibility as a father, a father who acts as a moral guide and who will provide his children with the knowledge and skills they require to manage as adult, independent individuals. In a Norwegian reality characterised by celebrity hysteria and hollow notions in youth circles that it is money and being popular that are important, he wants to act as a counterweight. He will stand for what is real and authentic in a healthy upbringing characterised by good values. He must keep his daughter away from potentially destructive sources of influence until she is mature enough to make her own decisions. As a good, ethically aware father, it is his duty.

It is common for the imprisoned fathers to argue in favour of child rearing based on a strong version of the patriarchal father. Some have realised that, in practice, this type of father role will be so difficult to act out in Norway that they will not, therefore, allow their children to grow up here. For others, like Tarik, it is more problematic. He is not unambiguously negative about Norwegian society's influence on children:

But it's not that simple. There are good things in Norway as well. I want my children to be able to eat with a knife and fork, but also with their hands, you know? Both. But it's not easy.

The Norwegian and the non-Norwegian can be mixed in fruitful ways; the children can acquire their own cross-cultural competence, which in itself is valuable. At the same time, some of the problems lie in the cross-cultural element itself. For Tarik, this is about practices that do not fit into the Norwegian cultural climate:

> We've grown up differently. If a child starts to veer off [as in off the straight and narrow] when they turn 15 or 16, with drugs for example, then the father steps in. It's he who decides. It's no. End of story. Then he keeps the child in. You're not going out! It's not like you hit just to hit, but that can also happen. And that's not wrong! We've grown up completely differently, remember that. And what happens in Norway is that children can say "You aren't allowed to do that, I'll tell the police." And that's true, they can do that. And then you end up with parents who cannot parent. After all, no father has said to his son: you will now become a criminal. None have. It is when the parents can't parent that that happens. And that happens when the parents can't parent as they are used to, when they don't understand the method that is normal in the new country. [...] They're in Norway, but they don't fit in in Norway.

The problem is the two cultures' different perceptions and expectations. Hailed as a Moroccan father, he feels obligations associated with the strong version of the patriarchal father. If he says no, then it is no, end of story. Those who do not understand that must accept their well-deserved punishment. Hailed as a Norwegian father, physical punishment is not part of the legitimate repertoire. In this case it is more important to give of your time and create a sense of intimacy and closeness with the child. In a Norwegian context, the physical punishment of children has been criminalised and marginalised in Norwegian culture. It is at these points of intersection that problems arise, but it is also here, where these lines cross, that Tarik believes his children can acquire valuable competence.

Child rearing clearly has a gendered dimension. Small girls' consumption of princess stuff and pink clothes, and small boys' love of toy guns and remote-controlled cars, are indications that young people are perceived to be, and related to as, gendered as well. Boys are expected and brought up to be active and willing to take risks, while girls perceive that care and relationship skills are validated. Asserting this does not mean that it is not easy to find exceptions, nor does it mean that great variation exists within these very broad brush strokes.

Prison fathers also perceive that girls and boys are different and that they must be brought up differently. For Erol, it is just as much about different duties and areas of responsibilities in the future as it is about there simply being a difference between boys and girls:

Erol: As far as my daughter is concerned, I'll be strict. You must be strict, man, it's not just, no, I've experienced far too much, I know way too much to let her experience something like that, to end up with a bloke like me, for example.

TU: There's a big difference between having a daughter and having a son?

Erol: That's totally natural, I mean, perhaps it is for me, because when my son was born, I didn't even think about it.

TU: No concerns?

Erol: None. I mean, he should just be hard, just as hard as he wants. He will be, like, determined, he will achieve what he wants, and he will not be a let-down; that's the most important thing. Letting people down and tricking them is unacceptable in my family; you must take responsibility for your actions, you must stand behind what you say.

TU: You'll teach him that.

Erol: He will learn that from me. But my daughter will be brought up to take care of others, to be loving, to look after others, and to take care of people; no trickery and trying to curry favour and that, no.

TU: So, as far as that is concerned, it is sort of the same?

Erol: Yes, it will be the same, but uh, my son can be dominant, but my daughter can't. She must set limits, but she must set limits within her boundaries, what applies to her as a female, not as a male. But my son is becoming a bit like that, and my wife doesn't really like it, she says why should my son be allowed to do everything, and...

TU: She wants them to be more equal in a way?

Erol: Yes, that's want she wants, but I say no, no, no, no. Instead they can, no, heck, man, my daughter, I have to be strict man; heck, I feel sorry for the boy who wants to be with her, heh heh heh.

TU: Oh yes? You're going to watch out for her?

Erol: Fuck yes. What is really good, because I've thought about this, is that I have chosen to have kids early, because when they are 20 I'll be 40. And when my daughter is 20, I'll be 43. So I'm thinking, when her time comes, and she, like, starts to look at boys and that, and those boys who think they can do something, they can't, because in my 40s I'll still be pretty hard, heh heh, and be able to stand my ground, and they won't have an opportunity to mess with my family, because it's like this, it's the daughter who must have the honour in the family, the boy must have respect. She must bear the family's honour and the boy the respect. To maintain that honour, you [daughters] must follow the family's rules and not dominate or anything else, and be loving and take care of the others in the family because the daughter is for selling away; she is not for my family. My daughter will be in another family, not mine. We used to say in Kosovo that the son is in the house, the daughter is temporary. She is for another family; she will make her own family. While the son carries our blood.

This is a clear example of the strong patriarchal father who is morally responsible for the entire family. Erol felt that attending to the child's moral upbringing is a key duty for fathers, and this is about a gendered morality; different norms apply for boys and girls. Sons should be tough, but fair; they should be trustworthy, honest and not let others down. Daughters should be obedient; they should care for those they love and take care of them when they need it. He paints a picture of a father who is not only interested in his children's welfare, but who watches out for them and who is responsible for ensuring they conduct themselves in line with the different expectations that apply for men and women. The difference between boys and girls, men and women, is fundamental and permanent. The different genders have different roles to play in family life and in society as a whole. Sons should be capable of assuming the role of head of their family in the future, with all the necessary strength, sense and respect. Daughters should be able, and want, to take care of their husband's family; they must learn to think of others before themselves. Erol emphasises that the ability to put the husband's family first is an important part of the praise he afforded his wife, the world's best:

> She makes me happy because I know she doesn't see my parents as strangers. Quite simply, she regards my parents as her own. That's all you could want.

Erol wanted to be the head of, and boss in, a well-functioning family. He wanted to be a family father who presides over his family, and who knows best. As a father he was also capable of physically defending his family and willing to sacrifice himself for his loved ones; a safe, good *pater familias* whom everyone could ask for advice, and who was willing to do anything to defend those he loved. Because having children, and especially daughters, is a high-risk project. Daughters are a treasure that must be guarded and which can be stolen or despoiled by boys who are lurking out there.

Again this is about a gendered morality. When a man does not have enough money to buy food for his family, it is emasculating, not least because it also breaches a gendered ethical imperative that says the man is responsible for taking care of family members. For Haug (1990), this morality, as it functions and creates social effects, is ambiguous and dualistic. The same values (such as honour, honesty, care and so on) differ in worth for men and women, and they refer to different practices. In Haug's analysis, the acquisition of property and public life function as the centres of men's morality, while the body and virtue are the capstones of women's morality. A woman's morality lies in her nature, her body and the relationship she has with her body. Conversely, there is a connection between the law and justice and masculine morality. Masculine morality refers to virtue, truthfulness and courage; it is linked to public life, money and wealth, and work.

For men, honour is associated with success; for women, sexual abstinence is most important.

The concept of honour is key here. It can, for example in a cultural context such as described by Wikan (2008), be understood as the name of an ethical standard that hails real men as honourable, that stipulates rules with which honourable men must comply (or at least appear to comply) to maintain their status, and which also, to some degree, sets sanctions associated with the loss of honour. A sense of honour, writes Wikan, is a specific masculine value with specific masculine obligations. A woman who does not yield, who impugns the *family's honour*, for which the father is responsible, must be corrected, must in the last resort be killed, for the sake of honour (Aase, 2007).

Tarik, the father of small children, worried about the future:

Tarik: I'm going to be a strict father, yeah, I probably am. If a boy came to my home and said, hi, I'm your daughter's boyfriend, that's it, I'd kill him [grins]. Just like that. I couldn't tolerate that. I would say to him, hi, it was nice to meet you. If I ever see you again, it'll be at your funeral, heh heh.

TU: What would a boy have to do then, if he was in love with your daughter?

Tarik: [Long pause while he thinks] He must come to me and show me that he loves her, that he cares about her, that he is right for her. And that's not about money and that. They must be right for each other. But, obviously, a slob wouldn't do [grins]. But, you know, it's her who must decide. It says so in the Qur'an; I cannot decide who she should marry. But if it is someone who is wrong for her, he will not get her. He won't. That's the very least I can do. In Norway, a girl can sleep with whoever she likes from when she turns 16. But, come on, that's before she can watch out for herself, her finances; she is not an adult. Can she get a loan from a bank? No. But she can sleep with as many people as she wants? I don't understand that. This [points at his crotch] is not a landfill. I have to make sure that no one pisses on my daughter. I can't allow that.

Part way through the above quote Tarik moderates himself somewhat; he went from half-jokingly wanting to kill anyone who tried it on, to its being his daughter who will decide herself, although he would guide her. It is not completely clear what "her who must decide" means here, given that Tarik still possesses the truth about what differentiates suitors who are "right" for her and those who are "wrong" for her.

In any case, it is clear that for Tarik, as it was for Erol, fathers are morally responsible for what other family members do. Sons must be trustworthy, because they are *their* sons, and were their sons the sort who betrayed people, this would mean that they were the head of a family of betrayers, who does not deserve respect. Daughters must be self-sacrificing and, not least, virtuous, because daughters who do not maintain their virtue properly have no honour. Daughters without honour come from a family without honour, led by a father without honour. Men are bound to their family and father, but still have an opportunity to act independently. Women are always fundamentally bound to their family, and cannot act as individuals in this sense. A daughter can, as Erol says, *drag down and sink a whole family so low that no one will want to speak to that family anymore.* [19] It is easy to associate this with Grosz's (1994) observation that a woman is like a sponge that can absorb and hold men's dirt, and who, every time she is used, is made dirtier and dirtier.

From the vantage point of a Norwegian cultural context on the outside of the prison walls, characterised by discourses about gender equality and laissez-faire parenting, Tarik and Erol are, to put it mildly, politically incorrect and very old-fashioned in their articulation of the strong, all-powerful, patriarchal father. At the same time, this is also part of their point; parenting strategies are expressly used to mark their ethical distance from (parts of) "the Norwegian culture", which for Tarik and Erol is a culture with the definite article, singular. They are fully aware of how their ideas are understood in a Norwegian context. Tarik, Erol and Ilir are making an explicit and considered ethical choice when they want to be fathers in a non-Norwegian manner. They want their children to experience a greater focus on moral, healthy values and a good upbringing than, in their opinion, Norwegian children experience. Above, Erol describes how he wanted his home to be some sort of "Albanian embassy" which the negative elements of Norwegian society are unable to permeate and destroy.

Erol's Albanian "embassy" is also interesting from another perspective. According to Aase (Aase, 2007), the sense of honour and honour-related crimes in Western society are not about what happens when prehistoric cultural ideas are placed in a modern Western context. Rather, a sense of honour is something that becomes important in situations where state control is weak or absent, whether it is in a village in Pakistan or inside Danish biker gangs: "Honour becomes a valid subject in societies that do not have a state [...], in groups that are positioned outside the state [...], or in circles that position themselves outside the state [...]. *In other words, honour is a phenomenon that appears at the peripheries of the state*" (Aase, 2007: 247, my translation, emphasis added). When the ideal is managing without state intervention, when the state and the System are even enemies, then honour becomes an important concept. Honour takes the place of the state safety net and power system. In this case, honour is about being able to demonstrate to your surroundings that you have the capacity and strength necessary to look after yourself and your family when the state does not.

It is important to stress that I do not interpret what the prison fathers have said above as a description of what are, or will become, the parenting practices in their homes. They all have very small children and it will be a long time before they actually have to worry about their sons' respect and their daughters' virtue. Nor is it unthinkable that the father figure they describe will encounter obstacles in practice; for example, might not the mothers want a say as well? The important thing here is how they use the figure of the father in their ethical self-positioning work in everyday prison life. By articulating a specific form of love and care, the prisoners are turning themselves into morally aware, responsible, strong and capable fathers who love their children, who care about how they are doing, who are trustworthy and who would do absolutely anything to ensure their lives are as good as possible, all this despite the fact that at this moment they are prisoners in Oslo Prison, placed outside the family's day-to-day life in a way they find physically painful. They take their role as fathers seriously and are authoritative and firm in relation to their wives and children, but this is always based on a deeply felt love for the people they care for the most. It is interesting to see the degree to which they stress a father's control and responsibility as an ideal, positioned as they are in a situation where they have largely been deprived of the opportunity to practise control and responsibility.

So, what about "Norwegian" fathers? How do their ideas on parenting differ from those of the "multicultural" fathers in this area? It is not easy to answer this on the basis of my data. It is not that Norwegian prisoners do not have children; both my experience and the Norwegian and Nordic living conditions surveys indicate that many of them have. But in my data they are not as interested in using children, the family and the father's role as positioning resources. The exceptions to this are missing their family as a portrayal of the pain of imprisonment, and some narratives about the System's representatives who are willing to go so far as to use children as bait to trick information out of them. Apart from this, they had less of a need to position themselves in relation to the creation of a father's role in daily life. Perhaps they had less day-to-day contact with their wives and children, such that the role of father became less important? Perhaps they assumed a level of agreement that made discussing this with me unnecessary?

Rapists

Above, I have shown how the prisoners establish similarity and difference relationships between themselves and other prisoners. This also takes place on an ethical level. In fact, one ethics-based difference is probably the most important to stress clearly and plainly in everyday life in the prison. Rapists are used as an example of a radical difference, an ethical peripheral figure. Unlike the difference relationships the prisoners create between themselves and the immature young prisoners or those serving time difficulty, the difference created between most prisoners and rapists is not a difference of degree; rather, it is a deep-running qualitative difference that makes rapists fundamentally and essentially different from the proper, normal prisoners.

First and foremost, the rapist is different because he hurts ordinary people and, as if that was not enough, he hurts ordinary *women*, who are weaker than him. Rapists are driven by motives that differ from those that drive other prisoners. Proper prisoners are driven by a profit motive: they want to make money, they are professionals. The rapist is evil, perverse, sick and crazy. He does what he does because he likes it, out of lust and desire, not because he makes money from it. Proper prisoners do not position themselves very far from the ordinary wage earner, not when it comes to motives anyway. Normal incentives work with people who can think rationally. On the other hand, the rapist is steered by his sick, perverse desires; he is a dangerous monster against which the prison community, like the rest of society, definitely must protect itself. The division that is established between proper criminals and "the sick" is absolutely vital in the prisoners' positioning work.

Being assigned the status of rapist has clear and tangible consequences in everyday life for these individuals. The other prisoners mark their distance and difference in many ways. Common to all of them is the fact that it is difficult not to notice them:

> I'm hanging out in the common area on the sofa with Tom. I see a young prisoner on the landing who is pointing or "aiming" at a third prisoner with his fingers and "shooting" him with an imaginary gun, complete with loud shooting noises. Tom explains what I have just observed.
>
> Tom: That one there, you know? He's one of those rapists. Fuck, he grabbed a 17-year-old girl and raped her for hours. Fuck! But he also got a real beating. An Albanian in here, who is as big as you and me put together, got him. Just one punch. That was enough; he went down. There was another bloke; he was shoved into a washing machine. They have those big washing machines down in the laundry. They just stuffed him in and turned it on.
>
> TU: What? But, I mean, that could kill you?
>
> Tom: Heh heh, yeah that could kill you; it gets so fucking hot. And it takes a few minutes to stop the machine again. And you can't open the door straight away because it's on a time lock. But it turned out okay this time.

Such violent anecdotes in which rapists are the victims are common, and are also something the prisoners share in good company. The stories are so common and retold so loudly that those who have been assigned the status of rapist cannot avoid hearing them. From this perspective, the anecdotes can function as poorly concealed threats. Coupled with the normal practice of banging loudly on the cell doors of those who have been labelled "rapist" when one walks past, a clear signal that communicates something along the lines of "don't forget we know what you did", it is impossible for those who have been assigned this status not to be aware of what the other prisoners are thinking. At the same time, they make it appear that avenging the victims by tormenting or punishing rapists is not just absolutely legitimate, but, quite simply, the right thing to do. When talking about this peripheral figure, vigilantism is presented as the only right course of action. Those who encounter something like this can and should take matters into their own hands.

This does not mean that it is actually common to beat up rapists. Such incidents are the exception (Hanoa, 2008). However, the fact that this is not an everyday occurrence does not mean that violence against rapists is not important in the construction of "the proper prisoner". There is obviously a difference between discourse and practice here; the two levels are intertwined, but are not "the same". Punching a rapist is not the same as talking about doing it. But nor is talking about it only just talking about it. This is also a form of practice; positioning that creates meaning, hierarchies and subject positions in relation to each other. The imaginary violence, the wished-for violence, the legitimate potential violence that prisoner culture enables and values in such cases is vital when distance from the rapist as a morally defective peripheral figure needs to be stressed:

> From the open cell door come displeased sounds from Tom, who has been put to work readying the newly vacated cell for its next occupant. [...] A group of other prisoners, who have started their daily workout session, gather outside the open door and keep Tom company.
> Erik: So, the rapist has moved out? Fuck, that's brilliant! We can't fucking have that sort here. It's fucking sickening! Fuck!
> Naveed: No, fuck, that's true, man. I've held myself back; I don't want to mess up my case, right? But once I've got my sentence...
> Erik: Agreed! If another one of those arrives, it's just... [demonstrates a hard elbow strike against his palm with a loud smack].
> Both grin, fired up by their workout. The sweat is running; they agree on their desire to beat up and hurt rapists. Tom nods from inside the cell. Luckily, they no longer have to live with someone like that on the wing. It has been trying. The session shifts to more general play fighting, fired up by the thought of hurting a sick bastard who deserves it. The mood is light. High kicks and Hong Kong film-like, kung fu sound effects fill the small cell.

They are proper, moral prisoners who have come together as proper, moral prisoners to share anecdotes about righteous violence against rapists. But the distance is stressed and re-created in several other ways as well. Rapists are excluded from most forms of normal association and interaction with the proper prisoners:

> I try the pool table again. I lose badly as usual. The winner stays on so I walk over to the others on the sofa. They have been sitting and chatting,

not following the game. "Next", I say. It's Morten's turn. "No," he says, "I'm not playing that one there." He looks away from the table; everyone looks away. The winner is left standing with his cue in his hand without anyone wanting to play him. No one is interested. You don't play with rapists. He remains standing for a bit longer, smiling, but unsure, before he puts down the cue and surrenders the table to the others. Within a few minutes two of them have started a new game. The rapist is in his cell.

This form of social exclusion from the community is normal and routine. Rapists are not allowed to play against proper prisoners. You would rather beat them up, but that is probably not a smart thing to do; it will just harm the person throwing the punch. But, at the very least, you do not play pool with people like that.

The prison cannot, at least not in the official script, acknowledge this exclusion, although the officers cannot avoid being aware of what is going on. A prefect scheme was established in the prison school during the year I spent at Oslo Prison. The various classes each had to choose a group representative. This caused problems when one of the groups chose the "wrong" prefect. The other prisoners brought this up with the officers in the following way:

Prisoner: At the first meeting of the full prefect group, that rapist, him from Somalia, walked in as if it was the most natural thing in the world. But, of course, no one would talk to him. Naturally, that makes it difficult to work with him. They should probably pick a new one.

[School's representative at the relevant meeting]: Oh, was that why? I thought it was just language problems.

Prisoner: Well, yeah, there is that too, after all, he speaks almost no Norwegian. But it was primarily because he is a rapist. He was in court the day before and got six years for rape, and then he strolls in and expects everything to be normal, like? That's not right.

Here the prisoner tries to win agreement that the rapist could obviously not be a prefect. But the representatives of the school and the prison's administration do not acknowledge, and cannot acknowledge, this line of reasoning:

[School's administration]: Well, we can't do that. We can't suddenly take who is doing time for what into consideration; that's not an option.

[Prison's administration]: No, we can't concern ourselves with such things. For us, you are all the same, so that won't work. We can't base things on those sorts of differences.

Later I was talking to the same prisoner in his cell. He was frustrated about having to deal with the rapist from Somalia in the prefect group, but also because the prison's representatives did not acknowledge the obvious difference between rapists and other proper prisoners like him.

> It's just stupid; no one wants anything to do with that Somalian. We found out what he is in for, that he got six years the day before, and then suddenly he is just sitting there, smiling. No one will talk to him; everyone turned their back on him. They say we're all the same, well, fine, so be it. But we're fucking not! And that means it will be nine against one in the prefect group. Is that really a good idea?

The "we" created by the exclusion of the category *rapists* has difficulties dealing with the prison placing an equals sign between groups that, for reasons that are obvious to them, should be kept strictly separate.

The division between rapists and proper prisoners was most clearly demonstrated towards the end of my fieldwork. Thanks to the newspapers' coverage of an ongoing court case, the prisoners realised that someone who had made himself out to be one of them, a proper prisoner, was in reality a disgusting rapist of the worst sort. For many months he had claimed that he was on remand because he had been mixed up in a "totally normal" violent episode. But when the case came up, it became impossible to maintain that story. The journalists who covered the court case tried to anonymise the defendant as well as they could, but the newspaper articles provided the prisoner group with more than enough information to put two and two together, and suddenly the revelation was the only thing everyone was talking about:

> That's the worst thing, the fucking worst, right? That he has always said something else, that he has been accepted as one of the boys. After all, he seems like a nice bloke, but fuck, what a swine, one of those, but he'll get his, it'll kick off, no doubt about it. Everyone in here is pissed off at him. [Prisoner X] is really angry. He's been at school with him, sat and talked to him, right? But we did wonder what he'd done. We realised that it was something bad, right? Just broke up a fight and dried up some spilled blood, and the prosecution asks for six years? Something didn't sound right there.

A while later I spoke to the prisoner concerned. Sure enough, he was furious with his friend who proved to be a rapist in disguise:

> I hate being fooled! It would be different if he had told the truth straight away, then we could have kept our distance, but we bonded with him. I thought he was a good man, with a good sense of humour, and it turns

out he is just the lowest of the low. I hate violence, but sometimes it's necessary in my business, right? But it's against men, and always men who are part of the same lifestyle. And when it happens, it's necessary. I get no pleasure from it, quite the contrary, but now and then it's necessary in order to work in this business. But violence against women and children, those who are weaker than you? Paedophiles and rapists should do their time alone, and they should do long stretches. Really long. I mean, you can't hurt him physically, not in here, the officers are guarding him now. But I will hurt him in other ways. Fuck, he should be so embarrassed; he ought to be hiding under his bed. I want him to think about it, not forget it, not believe that he is so fucking big; so I will make sure that he remembers what he has done. Fucking, fucking rapist! Talking about him almost makes me physically sick.

Rapists may be hiding among us. That was perhaps the worst thing for the prisoner concerned, the fact that he had accepted a rapist into a "we" relationship; he made him a person who meant something to him, whom he compared himself with. The rapist had broken fundamental masculine ethical requirements by hurting those who are weaker instead of protecting them. Again, it is clear how the rapist is a figure who marks a boundary, and on the other side of the boundary exists the unethical and unthinkable, but also the unmanly. Rape is something qualitatively different from what the *proper prisoner* does. Being associated with someone like that, being positioned in the same category as them by being ascribed the status of *general prisoner*, is painful, and it is necessary to create the maximum distance from them. It is as if rapists were carriers of some moral infection (Cohen and Taylor, 1981). When one has inadvertently positioned oneself as an equal in a relationship with someone like that, when one has acknowledged the person concerned as someone *who is like me*, and the mask then falls, the reaction is all the stronger.

What is to be gained from marking the distance between *myself* and *us prisoners* on one side, and *rapists* on the other? The necessary distance that is created is not about the rapists as individuals, nor is it really about what they have done; it is about what their actions make them. Rapists are a different sort of people. They are used as symbols of the fact that the proper prisoners feel that their surroundings regard them all as prisoners, but that they do not feel that they are: sick, evil bastards who are such a threat to their surroundings that they should be locked up indefinitely.

Snitches

Another morally peripheral figure commonly found in the prison is the snitch. The snitch has broken what is perhaps the prisoner community's most important rule by crossing the boundary between prisoners on the one side and the System and its representatives on the other. This boundary between prisoner and officer is supposed to be absolute. A prisoner should never do anything for officers that hurt fellow prisoners. The snitch has not just betrayed individual fellow prisoners; he has betrayed the entire prisoner community and crossed the line between prisoners and officers.

Such a breach of the prisoner community's most fundamental imperative is so serious that the prisoners accept that it could, in lieu of a better term, have what can be called existential effects. The person who snitches changes, and not just his status in the prisoner community, not just with respect to how the surroundings view him, but more fundamentally and deeply. The person who snitches becomes a snitch:

> I'm sitting talking to Erol in his cell. We start talking about a fellow prisoner who was suddenly and incomprehensibly released. He thinks the whole thing is suspicious.

> Erol: It makes you wonder. Fuck, I hate those people, man; they've tried it on with me as well. They badger me, but I tell them, listen, it's not my job to put others in prison, it's your job, you'll have to manage on your own. But hell, what are they thinking, those who do that sort of thing? I could get out of here today, no problem. I could just tell the police, listen, I'll give up all the Albanians who will be carrying drugs over the border this week. But, you know, I can't do it, what have they done to me? Who would I be then?

In general, within a group, a rule about solidarity and presenting a common front will be important for its construction and maintenance. A similar rule applies to officers in their relationship with the prisoner group (Lindberg, 2005; Nylander, Lindberg and Bruhn, 2011). Internal solidarity and loyalty are just as strong an imperative among officers as they are in prisoner culture. This rule is, in its various concrete configurations, extremely common and can be found on different levels, from nuclear families to multinational companies.

The group solidarity rule stands, in concrete cases, in a more or less balanced relationship with the individual's opportunities and rights. Being a member of a group brings with it benefits, but also obligations. Every group will have ideas about the individual's responsibilities in relation to the group, and the group's responsibilities in relation to individuals. And in the prisoner group, which is assumed and reconstructed through the collective condemnation of the snitch, the most important constituting rule is presenting a common front against a common enemy. The relationship between prisoners and officers is structured by the prohibition against prisoners talking to officers. Sometimes the prohibition against talking to the System's representatives has comical results:

> In frustration, Adem has broken two of his window panes. An officer goes in and starts giving him a serious talking to. Adem tries, almost jokingly, to explain what has happened:
>
> Adem: What do I know about what has happened? Someone must have thrown something from outside, or perhaps a bird flew into the window?

Adem admitted nothing to the officer, although of course his bird story was not believed. The bird story subsequently became a joke because it was such an overly creative excuse. The officers felt his frustration was understandable and did not regard it as a big deal. Dangerous birds became a joke on the wing that day.

Never say anything, is the imperative. Breaking this rule for your personal benefit means putting yourself before the group, an action that threatens the group's solidarity and the group members' position as members of the group. Snitching means breaching a bond of trust and loyalty. People who can bring themselves to do something like that are weak. Men, *real men*, definitely do not do that. The prohibition against snitching thus creates a difference between real men with the fortitude to withstand external pressures, who keep their word and who take loyalty and a sense of honour seriously, on the one side, and weak snitches who only think of themselves, and who buckle and allow themselves to be manipulated, on the other. Snitches put themselves before the group; they are selfish and have poor morals. On a remand wing, many of the prisoners will have been encouraged by the police to "give up" mates and colleagues. But you do not do that sort of thing, whatever they promise you and regardless of the potential benefit to you. The snitch does not care about others; he uses and sacrifices other people to improve his own situation. Snitching, as it is often put, means selling your soul. Mark has been snitched on by others, but, for him, it would be totally unthinkable to return the favour:

> Mark: [W]hen you make agreements, and you know what you are getting into, and you snitch then it's simply unacceptable. And many people still do it. I don't know why, because they don't have character, because they're weak, because they don't have principles, they think it's tough and cool to do criminal stuff, but when it really comes down to it, they don't have the heart or the guts or the balls.
>
> TU: Still, they get something out of it, a reduced sentence or whatever?
>
> Mark: Well most of the time, although it's often, it's not even worthwhile, I think. That's why I've been offered a few times in my life by the police to cooperate or just talk about all the things that I know and the people

that I know, and I've been offered quite good deals and very comfortable things. But for me it's an insult, even mentioning it. Get the fuck out of here, don't even say it, you know. I could have, my previous sentence I could have gotten a much lower sentence, but I just ... you don't snitch. You don't do that. I think it's something, it's very clear, when you do something, you stick to it. I mean, many people, they're talking, they cooperate, they don't have any pride or honour. Or any principles.

To Mark, the snitch is someone who does not take responsibility for his actions, someone who tries to push all or parts of the responsibility onto others. The snitch does not take responsibility for what he has done. He does not take responsibility for his actions; it is as if he regrets them and wishes they could be undone. He does not have the heart, guts or balls to work in Mark's business; he lacks pride, toughness and courage, and is thus not a real man.

Nonetheless, the snitch is, in a way, easier to understand than the rapist. Even though he does the unthinkable, his motives are easier to recognise. One does not snitch because one is a pervert and sick; one snitches because one wants to feather one's own nest or because one may buckle under the pressure that everyone feels. The desire to see family and friends again, and the pain of long-term isolation, can become too much, leaving the snitch unable to resist the police's offer. Anecdotes about snitches are, therefore, usually not anecdotes about evil, but, rather, about poor self-control and weakness. Because of this, the snitch is somewhat more understandable and therefore a more deeply tragic figure than, for example, the rapist. I spoke to Robert and Frode about this:

> Robert: Someone I knew in the seventies, he was the world's nicest bloke really, he snitched on me and some others. He couldn't live with himself afterwards; his bad conscience was too much for him, so in the end he took his own life. At the time I thought that it was the right thing for him to do, but now I've got a bit older, I see these sorts of things differently. I mean, it was tragic, really.
>
> Frode: So he took his own life because of a bad conscience? I couldn't live having to look over my shoulder all the time, man, watching for those who were after me. So instead I choose not to give anyone up.
>
> TU: So the police come and take you instead?
>
> Frode: Yes, I'd rather that. It's better, despite everything, heh heh.

The snitch Robert told about was doubly weak: first he buckled and snitched on his friends, then he could not live with his bad deed and took his own life. Doubly weak and doubly tragic. In this story, snitching became a personal tragedy and the solution, ending your life, was immediately understandable for both of them. By extension, snitching became a symptom of a general weakness that ultimately resulted in the person concerned choosing the way out of the weak. Mark also believed that the imperative about not snitching was about strength, and he explicitly associated it with masculinity:

> When you think about it thoroughly, you don't do that. And, it separates the weak from men. And I think many people are weak, in the end. I told you, you see it in all extreme situations, it doesn't have to be the criminal life, it's not many people who are courageous, or who take responsibility, cause it's all about taking responsibility and staying loyal. How many people in real life are like that, when it really comes down to it? Not many. It's, you know, I told you, the only thing is, in crime, the consequences are quite severe. Long sentences and so on and so forth, plus the betrayal goes, you know, that's why it's, it's, it cuts as deep as nothing else, you know. The consequences are so severe. And also, when you do criminal things, you often trust yourself with, you give your, your life is in someone else's hands. Or a big part of your life that can be taken away, so it's the worst betrayal there is.
>
> [...]
>
> I mean, it's like, be a man, you know. Not a bitch. Have honour, have loyalty, have some dignity. Stand by your word. I never lie. It isn't in my character.

There is a clear gendered element here too; a real man with enough balls is someone you can trust, someone who does the right thing, who keeps his word, who keeps quiet, and who is willing to sacrifice himself for the good of all. The snitch's loose lips are feminine.

Like rapists, snitches also provide grounds for legitimate violence. A snitch needs eyes in the back of his head, because the response to the challenge snitching represents is fair payback in the form of violence. This can cause problems when the snitch and the person who has been snitched on are put on the same prison wing. Sabri was despondent about having to be on the same wing as 'his' snitch, who was even in the cell right opposite his. He went to the wing's administration and asked to be transferred, at least up to the fourth floor. In the meantime, he promised not to do anything, although it wore on him:

> It has been fucking tiring. I can't understand how the prison doesn't have a better overview than that over who is doing time where. If anything happens to him, then, of course, they will come straight to me. I wouldn't do it, because I don't want to ruin things for myself. A lot of people have asked me if they can do him for me since he is a snitch, but I have said no. No one will do anything to him right now; I don't want to ruin my

case. I don't need to do more time than I'm going to get. But as soon as my sentence is final, then fuck it. [. . .] Thomas, oh, if I could have six minutes alone with him in a cell! Do you know what I would do to him in six minutes, eh? I don't dare even think about it [bites the back of his hand]. Having it done would be no problem; it would just be a case of getting him in the yard. After all, there are no officers there. So if you are a bit discreet, you have a whole hour to enjoy yourself. And even if they see it, then, you know, you have several minutes before they get their gear on and get ready. You can do a lot of things in five minutes [grins].

Sabri perceived the large-as-life and unharmed snitch to be a challenge that the surroundings demanded he got to grips with, an interpellation to unmanliness if he did not do something. At the same time, circumstances made it difficult for him to do what was demanded of him. Every second the snitch spent walking around, unharmed, on the wing together with him was a second during which he had not responded to an obvious and clear challenge from his surroundings. Settling things with snitches is an opportunity to do masculinity, but, if one has had the chance and not taken it, it is potentially emasculating. Sabri's position was problematic because he felt he had a duty to take action against "his" snitch; he was expected to avenge himself, but at the same time it was difficult to carry out such revenge without causing difficulties for himself. Sabri felt his responsibility as a man, but as a man he was also supposed to be sensible and not allow his feelings to run away with him. By holding back and not allowing the desire for revenge to get out of control, he showed he was in control of himself.

Prisoners achieve a number of things when they use the snitch as a distance marker. They become subjects who have clear rules concerning their activities, which only hurt those who deserve it, those who are part of the same game (not "ordinary people"), and they do not snitch on anyone. From this perspective, not snitching is about more than a perceived ethical challenge; keeping quiet is also closely associated with the status of professional criminal. Erol can serve as an example:

Erol: I mean, I see crime as a type of job. Some crime, not all of it. The reason is, well I look at you, you do what you are doing now, you have chosen that job. You have chosen to take the long way round to get where you are now, to earn money. While a criminal is not good at what you are good at, cannot read, doesn't have the resources, everything goes wrong for him; he also finds something that he's good at, selling, for example. Or carrying. Or something else. At the same time, he knows what the consequences might be, but he chooses to do it; there is money in it, he wants to live off it, so this is a type of job for him. As long as he keeps his word, then it's a type of job. If you don't keep your word, you're an arsehole, so it is not a job for you; you shouldn't stick your nose into it at all.

TU: You have to be professional?

Erol: It has to be professional, right, either way; you have to look at it as a thing you live off, and respect what you live off. You don't stick your arse in your money; you don't sit on your money or your bread. And a criminal wouldn't do that either. And for those who do, then it isn't, so they deserve to be here, to put it that way. Because, everyone knows that it's harmful, especially when it comes to drugs, but none of us forces anyone to do anything at all; those who do force, they aren't, I mean, they deserve to be here. But none of us forces anyone to use or take or whatever; everyone makes their own choice. I mean, I'm not exactly a street level seller, so I don't exactly know who uses what, but people, those who buy, they buy to make money. And those who buy from them, some of them do it to make money, some to use, I don't know.

TU: What sort of crimes wouldn't be a job?

Erol: Crimes that I don't think is a job is... murder for example. Killing a person is not worth, like billions, if you put it in front of me, so it's not worth killing a person. I mean, the worst thing you can do is to snitch on a person, the worst thing of all. Tricking your way into a field you shouldn't be in. That's a snitch. I mean you elicit an action, I don't know, trickery, snitching, killing someone, that's not, that's not crime, that's... and paedophiles, people who do things that hurt people, that is not legitimate. And nor should it be legitimate. Because, after all, you're hurting people, and you're doing it deliberately. As long as it's deliberate, then you're done; you are not even a criminal, you are just an idiot. You were born to be an idiot and so you deserve to be in prison, where the authorities decide.

TU: You don't deserve to be called a criminal?

Erol: No. I mean, criminals are people with brains, people who know what they are doing, people who do it for the money without hurting others.

TU: Like a job. Professional. Fair.

Erol: Yes, professional and fair. And that is also the type of criminal who gets respect, both from the police and from everyone who is after him.

TU: Because the police view those crimes and what you call idiots differently? The police view them differently?

Erol: Well, they are treated differently, put it that way. I have a specific reason, right. When it comes to me, it looks totally different than it does for others. As far as the case I'm suspected of is concerned, I was treated totally differently, spoken to totally differently, to the other people who they, like, think are errand boys.

TU: How?

Erol: Well, it was like more throwing things at them. We got the kingpin, like, so we couldn't give a toss about the rest of you, thanks for your help so far. But with me it can become a negotiation with them, I am offered negotiations with the police at any time, if I want. I can choose to get out [of prison]. If I want. But that would make me an arsehole, and I don't want that. Because then I would have to make some sort of...

TU: You'd have to cooperate.

Erol: I would have to cooperate, I would have to give them someone, and I'm not the type of person to give anyone anything at all.

A real professional criminal does not snitch, and nor do real men, although in their case it is called informing. This sort of thing is reserved for unmanly amateurs; real men are men of their word, they say what they mean, and stand behind what they have said. The subject that recognises that snitching is wrong is the subject that recognises the virtues of masculinity (Herzfeld, 1985), as well as the implicit contract between professional criminals who must not snitch on each other, which is the camaraderie on which the rule of not snitching relies. Imprisonment – especially in a remand prison – presents the subject with many opportunities to make himself into a subject who does not snitch, an ethical subject. This, again, has a gendered dimension. Ascribing unmanliness to "men who resist" is generally a very common resource for declassing and disavowing (Ekenstam, 2006).

The paradoxical thing, then, is that many of those who view themselves as professional criminals, as Erol describes it, all of whom strongly resist snitching and snitches, cooperate with the police in different ways. The question thus becomes: what do the rules that make it possible to snitch without becoming a snitch look like? What is the difference between snitching and other forms of cooperation with the police? It is one thing to fool the police into thinking that you want to cooperate in order to gain benefits (as in Nadir's anecdote in the Introduction, where he uses trickery to get himself a hamburger and a bottle of coke). But what are the rules when it comes to actually cooperating with the police without becoming a snitch? Can you testify against someone in a criminal case, for example, without being a snitch? Sometimes the answer is yes, as long as you stick to some clear rules. Below is an extract from a conversation with a prisoner that took place a few days before he was going to go to court to testify against three people who, among other things, were charged with extorting money from him. He showed me the transcripts of the interview of him in connection with the case.

Prisoner: It is important, you know? That it says that and that it wasn't me who went to the police.

TU: Because you are not a snitch?

Prisoner: Yeah, you shouldn't snitch; it's not done. And it says it right there, in black and white. That's good; there will be a lot of criminals in court, so it is important. The "B Gang" will be there, [a fellow prisoner] is also going to send someone. It's going to be full of criminals there, heh

heh. So it's important that I don't look like a snitch. I've told the police exactly how it happened. I've helped them a bit, yes I have. He said it, that detective, that you best keep away from my area in the future, keep away from me, I know you far too well now.

In order to understand this extract, it is essential to know that he believes the accused in the case broke a number of unwritten rules to start with by extorting money from him. The rule about not snitching on each other presupposes a *gentleman's agreement* about what one can and cannot do as part of one's illegal activities. In this case, the other party had already broken the rules. Testifying against them could, therefore, not be counted as snitching; their breach of the rules had already annulled the unwritten agreement. It is also important that it is clear to all involved, not least to his "colleagues" who were going to come and watch the case, that it was not he who had reported the matter to the police. Had they been going to meet in court at his initiative, it would have been snitching; that sort of thing is going too far, regardless of what the others have done.

Keeping quiet, not snitching, only works as a technique of the self because a specific culture has a norm about not snitching on each other that is associated with views about snitches, about the police trying to provoke snitching and so on. Not snitching is an ethical choice because it has consequences, because there is an ethical norm that can be breached, and because the individual who freely chooses to uphold the norm assumes responsibility for the consequences that might arise. Only when there are no consequences, when the ethical norm has in some way or other already been neutralised, or when those being snitched upon have no moral status, is it possible to cooperate with the police without being a snitch. In the encounter with the police who are trying to get you to cooperate, the subject who manages to keep quiet is a freedom and resistance subject, whether it plays out as totally laid-back silence or trickery to get a bottle of coke.

Victims

In the following I share Christie's (1997) observation that "monsters do not exist", in the sense that I did not meet prisoners who talked about their previous criminality as something they did because they wanted to be evil or to do evil. From such a perspective, victims of crime are a challenge for those who want to turn themselves into ethical prisoners. Hurting someone, thinking about those one has hurt, is basically hard to square with perceiving yourself as an ethically aware subject.

Many of the prisoners, whether they steal from companies or bring drugs into the country, are preoccupied with the idea that their criminality has no victims. But for those who have done something that has turned identifiable, private individuals into victims, people whom they might even know or who are family members, the victims personify and remind them that they are responsible for wronging someone. From the perspective of society as a whole or the System, what the prisoners have done is serious enough for them to be put in Oslo Prison. This also involves an inherent evaluation: the general status of prisoner indicates that prisoners are immoral people who are responsible for some very serious, sick and/or evil actions. Having one or more victims always simultaneously means being a perpetrator. Disturbing thoughts about the victims are, from such a perspective, also a reminder to the prisoners of how they are seen by others.

Many struggle with thoughts about "their" victims and are despondent about what they have done. Henning was among them. At the time of the extract below, he had just arrived in the prison. He had been remanded for domestic abuse and was still strongly affected by what had happened. He needed to talk to someone about what he had done, but did it in ways that broke a number of the informal rules that apply to such conversations on the wing.

> Henning: When I'm clean, I'm the world's calmest guy, my friends will confirm that, but when I'm high on speed, then my impulse control is poor, right? We, me and my lady, had been high, hadn't slept for four days. I was in the bathroom, she came in and started nagging me, right? I didn't want to hear it right then, I grabbed her arm hard, so she probably got really scared, right? And hit me. I snapped. We had been decorating, there was a rubber mallet there, I grabbed it and started hitting her. Fuck! [Buries face in hands] But she'll forgive me, she will. She said so. Our friends will understand as well: they understand me, she understands me, knows that I'm not really like that, that I'm really a nice guy. I was totally shocked when I saw what I had done to her.
>
> [...]
>
> Henning: She saw how sorry I was. I tried not to cry, I didn't want to, it was her who was hurt.
>
> The conversation is taking place in the common area; Henning and I are sitting opposite each other. Sitting next to us is [prisoner X], who is reading the newspaper and cannot mark the distance between him and Henning strongly enough. He constantly shifts position until, eventually, he is almost sitting with his back to Henning, even though they are sitting on the same sofa. He also sighs loudly and looks away. This sort of self-exposure and remorseful conversation is not everyday fare in socials. [Prisoner X] is demonstrating with his entire body, his whole attitude, what he thinks of Henning's story.

A number of elements of Henning's story made his fellow prisoner want to mark the distance he felt existed between them. His story was one of out-of-control drug addiction, of a person who could not control himself, who had poor impulse control, who had not intended things to work out as they did. He blamed his amphetamine use instead of taking responsibility for what he had done. He did not accept responsibility. He could not sufficiently control his emotions in the situation on the sofa either. He had also hurt a woman who was smaller and weaker than him. Not hurting women and children is basically a moral imperative that is strongly abided by in the prison (see the section on rapists above). Nor was there anything his girlfriend did in the story that could be used to make Henning's violence acceptable, or at least understandable. Henning's story was of an unpredictable and out-of-control Mr Hyde who hurt defenceless women and did not take responsibility for it afterwards either: a monster. The fact that Dr Jekyll was remorseful afterwards did not change anything.

Even though it is unusual to expose yourself in the common area as Henning did, it is probably not uncommon to have thoughts of guilt and remorse in relation to your victims (Leer-Salvesen, 1988a, 1988b). It is usually just not as obvious in day-to-day life on the wing. Daniel did not regret in public. However, alone in his cell with me, he became serious and thought about everyone whose credit cards he had emptied over the years:

> Daniel: Yeah, I think about everyone I've done this to [various credit card swindles and other forms of fraud]. Prison is far too good for me really. I deserve much worse.
> TU: So, you think about that sort of thing?
> Daniel: Yes, of course, of course I do. I think about all the families that have been affected. Yeah okay, it's only money, and, after all, they'll get it back from their insurance. But that sort of thing takes time and in the meantime they're poor. I think about the holiday that didn't happen. The whole family that has been looking forward to it, but suddenly the money is gone. I think about that sort of thing. All the people I have ruined things for. I deserve much worse.

Daniel was keeping accounts here. He based them on some sort of karmic idea. The total amount of pain he had caused should be reflected in his punishment. Given all of his victims, his punishment was not harsh enough. The number of months of imprisonment was not enough to cleanse him of his guilt. Such religious (in some sense or other of the word) notions are not uncommon.

Both Henning and Daniel thought and talked about their victims, albeit in different contexts and in different ways. The victims are a symbol of the harm caused. The imprisonment is a symbol of society's evaluation of the prisoners' harm-causing actions. The relationship with the victims, therefore, becomes an ethical problem. Many experience feelings of guilt, shame and grief in relation to the actions for which they are doing time in prison (Leer-Salvesen, 1988a). Below I will concentrate on what may be a possible solution to this point of departure, more specifically on prisoners who make use of a special type of transformation art: a form of neutralisation technique by which, after the fact, one changes the victim's narrative status in some way or other in order to position oneself as ethically superior. Please note that this does not mean that the prisoners have no regrets; it just means that they make use of this specific technique of the self.

From one perspective Trond had done much the same as Daniel above. But he described it in a completely different way, using other victim roles that in turn gave him an opportunity to position himself in an ethically far more advantageous way:

> Trond: People are so fucking naive. You just have to call and be polite, and you'll get everything you want. For example, I could call and pretend that I'm conducting a survey for MMI, and I would learn everything. Everything! Personal identification number, bank, and income, ta-da, your account is empty. It's fucking unbelievable how stupid people are. [...] However, I've completely stopped defrauding private people now. Although they are insured, having to wait six months before you get your money back can of course be fucking crap. So I only swindle large companies and I don't have many scruples when it comes to them, I really don't. For example, I swindled Aker Kværner out of quite a bit of money. The fact that Røkke[20] is an idol in Norway is just fucking stupid. I don't exactly have a problem swindling that sort of swindler, to put it that way. I have always voted well to the left of centre; I have always been bloody interested in injustice.

In the anecdote Trond relates, he is smart, not bad. Most people are naive; they need to be protected from themselves. Being as clever and smart as Trond is brings with it great responsibility; most people will fall for absolutely anything. Unfortunately, he was not aware of his responsibility before and he swindled private people. That was wrong. Therefore, he stopped doing it. Now, he only steals from those who deserve it, fair targets. He does what he calls a half Robin Hood. He only steals from those who have done something wrong and who can afford to be robbed; he just does not share the spoils with others poorer than himself. He is preoccupied with injustice and goes after the *real* crooks, the filthy rich who have swindled their way to enormous fortunes and got away with it.

This division between victims who deserve it and innocent victims who do not can also be found in Tom's anecdote about someone he knows who was on an underworld debt collection job and had been given the wrong information:

The job went really wrong. They got the wrong address, just broke down the door and started to wreck the flat, broke everything. When they found out it was the wrong bloke, he had nothing to do with the case, they didn't do things by half; they ordered the best door that day and sent the whole family on holiday to the Med. The whole family. That's the way it is; they didn't want having messed up an innocent person on their conscience. They just had to pay up. It's about honour, right? In those sort of circles [biker gangs] it guides everything. You just have to abide by the rules.

Tom's story is about maintaining a code of professionalism and a code of honour. You do not just break into anybody's home and start breaking things. You do that on the job, and only when it is well deserved because the owner is involved in a "case". It is okay to make mistakes, but if you do you have to put things right afterwards. There is a class of ordinary, inno-cent people out there, the sort who are not involved in the game between the criminals and the System. Those who accost people like that are nothing more than simple scoundrels. The home owners became *innocent* victims because of a mistake. Innocent victims are something altogether different, and deserve something else.

Presser (2004) has studied how men convicted of violence reconstruct themselves as morally superior in and through their interviews with her. She finds no transformation of the applicable moral codes; all the men she interviewed agreed that morally inferior people exist and that they can also be found in the prison. A common ethical technique Presser describes is how the men work to position themselves as something other than an example of these. It is about creating categories in and through the interviews, and asso-ciating yourself with the advantageous categories and marking the distance between you and less favourable ones.

Tom was on remand, charged with murdering an ex-girlfriend. One day, the two of us were in his cell talking about his case. The date of his court case was approaching and he was nervous about how he would act and come across in court. He spoke about what had happened and about the outcome he envisaged. After a while, the victim became something of an empty space in the conversation that we were circling around, without this being made explicit. I tried to move the conversation towards this, but my stammering indicates that I thought it was difficult to find a good way of doing so:

TU: He...this happened with...he had...
Tom: He...yeah, it was actually a woman, though. That's why I say the person. But we are talking about a person who had done time for mur-der, who had drilled people's joints using a hammer drill to destroy them. You have no idea how many female underworld debt collectors

work in Oslo today. There's no difference between men and women any more.

TU: So there is full equality, then?

Tom: There is. I mean, there are more men, but the women are just brutal. [...] The woman we are talking about was breaking the kneecaps of people as well, with the sort of hammers they have on buses. She hid the hammer in her sleeve and just walked over to you and swung away [points to my knee].

TU: The red ones, with the pointed tip?

Tom: Yeah, that sort. When it hits your kneecap, it smashes it into a thousand pieces. Then you've had it.

TU: Bloody hell [shaking my head].

At the time, we had spoken about his case several times over a longer period. This was the first time Tom had told me it was a woman, let alone an ex-girlfriend, he had killed. A murderer is basically positioned as dangerous, bad, sick and incomprehensible, someone who has done the worst thing you can do. For a murderer who has also killed a woman, and on top of that a woman he had had a personal relationship with, the position is even worse. Tom clearly knew this. He did not want the details to come out, for people to talk about it, and consistently referred to the victim as "the person". At the same time, he did not want to lie. After all, admitting what you have done, taking responsibility for it, is a value. As in the example above, the person who must take responsibility for something like this must do something or other to reduce the imbalance or, in the words of Sykes and Matza (1957), the *cognitive dissonance* that arises. It is wrong to hurt someone who is weaker than you. Tom did not disagree with this. It is also wrong not to take responsibility for what you have done. How can these contradictions best be reconciled in practice? Tom's solution was to position the victim as something entirely different from an ordinary woman. The physical advantage he had as a man was equalised; another time he said that she *perhaps weighed only 50 kilos and was 150 centimetres tall. A petite lady. But remember, you don't mess with a 50-kilo pit bull.* The ex-girlfriend was no defenceless, female victim, but a raving, foaming at the mouth, fighting dog. Thus, Tom's actions were imperceptibly creeping in the direction of understandable self-defence.

The victim was positioned as extremely dangerous, but also as morally inferior. After all, this was someone who had done time for murder (as he would; they are, as he said, equal in some sense). She was dangerous; she hurt other people and did so for money. Tom did not do that sort of thing. He wanted to stress that there are differences between murder cases and that he was not one of those who had hurt innocent or defenceless people. "His" victim was not a random person, not a *real* woman, almost not a person at all. The defeminisation and dehumanisation of the victim thus becomes a positioning tool for making one's own actions understandable and ethically acceptable.

Similar strategies are also brought into play when Tarik tells me about Youssuf's case:

> Tarik: Consider Youssuf, then. He has been in Norway for ever, almost 30 years in Norway. You can knock on every door in the Moroccan community in Oslo and they will say, Youssuf is a fine man, never any problems with him. Nothing to say; no one has anything to say against him. But what happened was that his wife went behind his back; she was unfaithful and also started stealing. That's okay; they get separated, no drama. But then she started taking his children stealing with her. He went to her and asked if she could please stop doing that, she mustn't get the children involved. That's when she got angry and came at him with a ... What's it called ... ? I'll have to draw it for you [draws a spanner].
>
> TU: A spanner?
>
> Tarik: Yes, a spanner; was going to hit him. He had been to the gym, he had a small knife that he used to cut fruit with after working out [makes a three or four-centimetre gap with his fingers] it was so small. That's when he totally lost it; he was knackered, he cut her face up. It had gone too far. He couldn't stop himself. And he gets six years for that. Six years!

Youssuf was presented as a fine man, a law-abiding, normal man who treats his wife well, even when she has been unfaithful and has started stealing. He even asked her, politely, to stop when she starting taking their children with her stealing. It was not until she attacked him with a spanner that he lost it. He could not stop himself. Obviously he should have, but it is easy to understand how things turned out as they did. That is how it looks, according to Tarik, when one looks at both sides of the case. Youssuf's ex-wife was no innocent, defenceless woman. She stole, she put her children in danger, and was a poor influence on them. She was, therefore, a poor mother, and she was fully capable of defending herself when she picked up the spanner. She also becomes equal, part of an environment that removed her from the category of "ordinary people". On the contrary, she was someone an "ordinary person" had to watch out for. Youssuf thus became a person, a fallible person, who was finally pushed too far by his dubious wife and who could not control himself. Even though he was convicted of attempted murder, he is not dangerous.

For his part, Youssuf is preoccupied with marking that he is not like the other prisoners in Oslo Prison. He especially targets those who are on remand for drug smuggling:

> Youssuf: I totally agree with the police, I totally agree with them. Crush all those who are fucking selling drugs! I totally agree; I don't like people

who earn money by killing others with drugs, I agree! One hundred per cent; I agree with them.

TU: The police should work against them as much as possible?

Youssuf: Against drugs? I think the police must. But there are other areas where they should totally relax. Try when it is a family conflict; try to see if you can resolve the problem. That's very good, that they can try to resolve the family problem before they perhaps destroy that family.

TU: Talking instead?

Youssuf: Talk with them and have a meeting, and, because, like I said to you, immigrants, it is a new society. It's true. I could live better in France; I could live better in Italy because they have the Mediterranean. People, they know what it means, they know our culture. Norway, it's just a little place on the fringe! Paysage, countryside. So, for example, the French, they call Norway le paysage de l'Europe.

Youssuf finds it morally reprehensible to make money from someone else's misfortune, from hurting or killing others. People who do things like that should be locked up. On the other hand, he believed family conflicts are a more problematic area when it comes to police intervention. The result can be destroyed families. It is best to get the parties to meet to talk through the conflict. The fact that Youssuf got as heavy a sentence as six years was due to us northerners not understanding the Mediterranean temperament. A more culturally sensitive solution would have attached importance to getting the parties together and resolving their problems, according to him. Instead, the Norwegian System, from that strange, little country in Northern Europe, stepped in and made him a hardcore assailant who deserves his long imprisonment. This is a position that Youssuf finds very difficult to reconcile with his self-image.

Erol's earlier description of the professional criminal was the opposite of Youssuf's categorisations:

> I don't know... killing someone, that's not, that's not crime, that's... and paedophiles, people who do things that hurt people, that is not legitimate. And nor should it be legitimate. Because, after all, you're hurting people, and you're doing it deliberately.

Erol differentiated between two groups of prisoners: the professionals, those for whom criminality is a job and who have not hurt other people; and those who have hurt others, murderers and paedophiles, are those who deserve to do time. Youssuf believed that drug smugglers should be in prison because they make money from other people's suffering. This was a legitimate job for Erol; it is about buying and selling a product for adults. He believed the opposite of Youssuf; those who hurt others physically are the ones who deserve to be in prison. Each of them elevated himself above what the other had done based on his ethical values. Both positioned themselves as ethical people by using the other's actions as a reference point for the unethical.

The common denominator in the ethical self-construction work described here is that the prisoners want to position themselves as not dangerous. By repositioning the victims, they turn themselves into not dangerous or not generally dangerous, normal, ethically aware subjects. From this perspective, the narratives about the dubious, dangerous and equal victims can be read as opposition to the status of prisoner, which entails being understood as a dangerous person it is best to avoid and who is in prison for good reason. The prison is also a moral space. Everyone who has grown up under the shadow of a prison wall knows this: be careful so you do not end up on the other side! Prison is where the bad people live. The sort who belong there are basically positioned at the bottom of the moral scale (Cohen and Taylor, 1981). Being positioned as unethical is painful. The institution's entire structure is based on the notion that prisoners, as untrustworthy bodies, cannot be trusted. As a prisoner, you are also positioned such that you cannot take care of your children, wife or partner, like a bad father and partner/spouse, thus demonstrating that you cannot be trusted. Prisoners are, from the start, positioned as dangerous individuals who present a risk, as people who deserve to be in prison, and who must be guarded so that society outside can feel safe.

Ethics in practice is key to the production of the ethical subject, the person who does the right thing, who is one of those who do the right thing, which, in other words, separates them from those who do the wrong thing. Ethics can function as a diacritical tool. Criminal law can be described as the institutionalisation of this type of diacritical ethics that prisoners have already felt physically, and are still feeling physically. The imprisoned subject is not cut off from society. On the contrary, as a prisoner one is positioned in relation to society in a new way, in relation to new discourses, with new consequences for how you perceive yourself and how others perceive you. Ethics is, therefore, front and centre in the prisoner group. Being branded immoral is a similarity prisoners share – as a prisoner you are a concrete example of abstract immorality. You start from the position of being one of "the unethical others". The prison is a system and an organisation that is organised on the basis of the notion that the prisoners have already, upon arrival at the institution, proven that they are untrustworthy. As an institution, a closed prison is built to cope with the *worst case scenario*, in order to ensure that the *worst case scenario* does not become a reality. The prisoners protest against the institutional mistrust the institution shows them. Brede's drawn-out sigh is illustrative: *Is everything we say just a lie then? Just because we are in prison that does not mean that we only lie, does it?*

As a prominent social example of "the unethical", being able to turn yourself into an ethical person is vital. One fundamental way is to introduce divisions between various prisoners based on morality. When the prison says that *you are all the same to us*, they are in some sense saying that you are all *equally bad* to us. *The hell we are,* respond the prisoners, knowing full well that, according to the rules of prisoner culture, the differences are clear. The problem is not that prisoners lack morals; on the contrary, there is a lot of morality in the prison. The prisoners associate themselves with and position themselves in relation to moral norms that are broadly recognised in society. What happens is that they feel pressure not to understand themselves as amoral or immoral people, and do something about it. In such a situation, repositioning yourself as an ethical person therefore becomes vital. This can be understood as resistance to the power that speaks the truth about you from the outside, that talks about you in the third person, but that equally positions you as someone/something you do not want to be, the power that speaks from above, and that through its speech nails you in place and fixes you as a member of a group you want to distance yourself from. Resistance consists of resolving and problematising the association that arises, saying that I am not like what they say I am; I am not like the other prisoners. In the ongoing ethical subjectification work, the professional criminals group together as professional criminals by marking their distance from snitches and rapists. This is done by putting categories that can be found culturally, in prisoner culture, to work. But such distancing also, simultaneously, strikes a note in a broader cultural context. As children learn in nursery school: "tell-tale tit, your tongue will split and all the little puppy dogs will have a little bit" and "do unto others as you would have them do unto you". The prisoners, whom the prison puts in the same pigeonhole (*you are all the same to us*), have, in turn, a need to highlight differences (*the hell we are!*) They may have contravened the Norwegian General Civil Penal Code, but breaking one rule does not mean that they have no rules. The prisoners put alternative moral codes to work and position themselves in relation to these. Whether it is the childhood rhyme above, or the Bible's Golden Rule, they re-create the difference between professional criminals and sick rapists, which the Norwegian General Civil Penal Code and prison have basically wiped out by treating them the same. The contempt for snitches reinstates a similar distance between professional criminals and the non-professionals who have broken the first rule of prisoner culture: keep quiet and take responsibility for what you have done.

Conclusion: To Be or Not to Be a Prisoner

I am hanging out with Daniel in his cell. He is telling me, half embarrassed but smiling, about a food-related near accident he had in his cell recently:

Daniel: *I almost made a complete fool of myself a couple of days ago. I was going to make pasta, but I wasn't concentrating and did it wrong. Sparks flew and the power went. I was sat there in the dark just saying "fuuuuuck". I waited and waited for some of the other cells to call. After all, three or four cells are linked and thus the power goes at the same time. They are on the same circuit. Finally him next to me called. They came and, of course, they searched his cell, since the power had gone, and found the cable he uses to listen to music on his TV. He was really pissed off; he banged on the wall and shouted: "Fuck, Daniel, that's the last time you make food! They took my music!" We are friends again now, heh heh. He's back at it; he plays music for me as well. Listen. [Bangs hard on the wall] Volume! Turn it up! [Shouts through the wall. The music can soon be heard more clearly. Daniel smiles.] When it's quiet in here, at night, you can hear everything quite clearly. I sorted it, heh heh. A couple of weeks ago, he was sitting in there and had smoked some cannabis. I shouted that I couldn't hear well enough and that he had to do something. So he broke four of his window panes, heh heh. I can get people to do anything I like in here. Now I can hear everything clearly. But, I know all the songs pretty well, to put it mildly. He doesn't have that many CDs and he has his favourites, to put it like that.*

TU: *Is there a lot of communication between the cells?*

Daniel: *Yes, lots; after the shift change in the evening you more or less have free rein. We just shout across the yard between the buildings. It's not hard. It gets a bit messy sometimes when several conversations are taking place at the same time. Occasionally someone will shout "shut up for five minutes, we have to finish talking! It's important!" Then you're quiet for a while. It works. Another lad involved in my case is in here, on the other side. Unfortunately, though, he is on the wrong side of the building. Luckily, there is another lad I know on*

236

the side across from here. So I talk to him and during the day he talks to the lad involved in the same case as me. It's a bit cumbersome, but it works well. We can prepare for court, coordinate our stories. I mean, it's worth its weight in gold, especially when, basically, we're not supposed to have met or spoken to each other. We call it the Internet, the conversations between the buildings. It's a bit slow, but it gets there. An officer has come in twice during the middle of conversations. I was lucky both times. They were pleasant officers, who I know well. They just looked at me sternly and said: "What are you doing? Be quiet!" I smiled and said that it wasn't me, it was the cell next door. And that was that. I waited 15 minutes and carried on. When [Officer X] was here, she was pretty strict; she can be a bit tough. But there were no consequences later. I like her. She has strength; she doesn't let herself be picked on. I mean, she is small and light, but it's clear that she's the one in charge. You can see some of the other female officers are anxious. Not [Officer X]. She knows she is in charge and she doesn't take crap from anyone. She doesn't let herself be pushed around. I like that.

TU: *I agree. She seems like she knows what she wants alright.*

Daniel: *In general, there is a difference between the officers in four and five. Us up in five are lucky. There are a few with bad attitudes in four, who just point and wave you into your cell, for example. Here in five, almost everyone is nice the whole time. They talk to you like a person; they don't just look at you like a dog.*

Transformation, adaptation, resistance

The fact that power does not necessarily produce conformity or the effects the power wants to produce is something that everyone who has felt that exciting feeling of breaking the rules knows, a feeling that comes directly from, and is totally dependent on, the rules being broken. However, power does, by necessity, position subjects in specific ways. From a Foucauldian perspective, resistance is a fundamental concept when it comes to understanding the practical and specific correlation between power and subjectivity. In the encounter between an individual and the power relationships they are involved in, resistance arises as a bridge between levels, and the result is the socially positioned subject. In other words, subjects are not a result of individuals quoting the culture's available subject positions like actors reading a film script. There are always several ways of articulating a specific position (Laclau and Mouffe, 2001), and even simply identifying (Neumann, 2001) with a longed-for subject position is not *that* simple. There are always alternative ways of reproducing, varying and adapting positions in and through social practices, depending on factors such as the specific context, other available positions to play off, and the collection of resources the individuals, with their specific bodies, backgrounds and experiences, constitute. In addition to this, counter-identification –

when an individual assumes a diametrically opposite position to that pre-scribed by the interpellation hail – and disidentification – where one pulls the offered position in a new direction, or combines positions from differ-ent hails into new hybrids – are always possible. It is not until the situated individuals encounter the relevant field in practice, when individuals (who are always already subjects) enter into, negotiate and relate to how positions should specifically be articulated, that the space for creativity, adaptation and resistance opens up.

The Norwegian Correctional Services' policy documents hail prisoners as people with problems and deficiencies, whom the correctional services hope to change, for the benefit of everyone. On the outside of the porous walls, the prisoners are understood as dangerous actors responsible for incompre-hensible and evil acts, members of a criminal class of inferior or defective members of society who, for good reason, must be kept apart from the major-ity of good citizens. In the daily encounters with the officers, the prisoners are turned into untrustworthy bodies that must be controlled and admin-istered. The encounters between prisoners produce smart and stupid, moral and immoral, weak and strong prisoners. At the same time, in many ways, prison life deprives prisoners of their responsibilities and capacity to act, and they are made passive and dependent. To put it in very simplistic terms, the status of prisoner, therefore, entails being positioned as either pitiful or dangerous.

According to Sykes (1958), one can say that being imprisoned entails a series of challenges that can be perceived as more or less painful: you are torn away from the daily routine you know, deprived of control over day-to-day life's many decisions, placed in a subordinate position in relation to a group of prison officers, a large proportion of whom in a contemporary Norwegian context are, to add insult to injury, women who are younger than you and who could, therefore, be perceived as challenges for the male pris-oners' subjectification work. From such a perspective, by doing resistance, one is also doing something else; these are freedom practices whereby the prisoners performatively do, for example, autonomy, resourcefulness and creativity: values that, by being done in specific contexts, can also be used to do masculinity.

The prisoners' everyday forms of adaptation, resistance and escape attempts are, seen from this vantage point, something far more than relatively harmless but irritating boundary testing. Such practices have fun-damental effects on the level of the ongoing work of transforming one's position in relation to, and with the aid of, the institution's material, discursive and social conditions of possibility. In this book I have shown how this transformation work plays out in practice and the consequences it has for the prisoners, who can thus become something other than a pitiful or evil prisoner. The prisoners experience the status of prisoner as intolerable. And they do something about it. They change the interpretive framework through the symbolic and performative power inherent in very different forms of resistance practices. By changing the situation, by participating in the prison's power relationships in ways that allow them to assume better alternative subject positions, they can transform themselves into responsible, autonomous, capable, ethically aware free men, albeit, of course, within the framework, and with the aid of, the resources a prison wing offers.

The forms of power are most visible precisely when they encounter their specific forms of resistance (Foucault, 2000c). The power can, thus, be understood as an offer that demands resistance. A person who is positioned as a prisoner may, for example, need to make it clear that the prison does not decide everything, and that the ability to decide things for himself and about his situation has not completely disappeared. He may wish to underscore that he neither wants nor needs to be changed, that he is not defective, inferior or incomplete. He may try to convince the relevant authorities that he is not one of the dangerous ones, that he will not commit crimes in the future, and that he can safely be allowed out among the public as one of "us".

Resistance can be so many things. It can be played out in many contexts and in opposition to, or as an extension of, many different forms of power. Resistance to a disciplinary power technique that focuses on the detailed control of the body's movements will have to be played out differently from resistance to responsibilisation techniques whose aim is to get individuals to exercise self-control. Sometimes resistance can take the form of simple opposition to the power. One struggles, one stands up and fights for what is right, one says *no*. Or one refuses to participate, one becomes mute and sits down, one refuses to acknowledge the rules of the game. The prisoner who refuses, who plays hardball, will in the vast majority of cases lose. This is usually clear to all involved. This is precisely why saying no can have large, expressive and symbolic consequences. The person who says no has been pushed to their limit and needs to demonstrate it. This need may be stronger than the fear of the unfortunate consequences that are bound to follow. Such resistance could be further refined into a counter-identification position; the person who does resistance can become someone who resists. Resistance is then (also) about turning yourself into a subject who manages, and wants, to avoid the institution's power or to deny its legitimacy, the subject who stands up to the (superior) power. It is through relating to the forms of power, through entering into concrete power and resistance relationships, that the subject, understood in this way, is produced.

Resistance can also, quite simply, be about demonstrating that you are someone who can tackle the prison-produced pain well. As previously mentioned, Crewe (2009) believes that "resistance" and "coping" are related phenomena, but not the same. The form of resistance that is closest to coping will be expressive practices that underscore and communicate strength and stamina in the encounter with the monotony and impassivity of the prison, and the police's attempts to get you to talk. Real men do not whine, they do not let themselves be broken, and they definitely do not snitch.

The fact that time is passing is not something that most of us on the outside think about on a daily basis. The time ahead and the time that has passed are at the forefront of prisoners' minds. Remand prisoners are also trapped in a monthly cycle of hope and disappointment, of which it is not easy to see the end. The prisoner who copes with this, who retains his sense of humour despite everything and does not allow himself to be broken by the System that is trying to break him (as they perceive the case to be), turns himself into the man who can endure. Real criminals keep quiet and do not allow themselves to be tempted by the police's offer to end their remand in return for information. At the same time, the time ahead is an enemy against which a man who resists can triumph. Every day that passes without you cracking and snitching on someone can, therefore, become a small victory.

The person who says no can appear principled and uncompromising, as someone who dares to say no. However, there is little room for mistake when finding a balance between being principled and being unnecessarily confrontational, childish and stupid in the eyes of both officers and fellow prisoners. Prisoners who "are stubborn" are often a nuisance for the officers and unintentionally funny or tragic to their fellow prisoners. In these circumstances, subtle forms of resistance that go below the institution's radar may be preferable. One example of this is the prisoners' discursive transformation of the relationship between prisoner and officer that turns the officers into caretakers, servants or pitiful, failed, not-quite-policemen, which has direct consequences for the associated prisoner position. Another is creative resistance practices that focus on achieving something, on doing something, even in a prison. Opening up space for opportunities is to become something other than a prisoner. A person who manages to take liberties, even in restrictive surroundings, becomes, at least partly and temporarily, free. The capable bricoleur is the master of his surroundings and transforms them to his benefit. The subject who thereby enables a disidentification position is the subject who makes creative use of the sparse resources available, the subject who manages to "make the best of it", the subject who will not allow himself to be broken, and who retains his optimism and his wit. The prison's rules and the daily control routines limit the prisoners' freedom of movement and action. However, it is the same rules and the same control that make it possible to turn yourself into a prisoner-subject who manages to resist the institution in many hidden ways; a smart, capable prisoner who always keeps his resistance practices hidden just under the surface.

The prisoners' resistance practices take place from a relatively subordinate position. Resistance, therefore, always entails some degree of risk. At the same time, and precisely for this reason, resistance is a potentially potent tool in the process of transforming your own position, regardless of the outcome. The victor laughing at his fleeing enemies has in common with a dying martyr that they are both positioned as subjects who dared and managed to resist, which simultaneously entails *doing* courage and vigour and thus *becoming* a courageous and vigorous subject in the specific situation. This will even be a by-product of resistance practices that do not achieve their goal. All in all, resistance practices are diverse, and resistance subjects are just as diverse in their creative production of resistance.

Many of the resistance practices I have described can be said to be fundamentally based on a desire for individualisation. They can, for example, be about making yourself into an individual when the surroundings only see you as part of a group. Being a unique individual becomes especially important in a context where you are seen as a number in a series, as an example of a larger unit. In prison, everything prisoners do will often be understood on the basis of the fact that it is being done by prisoners. A prisoner is turned into a cell number, an example of the set of prisoners. At the same time, prison life requires prisoners to stick together against their common enemy. The requirement for group solidarity is an essential part of what has been described as prison culture. From this perspective, prisoners must navigate between two important needs: being a unique individual and being part of a collective and a community of prisoners who share the same fate and who stand together.

Finally, the goal of resistance can be to reinstate a successful male subject. The prison's control practices position prisoners as unmanly in a number of ways. At the same time, what Kolnar (2006) has called a centripetal invitation is directed at the prisoners: do something about it! Be a real man, not a weak, beaten, immoral victim who is either pitied or whose malice is incomprehensible. The day-to-day forms of resistance can, correspondingly, be understood as attempts to restore the balance. In practice, prisoners are, because they are prisoners, deprived of the opportunity to perform many traditional male duties. They are unable to participate in the relationships that are usually among the most important for the day-to-day reproduction of masculinity; relationships with wives, sweethearts or live-in partners, parents and children. Their room for action and decision making has also contracted considerably. The prisoners are made dependent on a system that has great influence over their everyday lives. I have, a number of times, described how prison life can have an infantilising effect. Like most male victims of violence (Åkerström, 2007), the male victims of the mighty System must also find that difficult balance between the legitimate victim's role of passivity and impotency and the requirements of masculinity vis-à-vis vigour and strength. Some prisoners resign themselves and feel helpless. But most, instead, turn themselves into victims of an illegitimate system that cheats and breaks its own rules, at the same time as they manage to do some form or other of legitimate resistance. Thus, they do what men should do in such a situation.

As institutions that share specific characteristics, prisons produce similar conditions for the prisoners' subjectification work. The process is prison-specific, but this does not mean that the walls around an institution are so impermeable that the process is not intimately linked to the central perceptions of masculinity in the rest of society. For example, the conditions for safe, responsible, mature, parental masculinity are poor, although the prison fathers try to counter the frustration felt due to a lack of familial company in their everyday lives by overcompensating with regard to their poor future sons-in-law. The designations of involved fathers and understanding, equal husbands are placed in brackets, in the same way as successful employees, entrepreneurs and contractors are. In these circumstances, young masculinity that focuses on physical strength and spectacular actions can be an alternative. It is here you find the fights, challenges, wagers and breaching of taboos. Many of the forms of resistance I have described above can be understood as being adapted to the prison's conditions of possibility in this way.

Kelly (2009) differentiates between resistance on two different levels: one is the everyday micro-level of individual actions (what has been in focus so far) and the other is the overarching, strategic level of big important goals. From the vantage point of the latter, longer-term macro-level, the prisoners' small forms of resistance can be understood as absolutely necessary for the prison's continuation and possible success:

> Micro-resistance is regularly produced and therefore can be anticipated at the level of macro-power. The prison system qua strategic assemblage requires micro-resistance to function: resistance to the authorities is regularly produced, a justification for further disciplining, in which regular recidivism is produced in people caught in power relations in which others try explicitly at the macro-power to discourage reoffending. This is not to say that criminals would not commit crimes were they not punished, but rather that the existing system of punishment produces effects of criminality that it is not supposed to, which count as resistance at a micro-level, but at a macro-level are already accounted for in power's strategies.
>
> (Kelly, 2009: 110)

Resistance practices that provide results on the micro-level can, at the same time, be failures as macro-level resistance (Hollander and Einwohner, 2004). Rhodes (2004) describes how forms of resistance such as throwing excrement and self-harming, which, in some sense, both work as resistance within a very rigid control framework, can at the same time legitimise and necessitate new control measures. From this perspective, the prisoners' everyday forms of resistance can help demonstrate the necessity of prison and the fact that prison officers perform a vital job for society.

The everyday hidden resistance can also be understood as necessary for the operation of the institution in another way. Above, I quoted Cressey, who says that what is strange about prison, what must be explained, are not any extraordinary explosions, but the day-to-day, relatively well-functioning balance. I would claim that one of the reasons why such a balance is largely maintained is that relatively non-confrontational, day-to-day resistance can function as a safety valve. From this perspective, the everyday forms of resistance are, quite literally, necessary for the institution's operation.

At the same time as it is necessary, micro-resistance can help make it harder to achieve, and perhaps even counteract, the prison technology's overarching goal. For the Norwegian Correctional Services, a successful sentence, at least as it is described in its policy documents, depends on the prisoners allowing themselves to be positioned in what for many of them is an intolerable subject position: "the repentant sinner who will allow himself to be changed by a system that knows better". The goal is to release responsible, law-abiding people who exercise self-control, but the fundamental paternalistic attitude deeply embedded in the system that is meant to produce this result produces resistance, which, in turn, can be said to be directly counterproductive. In a system that is meant to cultivate responsibility in people, one removes most of the arenas for assuming responsibility in practice. This is yet another example of the point that the prison's different, and to some extent contradictory, goals can be said to cancel each other out. Punishment is burdened with tensions that cannot be resolved, paradoxes one cannot get past, writes Garland (1990).

The prisoners will find a way to express resistance; they do so even in Rhodes' (2004) high security prisons. Oslo Prison could move to different locations that would make talking between the cells harder. One could confiscate all the cables that make it possible to listen to music through a TV. One could eliminate the prisoners' ability to buy their own food. One could remove almost everything and ensure that what is left is unbreakable and harmless. But, even if the prisoners are left with an empty room, they will find cracks and escape routes that make it possible to do freedom in practice. A prison that eliminated every opportunity for this would no longer be a prison as we know it. On the path to a completely resistance-free prison, one would have to sacrifice any hope of facilitating rehabilitation and any human contact between prisoners and between prisoners and officers. As long as a prison is not completely totalitarian, one will find everyday forms of resistance and escape routes below the surface. If this is taken for granted, the challenge the correctional services face becomes constructing an institutional and structural framework and exercising power in ways that result in forms of resistance that are the best possible, or the least destructive possible, for all involved.

In any case, I have described how the prisoners' forms of resistance, freedom practices and escape attempts can play out in and through the concrete context a prison wing constitutes. The specific practices will vary. But, and this is the project's generalisable bottom line, in a certain sense, a prison is a prison is a prison. The prison's forms of power ascribe the status of prisoner to the prisoners. However, most prisoners do not wish to be prisoners and work to be something else. Through concrete, day-to-day practices, the prisoners produce alternatives to the prison power's objectification that enable them to transform themselves into unique, creative and ethically conscious people who do resistance and who are therefore free, and who thus cannot be (merely) prisoners.

This is the result of the level of ongoing practice, interaction and subjectification work on a prison wing, and I could have stopped here. But, by way of conclusion, I would like to change my focus somewhat and take a quick look at the prison from the outside of the walls and try to place the institution and its results in a broader social context.

The prison's cultural position

I have studied the way power works on a micro-level and its effects in and on people's daily lives. I have described what it means for the prisoners' self-perception to be turned into objects of the power assemblage the prison constitutes, and have shown what they do about it. From this point of departure, on the level of what Foucault called the microphysics of power, one can elevate one's gaze to see how what is happening forms part of larger mechanisms. What happens in prison is always affected by factors and circumstances outside the walls. For example, it depends on broader cultural discourses about crime, punishment, responsibility, ethics and masculinity that apply inside, as well as outside, the walls.

The prison is a kind of cultural trope, an "abstract place" (Rhodes, 2004) in the collective cultural consciousness that everyone can have an opinion about without having experienced it (other than through Hollywood films). Specific prisons also tell stories about the society of which they are a part (Garland, 1990). Some prisons are shiny and high-tech and tell stories about "the latest thing" and communicate that, finally, one has, with the aid of international research and cutting-edge science, come closer to the Solution. Others have walls covered in ivy and tell stories about solidity and durability, and an institution that has always been there and that will always, in some sense, remain what it is.

As a categorisation practice (Foucault, 2000c) the prison is a co-producer of three distinct, mutually exclusive, subject positions: first, the prisoner, second, the prison officer, and, third, "ordinary people". These are positions that in some sense do not exist without the prison as a categorisation practice. No prisoners exist before they are put in prison. Without the prison, there can be no prison officers either. And, perhaps most importantly of all, without a clear and plain reference point consisting of unethical, abnormal non-citizens, there can be no good, normal citizens. From this vantage point, prison is a definition machine that produces prisoners and set them apart from both prison officers and the normal population.

From this perspective, then, as a cultural figure, the prisoner is important as an abnormal, immoral constitutive exterior for moral and normal "proper people" in society outside, as the abnormal in general is part of the normal's condition of possibility. At the same time, "normal people" are made observable and validated as those who abide by the norms. Foucault ascribes a specific role to juridical practice in the constitution of modern subjects:

> Juridical practices, the manner in which wrongs and responsibilities are settled between men, the mode by which, in the history of the West, society conceived and defined the way men could be judged in terms of wrongs committed, the way in which compensation for some actions and punishment for others were imposed on specific individuals [...] seems to me to be one of the forms by which our society defined types of subjectivity, forms of knowledge, and, consequently, relations between men and truth which deserves to be studied.
>
> (Foucault, 2000d: 3)

The prison holds, as part of this juridical sphere Foucault describes, a central place in our society's subjectification processes in general. The prison's role as a cultural and symbolic variable, in relation to other variables like "freedom", "punishment", "guilt", "atonement", "responsibility" and "the good and honourable", indicates how important the institution can be said to be. From such a perspective, *Homo sapiens* has long ago turned into *Homo juridicus* (Supiot, 2007). The law as an institution has been, and is, important in the production of the stable self that has the freedom to choose good or evil, that remains itself over time, and which can, therefore, take responsibility for good and evil actions one has committed in the past. From this perspective, prison can be understood as a "moral technology", coupled to society's broader cultural reproduction of norms, morality, laws and so on.

One of prison's most important effects is the production of criminals, according to Foucault (1977a). This happens on various levels. People who are put in prison will, to some extent, be positioned in relation to the state and the state power in a new way, which, in turn, as I have shown, has a number of effects on the subjectification game that takes place there. Next, and as part of this, the prison helps to constitute a group by placing specific people together as a group through their being sentenced to a prison sentence. The prison produces a criminal class that also becomes a "class for itself".

As the concrete reasons for, and forms of, the punishment and power change, the correlating subject also changes. The power will, as it focuses on the rehabilitation and re-socialising of the criminal subject, set people apart and categorise them according to their various levels of potential and problems, deficiencies and opportunities. The state's gaze is a diagnostic and prognostic gaze that sees a criminal person as an opportunity for intervention. The criminal group thus plays a role in society that is not afforded enough attention, according to Foucault: "Illegality is not an accident, a more or less unavoidable imperfection. It's an absolute positive element of social functioning, whose role is allocated in the general strategy of society" (Foucault, 1996: 148). Prison makes a group of people visible, opens them up to observation and analysis, and binds them together as people of a certain type, a group that thus "exists" as a "thing" to do something about. This is prison's most important cultural effect: "producing manageable forms of difference" (Widder, 2004: 421–422). The "we" that thinks that something must be done about them – "the criminals" – can thus continue its reconstituting of itself as not (really) criminals, as people who want what is good, but at the same time as people positioned in relation to the state and the law as law-abiding citizens and, therefore, always as potential lawbreakers. As an adult member of a society with the state and the law, one is always a possible object for punishment. This potential punishability is absolutely key in the self-understanding of the adult members of society, associated with notions of their free will to choose good, and the degree of guilt that can be associated with those who do not do this.

At the same time as "criminals" are constituted as a group, they are removed from society and hidden from view. The prison has been described as a magic trick that makes social problems disappear (Rhodes, 2004), a form of collective forgetting technique. Prison both produces undesirable people and keeps them together and hidden in the same movement. The prison walls step forward and display their smooth, clean, solid surface to the rest of society, and at the same time communicate that, yes, we have crime and social problems, but we are also doing something about them. Every system will produce its deviants and every expectation produces people who are unable to live up to these expectations. Those who fail are, in some sense, just as necessary as the norms themselves in order for the ethical community to be able to perceive itself as a community. From this perspective, the prison is meant to function as an expressive or communicative tool. The prison is itself also a symbol of the state's potential concerning the legitimate use of violence – as an enormous sign in the middle of the city, Oslo Prison has, since it opened, functioned as a reminder of what is the final instance for bad boys.

The prison walls are tangible, but they also constitute a symbolic social boundary that changes the status of those who are placed behind them. A prison sentence exhibits the state's capacity; the visible prison walls incessantly rattle their sabres, which in itself is meant to function as part of a broader government strategy in relation to us others. One of the characteristics of the state is that it can lawfully use means of force and violence against people in its territory. This is not mutual; those who are violent towards the state in return have no such rights. The threat of punishment is a key part of the contract between the individual and the state. The goal of implementing punishment can also be said to strengthen the contract between citizens and the state, and show that it still applies. Individuals become the state's subjects precisely by being positioned in such a power relationship with the "authorities". The punishment, like the state's legitimate use of violence, constitutes and shapes the relationship between the authorities, the convicted and the rest of the population. The prison sentence simultaneously demonstrates both the state's problems and its ability to regain control.

The relationship between individuals and the state is thus understood as key to the constitution of modern subjects. The prison sentence, as something that happens in the relationship between "the state" and "the citizens", helps to constitute both of these variables. In some sense, the status of prisoner is characterised by the fact that they have not upheld their side of the agreement or contract they have entered into as citizens of the state. They are examples of people who attempt to live within the state's borders but outside the state's laws. By breaking the law, one falls outside the collective subject the social contract establishes. Foucault quotes Rousseau: "Again, every malefactor, by attacking social rights, becomes on forfeit a rebel and a traitor to his country; by violating its laws, he ceases to be a member of it [...]" (Foucault, 2007: 53n). From this perspective, offenders question the state itself and the state's legitimacy, and thus become a key project for state intervention. By forcing the state to draw boundaries, they demonstrate where the boundaries are. This is how boundaries emerge and are continued over time. Offenders are, thus, a crucial condition of possibility for the law.

As a modern institution, the prison assumes a modern perception of the self. The prison's subject, the imprisoned subject, is a subject who must, and can, take responsibility for their crimes and pay with the loss of their liberty, a subject who is fundamentally stable in time and space. Without such stability, any subsequent reaction that was implemented in a different place to the triggering act (the crime) would be completely meaningless. At the same time, the prison, as an expression of a social-technological desire to change and improve subjects, has helped to underscore the potential of knowledge and consolidate the belief in scientifically based forms of governing and administration. By demonstrating what a person with a stable self is, with personal responsibility, individual liberty and the ability to do right and wrong, the prison helps to re-create specific notions of freedom, responsibility and personality. This system, which was designed to intercept, punish and change people whose behaviour is unwanted, is a co-producer of the modern subject with personal responsibility and a stable personality and identity, who is free to do the right thing (Foucault, 2000d). At the same time, as a technology, the prison itself builds on a belief that the state can, and a wish that it should, intervene and change people and human actions for the better, which is a classic, modern goal. The prison has, thus, helped to structure notions of the self and the person, of the state and its sphere and duties, and of the relationship between individuals and the state.

At the same time, and for very this reason, the prison is perhaps our most important co-producer of freedom. The question about freedom can only be asked within the framework of potential restrictions on freedom. It is not before something or someone threatens to affect or intervene in my freedom that I have an opportunity to decide whether or not I am free. In some sense, the prison walls constitute, from an overarching perspective, a restriction that makes it possible for prisoners to conclude that no, they are obviously not free. It is not before power is concretised and exercised that the question of freedom can be asked in a meaningful way, and it is only through the concretisation of what it would mean to say no that it becomes possible to answer yes. From this vantage point, the prisoners form part of all "free people's" (those who are outside the walls at any given time) conditions of possibility as *free* people. Through the prison's confiscation of the prisoners' time, we on the outside are free to spend our time doing "what we want" (Hardt, 1997).

The individual who will not let himself be governed, on the other hand, who cannot exercise self-control, can, of course, always be subdued and disciplined. But these are at best temporary solutions as long as the individual will be released back into a society characterised by indirect governing strategies. Nonetheless, prison's hegemony continues, now intertwined with new governing techniques with new purposes and goals. One reason for this may be that the prison population is necessary for the freedom of the free society outside, given an understanding of freedom as being correlated with a modern control and power system with a focus on governing strategies, as they are put to work. Such has individual freedom become. The prison is a necessary reference for the continuous social construction of free people. The prison and its prisoners are, thus, key symbols. Being put in prison in such a context is also something other than being put in prison in earlier eras and in other contexts that value individual freedom differently. The fact that people are basically free and exercise self-control legitimises the control of the constitutive others who are not, or who cannot be, free. Note the crucial point: this can also be done as an integral part of the governing power directed at the rest of the population. The minority is, again, necessarily constitutive for its opposite, in this case the "majority" of normal, law-abiding, responsible and free citizens.

* * *

Last week of fieldwork. On my way out at the end of the working day I meet John, who is on his way in together with two strapping, uniformed police officers. He is walking down the ramp from the entrance door while I'm standing by the cupboard where staff leave their mobile phones before the working day starts. John was in wing four last summer. After a while he was transferred down to A unit, where I have met him a few times. So, he is back on remand then. He smiles when he sees me and stretches out his hands towards me. Shaking hands while handcuffed appears to be a bit awkward.

John: Hi, Thomas, are you still up here? Everything alright?
TU: Yes, everything is fine.
I smile. The obligatory reciprocal question seems out of place as John and his escort hurry on, past me, into reception. The seasons change. Snow falls on the walls that hide an inside with which very few are familiar. The tall trees along the avenue that runs up towards Oslo prison tower over four and five-storey blocks of flats on the other side of Grønlandsleiret. They are old, but deeply rooted. Like the prison.

Prison Glossary

2/3 time: Prisoners can apply to the prison for parole after serving two-thirds (and at least 60 days) of their sentence. If the prisoners are granted parole, they are transferred to the Norwegian Probation Service, which follows them up for the remaining sentence period.

A: Oslo Prison, A wing, generally referred to as "down on A" when seen from "up on B". A wing houses prisoners who are serving sentences of up to two years. A is also called Botsen since it is located in the old penitentiary (*botsfengsel*) part of the prison.

Administration time: When the prisoners are locked in their cells it is the officers' administration time. During administration time, the officers carry out all the tasks and routines necessary for the prison's day-to-day operation. Contact officer work on behalf of the prisoners is also a common task during administration time. It is a common joke that administration time is synonymous with a break.

Alarm: The personal assault alarm carried by each member of staff will peep when the alarm is triggered. Depending on the circumstances, the red lamp in the middle of the wing may also light. Most officers run as fast as they can to help their colleague who triggered the alarm. Those left on the wing lock the prisoners into their individual cells. The vast majority of alarms are false alarms or drills.

B: Oslo Prison, B unit, generally referred to as "up on B" when seen from "down on A". B unit is also called Bayern, since it is located in the newer buildings that were taken over from the Oslo Aktiebryggeri brewery in the 1930s. B mainly houses remand prisoners.

Bed with restraints: The cellar houses a bed with restraints to which prisoners can be strapped if they represent an acute danger to themselves. They are meant to simply lie strapped to the bed for as long as they represent a danger to themselves. Two officers must be in the room at all times. For this reason, some people believe that the bed with restraints is preferable to the security cell, which is also in the cellar.

Bøtta: Those who work in "Bøtta" (the bucket) are responsible for cleaning those areas of the prison that are not on a prison wing. Cleaning the prison wing's common area is the responsibility of the trustees; cleaning the cells is the responsibility of the individual cell occupant.

Case: All remand prisoners have an ongoing case. The case runs its course during remand as the police proceed with their investigations. When the case comes up, this means that the investigation has ended and that the court is ready to hear the case. Once the case is over, it can be appealed if the outcome is unsatisfactory. In these circumstances, remand continues and one must again wait for a new case to come up.

Cell: The prisoner's bedroom, workroom, toilet, living room and kitchen, all in one room. All prisoners in Oslo Prison have single cells. The most important distinguishing feature of a high security prison cell is that the metal door has a door handle and keyhole on the outside only.

Cell action: In the event of a cell action, a group of officers put on riot gear. The officers enter the cell as a team, use physical force to gain control of the prisoner who lives in it, and bring him out. Cell actions are not common, but officers practise them regularly.

Client: A prisoner is called a client by the child welfare services or social welfare office.

Court: The court decides whether or not the prisoners should be remanded and whether or not the remand should be extended. The court is the place where the case is heard and is the institution responsible for the case and its outcome. The court is usually defined as part of the System, together with, at the very least, the police and the prison.

Court psychiatrist: Prisoners who risk receiving a preventive custody sentence are likely to undergo a court psychiatric assessment during their remand. This assessment plays a key role in the assessment of danger that will form the basis for a preventive custody sentence.

Defence lawyer: See lawyer.

Detective: The person or people in the police responsible for leading and administering the work on the case against a remand prisoner. The prisoners often get to know their detectives quite well. According to prisoners, some detectives are organised and fair, others cheat or make a sport of catching you, but all of them are part of the System.

Down: Being moved down means being moved to wing two or three. One can also be moved right down to wing one, or down to A wing. As a rule, being moved to A wing is good because it means more time out of your cell and often access to a kitchen where you can make your own food. Being moved down to wing one, two or three is not good and is usually regarded as a punishment.

Effekten: The effects storeroom or "Effekten" is used to store the prisoners' surplus belongings for which there is no space in the cell. What, and how much, there is space for in a cell is regulated; it is not a practical question. The effects storeroom also administers the prisoners' incoming post. Visitors cannot bring belongings in for the prisoners; they have to be sent by post.

Escorted leave: A form of accompanied leave. You can get escorted leave to visit the dentist, purchase items you need or participate in family functions. Escorted leave is a scarce privilege. It is not uncommon for applications for escorted leave to be refused because of a lack of resources, since one prisoner must be accompanied by two officers.

Extra officer: An extra officer is an officer who does not have a full-time position. Extra officers have not attended the Correctional Service of Norway Staff Academy.

The number of extra officers rises rapidly in the summer when the full-time officers take their holidays. The extra officers' shirt shoulder straps are empty and have no cloth sleeves or other badges.

Four more weeks: Seen from inside Oslo Prison's B wing, four new weeks is easily the most frequent outcome of remand reviews.

Full lock-down: When the officers are ordered to implement a full lock-down, the red lamp on the wing lights, which means that they have to lock all the prisoners in their respective cells as quickly as possible. This can be a minor or a major job, depending on the circumstances. As a rule full lock-downs are drills, but they can also be ordered due to, for example, problems on another wing that mean officers have to be ready to go and provide assistance. The officers' ability to execute such orders is tested regularly.

Full-time officers: The full-time officers are full-time employees of the Norwegian Correctional Services. They have trained at the Correctional Service of Norway Staff Academy and wear a black cloth sleeve with a single yellow stripe on their shirt shoulder straps. Most on the officers on a prison wing are full-time officers, except during the summer holidays.

Hanging out: A provision for prisoners on the days they do not have a social, that is, every second day. When hanging out, two prisoners at a time are locked in one of their cells, voluntarily, for one hour. The door hatch is left open so that officers have some sort of control over what is going on.

Health: Short name used for the prison infirmary. The infirmary is run by one of the prison's so-called government partners, the Norwegian National Health Service. In other words, the infirmary staff are not employed by the prison; they are employed by Norway's ordinary National Health Service.

Inmate: The most commonly used term for prisoner. It is also the Norwegian Correctional Services' preferred designation. Some prisoners view "inmate" as a euphemism they refuse to use.

Judge: Prisoners meet judges frequently, usually every four weeks in the so-called remand reviews, where a decision is made about whether or not to extend their remand. When the case finally comes up, the prisoners attend court, where, depending on the seriousness of the case and its place in the legal system, they meet one, two or three professional juridical judges, as well as two, three or four lay judges, or possibly a jury consisting of ten lay people. When prisoners talk about their judge they mean a professional judge.

Keys: The most important material difference between prisoners and officers is their differing access to keys. Officers carry keys in a leather case attached to their belt by a solid chain. The prisoners have no keys. Thus, the noise the keys make differentiates between prisoners and officers, even when you cannot see who is coming.

Kitchen: Oslo Prison does not have a physical kitchen, so "the kitchen" is the name of the van that delivers food from a local hospital. Those assigned to work in the kitchen take receipt of the food and ensure it is forwarded to the individual wings, where the trustees take over.

Lawyer: As a rule, the remand prisoner's closest ally in the ongoing case against them. However, sometimes they are perceived as part of, or allied with, the System. In such circumstances, a new lawyer can be found from the list of lawyers.

Lawyer visits: Take place, like other visits, down in the visitation unit. There are special, small rooms designed for lawyer visits. During lawyer visits, the prisoner and his lawyer prepare for the upcoming court case. The preference is for the lawyer to come in person, but they often send a trainee lawyer in their place. The officers are supposed to be unable to monitor what is going on during lawyer visits.

Leave: Once prisoners have received their sentence and served a third of their time, they can apply for leave. If the sentence is longer than 12 years, the right to leave is earned after four years.

Lock-up: Describes the situation when all the prisoners are locked in their individual cells. Lock-up occurs routinely at fixed times each day. Apart from the time spent in school or on various work assignments in the prison (for those with these), the prisoners are locked in all day except for one hour of yard time and one hour for a social or hanging out in each other's cells, as well as for brief periods for showering, phone calls, cleaning cells and so on. In other words, prisoners are, in practice, locked in for most of the day.

Love room: The visiting room for conjugal visits. Spouses or registered partners can apply to use the love room.

The Norwegian Correctional Services: The official name of the National Correctional Services. Includes the correctional services in institutions (prisons) and the correctional services outside prisons (probation service).

Note: Every morning, prisoners who want to shower, participate in organised training, participate in religious services, use the phone and so on, must submit information about this in a note to the officers so that the officers can organise the working day as efficiently as possible.

Officer: In everyday speech, the term "officer" collectively refers to extra officers, trainees, and full-time officers. Thus, the hierarchy between these groups disappears when 'officer' is used generally. If one means a prison governor, one says so.

Out: Prisoners who are being released are going out. Prisoners who are on yard time are going out. Officers who are going out are going out into the town at the end of the working day. In a prison, being out is always better than being in.

The police: The driving part of the System. It is the police who take the initiative to open a case against the prisoners and it is the police who administer the work on the case and drive it forward. The police are, thus, the remand prisoners' most distinct counter-party in relation to their case.

Pork free: The most common alternative dietary need is a diet without pork. Pork free is not the same as halal, but it is the closest you can get.

Preventive custody: Unlike a prison sentence, preventive custody is a sanction based on an assessment of future danger. In practice, the main difference is that a prison sentence is for a fixed amount of time, while people sentenced to preventive custody are given a minimum amount of time and a maximum amount of time. After the maximum amount of time the court can extend the preventive custody as long as the convicted person is still deemed dangerous. In theory, this can be done for the rest of the person's life. Preventive custody is served at Ila Detention and Security Prison. Some remand prisoners do not know whether they will end up in prison or in preventive custody. For them, a prison sentence can be perceived as a semi-victory.

The prison: By the prison, the prisoners usually mean the entire abstract organisation that controls and administers the prison as a concrete place, as a whole. The prison is often referred to as if it were a person with motivations and capacity for actions; usually by the prisoners, but sometimes also by the staff.

Prisoner: The terms "prisoner" and "inmate" are largely interchangeable in the prison, but "inmate" is the most commonly used term. "Inmate" is also the official term used by the Norwegian Correctional Services. Some prisoners get very irritated about the term "inmate" because they think it functions as a euphemism.

Prison governor: The wings are headed by a principal prison officer who is responsible for its day-to-day operations. These governors are the prison's middle managers. When the definitive article, singular, is used, the governor usually refers to the prison staff member who, at any given time, actually makes the important decisions, that is, the position rather than a person. When an irritated prisoner says "I want to talk to the governor", this can be interpreted as "I want to talk to the person who is really in charge". Prison governors wear a cloth sleeve with a single gold star on their shoulder straps.

Prison yard: B unit has two prison yards. Wings four and five have the use of a sand volleyball court, two small football goals, a couple of benches and an open space they can walk around.

Programme: As part of its rehabilitation work, the Norwegian Correctional Services provides various so-called cognitive skills programmes. Participation in the programmes is voluntary, but can seem such a smart choice that participation can be strategic. It is unusual for remand prisoners to participate in programmes, but in wings four and five they regularly offer Agression Replacement and management Training (ART).

Pupil: A prisoner who is attending the prison school.

Red lamp: When the red lamp in the middle of the wing lights, it means full lockdown. The officers have to lock the prisoners into their individual cells as soon as possible. All activities, including hanging out, must end.

Red note: A red note on a cell door in addition to a white or yellow one means that the prisoner inside is subject to a disciplinary sanction. The red note also contains information about the authority in the *Norwegian Execution of Sentences Act* being applied, usually sections 37 or 39.

Rehabilitation: The desired outcome of imprisonment, from the perspective of the Norwegian Correctional Services. Rehabilitation involves putting the prisoner in a position where he no longer breaks the law. According to key governing documents, everything the correctional services do should be measured against its ability to rehabilitate the prisoners.

Release: The imprisonment's ultimate goal, from the perspective of the prisoners. Release is many years away for most remand prisoners in wings four and five. Sometimes people are released directly from remand. This can be suspicious because it suggests snitching.

Remand review: Remand prisoners are regularly taken to remand reviews at court, usually every four weeks, where the question of whether or not to extend their remand is decided. Participation is voluntary, but most prisoners attend, not least to get out of the prison and perhaps even meet their family and friends.

Report: Unwanted incidents often end up with one or more prisoners being put on report. The report can also lead to the prisoner concerned being disciplined. This sanction will stay on the prisoner's file and may have consequences for decisions later on during their imprisonment.

Restrictions: Remand prisoners are often subject to restrictions at the beginning of their remand, usually bans on letters and visits.

Room: Synonym, some would say a euphemism, for cell.

Sats: Prison hooch. Also called wine. Sats can be made from anything you can get to ferment, such as fruit and leftover bread.

School: The prison's school unit is run by Grønland Adult Education Centre, which is based in Grønland in Oslo. The school is one of the prison's government partners and part of the ordinary school system on the outside. In other words, the school's teachers are not employed by Oslo Prison.

Search: When a cell is going to be searched, two officers enter while the occupant is elsewhere, usually outside on yard time. The officers search through the cell thoroughly, or less thoroughly, hunting for irregularities or breaches of the rules. When a prisoner is searched, often on his way back from a visit, this means that the prisoner must fully undress and be examined visually by two officers to ensure that he is not trying to smuggle something, usually drugs, up to the wing. Officers are not allowed to search body cavities directly; only health professionals can do this.

Section 12: Serving a prison sentence in an institution other than a prison, typically a drug treatment institution, ref. section 12 of the *Norwegian Execution of Sentences Act*.

Sentence: When a case is over it often ends with the prisoner receiving a sentence. Those who are serving a sentence are no longer on remand. Prisoners who have received a sentence are usually transferred quite quickly from B, either down to A, if they have received a sentence of two years or less, or to another prison.

Serving one's sentence: One starts serving a sentence when remand ends. Upon transfer, many prisoners say that it will be nice to start serving their sentence. The term "serving a sentence" can also be used in a joking way about being locked into your cell alone. "Have a nice evening. I have to go and serve my sentence" is not an unusual refrain during locking in at the end of the day.

Shopping: The prisoners can shop from the prison store every Monday. The range carried is comparable with a normal, small local store. In practice, prisoners must submit an order form the day before. The goods are then normally delivered to each wing at lunch time on Mondays. The officers check every bag to ensure the contents are right before they deliver the bags to the correct cell. For practical reasons, shopping is limited to NOK 850 per week.

Social: Is the name given to a prisoner privilege on the days when they cannot hang out in another prisoner's cell, that is, every second day. Eight to ten prisoners are let out of their cells for a social at the same time so that they can, together, take advantage of the opportunities offered by the common room: gym equipment, table tennis, foosball, pool and the common area's big TV.

Spinning: Once a week the prisoners have an opportunity to participate in a spinning lesson (indoor group cycling). Prisoners who want to take advantage of the offer must submit a note.

The System: The total state power system the prisoners encounter from an abstract perspective, especially the parts that can have unfavourable consequences for the prisoners. The prison, the police, the courts and the Norwegian Directorate of Immigration are all parts of the System.

Trainee: A trainee is a prisoner officer in training. It takes two years to qualify as a prison officer in Norway. Following a short induction course, the trainees spend their first year in the field in supervised professional training. Trainees wear black cloth sleeves on their shoulder straps without other distinguishing marks.

Transfer: Transfer is more permanent than moving up or down. Transfer occurs when prisoners have received their sentence and are going to the prison where they will serve their sentence.

Trustee: A work assignment as a sort of odd job man on a wing. Their main duties involve cleaning common areas and distributing food. From the prison's perspective, being a trustee is a position of trust reserved for the "best" prisoners. From the prisoners' perspective, being a trustee is attractive because it also involves spending a lot of time out of your cell. This is a privilege that must be managed with care; the trustees must ensure that all the benefits that come with the position do not result in the status of "brown noser" or "model prisoner". More informally, the trustees also often function as psychologists, the prison grapevine and providers of amusement. A good trustee is important for the satisfaction on the wing, as both prisoners and officers will agree. Conversely, a bad trustee can poison the mood in record time.

UDI (Norwegian Directorate of Immigration): For many prisoners, the Norwegian Directorate of Immigration is a key part of the System. As a rule, remand prisoners who are not Norwegian citizens receive prior notice of deportation, which in most cases ends, quite a long time later, in a deportation order. Those who have received a deportation order must leave the country upon release.

Visiting unit: The visiting unit is the arena in the prison where most of the contact takes place between prisoners and people from the world outside. Visits from family members take place in a common area that has space for five to six prisoners and their families at a time. So-called intimate visits (conjugal visits) take place in separate rooms adjacent to the common area (see the love room). There are also special, small rooms for lawyer visits.

Waffle prison: Serving a sentence in a lower security unit is very easy. Those serving their sentence in these circumstances often participate in various activities and things outside the prison. They also seem to be eating waffles a lot. From this perspective, "waffle prison" is clearly preferable to proper prison, although not very masculine.

Water round: Every day, the trustees deliver hot water to the individual cells from a large metal urn. The water is poured into the thermos found in each cell. Between water rounds the water urn is plugged in to keep the water hot.

White note: Those who are on remand have a white note on their cell door. The white note also contains information about the prisoners' wishes vis-à-vis alternative and special diets.

Yellow note: Those serving a sentence have a yellow note on their cell door. The yellow note also contains information about the prisoners' wishes vis-à-vis alternative and special diets.

Notes

Introduction: Power, Resistance and Freedom in Prison

1. How is freedom measured in individuals as in peoples? It is measured by the resistance that needs to be overcome, by the effort that it costs to stay on *top*. Look for the highest type of free human beings where the highest resistance is constantly being overcome: five paces away from tyranny, right on the threshold, where servitude is danger.

    (Nietzsche, 2005: 213–14)

2. The *Prisoner's Handbook* is a practical guide to life in prison with an emphasis on the relevant laws, rules and regulations. It is published by Jussbuss, a free legal aid service run by law students, and is available on most Norwegian prison wings.
3. The prisoner's catch-all term "the System" is used as a proper name. For more on this, see the section on "The Prisoner and the System" below. This and other prison-related terms are also explained in the glossary at the back of this book.
4. Chandala is the name of an Indian lower caste, the "untouchables".
5. However, compared with the thesis (Ugelvik, 2010) that provides the basis for this book, this point is played down considerably. Norwegian-speaking readers interested in Foucauldian and post-structuralist hair-splitting can find many examples in the original thesis.

1   Implementation

1. However, interest was soon lost in the penitentiary concept and Oslo Prison was the only one that was actually built, but that is another story (Schaanning, 2007b).
2. See, for example, Christie (2007).
3. It was different for Holmberg (2001), who conducted his prison research as a teacher in a prison school in the American Midwest. As a teacher, he was expected to help control the prisoners in a crisis situation. A mandatory firearms test showed that, despite his pacifist convictions, he was the best shot of all the new members of staff. As a result, he was told that he had to immediately come and collect a rifle if there was ever a riot. The prisoners respected him for this. The officers disliked it; they felt insecure about being beaten by a civilian.
4. Many prisoners suggested I should spend a couple of weeks, or at least a weekend, as a prisoner in order to feel what it is "really" like to be in prison:

    Prisoner: You should do some time here, you know? You know nothing until you've tried it yourself. It is easy, just walk up to a police officer and hit him in the face, heh heh, and you'll be here before you know it. You don't have a previous record?
    TU: No, nothing.
    Prisoner: Yeah, well then you'll get four to six weeks for something like that. That's perfect for gaining an insight. You ought to get going and find some bloke in uniform, heh heh.

Since the Norwegian Correctional Services would never have let me have a cell (and since I felt that hitting a police officer in the name of penology would present a problem from a research ethics point of view), I did not even consider this. Meanwhile, this does not appear to be an unusual message for prison researchers to get. Jacobs (1977: 223) was told: "[I]nstead of doing your bull shit research from an armchair, why didn't you come in as an inmate so you could find out what it's all about, you phoney cock sucker." The following tirade was directed at Bosworth (Bosworth et al., 2005: 252): "How much time have you did? How many strip searches? How many hours in chains? How many beatings? How many brutalities? You know nothing! All that you know [of the truth] is what we tell you! Are you listening? Are you really listening?".

5. Both prisoners and officers shared this kind of scepticism about academics. My only allies in this respect were the extra officers who worked part-time in the prison while studying; on the other hand, they were relatively marginal allies. I exchanged many a knowing look with an extra officer after we had been the targets of jokes about academics in an environment where too many academic credits basically make you a vague and professorial windbag.

2   The Forms of Power in Prison

1. This is not necessarily problematic. For an alternative typology of resistance that also encompasses "coping" practices, see Cohen and Taylor (1981).
2. This particular practice is not a big theme in this book. Drug use appears to be less prevalent in Oslo Prison's remand units than in Crewe's British medium security prisons, although it does exist. Part of the reason for this, of course, is the fact that prisoners in Oslo are subject to a far stricter regime of control with far less freedom of movement around the prison, which makes large-scale drug dealing difficult. However, making something more difficult increases its symbolic weight. From this perspective, drug use could have greater value as a form of resistance in Oslo Prison than it has in Crewe's prisons.
3. Kelly (2009) discusses this further with the aid of an extremely hypothetical but illustrative example borrowed from Locke: if a man voluntarily walks into a room and for some reason does not wish to leave it (he does not touch the door either, but in this case because he does not *want* to leave), and if another wrongly believes that the room is empty and therefore locks it without the knowledge of the man inside, this is not an instance of power. The action, turning the key in the lock, is the same, but in this case there is no action on action.
4. Note that Foucault is not completely clear about how large or clear the potential for action must be in order for it to be possible to say that a power relationship exists: "[S]lavery is not a power relationship when a man is in chains, only when he has some possible mobility, even a chance of escape" (Foucault, 2000c: 342). I suppose it depends on the chains; as long as the slave in chains has a chance of, for example, retorting verbally, resistance is possible and therefore it is just as much a power relationship, even though the slave has been deprived of all possible mobility.
5. The Norwegian Execution of Sentences Act also enables the establishment of special maximum security units. At the time of writing there are two such units. One is in Ringerike Prison; the other, in Ila Prison, is designed specifically for one prisoner only, the terrorist and mass-murderer Anders Behring Breivik.

6. At the same time, this creates a division between the serious, full-time officers with correctional service qualifications and the less professional, temporary officers who are "really" students doing a summer job. The more full-time an employee you are, the more likely it is that you will be wearing steel-toecapped safety footwear. Extra officers can get away with slightly worn black trainers.
7. Aggression Replacement and management Training is one of the cognitive skills programmes that the Norwegian correctional services or external partners offer prisoners in Norwegian prisons.
8. Abu Ghraib appears to be an example of what can happen in a tyrannical prison.

3 Taking Liberties

1. http://www.aftenposten.no/nyheter/uriks/UNDP-Norge-er-fortsatt-verdens-beste -land-7147646.html#.U6bLIXY4UdU (Accessed: 22 June 2014).
2. http://shiva82.blogspot.com/2009/10/gratulerer-du-er-norsk.html (Accessed: 22 June 2014).
3. Smoking is (at least for now) permitted in the cells. The common area, on the other hand, is a smoke-free zone, as is the officers' room. This permits one of the most common forms of fraternisation across the officer/prisoner boundary (which, of course, is not particularly common either). The officers who smoke can have a cigarette in a cell rather than having to go all the way down the stairs and outside. From this perspective, this is one of the many positive effects of the law banning smoking in public indoor places.
4. He said this to me while I was sitting in his chair.
5. Døving, based on his data from a smaller town in the county of Østfold, primarily views this as a female requirement. In the prison this is placed in a different context. See the section on food, resistance and masculinity for more.
6. The power in the food/emotions/memory association is so strong that various industries started taking advantage of it long ago. Vanilla is an example that is popular in perfume because vanilla creates associations with childhood, security and home-baked cakes, according to Lupton.
7. Food can, however, be used as a reward, although this is unusual. During my fieldwork, hand-picked prisoners who participated in the prison's so-called "open day", where invited guests got guided tours of the prison, were "paid" in pizza afterwards. This was, however, an exception.
8. The strong symbolic connection between prison and porridge (e.g. referring to going to prison as "doing porridge") does not exist in Norway.
9. FOR 2002-02-22 no. 183, *Regulations to the Execution of Sentences Act.*
10. *Diet: Guidelines for section 3–23 of the Regulations to the Execution of Sentences Act* 2004.
11. Reference the so-called *principle of less eligibility*, which is well known in the history of prisons. The argument is that the conditions in a prison must be poorer than the living conditions of poor people on the outside in order to have a deterrent effect.
12. A Croatian spice mix which is very popular in the Balkans and Turkey.
13. Milk's status was changed from being somewhat "unclear and potentially dangerous" to "pure, safe and healthy, even in its fresh form". Interestingly, this was achieved by an advertising campaign in which the bottles of milk were depicted as prison officers who kept the unhealthy coffee under lock and key (Lyngø, 2007).

14. The terms Scott uses are "public transcript" and "hidden transcript". "Transcript" is difficult to translate into Norwegian in the sense he uses it. I have chosen to use the term *script*, even though it carries with it the risk of associations with the theatre and acting. Scott does not think that one is an expression of what people *really* think, while the other is manipulation or an expression of ideology and false consciousness. Both scripts must be understood from a contextual and relational perspective.

15. There are a number of webshops that specialise in equipment for military personnel and police and prison officers. In other words, this is equipment one can purchase as a private person. Those who are interested can, for example, take a look at the Norwegian online store Capsicum (http://www.capsicumnordic.com/ (Accessed: 22 June 2014)). See also Finstad's (2000) description of the so-called "city centre rig" in the police.

16. The Pacto toilet was used a total of 19 times (all Norwegian prisons) in 2008, with a hit rate of 73.7 per cent, according to the *Norwegian Correctional Services' Annual Statistics 2008*.

17. Nonetheless, this does not entail a complete dissolution of the concept. This does not mean that freedom practices are not "really" free, just that "free" is problematic as a concept in an ahistorical, absolute sense. One can also talk about being more or less free. Foucault's great advantage is showing how we may have a history of this by looking at the techniques that are in use and that have been used when people have made themselves into ethical subjects in specific situations.

18. Note that the neutralisation techniques theory was thus an attempt to construct a causal explanation – the article's subheading is "A theory of Delinquency". When the neutralisation techniques exist prior to the deviant action, they can be understood as (one of many) causes behind the action occurring. I do not assert such a causal relationship in the following, but, instead, focus on how the prisoners I have spoken to use the techniques in their ongoing positioning work. The fact that the prisoner below, for example, transforms his partner's status from murder victim to "a 50-kilo pit bull" (an example of what Sykes and Matza call *denial of the victim*) says something about the relevant situation and his desire to be seen by me in a particular way. I do not mean by this that one can conclude that this rewriting was important to him in the specific situation when he killed his former partner.

19. In other words, these are two completely different systems of morality. The boys must have respect; the girls must ensure that honour is maintained:

    TU: You say that if your wife does something wrong, it affects your honour. Does it affect her respect if you do something wrong?

    Erol: No, no, respect is only about the man. She may, perhaps, even gain recognition from having the strength to live with someone like me, for holding out, if I do something wrong.

20. Ref. note 56 – Trond had never, as far as I know, met Kjell Inge Røkke in person either.

Bibliography

Aase, T.H. (2007). "Ærens grammatikk". Ø. Fuglerud and T.H. Eriksen (eds), *Grenser for kultur? Perspektiver fra norsk minoritetsforskning*. Oslo: Pax.

Åkerström, M. (2007). "Coola offer: Unga mäns balansering av brottsofferidentiteten". Hv. Hofer and A. Nilsson (eds), *Brott i välfärden: Om brottslighet, utsatthet och kriminalpolitik*. Stockholm: Kriminologiska institutionen, Stockholms universitet.

Althusser, L. (1971). *Lenin and Philosophy, and Other Essays*. London: New Left Books.

Andersen, N.Å. (1999). *Diskursive analysestrategier: Foucault, Koselleck, Laclau, Luhmann*. København: Nyt fra Samfundsvidenskaberne.

Anderson, B. (1983). *Imagined Communities: Reflections on the Origin and Spread of Nationalism*. London: Verso.

Andersson, R. (2011). "A Blessing in Disguise: Attention Deficit Hyperactivity Disorder Diagnosis and Swedish Correctional Treatment Policy in the Twenty-First Century". T. Ugelvik and J. Dullum (eds), *Penal Exceptionalism? Nordic Prison Policy and Practice*. London, NY: Routledge.

Baer, L.D. (2005). "Visual Imprints on the Prison Landscape: A Study on the Decorations in Prison Cells". *Tijdschrift voor economische en sociale geografie* 96 (2), 209–217.

Baer, L.D. and B. Ravneberg. (2008). "The Outside and Inside in Norwegian and English Prisons". *Geografiska Annaler, serie B* 90 (2), 205–216.

Bakhtin, M. (2003). *Latter og dialog: Utvalgte skrifter*. Oslo: Cappelen akademisk.

Bandyopadhyay, M.M. (2006). "Competing Masculinities in a Prison". *Men and Masculinities* 9 (2), 186–203.

Barth, F. (1996). "Ethnic Groups and Boundaries". J. Hutchinson and A.D. Smith (eds), *Ethnicity*. Oxford, NY: Oxford University Press.

Barthes, R. (1961). "Toward a Psychosociology of Contemporary Food Consumption". R. Forster and O. Ranum (eds), *Food and Drink in History*. Baltimore: John Hopkins University Press.

Barthes, R. (1973). *Mythologies*. London: Paladin.

Barthes, R. (1979). "Matens 'grammatikk'". *Samtiden* 88 (6), 32–39.

Basberg, C.E. (1999). *Omsorg i fengsel?* Oslo: Pax.

Beauvoir, S.D. (1953). *The Second Sex*. New York: Alfred A. Knopf.

Becker, H.S. (1967). "Whose Side Are We On?". *Social Problems* 14 (3), 234–247.

Belmonte, T. (1989). *The Broken Fountain*. New York: Columbia University Press.

Bentham, J. (1995). *The Panopticon Writings*. London, NY: Verso.

Beyers, L. (2008). "Creating Home: Food, Ethnicity and Gender among Italians in Belgium since 1946". *Food, Culture and Society* 11 (1), 8–27.

Bordo, S. (1998). " 'Material Girl': The Effacements of Postmodern Culture". D. Welton (ed.), *Body and Flesh: A Philosophical Reader*. Malden: Blackwell.

Bosworth, M. (1999). *Engendering Resistance: Agency and Power in Women's Prisons*. Aldershot: Ashgate.

Bosworth, M. and E. Carrabine. (2001). "Reassessing Resistance: Race, Gender and Sexuality in Prison". *Punishment & Society* 3 (4), 501–515.

Bosworth, M. et al. (2005). "Doing Prison Research: Views from Inside". *Qualitative Inquiry* 11 (2), 249–264.

Bourdieu, P. (1984). *Distinction: A Social Critique of the Judgement of Taste*. London: Routledge & Kegan Paul.

Bourdieu, P. (1990). "Kroppens sosiale persepsjon: Noen foreløpige bemerkninger". *Sosiologi i dag* 20 (3), 3–11.

Brandth, B. and E. Kvande. (2003). *Fleksible fedre: Maskulinitet, arbeid, velferdsstat*. Oslo: Universitetsforlaget.

Brownlie, D. and P. Hewer. (2007). "Prime Beef Cuts: Culinary Images for Thinking 'Men' ". *Consumption, Markets and Culture* 10 (3), 229–250.

Butler, J. (1993). *Bodies That Matter: On the Discursive Limits of "Sex"*. New York: Routledge.

Butler, J. (1995). "Conscience Doth Make Subjects of Us All". *Yale French Studies* (88), 6–26.

Butler, J. (1997). *The Psychic Life of Power: Theories in Subjection*. Stanford: Stanford University Press.

Butler, J. (2006). *Gender Trouble: Feminism and the Subversion of Identity*. New York: Routledge.

Caputo-Levine, D.D. (2012). "The Yard Face: The Contributions of Inmate Interpersonal Violence to the Carceral Habitus". *Ethnography* 14 (2), 165–185.

Carrabine, E. and B. Longhurst. (1998). "Gender and Prison Organisation: Some Comments on Masculinities and Prison Management". *The Howard Journal* 37 (2), 161–176.

Cavadino, M. and J. Dignan. (2006). *Penal Systems: A Comparative Approach*. London: Sage.

Cavanagh, K., R.E. Dobash, R.P. Dobash and R. Lewis. (2001). " 'Remedial Work': Men's Strategic Responses to Their Violence against Intimate Female Partners". *Sociology* 35 (3), 695–714.

Christie, N. (1997). Gi meg et monster. http://www.apollon.uio.no/portretter/1997/monster.html (Accessed: 18 March 2014).

Christie, N. (2000). *Crime Control as Industry: Towards Gulags, Western Style*. London: Routledge.

Christie, N. (2007). *Limits to Pain*. Eugene: Wipf & Stock.

Clemmer, D. (1940). *The Prison Community*. New York: Holt, Rinehart & Winston.

Coffey, A. (1999). *The Ethnographic Self: Fieldwork and the Representation of Identity*. London: Sage.

Coggeshall, J.M. (2004). "Closed Doors: Ethical Issues with Prison Ethnography". L. Hume and J. Mulcock (eds), *Anthropologists in the Field: Cases in Participant Observation*. New York: Columbia University Press.

Cohen, A.K. (1955). *Delinquent Boys: The Culture of the Gang*. New York: The Free Press.

Cohen, S. and L. Taylor. (1976). *Escape Attempts: The Theory and Practice of Resistance to Everyday Life*. Harmondsworth: Penguin.

Cohen, S. and L. Taylor. (1981). *Psychological Survival: The Experience of Long-Term Imprisonment*. Harmondsworth: Penguin.

Collins, H.M. (1991). "Captives and Victims: Comment on Scott, Richards, and Martin". *Science, Technology & Human Values* 16 (2), 249–251.

Comfort, M. (2002). " 'Papa's House': The Prison as Domestic and Social Satellite". *Ethnography* 3 (4), 467–499.

Connell, R.W. (1983). "Men's Bodies". R.W. Connell (ed.), *Which Way Is Up? Essays on Sex, Class and Culture*. Sydney, London: Allen & Undwin.

Connell, R.W. (2005). *Masculinities*. Cambridge: Polity Press.

Connolly, W.E. (1991). *Identity/Difference: Democratic Negotiations of Political Paradox.* Ithaca, NY: Cornell University Press.

Connor, W. (1996). "Beyond Reason: The Nature of the Ethnonational Bond". J. Hutchinson and A.D. Smith (eds), *Ethnicity.* Oxford, NY: Oxford University Press.

Cowburn, M. (1998). "A Man's World: Gender Issues in Working with Male Sex Offenders in Prison". *The Howard Journal* 37 (3), 234–251.

Crewe, B. (2005). "Prisoner Society in the Era of Hard Drugs". *Punishment & Society* 7 (4), 457–481.

Crewe, B. (2009). *The Prisoner Society: Power, Adaptation, and Social Life in an English Prison.* Oxford: Oxford University Press.

Crewe, B. (2011). "Soft Power in Prison: Implications for Staff-Prisoner Relationships, Liberty and Legitimacy". *European Journal of Criminology* 8 (6), 455–468.

Daly, K. (1997). "Different Ways of Conceptualizing Sex/Gender in Feminist Theory and Their Implications for Criminology". *Theoretical Criminology* 1 (1), 24–53.

Davidson, A.I. (1986). "Archaeology, Genealogy, Ethics". D.C. Hoy (ed.), *Foucault: A Critical Reader.* Oxford, Cambridge: Blackwell.

Derrida, J. (1981). *Positions.* Chicago: University of Chicago Press.

Derrida, J. (1988). *Limited Inc.* Evanston: Northwestern University Press.

Derrida, J. (2006). "Différance". K. Gundersen (ed.), *Dekonstruksjon: Klassiske tekster i utvalg.* Oslo: Spartacus.

Douglas, M. (1970). *Purity and Danger: An Analysis of Concepts of Pollution and Taboo.* Harmondsworth: Penguin.

Døving, R. (2003). *Rype med lettøl: En antropologi fra Norge.* Oslo: Pax.

Døving, R. (2007). "Fedmens politiske sårdannelser". *Arr: idéhistorisk tidsskrift* 19 (2–3), 75–82.

Drake, D.H. (2012). *Prisons, Punishment and the Pursuit of Security.* Basingstoke: Palgrave Macmillan.

Duguid, S. (2000). *Can Prisons Work? The Prisoner as Object and Subject in Modern Corrections.* Toronto: University of Toronto.

Edel, M. and A. Edel. (1959). *Anthropology and Ethics.* Springfield: Charles C. Thomas.

Ekenstam, C. (1998). "Kroppen, viljan och skräcken för att falla: Ur den manliga självbehärskningens historia". C. Ekenstam, J. Frykman, T. Johansson, J. Kuosmanen, J. Ljunggren and A. Nilsson (eds), *Rädd att falla: Studier i manlighet.* Stockholm: Gidlund.

Ekenstam, C. (2006). "Mansforskningens bakgrund och framtid: Några teoretiska reflexioner". *Norma: Nordisk tidsskrift for maskulinitetsstudier* 1 (1), 6–23.

Elias, N. (1994). *The Civilizing Process: Sociogenetic and Psychogenetic Investigations.* Malden, Oxford, Victoria: Blackwell.

Ericsson, K. and N. Jon. (2006). "Gendered Social Control: 'A Virtuous Girl' and 'a Proper Boy'". *Scandinavian Journal of Studies in Criminology and Crime Prevention* 7 (2), 126–141.

Finstad, L. (2000). *Politiblikket.* Oslo: Pax.

Fischler, C. (1988). "Food, Self and Identity". *Social Science Information* 27 (2), 275–292.

Forsberg, L. (2007). "Negotiating Involved Fatherhood: Household Work, Childcare and Spending Time with Children". *Norma: Nordisk tidsskrift for maskulinitetsstudier* 2 (2), 109–126.

Foucault, M. (1976). *The Birth of the Clinic.* London: Tavistock.

Foucault, M. (1977a). *Discipline and Punish: The Birth of the Prison.* London, NY: Penguin.

Foucault, M. (1977b). "Nietzsche, Genealogy, History". D.F. Bouchard (ed.), *Language, Counter-Memory, Practice: Selected Essays and Interviews*. Ithaca: Cornell University Press.

Foucault, M. (1980). "Prison Talk". C. Gordon (ed.), *Power/Knowledge: Selected Interviews and Other Writings 1972–1977*. New York: Pantheon Books.

Foucault, M. (1988). "The Ethic of Care for the Self as a Practice of Freedom: An Interview with Michel Foucault on January 20, 1984". J. Bernauer and D. Rasmussen (eds), *The Final Foucault*. Cambridge, MA: MIT Press.

Foucault, M. (1990a). *The Care of the Self: The History of Sexuality Volume 3*. London: Penguin.

Foucault, M. (1990b). *The Will to Knowledge: The History of Sexuality Volume 1*. London: Penguin.

Foucault, M. (1992). *The Use of Pleasures: The History of Sexuality Volume 2*. London: Penguin.

Foucault, M. (1996). "From Torture to Cellblock". S. Lotringer (ed.), *Foucault Live: Interviews, 1961–1984*. New York: Semiotext(e).

Foucault, M. (1997). "Sex, Power, and the Politics of Identity". P. Rabinow (ed.), *Ethics, Subjectivity and Truth: Essential Works of Foucault 1954–1984 I*. New York: The Free Press.

Foucault, M. (2000a). "Lives of Infamous Men". J.D. Faubion (ed.), *Power: Essential Works of Foucault 1954–1984 III*. New York: The New Press.

Foucault, M. (2000b). " 'Omnes Et Singulatim': Toward a Critique of Political Reason". J.D. Faubion (ed.), *Power: Essential Works of Foucault 1954–1984 III*. New York: The New Press.

Foucault, M. (2000c). "The Subject and Power". J.D. Faubion (ed.), *Power: Essential Works of Foucault 1954–1984 III*. New York: The New Press.

Foucault, M. (2000d). "Truth and Juridical Forms". J.D. Faubion (ed.), *Power: Essential Works of Foucault 1954–1984 III*. New York: The New Press.

Foucault, M. (2003). *Abnormal: Lectures at the Collège De France 1974–1975*. New York: Picador.

Foucault, M. (2007). *Security, Territory, Population: Lectures at the Collège De France 1977–1978*. Basingstoke, NY: Palgrave Macmillan.

Fox, N.J. (1998). "Foucault, Foucauldians and Sociology". *The British Journal of Sociology* 49 (3), 415–433.

Friestad, C. and I.L.S. Hansen. (2004). *Levekår blant innsatte*. Oslo: Fafo.

Fürst, E.L.O. (1993). "Mat: Et annet språk". *Sosiologi i dag* 23 (1), 27–46.

Fürst, E.L.O. (1997). "Cooking and Femininity". *Women's Studies International Forum* 20 (3), 10.

Galtung, J. (1959). *Fengselssamfunnet: Et forsøk på analyse*. Oslo: Universitetsforlaget.

Garland, D. (1990). *Punishment and Modern Society: A Study in Social Theory*. Chicago: University of Chicago Press.

Garland, D. (2001). *The Culture of Control: Crime and Social Order in Contemporary Society*. Chicago: University of Chicago Press.

Geertz, C. (1973a). "Deep Play: Notes on the Balinese Cockfight". C. Geertz (ed.), *The Interpretation of Cultures: Selected Essays by Clifford Geertz*. New York: Basic Books.

Geertz, C. (ed.) (1973b). "Thick Description: Toward an Interpretive Theory of Culture". *The Interpretation of Cultures: Selected Essays of Clifford Geertz*. New York: Basic Books.

Geertz, C. (2000). *Available Light: Anthropological Reflections on Philosophical Topics*. Princeton: Princeton University Press.

Godderis, R. (2006). "Dining In: The Symbolic Power of Food in Prison". *The Howard Journal of Criminal Justice* 45 (3), 255–267.

Goffman, E. (1961). *Asylums: Essays on the Social Situation of Mental Patients and Other Inmates*. Harmondsworth: Penguin.

Goffman, E. (1963). *Stigma: Notes on the Management of Spoiled Identity*. Englewood Cliffs: Prentice-Hall.

Grosz, E. (1994). *Volatile Bodies: Toward a Corporeal Feminism*. Bloomington, IN: Indiana University Press.

Gullestad, M. (1989). *Kultur og hverdagsliv: På sporet av det moderne Norge*. Oslo: Universitetsforlaget.

Gullestad, M. (2002). "Invisible Fences: Egalitarianism, Nationalism and Racism". *The Journal of the Royal Anthropological Institute* 8 (1), 45–63.

Hammerlin, Y. and R. Kristoffersen. (2001). *Vold og trusler mot tilsatte i Kriminalomsorgen*. Oslo: KRUS.

Hammerlin, Y. and T. Rokkan. (2007). *Vold og trusler mot tilsatte i Kriminalomsorgen 2007*. Oslo: KRUS.

Hammerlin, Y. and T.W. Strand [Ugelvik]. (2005). *Vold mot tilsatte i Kriminalomsorgen 2004*. Oslo: KRUS.

Hammerlin, Y. and T.W. Strand [Ugelvik]. (2006). *Vold mot tilsatte i Kriminalomsorgen 2005*. Oslo: KRUS.

Hanoa, K. (2008). *Vold og trusler mellom innsatte: En intervjuundersøkelse*. Oslo: KRUS.

Hardt, M. (1997). "Prison Time". *Yale French Studies* (91), 64–79.

Haug, F. (1990). "Moralens tvekjønn". *Sosiologi i dag* 20 (3), 12–34.

Hayslett-McCall, K.L. and T.J. Bernard. (2002). "Attachment, Masculinity, and Self-Control: A Theory of Male Crime Rates". *Theoretical Criminology* 6 (1), 5–33.

Herzfeld, M. (1985). *The Poetics of Manhood: Contest and Identity in a Cretan Mountain Village*. Princeton: Princeton University Press.

Heyes, C.J. (2007). *Self-Transformations: Foucault, Ethics, and Normalized Bodies*. Oxford, NY: Oxford University Press.

Høigård, C. and L. Finstad. (1992). *Backstreets: Prostitution, Money, and Love*. Cambridge: Polity Press.

Hollander, J. and R. Einwohner. (2004). "Conceptualizing Resistance". *Sociological Forum* 19 (4), 533–554.

Holm, L. and S. Smidt. (1993). "Livet, døden og maden". *Sosiologi i dag* 23 (1), 11–26.

Holmberg, C.B. (2001). "The Culture of Transgression: Initiations into the Homosociality of a Midwestern State Prison". D. Sabo, T.A. Kupers and W. London (eds), *Prison Masculinities*. Philadelphia: Temple University Press.

Holter, Ø.G., H. Svare and C. Egeland. (2008). *Likestilling og livskvalitet 2007*. Oslo: Arbeidsforskningsinstituttet.

Hood-Williams, J. (2001). "Gender, Masculinities and Crime: From Structures to Psyches". *Theoretical Criminology* 5 (1), 24.

Ibsen, A.Z. (2012). "Ruling by Favors: Prison Guards' Informal Exercise of Institutional Control". *Law & Social Inquiry* 38 (2), 342–363.

Jacobs, J.B. (1977). *Stateville: The Penitentiary in Mass Society*. Chicago, London: The University of Chicago Press.

James, A. (2005). "Identity and the Global Stew". C. Korsmeyer (ed.), *The Taste Culture Reader: Experiencing Food and Drink*. Oxford, New York: Berg.

Jefferson, T. (1998). "Muscle, 'Hard Men' and 'Iron' Mike Tyson: Reflections on Desire, Anxiety and the Embodiment of Masculinity". *Body & Society* 4 (1), 77–98.

Jewkes, Y. (2002). *Captive Audience: Media, Masculinity and Power in Prisons*. Cullompton: Willan.

Jewkes, Y. (2005). "Men behind Bars: 'Doing' Masculinity as an Adaptation to Imprisonment". *Men and Masculinities* 8 (1), 44–63.

Johansson, E. (2006). "Arbetare". J. Lorentzen and C. Ekenstam (eds), *Män i Norden: Manlighet och modernitet 1840–1940*. Stockholm: Gidlunds.

Johansson, T. (1998). "Pappor och deras pappor". C. Ekenstam, J. Frykman, T. Johansson, J. Kuosmanen, J. Ljunggren and A. Nilsson (eds), *Rädd att falla: Studier i manlighet*. Stockholm: Gidlunds.

Johansson, T. (2001). "Fadern som försvann". C. Ekenstam, T. Johansson and J. Kuosmanen (eds), *Sprickor i fasaden: Manligheter i förandring*. Stockholm: Gidlunds.

Johnsen, B. (2001). *Sport, Masculinities and Power Relations in Prison*. Oslo: Norwegian University of Sport and Physical Education.

Kelly, M.G.E. (2009). *The Political Philosophy of Michel Foucault*. New York: Routledge.

Kimmel, M.S. (2006). *Manhood in America: A Cultural History*. New York: Oxford University Press.

Klare, H.J. (1960). *Anatomy of Prison*. London: Hutchinson.

Klein, J. and L.S. Chancer. (2006). "Normalized Masculinity: The Ontology of Violence Rooted in Everyday Life". B.A. Arrigo and C.R. Williams (eds), *Philosophy, Crime, and Criminology*. Urbana, Chicago: University of Illinois Press.

Kollhöj, J.P. (2005). "To bilder av norske soldater i 1914: Ulike maskulinitetsformer og voldsbevegelser". *Nätverket* (14), 115–133.

Kolnar, K. (2005a). *Mannedyret: Begjær i moderne film*. Oslo: Spartacus.

Kolnar, K. (2005b). "Når volden skaper mannen". *NIKKmagasin* (1), 31–34.

Kolnar, K. (2006). "Volden". J. Lorentzen and C. Ekenstam (eds), *Män i Norden: Manlighet och modernitet 1840–1940*. Stockholm: Gidlunds.

Kupers, T.A. (2005). "Toxic Masculinity as a Barrier to Mental Health Treatment in Prison". *Journal of Clinical Psychology* 61 (6), 713–724.

Lacey, N. (2008). *The Prisoners' Dilemma: Political Economy and Punishment in Contemporary Democracies*. Cambridge: Cambridge University Press.

Laclau, E. and C. Mouffe. (2001). *Hegemony and Socialist Strategy: Towards a Radical Democratic Politics*. London: Verso.

Laidlaw, J. (2002). "For an Anthropology of Ethics and Freedom". *The Journal of the Royal Anthropological Institute* 8 (2), 311–332.

Latour, B. (1992). "Where Are the Missing Masses? The Sociology of a Few Mundane Artifacts". W.E. Bijker and J. Law (eds), *Shaping Technology/Building Society: Studies in Sociotechnical Change*. Cambridge, London: MIT Press.

Lauesen, T. (1998). *Fra forbedringshus til parkeringshus: Magt og modmagt i Vridsløselille Statsfængsel*. København: Hans Reitzel.

Leer-Salvesen, P. (1988a). *Etter drapet: Samtaler om skyld og soning*. Oslo: Universitetsforlaget.

Leer-Salvesen, P. (1988b). "Kan et monster sørge?". E. Skærbæk and E.J. Stabrun (eds), *Forbryteralbum: Alternative fengselsbilder ved danske og norske fengselsprester*. Oslo: Pax.

Lévi-Strauss, C. (1966). *The Savage Mind*. London: Weidenfeld and Nicolson.

Levit, N. (2001). "Male Prisoners: Privacy, Suffering, and the Legal Construction of Masculinity". D. Sabo, T.A. Kupers and W. London (eds), *Prison Masculinity*. Philadelphia: Temple University Press.

Liebling, A. (2001). "Whose Side Are We On? Theory, Practice and Allegiances in Prisons Research". *British Journal of Criminology* 41 (3), 472–484.

Liliequist, J. (1999). "Från niding till sprätt: En studie i det svenska omanlighetsbe-greppets historia från vikingatid till sent 1700-Tal". A.-M. Berggren (ed.), *Manligt och omanligt i ett historiskt perspektiv*. Stockholm: FRN.

Lindberg, O. (2005). "Prison Cultures and Social Representations: The Case of Hinseberg, a Women's Prison in Sweden". *International Journal of Prisoner Health* 1 (2–4), 143–161.

Lorentzen, J. (2004). *Maskulinitet: Blikk på mannen gjennom litteratur og film*. Oslo: Spartacus.

Lorentzen, J. (2005). "Mannforskningens Historie". *Arr: Idéhistorisk idsskrift* 17 (3), 3–16.

Lorentzen, J. (2006). "Fedrene". J. Lorentzen and C. Ekenstam (eds), *Män i Norden: Manlighet och modernitet 1840–1940*. Stockholm: Gidlunds.

Lupton, D. (2005). "Food and Emotion". C. Korsmeyer (ed.), *The Taste Culture Reader: Experiencing Food and Drink*. Oxford, New York: Berg.

Lyngø, I.J. (2007). "Et melkedrikkende folk: Melkens nye status i mellomkrigstidens Norge". *Arr: Idéhistorisk tidsskrift* 19 (2–3), 27–40.

Majors, R. (2001). "Cool Pose: Masculinity and Sports". S.M. Whitehead and F.J. Barret (eds), *The Masculinities Reader*. Cambridge, Malden: Polity Press.

Mathiassen, C. (2004). *Fanget i tilværelsen? Casestudier om fastlåsthed og forsøg på frigørelse*. København: Institut for psykologi, Københavns universitet.

Mathiesen, T. (1965). *The Defences of the Weak: A Sociological Study of a Norwegian Correctional Institution*. London: Tavistock.

Mauss, M. (1954). *The Gift: Forms and Functions of Exchange in Archaic Societies*. London: Cohen & West.

Mauss, M. (2006). "Techniques of the Body". N. Schlanger (ed.), *Techniques, Technology and Civilization*. New York, Oxford: Berghahn Books.

McCorkle, L.W. and R. Korn. (1954). "Resocialization within Walls". *Annals of the American Academy of Political and Social Science* 293, 88–98.

Messerschmidt, J.W. (1993). *Masculinities and Crime: Critique and Reconceptualization of Theory*. Lanham: Rowman & Littlefield.

Messerschmidt, J.W. (2000). *Nine Lives: Adolescent Masculinities, the Body, and Violence*. Boulder: Westview Press.

Messerschmidt, J.W. (2001). "Masculinities, Crime and Prison". D. Sabo, T.A. Kupers and W. London (eds), *Prison Masculinities*. Philadelphia: Temple University Press.

Messerschmidt, J.W. (2004). *Flesh and Blood: Adolescent Gender Diversity and Violence*. Lanham: Rowman & Littlefield Publishers.

Miller, J. (2002). "The Strengths and Limits of 'Doing Gender' for Understanding Street Crime". *Theoretical Criminology* 6 (4), 433–460.

Moran, D. (2012). "'Doing Time' in Carceral Space: Timespace and Carceral Geography". *Geografiska Annaler: Series B. Human Geography* 94 (4), 305–316.

Moran, D., J. Pallot and L. Piacentini. (2013). "Privacy in Penal Space: Women's Imprisonment in Russia". *Geoforum* 47 (4), 138–146.

Mysterud, I. (2007). "Hva er mennesket tilpasset å spise?". *Arr: Idéhistorisk tidsskrift* 19 (2–3), 15–26.

Nelken, D. (2010). *Comparative Criminal Justice: Making Sense of Difference*. Los Angeles, London, New Delhi, Singapore, Washington, DC: Sage.

Neumann, I.B. (1998). *Uses of the Other: "The East" in European Identity Formation*. Minneapolis: University of Minnesota Press.

Neumann, I.B. (2001). *Mening, materialitet, makt: En innføring i diskursanalyse.* Bergen: Fagbokforlaget.

Newburn, T. and E.A. Stanko. (1994). *Just Boys Doing Business? Men, Masculinities and Crime.* London: Routledge.

Newton, C. (1994). "Gender Theory and Prison Sociology: Using Theories of Masculinities to Interpret the Sociology of Prisons for Men". *The Howard Journal* 33 (3), 193–202.

Nielsen, M. (2011). "On Humour in Prison". *European Journal of Criminology* 8 (6), 500.

Nietzsche, F. (2005). *The Anti-Christ, Ecce Homo, Twilight of the Idols, and Other Writings.* Cambridge, NY: Cambridge University Press.

Norton, A. (1988). *Reflections on Political Identity.* Baltimore: Johns Hopkins University Press.

Nylander, P-Å., O. Lindberg and A. Bruhn. (2011). "Emotional Labour and Emotional Strain among Swedish Prison Officers". *European Journal of Criminology* 8 (6), 469–483.

Ochs, E. (1993). "Constructing Social Identity: A Language Socialization Perspective". *Research on Language and Social Interaction* 26 (3), 287–306.

Olsen, B.M. and H. Aarseth. (2006). "Mat og maskulinitet i senmoderne familieliv". *Norma: Nordisk tidsskrift for maskulinitetsstudier* 1 (1), 42–61.

Øverland, I. (2003). "Regjering av liminaritet: Urfolk, minoriteter og innvandrere". I.B. Neumann and O.J. Sending (eds), *Regjering i Norge.* Oslo: Pax.

Øygarden, G.A. (2001). *Den brukne neses estetikk: En bok om boksing.* Oslo: Solum.

Pratt, J. (1999). "Norbert Elias and the Civilized Prison". *The British Journal of Sociology* 50 (2), 271–296.

Pratt, J. (2008a). "Scandinavian Exceptionalism in an Era of Penal Excess: Part I: The Nature and Roots of Scandinavian Exceptionalism". *The British Journal of Criminology* 48 (2), 119–137.

Pratt, J. (2008b). "Scandinavian Exceptionalism in an Era of Penal Excess: Part II: Does Scandinavian Exceptionalism Have a Future?". *The British Journal of Criminology* 48 (3), 275–292.

Presser, L. (2004). "Violent Offenders, Moral Selves: Constructing Identities and Accounts in the Research Interview". *Social Problems* 51 (1), 82–101.

Proudhon, P.-J. (1989). *General Idea of the Revolution in the Nineteenth Century.* London: Pluto Press.

Rhodes, L.A. (2004). *Total Confinement: Madness and Reason in the Maximum Security Prison.* Berkeley: University of California Press.

Roos, G. and M. Wandel. (2005). " 'I Eat Because I'm Hungry, Because It's Good, and to Become Full': Everyday Eating Voiced by Male Carpenters, Drivers, and Engineers in Contemporary Oslo". *Food & Foodways* 13 (1), 169–180.

Ross, J.I. and S.C. Richards. (2003). *Convict Criminology.* Belmont, CA: Wadsworth/Thomson Learning.

Rozin, E. and P. Rozin. (2005). "Culinary Themes and Variations". C. Korsmeyer (ed.), *The Taste Culture Reader: Experiencing Food and Drink.* Oxford, New York: Berg.

Sabo, D. (2001). "Doing Time, Doing Masculinity: Sports and Prison". D. Sabo, T.A. Kupers and W. London (eds), *Prison Masculinities.* Philadelphia: Temple University Press.

Said, E.W. (1979). *Orientalism.* New York: Vintage Books.

Sandberg, S. (2010). "What Can 'Lies' Tell Us about Life? Notes towards a Framework of Narrative Criminology". *Journal of Criminal Justice Education* 21 (1), 447–465.

Schaanning, E. (2007a). "Mat og makt". *Arr: Idéhistorisk tidsskrift* 19 (2–3), 83–98.

Schaanning, E. (2007b). *Menneskelaboratoriet: Botsfengslets historie*. Oslo: Scandinavian Academic Press.

Schwalbe, M. and M. Wolkomir. (2001). "The Masculine Self as Problem and Resource in Interview Studies of Men". *Men and Masculinities* 4 (1), 90–103.

Scott, J.C. (1985). *Weapons of the Weak: Everyday Forms of Peasant Resistance*. New Haven: Yale University Press.

Scott, J.C. (1990). *Domination and the Arts of Resistance: Hidden Transcripts*. New Haven: Yale University Press.

Shalev, S. (2009). *Supermax: Controlling Risk through Solitary Confinement*. Cullompton: Willan.

Sim, J. (1994). "Tougher than the Rest? Men in Prison". T. Newburn and E.A. Stanko (eds), *Just Boys Doing Business? Men, Masculinities and Crime*. London: Routledge.

Sim, J. (2003). "Whose Side Are We Not On? Researching Medical Power in Prison". S. Tombs and D. Whyte (eds), *Unmasking the Crimes of the Powerful: Scrutinizing States and Corporations*. New York: Peter Land.

Simmel, G. (1997). *Simmel on Culture: Selected Writings*. London: Sage.

Skardhamar, T. (2002). *Levekår og livssituasjon blant innsatte i norske fengsler*. Oslo: Department of Criminology and Sociology of Law.

Skrinjar, M. (2003). "Forskare eller 'babe'? Om genuskonstruktioner i intervjusituationer". I. Lander, T. Pettersson and E. Tiby (eds), *Femininiteter, maskuliniteter och kriminalitet: Genusperspektiv inom svensk kriminologi*. Lund: Studentlitteratur.

Smith, C. (2002). "Punishment and Pleasure: Women, Food and the Imprisoned Body". *The Sociological Review* 50 (2), 197–214.

Sollund, R. (2006): "Racialisation in Police Stop and Search Practice: The Norwegian Case". *Critical Criminology* 14, 265–292.

Søndergaard, D.M. (2002). "Poststructuralist Approaches to Empirical Analysis". *Qualitative Studies in Education* 15 (2), 187–204.

Søndergaard, D.M. (2006). *Tegnet på Kroppen: Køn: Koder og konstruktioner blandt unge voksne i akademia*. København: Museum Tusculanum.

Sparks, R., A.E. Bottoms and W. Hay. (1996). *Prisons and the Problem of Order*. Oxford, England; New York: Clarendon Press.

St.meld. nr. 37. (2007–2008). *Straff Som Virker – Mindre Kriminalitet – Tryggere Samfunn*. Oslo: Justis- og politidepartementet.

Stene-Johansen, K. (2007). "Smakens fysiologi som estetisk erfaring". *Arr*. 19 (2–3), 5–14.

Supiot, A. (2007). *Homo Juridicus*. London: Verso.

Sutton, D.E. (2005). "Synthesia, Memory and the Taste of Home". C. Korsmeyer (ed.), *The Taste Culture Reader: Experiencing Food and Drink*. Oxford, NY: Berg.

Sykes, G.M. (1958). *The Society of Captives: A Study of a Maximum Security Prison*. Princeton: Princeton University Press.

Sykes, G.M. and D. Matza. (1957). "Techniques of Neutralization: A Theory of Delinquency". *American Sociological Review* 22 (6), 664–670.

Theweleit, K. (1998). "Male Bodies and the 'White Terror' ". D. Welton (ed.), *Body and Flesh: A Philosophical Reader*. Malden: Blackwell.

Thompson, K. (2003). "Forms of Resistance: Foucault on Tactical Reversal and Self-Formation". *Continental Philosophy Review* 36 (2), 113–138.

Ugelvik, T. (2006). *Vend om i tide: En evaluering av Snu-prosjektene i Trondheim og Bergen*. Oslo: KRUS.

Ugelvik, T. (2010). *Å være eller ikke være fange: Frihet som praksis i et norsk mannsfengsel*. Oslo: Institutt for kriminologi og rettssosiologi, UiO.

Valentine, G. and B. Longstaff. (1998). "Doing Porridge: Food and Social Relations in a Male Prison". *Journal of Material Culture* 3 (2), 131–152.

Wacquant, L.J.D. (2002). "The Curious Eclipse of Prison Ethnography in the Age of Mass Incarceration". *Ethnography* 3 (4), 371–397.

Waldram, J. (2009). "Challenges of Prison Ethnography". *Anthropology News* [unknown volume] (1), 4–5.

Warnier, J.-P. (2001). "A Praxeological Approach to Subjectivation in a Material World". *Journal of Material Culture* 6 (1), 5–24.

Warnier, J.-P. (2009). "Technology as Efficacious Action on Objects...and Subjects". *Journal of Material Culture* 14 (4), 459–470.

Weinberg, M.S. and C.J. Williams. (2005). "Fecal Matters: Habitus, Embodiments, and Deviance". *Social Problems* 52 (3), 315–336.

West, C. and S. Fenstermaker. (1995). "Doing Difference". *Gender & Society* 9 (1), 8–37.

West, C. and D.H. Zimmerman. (1987). "Doing Gender". *Gender & Society* 1 (2), 125–151.

Wheeler, S. (1961). "Role Conflict in Correctional Communities". D.R. Cressey (ed.), *The Prison: Studies in Institutional Organization and Change*. New York: Holt, Rinehart & Winston.

Whitehead, S.M. (2002). *Men and Masculinities: Key Themes and New Directions*. Cambridge: Polity Press.

Whyte, W.F. (1955). *Street Corner Society: The Social Structure of an Italian Slum*. Chicago: University of Chicago Press.

Widder, N. (2004). "Foucault and Power Revisited". *European Journal of Political Theory* 3 (4), 411–432.

Wikan, U. (2008). *In Honor of Fadime: Murder and Shame*. Chicago: University of Chicago Press.

Willis, P.E. (1977). *Learning to Labour: How Working Class Kids Get Working Class Jobs*. Farnborough, Hants: Saxon House.

Young, I.M. (2005a). "House and Home: Feminist Variations on a Theme". *On Female Body Experience: "Throwing Like a Girl" and Other Essays*. Oxford, NY: Oxford University Press.

Young, I.M. (2005b). "A Room of One's Own: Old Age, Extended Care, and Privacy". *On Female Body Experience: "Throwing Like a Girl" and Other Essays*. Oxford, NY: Oxford University Press.

Young, I.M. (2005c). "Throwing Like a Girl: A Phenomenology of Feminine Body Comportment, Motility and Spatiality". *On Female Body Experience: "Throwing Like a Girl" and Other Essays*. Oxford, NY: Oxford University Press.

Index

Note: Locators followed by the letter 'n' refer to notes

Printed and bound by CPI Group (UK) Ltd, Croydon, CR0 4YY